Neighborly
Adversaries

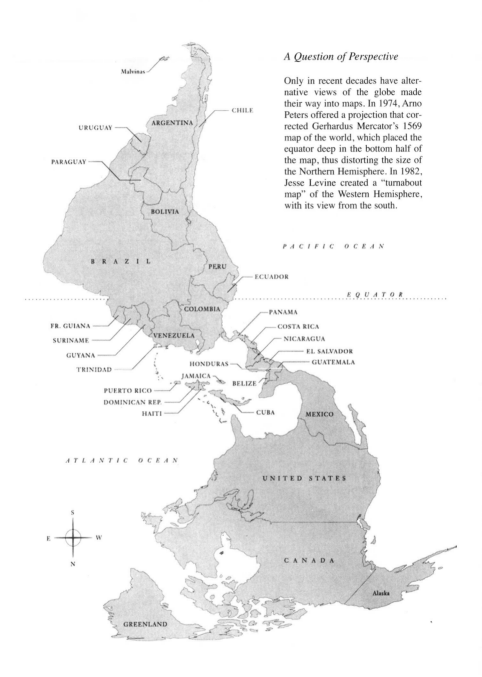

A Question of Perspective

Only in recent decades have alternative views of the globe made their way into maps. In 1974, Arno Peters offered a projection that corrected Gerhardus Mercator's 1569 map of the world, which placed the equator deep in the bottom half of the map, thus distorting the size of the Northern Hemisphere. In 1982, Jesse Levine created a "turnabout map" of the Western Hemisphere, with its view from the south.

Malvinas

CHILE

URUGUAY

ARGENTINA

PARAGUAY

BOLIVIA

PACIFIC OCEAN

B R A Z I L

PERU

ECUADOR

E Q U A T O R

COLOMBIA

PANAMA

FR. GUIANA

COSTA RICA

SURINAME

VENEZUELA

NICARAGUA

GUYANA

EL SALVADOR

HONDURAS

GUATEMALA

TRINIDAD

JAMAICA

PUERTO RICO

BELIZE

DOMINICAN REP.

HAITI

CUBA

MEXICO

ATLANTIC OCEAN

S

E ✦ W

N

UNITED STATES

CANADA

Alaska

GREENLAND

Neighborly Adversaries

Readings in U.S.–Latin American Relations

Second Edition

Edited by Michael LaRosa and Frank O. Mora

ROWMAN & LITTLEFIELD PUBLISHERS, INC.
Lanham • Boulder • New York • Toronto • Oxford

ROWMAN & LITTLEFIELD PUBLISHERS, INC.

Published in the United States of America
by Rowman & Littlefield Publishers, Inc.
A wholly owned subsidiary of The Rowman & Littlefield Publishing Group, Inc.
4501 Forbes Boulevard, Suite 200, Lanham, Maryland 20706
www.rowmanlittlefield.com

P.O. Box 317, Oxford OX2 9RU, UK

British Library Cataloguing in Publication Information Available

Library of Congress Cataloging-in-Publication Data

Neighborly adversaries : readings in U.S.–Latin American relations / edited by Michael
LaRosa and Frank O. Mora.— 2nd ed.
    p. cm.
Includes bibliographical references and index.
ISBN-13: 978-0-7425-4046-0 (cloth : alk. paper)
ISBN-10: 0-7425-4046-4 (cloth : alk. paper)
ISBN-13: 978-0-7425-4047-7 (pbk. : alk. paper)
ISBN-10: 0-7425-4047-2 (pbk. : alk. paper)
    1. Latin America—Foreign relations—United States. 2. United States—Foreign rela-
tions—Latin America. I. LaRosa, Michael (Michael J.) II. Mora, Frank O.
F1418.N397 2007
327.8073—dc22   2006007883

Printed in the United States of America

∞™ The paper used in this publication meets the minimum requirements of American
National Standard for Information Sciences—Permanence of Paper for Printed Library
Materials, ANSI/NISO Z39.48-1992.

To the Memory of a Teacher, Scholar, and Mentor
Enrique A. Baloyra

Contents

Preface and Acknowledgments

We are pleased to release the second edition of *Neighborly Adversaries: Readings in U.S.–Latin American Relations*. The first edition, published in October 1999, has been used as an accompanying text of readings for college courses in the United States that deal with Latin American politics, history, and geography/culture. We are thankful to the professors and students who read the book and made critical comments. Many of those comments and suggestions have been incorporated in this second edition. We have also listened carefully to the scholars who reviewed the book, and their helpful critiques have made this second edition stronger than the first. As in the first edition, we have chosen to edit out most of the notes from the original texts; however, in some places—in order to preserve clarity—we have included notes that offer important explanatory or background information.

The world has changed so much since the first edition of this book that the task of producing a second edition was somewhat daunting. So many new, important, and defining issues developed during the 1990s to the present. This second edition reflects new scholarship in the field of U.S.–Latin American relations and part VI of this book is completely redesigned. We have included chapters that deal with FTAs (Free Trade Agreements) in the Americas, immigration reform, and the environment. All of these issues are currently being debated in academic and policy-making circles, both in the United States and Latin America. Three chapters deal exclusively with the administration of George W. Bush and his post-9/11 policies toward Latin America. Of course, this is an ongoing, developing story, and the chapters that deal with the contemporary relationship express some degree of apprehension about the current state of affairs in terms of hemispheric relations.

This volume is interdisciplinary: readings have been purposely drawn from writers who are trained in history, political science, sociology, or environmental science. This allows for a wider interpretive framework in courses concerned with the development and evolution of U.S.–Latin American relations over a long period of time.

The coeditors of this book are trained in international relations and history (LaRosa) and international relations/political science (Mora). We have a twenty-three-year collaborative relationship, dating back to our undergraduate work at The George Washington University. Our students at the University of Miami (Coral Gables), Miami-Dade Community College, Rhodes College, and the National War College (Washington, D.C.) have helped us to design this book through their questions, critical comments, and reflections. Their enthusiasm and input have both encouraged and inspired us.

Many individuals helped us in preparing this second edition. At Rhodes College in Memphis we counted on financial support from the Office of the Associate Dean of Undergraduate Research, Robert Strandburg. Dorian M. Ellis helped with administrative details. Rhodes College student Jeffrey Austin Knowles has done much of the heavy lifting in helping us prepare this book; he edited our prose, corrected sections of the book, and organized the securing of permissions. He worked with great patience and diligence during the course of an entire school year.

We are very fortunate to count on the support of Susan McEachern at Rowman & Littlefield, who has been with us since the planning stages of the first edition of *Neighborly Adversaries* back in 1997. She has been a wise, careful, and patient editor: Susan understands the importance of "books" in this new era of "point and click" research.

Like the first edition, this book is dedicated to the memory of Enrique A. Baloyra, professor of political science at the University of Miami, who helped us understand why Latin America matters.

1

Introduction: Contentious Neighbors in the Western Hemisphere

Michael LaRosa and Frank O. Mora

The history of U.S.–Latin American relations has been one of tension, misperception, intervention, and cooperation. *Neighborly Adversaries* explores that relationship utilizing a methodology that can be characterized as interdisciplinary, analytical, and historical.

In the six parts that follow, the reader will have the opportunity to understand the history of U.S.–Latin American relations and how that relationship has evolved, changed, and been reinterpreted and negated over the decades. This volume is unique in that the positions of leading scholars, policymakers, and theorists are juxtaposed in a compelling fashion to show the wide diversity of existent opinion on a given topic. Juxtaposition of diverse views not only characterizes an element of this text's methodology but in many ways exemplifies the nature and structure of U.S.–Latin American relations since the early nineteenth century.

HISTORY IN ACTION

Almost one hundred years separates the fall of Tenochtitlán in the Central Valley of Mexico (1521) from the settlement of Jamestown (1607). The Spaniards who came to America were motivated by economic and religious considerations and constructed societies based on Iberian institutions and priorities. Thus the *encomienda*, or labor grant, became a way to organize work and was found principally in areas where large numbers of settled Native American civilizations were firmly established. The two poles of Hispanic society were found at the base of the Aztec Empire (modern-day Mexico City) and the Inca Empire (Peru). Spain controlled an overseas empire that extended from what today is northern California to the southern tip of Chile. Latin America's three-hundred-year colonial history (1521–1824) allowed for the establishment of institutions such as the *encomienda*, provided space for the Roman Catholic Church to dominate "formal" religious identification while controlling education and social life. Spanish policy in America was characterized by a caste that placed white Europeans at the apex of a structure in which those of mixed blood, Native Americans, and black Africans occupied lower social and economic rungs. Many Spaniards who came to America arrived to work as hacendados (land holders, administrators of plantations, or both), merchants, or mine operators; many amassed huge fortunes and were able to return to Spain where they could purchase titles and live out their lives on vast country estates as hidalgos.[1]

North America had a very different trajectory. Settled by the British and the Dutch, the first of the original colonies—particularly Massachusetts, Rhode Island, and Pennsylvania—were colonized by religious dissidents whose religious devotion had been persecuted in Europe, and no central religious institution facilitated or organized settlement, as was the case with the Catholic Church in Spanish America. The relationship between Native Americans and colonists were generally hostile and led to warfare that lasted until the end of the nineteenth century. Unlike the Spaniards, however, the North American settlers made no attempt to enslave Native Americans. Instead, there was a continuous push-concentrate process, the motive and goal of which was to expropriate land from the Native Americans.

The European North American colonists tended to question central authority and monarchies. They sought community in small groups of like-minded individuals, and this structure provided the framework for the individual "colonies" or states, each with a distinct personality. The colonial history of the thirteen colonies that achieved independence from Great Britain was shorter (by about 150 years) than the colonial history of Spain in America; this meant North American institutional and cultural ties with the mother country were weaker, easier to break away from, and more flexible than those in the South American case.

Rather than apply value judgments of Spain in America versus Britain in America, it is safer and more succinct to say that sharp differences in the economic, cultural, and religious makeup of the South and the North differentiated Latin American historical development from that of Anglo America.[2] An understanding of the eighteenth- and early nineteenth-century Wars of Independence provides further historical evidence of the dissimilar historical trajectory between and among the Americas.

The thirteen British colonies achieved political independence from Great Britain after an eight-year war, a brief experiment with a decentralized system under the Articles of Confederation, and final settlement on the republican form of government with a strong executive and a guiding constitution written in Philadelphia in 1787. This "experiment" in self-government was centered on a tradition of self-confidence, an inclination toward individualism, and a clear conception that America (the United States) was blessed with a divine spirit, stocked with abundant and seemingly endless natural resources, and youthfully vigorous compared with Europe—which was viewed as tradition bound, tired, and war-torn. African slaves and continual flows of migrants from Europe provided a constant source of labor that sustained not only a growing economy but America's sense of its own self-importance. Political independence from Great Britain—in the colonies—was perceived as a clean break and a fresh start, especially after the ego-boosting War of 1812, sometimes referred to as a Second War of Independence.

John Lynch, a scholar of Latin American independence, has characterized Latin American independence with the phrase "same mule, different rider."[3] Lynch was referring to the fact that with independence little actually changed in terms of economic and social development. Politically, clear changes could be seen in that Spaniards were no longer welcome, but those who replaced them in office were essentially Creoles (American-born whites) who looked to France, Great Britain, and—to a lesser but increasing extent—the new nation to the north for inspiration and guidance. Many early constitutions of the new republics in Latin America were verbatim copies of the documents of the French Revolution (1789), "The Universal Declaration of the Rights of Man," or the U.S. Constitution (1787).

Part of the reason, then, that Latin America's nineteenth century was so complicated, contentious, and catastrophic involved the fact that "independence" never brought true independence to the popular classes; never dealt with enormous yet institutionalized social, economic, and racial inequalities; and was based on theories and constitutions that had been developed and implemented in other parts of the world. A struggle with identity further marked and differentiated Latin America's development from development in the North.[4] From the earliest days of European invasion, Latin American history depended on and imported many intellectual, political, and economic features of Europe. Latin American culture and identity, then, became a curious but rich mixture of African, Native American, and European characteristics. This meant that during the nineteenth century Latin American elites, rather than building stable societies with clear priorities, spent much time distancing themselves from the numerous Native Americans among whom they had recently rebelled.[5] After 1824 economic and political identity came increasingly from abroad—from England and the United States.

LATIN AMERICAN INDEPENDENCE AND THE MONROE DOCTRINE

The U.S. expressed sympathy for the Latin American independence movements. However, U.S. reluctance to wholeheartedly support the process resulted mostly from a general policy of isolationism during the early days of the republic. Latin American independence did become a source of debate and tension in the United States—particularly between Henry Clay, speaker of the House of Representatives, who strongly favored recognizing Latin American independence (he even called for providing military assistance), and John Quincy Adams, secretary of state, who was suspicious of both Clay's motives and Latin America's ability to achieve representative government. Latin Americans, for their part, were equally suspicious of the United States. Simón Bolívar was one of the more vocal critics; he advised caution in dealing with the neighbor to the north in his often repeated 1829 phrase that "the United States appear to be destined by Providence to plague America with misery in the name of liberty."[6]

What was clear from the time of Latin American independence was that U.S.–Latin American relations would be shaped and framed within the context of hemispheric threats emanating from Europe. The No-Transfer Resolution of 1811 and the Monroe Doctrine of 1823 became the cornerstones of U.S. policy toward Latin America, dominated by the goal of keeping extrahemispheric rivals from threatening U.S. security in the Western Hemisphere. In short, Washington's policy toward Latin America "rarely focused upon Latin America per se, but upon what extra-hemispheric rivals might do in Latin America that could affect the security of the United States."[7]

The Monroe Doctrine became the cornerstone of the relationship that developed between the United States and Latin America more than a century and a half ago. Although few took notice of President James Monroe's message in 1823, the doctrine was a statement of intentions and was directed more to European powers than to the newly emerging Latin American republics. Written by John Quincy Adams, U.S. secretary of state under Monroe, the doctrine stated that any attempt by a European power to recolonize territory in Latin America would be considered a hostile act by the United States. The Monroe Doctrine was not law, was not voted on by Congress, and was little discussed at the time; it was merely a statement but one that was debated and reinterpreted for decades in the United States, Europe, and Latin America.

Part I of this volume is organized around the writings of three thinkers—Josiah Strong, José Enrique Rodó and Fredrick Pike—all of whom offer divergent interpretations of the U.S. role as hemispheric integrator or dominator. Part II captures the essence of the debate surrounding the Monroe Doctrine. Dexter Perkins, Elihu Root, and Gaston Nerval wrote extensively on the doctrine: Perkins as a scholar, Root as statesman, and Nerval as a Latin American critic of the document. Through the juxtaposition of these three distinct views the reader comes to a fuller understanding of the complexity of the doctrine itself and of the entire social and political milieu in which it was created.

Relations between the United States and Latin America were compelling and dramatic in the 1830s and 1840s, particularly concerning the annexation of

Texas. The resultant Mexican-American War (1846–1848) left Mexico vanquished, losing about half of its national territory, whereas the United States grew by about one-third in terms of territorial acquisition. The damage this war did to U.S.–Latin American relations was, some have argued, irreparable.[8] U.S. ambition and desire for territorial expansion, fueled by a theory of "Manifest Destiny," were pitted against a politically weaker and more fragmented Mexico.[9] The United States triumphed on the battlefield, and theoreticians and scholars debated the lasting impact of the war—and U.S. territorial expansion during the nineteenth century in general—during the decades that followed. The widely contrasting theories of Josiah Strong, José Enrique Rodó, and Fredrick Pike help to put this era in perspective for the reader. The diversity of opinion and passion of rhetoric provide a glimpse at the intensity engendered by issues of territory and politics among the United States, Mexico, and Latin America. We have placed this debate at the beginning of the volume because the theoretical issues covered provide a unifying framework for the volume as a whole.

MIXED MESSAGES: FROM BIG STICK TO GOOD NEIGHBOR

The period between 1898 and 1903 represented dramatic implementation of U.S. policy toward Latin America. Three important episodes—the Spanish-American War (1898), Theodore Roosevelt's rise to the presidency (1901), and Panama's "independence" (1903)—forever defined U.S.–Latin American relations. Taken together, these three episodes clearly established a relationship of antagonism between the United States and Latin America with the former appearing far more concerned with profitability, business, and security than with the ideology of democracy or sovereignty.[10] Part III in this volume focuses on the period from the presidency of Theodore Roosevelt to that of Franklin Delano Roosevelt (FDR) and shows the reader how policy changed more in style than in priority during that time. FDR's Good Neighbor policy was an attempt to change strategy without altering the ultimate objective—securing a sphere of influence in Latin America. The Great Depression (1929) and the need to fuel growth through reciprocal trade agreements, along with ominous threats from Europe, required an approach that made the United States seem less of a threat and more of a partner.[11] Fredrick Pike's important work on FDR and the Good Neighbor policy suggests that political and economic cooperation was more the result of a confluence of cultural values and U.S. appreciation of Latin America's spiritual and nonmaterial life.[12] The impoverishing effect of the Great Depression brought the Americas closer together, allowing for greater cultural cooperation and less direct military intervention.[13]

The Langley chapter, published in part III, demonstrates the difficulties, confusions, missteps, and successes during the initial days of U.S. occupation of

Cuba in the wake of the Spanish-American War. U.S. troops left Cuba in 1902, but for four years, the United States governed the island, yet U.S. administrators were unprepared for the tropical climate, the informality of social relations, and the relative lack of infrastructure on the island. Samuel Flagg Bemis, who published an overarching synthesis of hemispheric relations in 1936, focuses on the political, diplomatic, and strategic concerns; his chapter presented in part III offers a more traditional approach and interpretation that would be challenged by the revisionist economic historians of the 1960s and later. Walter LaFeber's 1984 pathbreaking *Inevitable Revolutions* is an example of scholarship that focused on economic and social history, and challenged the more genteel vision of earlier diplomatic historians.

THE COLD WAR: LATIN AMERICA IN THE EAST-WEST STRUGGLE

Parts IV and V delve into the Cold War and the impact of the East-West struggle on U.S.–Latin American relations. As Latin America became one of several battlefields in this global struggle, the attention and resources devoted to studying the region expanded rapidly, particularly after the Cuban Revolution (1959). A number of research centers, universities, and think tanks grew from the need to understand the causes of instability and social struggle that threatened to undermine political and economic interests in the region. During the 1960s theoretical and empirical studies of Latin American political development became part of U.S. mainstream academia. Much of the work was financed by the government, seeking answers to public policy questions. Specifically, questions centered on how to reverse or contain revolutionary forces from overwhelming Latin American societies and potentially threatening U.S. interests.[14]

The United States launched an anticommunist crusade, often collaborating with friendly authoritarian regimes to crush all "leftist" threats emanating from any sector of society, including many democratic and reformist forces. In many ways U.S. policy contributed to the societal polarization it was attempting to contain. The United States set out to assert its hegemony by establishing a security zone in Latin America (the Inter-American Treaty of Reciprocal Assistance or Rio Treaty in 1947) while exhuming elements of the Monroe Doctrine. Military intervention was viewed as a policy option during much of the Cold War, as the cases of Guatemala (1954), Cuba (1961), the Dominican Republic (1965), and Chile (1973) demonstrate. Policymakers in Washington were not averse to supporting military coups, as in Brazil (1964), when they believed communists were attempting to use their influence in the Goulart government to destroy democracy.[15]

The need to support anticommunist regimes often led to acquiescence with dictatorships. In 1950 one of the most important architects of U.S. Cold War policy,

George Kennan, stated that Washington policymakers had no choice but to support authoritarian regimes in Latin America. These governments, according to Kennan, were certain to ensure stability and protect vital interests in the region.[16] Kennan stated that Latin American nations had not yet come to maturity and at the present demonstrated no cultural inclination toward democratic rule. This policy of supporting military regimes while remaining suspicious of and vigilant toward Latin America's "democratic experiments" became known as the Kennan Corollary to the Monroe Doctrine.[17] In short, embracing dictatorships like those of Duvalier in Haiti, Somoza in Nicaragua, Trujillo in the Dominican Republic, and the military regimes of the 1960s and 1970s in Argentina, Brazil, Chile, and Uruguay was a cold-blooded calculation—dictatorial regimes would be more strongly and efficiently anticommunist than other types of governance.[18]

Part IV examines U.S. policy toward three revolutionary processes and regimes—Bolivia, Guatemala, and Cuba—previously governed by strong anticommunist dictatorships aligned with the United States. The section begins with two chapters that express U.S. sentiment toward Latin American in the period immediately following the World War II. Roger Trask focuses on the Cold War's impact on Latin America, and George Kennan, venerable State Department official and foreign policy intellectual, offers a damning critique of the Latin American region and people. He feared that communism would spread throughout the region and prescribed support for repressive (noncommunist) regimes. By the early 1950s, Washington was faced with political and social crises in Latin America, and three cases were of particular importance during the 1950s: Bolivia, Guatemala, and Cuba. In each case Washington responded differently to nationalist, revolutionary regimes, and attempted to destroy the regime of Fidel Castro by the same means it had used to successfully undermine the regime of reform-minded Guatemalan president Jacobo Arbenz. By closely analyzing these three cases the reader will understand the disparate forces and actors that led to U.S. reconciliation with Bolivia in the period 1952–1960, the overthrow of Arbenz in Guatemala in 1954, and failure and embarrassment in Cuba in the period of 1959–1961.

Part V examines a long and critical period in U.S.–Latin American relations during the Cold War (1962–1989). In the area of development during the early days of the Cold War, the message to Latin America was clear—no aid but trade. Washington urged Latin America to open its economies to trade and investments to generate growth and development. Expectations of a Marshall Plan for Latin America were quickly dashed at the Bogotá Conference in 1948. Only during the Kennedy administration—and after the Cuban Revolution—did a change in policy develop. In an interesting convergence of academia and policy, President Kennedy followed the advice of the modernizationists in his administration, who believed an injection of capital would contribute to growth and development and, in turn, to stability and democracy in the developing world.[19] A multi-billion-dollar assistance program sought to avoid the creation of "second Cubas" but instead led to the conditions that fostered revolution and military governments in Latin America. The Alliance for Progress, a Kennedy-initiated program that promised more than $20 billion for Latin American social development, demonstrated the degree of misunderstanding between Washington policymakers and Latin Americans.[20] The alliance also featured a military component through which the Kennedy administration hoped to "professionalize" the armed forces by providing them with aid, training, and the capacity to conduct civic action and counterinsurgency operations. This "new professionalism" also had the opposite effect. Throughout the 1960s and 1970s Latin American militaries assumed the reins of power, establishing themselves as a more permanent political force. Jerome Levinson and Juan de Onís's work, excerpted in this volume, examines the failures and miscalculations of the Alliance for Progress.

The Johnson and Nixon administrations, recognizing the failures of the alliance, pulled back from the program and reinstated the Kennan Corollary. Thomas Mann, assistant secretary of state for inter-American affairs in the Johnson administration, made sure lofty attempts toward democracy and development did not get in the way of U.S. security priorities. He claimed to know what Latin Americans wanted and needed, and he stated that "a buck in the pocket and a kick in the ass" would suffice. In 1966 Mann articulated the Johnson administration's Latin American policy (the Mann Doctrine) whereby military or rightist regimes would be tolerated if they followed a strong anticommunist line (i.e., Brazil in 1964). The policy was merely a reaffirmation of Washington's Cold War policy, which had been somewhat slighted by the previous administration. President Johnson—preoccupied with Southeast Asia—either neglected Latin America, supporting anticommunist allies in the region, or intervened militarily, as in the Dominican Republic in 1965.

President Richard Nixon made several attempts to establish a new "special relationship" with Latin America, but they came to naught. The Rockefeller Commission on Latin America called for greater economic engagement through trade and aid; however, in the area of politics the report reinforced the position taken by Kennan and Mann. The economic component of the report was disregarded, but the Nixon administration accepted the warning of communist penetration in Latin America. The U.S. role in the overthrow of Chilean president Salvador Allende in 1973 was consistent with both the report's recommendations and Cold War policy.[21]

Meanwhile, during this period Latin Americans sought to find a way out of their asymmetrical relationship with the United States. Most intellectuals and politicians viewed U.S. policy, as Peter Smith states, with "apprehension, alarm, and disdain."[22] Latin Americans began to develop options for confronting and mitigating U.S. power. One option was to undertake revolutionary change in the name of social justice and Marxism, mixed with nationalism, against U.S. interests and allies in Latin America. Guerrilla movements emerged throughout Latin America, espousing nationalism and populist causes. The other option, offered by nationalist leaders such as Venezuelan president Carlos Andrés Pérez and Luis Echeverria of Mexico, was the Nonaligned Movement, which sought to establish a "third way"—an independent and neutral foreign policy and a new economic development model. Latin America became a strong proponent of the New International Economic Order, which many in the region believed was Latin America's best hope for diminishing its economic dependence on the United States.

The election of Jimmy Carter as U.S. president in 1977 and the immediate announcement of a dramatic shift in foreign policy in favor of human rights and democracy indicated an end to the old policy of coddling anticommunist dictators. The Carter administration not only withheld economic and military aid but also pressured regimes in Argentina, Brazil, Chile, Guatemala, Nicaragua, and Paraguay to respect human rights. The White House argued that pressuring those regimes to cede power to trusted centrists in a process of gradual political liberalization would avoid polarization and thus prevent a communist victory.[23] Carter and his advisers believed this policy would regain support for the United States in Latin America and hoped that finalizing an agreement on the Panama Canal would repair Washington's tarnished image in the region. By the final two years of Carter's presidency, however, revolutions in Central America had become a top policy priority. Carter wished to remain true to his human rights policy by pressuring illegitimate, reactionary regimes in El Salvador, Guatemala, and Nicaragua to liberalize, but in these highly polarized societies the only alternative was often radical, Marxist revolutionaries. President Carter's attempt to find a middle course in El Salvador and Nicaragua is generally viewed as too little, too late. In the end he felt he had no choice but to restore economic and military aid to the military government in El Salvador, whereas in Nicaragua he attempted to moderate the course of the Sandinista Revolution by providing US $75 million in aid. In Guatemala in 1978, President Carter cut off aid to the administration of General Romeo Lucas, who was one of the worst human rights abusers in modern Guatemalan history.

In Washington, the Carter administration came under heavy attack from conservative forces in Congress and the media. Many called for the administration to restore the Kennan Corollary and the Mann Doctrine. This case was made in a highly critical article by Georgetown University professor Jeane Kirkpatrick entitled "Dictatorship and Double Standards," which appeared in *Commentary* in 1979.[24] Kirkpatrick criticized the Carter administration for undermining allies through its human rights policy while tolerating what she described as tyrannical, totalitarian regimes bent on destroying the United States (i.e., Castro's Cuba). According to Kirkpatrick, the double standard involved Carter's failure to distinguish between the two types of dictatorship. Her recommendation was merely the restatement of an old policy: to provide support and aid to authoritarian regimes that are almost always anticommunist and friendly to the United States. Kirkpatrick's argument, like those earlier espoused by Kennan and Mann, was based on the premise that Latin America was a traditional society not yet prepared for democracy. Therefore, rather than attempting to impose democracy (which would be hopeless), the United States must protect and ensure its security interests in Latin America. Kirkpatrick's argument was important in shaping Ronald Reagan's policies toward Latin America. Moreover, Kirkpatrick's thesis that totalitarian regimes were incapable of democratic change was consistent with what would soon be hailed as the Reagan Doctrine.[25]

REAGAN'S ELECTION

Immediately after taking office in 1981, the Reagan administration went on the offensive in Central America and the Caribbean. There was a marked change in the tone and style of U.S. policy.[26] The White House was determined to purge "communism" from the hemisphere, even supporting armed minorities (the contras) in their attacks on leftist governments (i.e., the Sandinistas in Nicaragua). The first test of U.S. policy and resolve came in Grenada in October 1983. Warning that Soviet-Cuban support existed for the coup against Maurice Bishop by an "ultra-radical" group led by Bernard Coard, President Reagan deployed troops to "thwart the USSR from establishing another base in the Caribbean and restore democracy to the island."[27]

On the heels of a successful quick-fix solution in Grenada, the administration turned aggressively to helping El Salvador defeat the leftist insurgency and undermining the Sandinista government in Nicaragua by financing and supporting a counterrevolutionary movement known as the *contra-revolucionarios*, or contras. In Central America as in other regions of the Third World, the administration stressed the global and strategic implications of local conflicts that were rooted not in the East-West struggle but in the region's lack of political legitimacy and socioeconomic equity.[28]

In 1983 President Reagan called on former secretary of state Henry Kissinger to chair a bipartisan commission on Central America to "study the nature of United States interests in the Central American region and the threats now posed to those interests." Although the commission's report noted some of the region's endemic political and socioeconomic problems and recommended an economic aid program of around $8 billion, it still reaffirmed the old policy of supporting friendly anticommunist governments regardless of their record on democracy and human rights.[29] Like the earlier Rockefeller Commission, Kissinger's bipartisan group warned of Soviet and Cuban influence and urged the United States to develop a comprehensive response to communist subversion in the region.

Meanwhile, Latin America feared that continued internationalization of the Central American crisis not only threatened to trigger an expansion of fighting that might engulf the entire region but also prevented the United States and Latin America from focusing on other, more critical social and economic issues, such as burgeoning debt. In 1984 the Contadora countries—Colombia, Mexico, Panama, Venezuela—worked hard to find a negotiated solution to the Central American crisis, putting forth a list of twenty-one principles emphasizing the need for all extraregional powers to withdraw from the isthmus and for Central Americans to hold "free and fair elections" ensuring equal participation for all parties.[30] Strong backing from a support group composed of representatives of Argentina, Brazil, Peru, and Uruguay gave the process further impetus and legitimacy. This attempt at regional mediation was unique in its effort to establish a new form of cooperation among Latin American countries. Unfortunately, the process failed because of resistance from the Reagan administration together with the Sandinistas and contras inability to arrive at a negotiated settlement of war in Nicaragua. Robert Pastor, who served as director of Latin American affairs in the Carter administration and currently works as professor of international relations at American University in Washington, D.C., provides a careful analysis—in part V—that helps the reader understand the development of U.S. policy toward Nicaragua; he notes the essential continuities in policy during the 1970s and 1980s and looks at the Nicaragua policy as reacting to the Cuban Revolution of the late 1950s.

Only in 1986, with the Reagan administration distracted by the Iran-Contra fiasco and the U.S. Congress reasserting its foreign policy responsibilities (i.e., shifting its opinion on contra aid), did Central Americans have an opportunity to solve the crisis through a negotiated settlement. Costa Rican president Oscar Arias initiated the peace process in 1987, presenting his weary colleagues with a plan to bring an end to conflicts in these war-torn societies. The Esquipulas accords—signed in August 1987—called for cease-fire, political dialogue among all groups, prohibition of irregular guerrilla forces, and free elections. The White House preoccupation with the political fallout from Iran-Contra and Congressional support for a Central American solution helped to ensure the plan's success.

DEBT, 1980s STYLE

The debt crisis of the 1980s and the Reagan administration's unwillingness to accept blame for the severity of the problem also contributed to the animosity that characterized U.S.–Latin American relations in the 1980s. Latin America's foreign debt brought financial and social ruin. The region's standard of living plummeted as the capacity of governments to invest in infrastructure and social services declined as a result of extremely high debt servicing, usually around 35 percent of export revenues. As many analysts have pointed out, including Riordan Roett in a chapter included in this volume, the debt crisis ravished and negated every social and economic gain achieved by the region during the 1950s and 1960s.[31] It was not until 1987 that the United States, along with the region's European creditors, worked to devise plans to alleviate the financial and social burdens caused by the debt crisis.

The debt crisis and Central America were not the only issues of discontent between the Americas during the 1980s; drug trafficking also created tensions in the relationship. As Bruce Bagley and Juan Tokatlian note, the U.S. supply-side policy of punishing countries for "not doing their part" in the so-called drug war has been not only counterproductive but also antithetical to cooperative relations between Washington and Latin America. In the end, drug policy regarding Latin America in the 1980s neither resolved the drug problem in the United States nor helped to consolidate strong democratic institutions in drug-producing countries.

The foreign debt, the Cold War, the "hot wars" in Central America during the 1980s, and the war on drugs took a heavy toll on Latin America and its relationship with the United States. The policy of unabashedly supporting anticommunist regimes not only contributed to undermining democratic political forces and deepening a process of polarization that benefited the most reactionary groups, but also postponed or set back the cause of economic development and social justice in the region. Margaret Daly Hayes perhaps stated it best when she described the 1980s as "the lost decade" in her 1988/89 *Foreign Affairs* article.

POST–COLD WAR OPTIMISM AND UNCERTAINTY

Part VI focuses on U.S.–Latin American relations from the 1990s to the post-9/11 period. While the 1980s might have been a "lost decade" because of debt, drugs, and despair, the 1990s was a more optimistic period in U.S.–Latin American relations. Democracy returned to Chile, the Sandinistas were elected out of power in 1990 and they left office peacefully, and serious negotiations were under way to end the endemic bloodshed in the other Central American countries, El Salvador and Guatemala. Peace accords were finally signed in 1992 in El Salvador and 1996 in Guatemala. Washington pushed Latin America to adopt administrative, fiscal, and other reforms in the name of what came to be known as "the Washington Consensus." Latin American governments, since the 1980s, were encouraged by the United States to privatize their banking sectors, their utilities, and other state-run entities that could be managed by the private sector (airlines, electric works, and oil and natural gas companies). Privatization in Latin America led to an infusion of outside investment, and profits soared for investors. Unfortunately, poverty continued, and today, approximately 43 percent of Latin Americans are categorized as living below the poverty line—a staggering 224 million citizens.

Bill Clinton, elected president in 1992, was enthusiastically embraced by Latin American leaders: he was an articulate leader who spoke extemporaneously about a wide variety of complex social, political, and economic issues. His charisma and story of growing up poor in rural Arkansas resonated with Latin Americans who viewed his election to the presidency as a clear example of how the United States "differed" from Latin America (where, historically, most leaders emerge from the elite classes). Clinton's initial outreach to Latin America involved trade—he was determined to secure passage of the North American Free Trade Agreement, or NAFTA (negotiations for which had begun in the 1980s). NAFTA would create a free trade zone between the United States, Canada, and Mexico, but opposition in the United States was significant and organized. Labor unions were opposed, for they feared that U.S. workers would lose their jobs as manufacturing plants moved south of the border. Texas billionaire Ross Perot famously predicted that, if passed, NAFTA would create a "giant sucking sound" as jobs, financing, and industry moved from the U.S. industrial heartland to the south side of the U.S.-Mexican border. Environmental organizations worried about lax environmental standards in Mexico, and predicted that hazardous smog, polluted water, and other contaminants would characterize the Mexico-U.S. border and would seep into the U.S. mainland.

NAFTA did pass, and went into effect on 1 January 1994. That same day, a Mexican revolutionary group called the EZLN (Zapatista Army of National Liberation) emerged and announced to the world that it was in armed opposition to NAFTA and free trade in general. The EZLN represented the poor of southern Mexico—people who had, historically, been forgotten about by Mexican elites in the capital city. They asked, via their January uprising, how they would in fact benefit from NAFTA and predicted that they would never be able to compete, agriculturally, with imported Kansas wheat and Nebraska corn. One of the chapters in part VI is an effective critique of the trend toward "globalization"; Professor Richard Harris of California State University at Monterey Bay focuses on some of the Latin American responses to globalization, and the EZLN is just one of the groups he studies. Professor Harris calls for peaceful resistance and "popular mobilization" throughout the Americas as a way to militate against the challenges of the relentless push toward globalization.

Trade, then, became a key issue in the early to mid-1990s, and Luisa Angrisani writes about the myriad of trade partnerships that developed throughout the Latin American region beginning in the mid-1990s as a way of building on NAFTA's energy and infrastructure. Other important issues to emerge in U.S.–Latin American relations involved immigration and the environment. Our second edition of *Neighborly Adversaries* includes an original chapter on each topic. Immigration remains, as of this writing, a critically important concern in the United States and Latin America. The mid-1990s witnessed an especially hostile period, culminating in the passage of the 1994 California Ballot Initiative Proposition 187 (which attempted to deny education and health care to undocumented adults—and children—living in California). The initiative never went into effect and was, by 1999, declared unconstitutional by the Courts. Conservative political commentator Pat Buchanan launched a 1996 presidential candidacy based on an essentially "anti-immigration" platform. He lost, but the rhetoric became vitriolic for a few years during the 1990s, and the chapter by Michael LaRosa and Lance R. Ingwersen presents the immigration debate in historic perspective. Environmental concerns could not be ignored by the early 1990s, especially with the passage of NAFTA. Wesley Ingwersen and Laura Ávila have contributed a chapter that focuses on the environmental challenges imposed by free or freer trade and they present some of the specific problems, concerns, and policies that have emerged over the past few years. The chapter is organized around specific policies and case studies, and focuses on the period since June 1992, when the Rio Treaty was ratified. Essentially, the Rio conference dealt with changes in the global climate due to human intervention, though the treaty to emerge out of this meeting had been worked on at the United Nations General Assembly prior to the Rio meeting. By the early 1990s, with rapidly expanding trade and increased purchasing power in places like Brazil and Mexico, new standards and cooperative agreements had to be developed as a way to protect natural resources—many of which cannot be renewed.

When George W. Bush arrived to the presidency by January 2001, it appeared that Latin America would be a central concern of his administration. The first state visit, in September 2001, was in honor of Mexican President Vicente Fox. Fox and Bush famously displayed their cowboy boots, and talked openly about how they preferred the quiet life of the ranch to the hustle of the big city. President Fox addressed a joint session of Congress on September 7, 2001, and talked clearly about the need for innovative immigration reform between the United States and Mexico. Four days later, of course, Latin America moved immediately to the back burner of U.S. priorities, and three chapters in part VI by Jorge Castañeda (former Foreign Minister in the Fox administration), and U.S.-based scholars and "Washington insiders" Michael Shifter and Arturo Valenzuela present U.S. policy toward Latin America in the post-9/11 world. The news, of course, is not good, and taken together, the three chapters paint a grim picture of missed opportunities, mistrust, and misplaced priorities. The three authors are not optimistic about the immediate future of U.S.–Latin American relations, and if the November 4, 2005, summit at Mar del Plata (Argentina) is any indication, U.S. prestige in the region has been seriously damaged by the War in Iraq and the U.S. insistence on pushing Free Trade Agreements that have failed to create prosperity and security for the majority of Latin American citizens. Hugo Chávez—the leftist/populist president of oil-rich Venezuela—was able to mobilize 20,000 people at the soccer stadium of Mar del Plata on the day of the summit to peacefully denounce globalization and U.S. policies in Latin America and the world. At the same time, hundreds of Argentines came out to protest against President Bush, and the U.S. president seemed alone, tired, and frustrated at the Argentine meeting—no significant policies or initiatives emerged at the summit. This meeting might come to foreshadow the deterioration of hemispheric relations—as predicted by several of the authors in part VI—in the absence of serious, committed leadership in Washington.

We believe the chapters in this volume capture the dichotomous and at times contradictory nature of U.S.–Latin American relations since the 1820s. This explains the incongruous title of the volume—*Neighborly Adversaries*. The relationship is filled with peaks and valleys that are often difficult to follow, but we have also sought to point out in the readings and editorial comments certain consistent traits in the relationship. We anticipate that this volume will add to increased discussion, debate, and scrutiny of an exciting and increasingly important relationship that is at once neighborly and adversarial, and as time goes by, increasingly difficult to characterize.

I

Disparate Perceptions:
Expansionism versus Arielismo

Misunderstandings between the United States and Latin America date back to the earliest days of independence, which was finalized in Latin America with the battle of Ayacucho (Peru) in 1824. Conflicting regional interests in Latin America led to a long period of caudillo rule, economic insecurity, and grinding poverty for rural residents. The Mexican-American War (1846–1848)—in which Mexicans lost about half of their national territory to the United States—demonstrated the difficult and usually contradictory aims of the Americas. By the mid-nineteenth century Simón Bolívar's remark that the United States appeared "destined by Providence to plague America with torments in the name of freedom" seemed almost prophetic.[1]

U.S. expansion was driven by a spirit of Manifest Destiny, a term coined in the 1840s by journalist John O'Sullivan. Manifest Destiny suggested that it was the destiny of Anglo-Saxon Americans to civilize and conquer the "barbaric" Native Americans and that this civilizing mission was guided and supported by the laws of God and man. Josiah Strong is perhaps best representative of this spirit of westward expansion during the nineteenth century, although his views were far from mainstream. Many intellectuals in Latin America and elsewhere criticized the crass materialist spirit that seemed to be driving U.S.–Latin American policy during the nineteenth century and particularly in the period after the U.S. Civil War (1861–1865). José Enrique Rodó offered one such criticism in the important treatise *Ariel*. Rodó faulted the United States for its proclivity to place material and strictly "utilitarian" values above all else. Taken together, Strong and Rodó offer a compelling glimpse at the differing historical trajectories that shaped U.S. and Latin American societies, as well as an outline of future tensions and misunderstandings. Fredrick Pike's work represents a contemporary scholarly exploration of the origins of negative U.S. stereotyping of Latin Americans during the nineteenth century.

2

The Anglo-Saxon and the World's Future

Josiah Strong

Josiah Strong, a Congregational minister, advocated rapid territorial expansion of the United States based on Darwinism, Protestantism, and the supposed superiority of the Anglo-Saxon "race." North America, according to Strong, "is to be the great home of the Anglo-Saxon, the principal seat of his power, the center of life and influence." In 1885 Strong published his ideas in the book Our Country, *which sold more than 167,000 copies. Strong believed the United States would take over the world and that "the powerful race will move down upon Mexico, down upon Central and South America, out upon the islands of the sea, over upon Africa and beyond."[1] John Fiske and Senator Albert Beveridge of Indiana echoed Strong's views; Admiral Alfred T. Mahan and President Theodore Roosevelt would build naval and political strategies based on his ideas. Strong's ideology is remarkable considering that racism, religion, science, and imperialism converge, reflecting both popular and academic thinking at the time.*

Every race which has deeply impressed itself on the human family has been the representative of some great idea—one or more—which has given direction to the nation's life and its form of civilization. Among the Egyptians this seminal idea was life, among the Persians it was light, among the Hebrews it was purity, among the Greeks it was beauty, among the Romans it was law. The Anglo-Saxon is the representative of two great ideas, which are closely related. One of them is that of civil liberty. Nearly all of the civil liberty in the world is enjoyed by Anglo-Saxons: the English, the British colonists, and the people of the United States. To some, like the Swiss, it is permitted by the sufferance of their neighbors; others, like the French, have experimented with it; but, in modern times, the people whose love of liberty has won it, and whose genius for self-government has preserved it, have been Anglo-Saxons. The noblest races have

19

always been lovers of liberty. That love ran strong in early German blood, and has profoundly influenced the institutions of all branches of the great German family; but it was left for the Anglo-Saxon branch fully to recognize the right of the individual to himself, and formally to declare it the foundation stone of government.

The other great idea of which the Anglo-Saxon is the exponent is that of a pure spiritual Christianity. It was no accident that the great reformation of the sixteenth century originated among a Teutonic, rather than a Latin people. It was the fire of liberty burning in the Saxon heart that flamed up against the absolutism of the Pope. Speaking roughly, the peoples of Europe which are Celtic are Catholic, and those which are Teutonic are Protestant; and where the Teutonic race was purest, there Protestantism spread with the greatest rapidity. But, with rare and beautiful exceptions, Protestantism on the continent has degenerated into mere formalism. By confirmation at a certain age, the state churches are filled with members who generally know nothing of a personal spiritual experience. In obedience to a military order, a regiment of German soldiers files into church and partakes of the sacrament, just as it would shoulder arms or obey any other word of command. It is said that, in Berlin and Leipsic, only a little over one percent of the Protestant population are found in church. Protestantism on the continent seems to be about as poor in spiritual life and power as Catholicism. That means that most of the spiritual Christianity in the world is found among Anglo-Saxons and their converts; for this is the great missionary race. If we take all of the German missionary societies together, we find that, in the number of workers and amount of contributions, they do not equal the smallest of the three great English missionary societies. The year that Congregationalists in the United States gave one dollar and thirty-seven cents per caput to foreign missions, the members of the great German State Church gave only three-quarters of a cent per caput to the same cause. Evidently it is chiefly to the English and American peoples that we must look for the evangelization of the world.

It is not necessary to argue to those for whom I write that the two great needs of mankind, that all men may be lifted up into the light of the highest Christian civilization, are, first, a pure, spiritual Christianity, and, second, civil liberty. Without controversy, these are forces which, in the past, have contributed most to the elevation of the human race, and they must continue to be, in the future, the most efficient ministers to the progress. It follows, then, that the Anglo-Saxon, as the great representative of these two ideas, the depositary of these two greatest blessings, sustains peculiar relations to the world's future, is divinely commissioned to be, in a peculiar sense, his brother's keeper. Add to this the fact of his rapidly increasing strength in modern times, and we have well nigh a demonstration of his destiny. In 1700 this race numbered less than 6,000,000 souls. In 1800, Anglo-Saxons (I use the term somewhat broadly to include all

English-speaking peoples) had increased to about 20,500,000, and in 1880 they numbered nearly 100,000,000, having multiplied almost five-fold in eighty years. At the end of the reign of Charles II, the English colonists in America numbered 200,000. During these two hundred years, our population has increased two hundred and fifty-fold. And the expansion of this race has been no less remarkable than its multiplication. In one century the United States has increased its territory ten-fold, while the enormous acquisition of foreign territory by Great Britain—and chiefly within the last hundred years—is wholly unparalleled in history. This mighty Anglo-Saxon race, though comprising only one-fifteenth part of mankind, now rules more than one-third of the earth's surface, and more than one-fourth of its people. And if this race, while growing from 6,000,000 to 100,000,000, thus gained possession of a third portion of the earth, is it to be supposed that when it numbers 1,000,000,000, it will lose the disposition, or lack the power to extend its sway?

This race is multiplying not only more rapidly than any other European race, but far more rapidly than all the races of continental Europe. There is no exact knowledge of the population of Europe early in the century; we know, however, that the increase on the continent during the ten years from 1870 to 1880 was 6.89 percent. If this rate of increase is sustained for a century (and it is more likely to fall, as Europe becomes more crowded), the population on the continent in 1980 will be 534,000,000; while the one Anglo-Saxon race, if it should multiply for a hundred years as it increased from 1870 to 1880, would, in 1980, number 1,343,000,000 souls; but we cannot reasonably expect this ratio of increase to be sustained so long. What, then, will be the probable numbers of this race a hundred years hence? In attempting to answer this question, several things must be borne in mind. Heretofore, the great causes which have operated to check the growth of population in the world have been war, famine, and pestilence; but, among civilized peoples, these causes are becoming constantly less operative. Paradoxical as it seems, the invention of more destructive weapons of war renders war less destructive; commerce and wealth have removed the fear of famine, and pestilence is being brought more and more under control by medical skill and sanitary science. Moreover, Anglo-Saxons, with the exception of the people of Great Britain, who now compose only a little more than one-third of this race, are much less exposed to these checks upon growth than the races of Europe. Again, Europe is crowded and becoming more so, which will tend to reduce continually the ratio of increase; while nearly two-thirds of the Anglo-Saxons occupy lands which invite almost unlimited expansion—the United States, Canada, Australia, and South Africa. Again, emigration from Europe, which is certain to increase, is chiefly into Anglo-Saxon countries; while these foreign elements exert a modifying influence on the Anglo-Saxon stock, their descendants are certain to be Anglo-Saxonized. From 1870 to 1880, Germany lost 987,000 inhabitants by emigration; in one generation, their children will be counted Anglo-Saxons. This race has been undergoing an unparalleled expansion during the eighteenth and nineteenth centuries, and the conditions for its continued growth are singularly favorable.

We are now prepared to ask what light statistics cast on the future. In Great Britain, from 1840 to 1850, the ratio of increase of the population was 2.49 percent; during the next ten years, it was 8.60; and from 1870 to 1880, it was 10.57 percent. That is, for forty years the ratio of increase has been rapidly rising. It is not unlikely to continue rising for some time to come; but, remembering that the population is dense, in making our estimate for the next hundred years, we will suppose the ratio of increase to be only one-half as large as that from 1870 to 1880, which would make the population in 1980, 57,000,000. All the great colonies of Britain, except Canada, which has a great future, show a very high ratio of increase in population; that of Australia, from 1870 to 1880, was 56.50 percent; that of South Africa was 73.28. It is quite reasonable to suppose that the colonies, taken together, will double their population once in twenty-five years for the next century. In the United States, population has, on average, doubled once in twenty-five years since 1685. Adopting this ratio, then, for the English colonies, their 11,000,000 in 1880 will be 176,000,000 in 1980. [. . .] It is not unlikely that, before the close of the next century, this race will outnumber all the other civilized races of the world. Does it not look as if God were not only preparing in our Anglo-Saxon civilization the die with which to stamp the peoples of the earth, but as if he were also massing behind that die the mighty power with which to press it? My confidence that this race is eventually to give its civilization to mankind is not based on mere numbers—China forbid! I look forward to what the world has never yet seen united in the same race; viz., the greatest numbers, and the highest civilization.

There can be no reasonable doubt that North America is to be the great home of the Anglo-Saxon, the principal seat of his power, the center of life and influence. Not only does it constitute seven-elevenths of his possessions, but his empire is unsevered, while the remaining four-elevenths are fragmentary and scattered over the earth. Australia will have a great population; but its disadvantages, as compared with North America, are too manifest to need mention. Our continent has room and resources and climate, it lies in the pathway of nations, it belongs to the zone of power, and already, among Anglo-Saxons, do we lead in population and wealth. Of England, Franklin once wrote: "That pretty island which, compared to America, is but a stepping-stone in a brook, scarce enough of it above water to keep one's shoes dry." England can hardly hope to maintain her relative importance among Anglo-Saxon peoples when her "pretty island" is the home of only one-twentieth part of that race. With the wider distribution of wealth, and increasing facilities of intercourse, intelligence and influence are less centralized, and peoples become more homogeneous; and the more nearly homogeneous peoples are, the more do numbers tell. America is to have the great preponderance of numbers and of wealth, and by the logic of events will follow the scepter of controlling influence. This will be but the consummation of a movement as old as civilization—a result to which men have looked forward for centuries. John Adams records that nothing was "more ancient in his memory than the observation that arts, sciences, and empire had traveled westward; and in conversation it was always added that their next leap would be over the Atlantic into America." He recalled a couplet that had been "inscribed, or rather drilled, into a rock on the shore of Monument Bay in our old colony of Plymouth:

'The Eastern nations sink, their glory ends,
And empire rises where the sun descends.'"

The brilliant Galiani, who foresaw a future in which Europe should be ruled by America, wrote, during the Revolutionary War, "I will wager in favor of America, for the reason merely physical, that for 5,000 years genius has turned opposite to the diurnal motion, and traveled from the East to the West." Count d'Aranda, after signing the Treaty of Paris of 1773, as the representative of Spain, wrote his king: "This Federal Republic is born a pigmy. . . . A day will come when it will be a giant, even a colossus formidable in these countries."

Adam Smith, in his "Wealth of Nations," predicts the transfer of empire from Europe to America. The traveler, Burnaby, found, in the middle of the last century, that an idea had "entered into the minds of the generality of mankind, that empire is traveling westward; and everyone is looking forward with eager and impatient expectation to that destined moment when America is to give the law to the rest of the world." Charles Sumner wrote of the "coming time when the whole continent, with all its various states, shall be a Plural Unit, with one Constitution, one Liberty, and One Destiny," and when "the national example will be more puissant than army or navy for the conquest of the world." It surely needs no prophet's eye to see that the civilization of the United States is to be the civilization of America, and that the future of the continent is ours. In 1880, the United States was the home of more than one-half of the Anglo-Saxon race; and, if the computations already given are correct, a much larger proportion will be here a hundred years hence. It has been shown that we have room for at least a thousand millions. According to recent figures, there is in France a population of 180.88 to the square mile; in Germany, 216.62; in England and Wales, 428.67; in Belgium, 481.71; in the United States—not including Alaska—16.88. If our population were as dense as that of France, we should have, this side of Alaska, 537,000,000; if as dense as that of Germany, 643,000,000; if as dense as that of England and Wales, 1,173,000,000; if as dense as that of Belgium, 1,430,000,000.

But we are to have not only the larger portion of the Anglo-Saxon race for generations to come, we may reasonably expect to develop the highest type of Anglo-Saxon civilization. If human progress follows a law of development, if

"Time's noblest offspring is the last,"

our civilization should be the noblest; for we are

"The heirs of all the ages in the foremost files of time,"

and not only do we occupy the latitude of power, but *our land is the last to be occupied in that latitude*. There is no other virgin soil in the North Temperate Zone. If the consummation of human progress is not to be looked for here, if there is yet to flower a higher civilization, where is the soil that is to produce it? Whipple says: "There has never been a great migration that did not result in a new form of national genius." Our national genius is Anglo-Saxon, but not English, its distinctive type is the result of a finer nervous organization, which is certainly being developed in this country. "The history of the world's progress from savagery to barbarism, from barbarism to civilization, and, in civilization, from the lower degrees toward the higher, is the history of increase in average longevity, corresponding to, and accompanied by, increase of nervousness. Mankind has grown to be at once more delicate and more enduring, more sensitive to weariness and yet more patient of toil, impressible but capable of bearing powerful irritation; we are woven of finer fiber, which, though apparently frail, yet outlasts the coarser, as rich and costly garments oftentimes wear better than those of rougher workmanship." The roots of civilization are the nerves; and other things being equal, the finest nervous organization will produce the highest civilization. Heretofore, war has been almost the chief occupation of strong races. England, during the past sixty-eight years, has waged some seventy-seven wars. John Bright said recently that, during Queen Victoria's reign, $750,000,000 had been spent in war and 68,000 lives lost. The mission of the Anglo-Saxon has been largely that of the soldier; but the world is making progress, we are leaving behind the barbarism of war; as civilization advances, it will learn less of war, and concern itself more with the arts of peace, and for these the massive battle-ax must be wrought into tools of finer temper. The physical changes accompanied by mental, which are taking place in the people of the United States, are apparently to adapt men to the demands of a higher civilization. But the objection is here interposed that the "physical degeneracy of Americans" is inconsistent with the supposition of our advancing to a higher civilization. Professor Huxley, when at Buffalo he addressed the American Association for the Advancement of Science, said he had heard of the degeneration of the original American stock, but during his visit to the states he had failed to perceive it. We are not, however, in this matter, dependent on the opinion of even the best observers. During the War of the Confederacy, the Medical Department of the Provost Marshal General's Bureau gathered statistics from the examination of over half a million of men, native and foreign, young and old, sick and sound, drawn from every rank and condition of life, and, hence, fairly representing the whole people. Dr. Baxter's Official Report shows that our native whites were over an inch taller than the English, and nearly two-thirds of an inch taller than the Scotch, who, in height, were superior to all other foreigners. At the age of completed growth, the Irish, who were the stoutest of the foreigners, surpassed the native whites, in girth of chest, less than a quarter of an inch. Statistics as to weight are meager, but Dr. Baxter remarks that it is perhaps not too much to say that the war statistics show "that the mean weight of the white native of the United States is not disproportionate to his stature." Americans were found to be superior to Englishmen not only in height, but also in chest-measurement and weight. Such facts afford more than a hint that the higher civilization of the future will not lack an adequate physical basis in the people of the United States.

Mr. Darwin is not only disposed to see, in the superior vigor of our people, an illustration of his favorite theory of natural selection, but even intimates that the world's history thus far has been simply preparatory for our future, and tributary to it. He says: "There is apparently much truth in the belief that the wonderful progress of the United States, as well as the character of the people, are the results of natural selection; for the more energetic, restless, and courageous men from all parts of Europe have emigrated during the last ten or twelve generations to the great country, and have there succeeded best. Looking at the distant future, I do not think that the Rev. Mr. Zincke takes an exaggerated view when he says: 'All other series of events—as that which resulted in the culture of mind in Greece, and that which resulted in the Empire of Rome—only appear to have purpose and value when viewed in connection with, or rather as subsidiary to, the great stream of Anglo-Saxon emigration to the West.'"

There is abundant reason to believe that the Anglo-Saxon race is to be, is, indeed, already becoming, more effective here than in the mother country. The marked superiority of this race is due, in large measure, to its highly mixed origin. Says Rawlinson: "It is a general rule, now almost universally admitted by ethnologists, that the mixed races of mankind are superior to the pure ones"; and adds: "Even the Jews, who are so often cited as an example of a race at once pure and strong, may, with more reason, be adduced on the opposite side of the argument." The ancient Egyptians, the Greeks, and the Romans were all mixed races. Among modern races, the most conspicuous example is afforded by the Anglo-Saxons. Mr. Green's studies show that Mr. Tennyson's poetic line,

"Saxon and Norman and Dane are we,"

must be supplemented with Celt and Gaul, Welshman and Irishman, Frisian and Flamand, French Huguenot and German Palatine. What took place a thousand years ago and more in England again transpires today in the United States. "History repeats itself"; but, as the wheels of history are the chariot wheels of the Almighty, there is, with every revolution, an onward movement toward the goal of his eternal purposes. There is here a new commingling of races; and, while the largest injections of foreign blood are substantially the same elements that constituted the original Anglo-Saxon admixture, so that we may infer the general type will be preserved, there are strains of other bloods being added, which, if Mr. Emerson's remark is true, that "the best nations are those most widely related," may be expected to improve the stock, and aid it to a higher destiny. If the dangers of immigration, which have been pointed out, can be successfully met for the next few years, until it has passed its climax, it may be expected to add value to the amalgam which will constitute the new Anglo-Saxon race of the New World. Concerning our future, Herbert Spencer says: "One great result is, I think, tolerably clear. From biological truths it is to be inferred that the eventual mixture of the allied varieties of the Aryan race, forming the population, will produce a more powerful type of man than has hitherto existed, and a type of man more plastic, more adaptable, more capable of undergoing the modifications needful for complete social life. I think, whatever difficulties they may have to surmount, and whatever tribulations they may have to pass through, the Americans may reasonably look forward to a time when they will have produced a civilization grander than any the world has known." [. . .]

Some of the stronger races, doubtless, may be able to preserve their integrity; but, in order to compete with the Anglo-Saxon, they will probably be forced to adopt his methods and instruments, his civilization and his religion. Significant movements are now in progress among them. While the Christian religion was never more vital, or its hold upon the Anglo-Saxon mind stronger, there is taking place among the nations a widespread intellectual revolt against traditional beliefs. "In every corner of the world," says Mr. Foude, "there is the same phenomenon of the decay of established religions. . . . Among Mohammedans, Jews, Buddhists, Brahmins, traditionary creeds are losing their hold. An intellectual revolution is sweeping over the world, breaking down established opinions, dissolving foundations on which historical faiths have been built up." The contact of Christian with heathen nations is awaking the latter to new life. Old superstitions are loosening their grasp. The dead crust of fossil faiths is being shattered by the movements of life underneath. In Catholic countries, Catholicism is losing its influence over educated minds, and in some cases the masses have already lost all faith in it. Thus, while on this continent God is training the Anglo-Saxon race for its mission, a complemental work has been in progress in the great world beyond. God has two hands. Not only is he preparing in our civilization the die with which to stamp the nations, but, by what Southey called the "timing of Providence," he is preparing mankind to receive our impress.

3

Ariel

José Enrique Rodó

Uruguayan intellectual José Enrique Rodó published Ariel *in 1900. This chapter emphasizes the strength and unifying power of Latin American spirituality and contrasts it with North American materialism and practical-mindedness. Critical yet optimistic, Rodó hoped "Arielism" would emerge as a unique fusion of the two tendencies. His work can be seen as an attempt to bridge, culturally and intellectually, the growing economic and political chasm that separated and divided the Americas. Although remarkably divergent in tone and emphasis, the published works of Strong and Rodó offer two distinct yet searing searches for identity. Rodó's reliance on French authors to build his thesis (to the nearly complete exclusion of Spanish and Spanish American thinkers) is somewhat typical of turn-of-the-century Latin American intellectuals who uncritically accepted French literature, language, and philosophy. Referring to North American culture as "admirably efficient," Rodó states that "our confidence and our opinion must incline us to believe . . . that in an inferred future their civilization is destined for excellence." A narrow reading of Rodó might focus only on his criticism of the United States; a more complete reading would frame his work within a wider search for identity, meaning, and fusion between south and north.*

The inextricably linked concepts of utilitarianism as a concept of human destiny and egalitarian mediocrity as a norm for social relationships compose the formula for what Europe has tended to call the spirit of *Americanism*. It is impossible to ponder either inspiration for social conduct, or to compare them with their opposites, without their inevitable association with that formidable and productive democracy to our North. Its display of prosperity and power is dazzling testimony to the efficacy of its institutions and to the guidance of its concepts. If it has been said that "utilitarianism" is the word for the spirit of the English, then the United States can be considered the embodiment of the word. And

the Gospel of that word is spread everywhere through the good graces of its material miracles. Spanish America is not, in this regard, entirely a land of hea-
thens. That powerful federation is effecting a kind of moral conquest among us.
Admiration for its greatness and power is making impressive inroads in the
minds of our leaders and, perhaps even more, in the impressionable minds of the
masses, who are awed by its incontrovertible victories. And from admiring to
imitating is an easy step. A psychologist will say that admiration and conviction
are passive modes of imitation. "The main seat of the imitative part of our nature is our belief," said Bagehot. Common sense and experience should in themselves be enough to establish this simple relationship. We imitate what we believe to be superior or prestigious. And this is why the vision of an America
de-Latinized of its own will, without threat of conquest, and reconstituted in the
image and likeness of the North, now looms in the nightmares of many who are
genuinely concerned about our future. This vision is the impetus behind an abundance of similar carefully thought-out designs and explains the continuous flow
of proposals for innovation and reform. We have our *USA-mania*. It must be limited by the boundaries our reason and sentiment jointly dictate.

When I speak of boundaries, I do not suggest absolute negation. I am well
aware that we find our inspirations, our enlightenment, our teaching, in the example of the strong; nor am I unaware that intelligent attention to external events
is singularly fruitful in the case of a people still in the process of forming its national entity. I am similarly aware that by persevering in the educational process
we hope to modulate the elements of society that must be adapted to new exigencies of civilization and new opportunities in life, thus balancing the forces of
heritage and custom with that of innovation. I do not, however, see what is to be
gained from denaturalizing the character—the *personality*—of a nation, from
imposing an identification with a foreign model, while sacrificing irreplaceable
uniqueness. Nor do I see anything to be gained from the ingenuous belief that
identity can somehow be achieved through artificial and improvised imitation.
Michelet believed that the mindless transferral of what is natural and spontaneous in one society to another where it has neither natural nor historical roots
was like attempting to introduce a dead organism into a living one by simple im-
plantation. In a social structure, as in literature and art, forced imitation will
merely distort the configuration of the model. The misapprehension of those
who believe they have reproduced the character of a human collectivity in its
essence, the living strength of its spirit, as well as the secret of its triumphs and
prosperity, and have exactly reproduced the mechanism of its institutions and the
external form of its customs, is reminiscent of the delusion of naive students
who believe they have achieved the genius of their master when they have
merely copied his style and characteristics.

In such a futile effort there is, furthermore, an inexpressible ignobility. Eager
mimicry of the prominent and the powerful, the successful and the fortunate,

must be seen as a kind of political snobbery; and a servile abdication—like that of some snobs condemned by Thackeray in *The Book of Snobs* to be satirized for all eternity—lamentably consumes the energies of those who are not blessed by nature of fortune but who impotently ape the caprices and foibles of those at the peak of society. Protecting our internal independence—independence of personality and independence of judgement—is a basic form of self-respect. Treatises on ethics often comment on one of Cicero's moral precepts, according to which one of our responsibilities as human beings is zealously to protect the uniqueness of our personal character—whatever in it that is different and formative— while always respecting Nature's primary impulse: that the order and harmony of the world are based on the broad distribution of her gifts. The truth of this precept would seem even greater when applied to the character of human societies. Perhaps you will hear it said that there is no distinctive mark or characteristic of the present ordering of our peoples that is worth struggling to maintain. What may perhaps be lacking in our collective character is a sharply defined "personality." But in lieu of an absolutely distinct and autonomous particularity, we Latin Americans have a heritage of race, a great ethnic tradition, to maintain, a sacred place in the pages of history that depends upon us for its continuation. Cosmopolitanism, which we must respect as a compelling requisite in our formation, includes fidelity both to the past and to the formative role that the genius of our race must play in recasting the American of tomorrow.

More than once has it been observed that the great epochs of history, the most luminous and fertile periods in the evolution of humankind, are almost always the result of contemporaneous but conflicting forces that through the stimulus of concerted opposition preserve our interest in life, a fascination that would pale in the placidity of absolute conformity. So it was that the most genial and civilizing of cultures turned upon an axis supported by the poles of Athens and Sparta. America must continue to maintain the dualism of its original composition, which re-creates in history the classic myth of the two eagles released simultaneously from the two poles in order that each should reach the limits of its domain at the same moment. Genial and competitive diversity does not exclude but, rather, tolerates, and even in many aspects favors, solidarity. And if we could look into the future and see the formula for an eventual harmony, it would not be based upon the unilateral imitation—as Gabriel Tarde would say—of one people by another, but upon a mutual exchange of influences, and the fortuitous fusion of the attributes that gave each its special glory. [. . .]

Any criticism of the Americans to our north should always be accompanied, as in the case of any worthy opponent, with the chivalrous salute that precedes civilized combat. And I make that bow sincerely. But to ignore a North American's defects would seem to me as senseless as to deny his good qualities. Born—calling upon the paradox that Baudelaire employed in a different context— with the *innate experience* of freedom, they have remained faithful to the laws of their origins and with the precision and sureness of a mathematical progression have developed the basic principles of their formation. Subsequently, their history is characterized by a uniformity that, although it may lack diversity in skills and values, does possess the intellectual beauty of logic. The traces of their presence will never be erased from the annals of human rights. From tentative essays and Utopian visions, they were the first to evoke our modern ideal of liberty, forging imperishable bronze and living reality from concepts. With their example they have demonstrated the possibility of imposing the unyielding authority of a republic upon an enormous national organism. With their federation they have demonstrated—recalling de Tocqueville's felicitous expression—how the brilliance and power of large states can be reconciled with the happiness and peace of the small. Some of the boldest strokes in the panorama of this century, deeds that will be recorded through all time, are theirs. Theirs, too, the glory of having fully established—by amplifying the strongest note of moral beauty in our civilization—the grandeur and power of work, that sacred power that antiquity degraded to the abjectness of slave labor, and that today we identify with the highest expression of human dignity, founded on the awareness of its intrinsic worth. Strong, tenacious, believing that inactivity is ignominious, they have placed in the hands of the mechanic in his shop and the farmer in his field the mythic club of Hercules and have given human nature a new and unexpected beauty by girding onto it the blacksmith's leather apron. Each of them marches forward to conquer life in the same way the first Puritans set out to tame the wilderness. Persevering devotees of that cult of individual energy that makes each man the author of his own destiny, they have modeled their society on an imaginary assemblage of Crusoes who, after gaining their crude strength by looking out for their self-interests, set to weaving the stout cloth of their society. Without sacrificing the sovereign concept of individualism, they have at the same time created from the spirit of association the most admirable instrument of their grandeur and empire. Similarly, from the sum of individual strengths subordinated to a plan of research, philanthropy, and industry, they have achieved marvelous results that are all the more remarkable, considering that they were obtained while maintaining the absolute integrity of personal autonomy. There is in these North Americans a lively and insatiable curiosity and an avid thirst for enlightenment. Professing their reverence for public education with an obsessiveness that resembles monomania—glorious and productive as it may be—they have made the school the hub of their prosperity, and a child's soul the most valued of all precious commodities. Although their culture is far from being refined or spiritual, it is admirably efficient as long as it is directed to the practical goal of realizing an immediate end. They have not added a single general law, a single principle, to the storehouse of scientific knowledge. They have, however, worked magic through the marvels of their application of general knowledge. They have grown tall as giants in the domains of utility; and in the steam engine and electric generator they have given the world billions of invisible slaves to save the human Aladdin, increasing a hundredfold the power of the magic lamp. The extent of their greatness and strength will amaze generations to come. With their prodigious skill for improvisation, they have invented a way to speed up time; and by the power of will in one day they have conjured up from the bosom of absolute solitude a culture equal to the work of centuries. The liberty of Puritanism, still shedding its light from the past, joined to that light the heat of a piety that lives today. Along with factories and schools, their strong hands have also raised the churches from which rise the prayers of many millions of free consciences. They have been able to save from the shipwreck of all idealisms the highest idealism, keeping alive the tradition of a religion that although it may not fly on wings of a delicate and profound spiritualism does, at least, amid the harshness of the utilitarian tumult, keep a firm grip on the reins of morality. Surrounded by the refinements of civilized life, they have a pagan cult of health, of skill, of strength; they temper and refine the precious instrument of will in muscle; and obliged, by their insatiable appetite for dominance, to cultivate all human activities with obsessive energy, they build an athlete's torso in which to shelter the heart of free man. And from the concord of their civilization, from the harmonious mobility of their culture, sounds a dominant note of optimism and confidence and faith that expands their hearts; they advance toward the future under the power of a stubborn and arrogant expectation. This is the note of Longfellow's "Excelsior" and "A Psalm of Life," which their poets, in the philosophy of strength and action, have advocated as an infallible balm against all bitterness. [. . .]

The idealism of beauty does not fire the soul of a descendant of austere Puritans. Nor does the idealism of truth. He scorns as vain and unproductive any exercise of thought that does not yield an immediate result. He does not bring to science a selfless thirst for truth, nor has he ever shown any sign of revering science for itself. For him, research is merely preparation for a utilitarian application. His grandiose plans to disseminate the benefits of popular education were inspired in the noble goal of communicating rudimentary knowledge to the masses; but although those plans promote the growth of education, we have seen no sign that they contain any imperative to enhance selective education, or any inclination to aid in allowing excellence to rise above general mediocrity. Thus the persistent North American war against ignorance has resulted in a universal semiculture, accompanied by the diminution of high culture. To the same degree that basic ignorance has diminished in that gigantic democracy, wisdom and genius have correspondingly disappeared. This, then, is the reason that the trajectory of their intellectual activity is one of decreasing brilliance and originality. While in the period of independence and the formation of their nation many illustrious names emerged to expound both the thought and the will of that people, only a half century later de Tocqueville could write of them, *the gods have departed*. It is true, however, that even as de Tocqueville was writing his masterpiece, the rays of a glorious pleiad of universal magnitude in the intellectual history of this century were still beaming forth from Boston, the *Puritan citadel*, the city of learned traditions. But who has come along to perpetuate the bequest of a William Ellery Charming, an Emerson, a Poe? The bourgeois leveling process, ever-swifter in its devastation, is tending to erase what little character remains of their precarious intellectualism. For some time now North American literature has not been borne to heights where it can be perceived by the rest of the world. And today the most genuine representation of American taste in belles lettres is to be found in the gray pages of a journalism that bears little resemblance to that of the days of the *Federalist*.

In the area of morality, the mechanistic thrust of utilitarianism has been somewhat regulated by the balance wheel of a strong religious tradition. We should not, nevertheless, conclude that this tradition has led to true principles of self-lessness. North American religion, a derivation from and exaggeration of English religion, actually serves to aid and enforce penal law that will relinquish its hold only on the day it becomes possible to grant to moral authority the religious authority envisioned by John Stuart Mill. Benjamin Franklin represents the highest point in North American morality: a philosophy of conduct whose ideals are grounded in the normality of honesty and the utility of prudence. His is a philosophy that would never give rise to either sanctity or heroism, one that although it may—like the cane that habitually supports its originator—lend conscience support along the everyday paths of life is a frail staff indeed when it comes to scaling the peaks. And these are the heights; consider the reality to be found in the valleys. Even were the moral criterion to sink no lower than Franklin's honest and moderate utilitarianism, the inevitable consequence— already revealed in de Tocqueville's sagacious observation—of a society educated in such limitations of duty would not inevitably be that state of proud and magnificent decadence that reveals the proportions of the satanic beauty of evil during the dissolution of empires; it would, instead, result in a kind of pallid and mediocre materialism and, ultimately, the lassitude of a lusterless enervation resulting from the quiet winding-down of all the mainsprings of moral life. In a society whose precepts tend to place the demonstration of self-sacrifice and virtue outside the realm of obligation, the bounds of that obligation will constantly be pushed back. And the school of material prosperity—always an ordeal for republican austerity—that captures minds today has carried the simplistic concept of rational conduct even farther. In their frankness other codes have surpassed even Franklin as an expression of the national wisdom. And it is not more than five years ago that in all of North America's cities public opinion consecrated, with the most unequivocal demonstration of popular and critical acclaim, the new moral law: from the Boston of the Puritans, Orison Swett Mardin wrote a learned book entitled *Pushing to the Front*, solemnly announcing that *success* should be considered the supreme goal of life. His "revelation" echoed even in the bosom of Christian fellowship, and once was cited as being comparable to Thomas à Kempis' *The Imitation of Christ*. [. . .]

I want each of you to be aware that when in the name of the rights of the spirit I resist the mode of North American utilitarianism, which they want to impose on us as the summa and model of civilization, I do not imply that everything they have achieved in the sphere of what we might call *the interests of the soul* has been entirely negative. Without the arm that levels and constructs, the arm that serves the noble work of the mind would not be free to function. Without a certain material well-being, the realm of the spirit and the intellect could not exist. The aristocratic idealism of Renan accepts this fact when it exalts — in relation to the moral concerns of the species and its future spiritual selection — the importance of the utilitarian work of this century. "To rise above necessity," the master adds, "is to be redeemed." In the remote past, the effects of the prosaic and self-interested actions of the merchant who first put one people in contact with others were of incalculable value in disseminating ideas, since such contacts were an effective way to enlarge the scope of intelligence, to polish and refine customs, even, perhaps, to advance morality. The same positive force reappears later, propitiating the highest idealism of civilization. According to Paul de Saint-Victor, the gold accumulated by the mercantilism of the Italian republics financed the Renaissance. Ships returning from the lands of the Thousand and One Nights laden with spices and ivory to fill the storehouses of the Florentine merchants made it possible for Lorenzo de Medici to renew the Platonic feast. History clearly demonstrates a reciprocal relationship between the progress of utilitarianism and idealism. And in the same way that utility often serves as a strong shield for the ideal, frequently (as long as it is not specifically intended) the ideal evokes the useful. Bagehot, for example, observed that mankind might never have enjoyed the positive benefits of navigation had there not in primitive ages been idle dreamers — surely misunderstood by their contemporaries — who were intrigued by contemplating the movement of the planets. This law of harmony teaches us to respect the arm that tills the inhospitable soil of the prosaic and the ordinary. Ultimately, the work of North American Positivism will serve the cause of Ariel. What the Cyclopean nation, with its sense of the useful and its admirable aptitude for mechanical invention, has achieved directly in the way of material well-being, other peoples, or they themselves in the future, will effectively incorporate into the process of selection. This is how the most precious and fundamental of the acquisitions of the spirit — the alphabet, which lends immortal wings to the word — was born in the very heart of Canaanite trading posts, the discovery of a mercantile civilization that used it for exclusively financial purposes, never dreaming that the genius of superior races would transfigure it, converting it into a means of communicating mankind's purest and most luminous essence. The relationship between material good and moral and intellectual good is, then, according to an analogy offered by Fouillée, nothing more than a new aspect of the old equivalence of forces; and, in the same way that motion is transformed into heat, elements of spiritual excellence may also be obtained from material benefits.

As yet, however, North American life has not offered us a new example of that incontestable relationship, nor even afforded a glimpse of a glorious future. Our confidence and our opinion must incline us to believe, however, that in an inferred future their civilization is destined for excellence. Considering that under the scourge of intense activity the very brief time separating them from their dawn has witnessed a sufficient expenditure of life forces to effect a great evolution, their past and present can only be the prologue to a promising future. Everything indicates that their evolution is still very far from definitive. The assimilative energy that has allowed them to preserve a certain uniformity and a certain generic character in spite of waves of ethnic groups very different from those that have until now set the tone for their national identity will be vitiated in increasingly difficult battles. And in the utilitarianism that so effectively inhibits idealism, they will not find an inspiration powerful enough to maintain cohesion. An illustrious thinker who compared the slave of ancient societies to a particle undigested by the social system might use a similar comparison to characterize the situation of the strong Germanic strain now identifiable in the mid- and far West. There, preserved intact—in temperament, social organization, and customs—are all the traits of a German nature that in many of its most profound and most vigorous specificities must be considered to be antithetical to the American character. In addition, a civilization destined to endure and expand in the world, a civilization that has not, in the manner of an Oriental empire, become mummified, or lost its aptitude for variety, cannot indefinitely channel its energies and ideas in one, and only one, direction. Let us hope that the spirit of that titanic society, which has until today been characterized solely by *Will* and *Utility*, may one day be known for its intelligence, sentiment, and idealism. Let us hope that from that enormous crucible will ultimately emerge the exemplary human being, generous, balanced, and select, whom Spencer predicted would be the product of the costly work of the melting pot. But let us not expect to find such a person either in the present reality of that nation or in its immediate evolution. And let us refuse to see an exemplary civilization where there exists only a clumsy, though huge, working model that must still pass through many corrective revisions before it acquires the serenity and confidence with which a nation that has achieved its perfection crowns its work—the powerful ascent that Leconte de Lisle describes in "Le sommeil du condor" [The Dream of the Condor] as an ascent that ends in Olympian tranquility.

4

Wild People in Wild Lands: Early American Views of Latin Americans

Fredrick Pike

Fredrick Pike's masterful The United States and Latin America: Myths and Stereotypes of Civilization and Nature *(1992) draws on decades of scholarship involving a wide variety of themes. Pike earned his Ph.D. at the University of Notre Dame in 1963 and has written extensively on church-state relations in Latin America, and political/cultural relations between the United States and Latin America. His* The United States and the Andean Republics: Peru, Bolivia, and Ecuador *(1977) is considered a classic and Pike's work on Peruvian populist leader Victor Raul Haya de la Torre* (The Politics of the Miraculous in Peru: Haya de la Torre and the Spiritualist Tradition, *1986) demonstrate the range, depth, and creativity of his scholarship. In the excerpt below Pike combines literary, artistic, and historical interpretations to show the complexity and history of negative U.S. stereotyping of Latin Americans. His work illustrates how during the nineteenth century most Americans viewed Latin Americans as "hopelessly inept and chaotic in their economic practices as in their politics." Many of these stereotypes, cogently analyzed by Pike, remain a central feature of modern U.S.–Latin American relations.*

Since ancient times, groups or "races" arriving at some sense of identity or "peoplehood" have turned to nature-and-civilization imagery as the basis for stereotyping. To those beyond the pale of their own peoplehood, they have attached pejorative stereotypes. Often for the Western world's Christian people, the Jew became the reviled Other who somehow could not measure up to the standards required by civilization. In the nineteenth century when unabashed anti-Semitism thrived among North Americans, Gentile native sons and daughters categorized newly arriving Jewish male immigrants as sneaky and conniving, resembling such denizens of the wild as weasels and foxes—the predators of wilderness or jungle rather than the noble and courageous killers. According to the stereotypes of American nativism, Jewish women were lascivious creatures of unbridled sexuality. In different ways, then, both Jewish men and women were dismissed as unredeemed creatures of nature.

The time finally came when Jews had the chance to avenge the decades and centuries in which they had suffered rejection as despicable Others. In the second half of the twentieth century, the Jews of Israel took to depicting Arab adversaries as "primitive and tribal," as brutal and bloodthirsty and less-than-human predators, as people who "don't respect reason," as emotional creatures easily incited and manipulated by monstrous leaders, as wily and cunning in battle but basically cowardly and not truly manly, as undisciplined, illogical, unable to distinguish between fact and fantasy, as threatening machos lusting after pure and refined Jewish women. On one hand, according to Jewish stereotypes, the Arab might benefit from contact with Israeli "civilization"; on the other, the Arab might be hopelessly refractory to civilization and therefore basically undeserving of full-scale human rights. In consequence, agents of progress could kill the Arab with impunity.

Jewish stereotypes of Arabs resemble those that Americans attached to Negroes and also to the Indians and Latins who at one time ringed their borders and held the land the emissaries of civilization coveted, ostensibly because they alone understood how to improve that land and thereby fulfill the moral injunctions of the true religion. Indeed, Jewish stereotypes of the Arab bear striking similarity to those that virtually all colonialists have attached to colonials. In approaching American stereotypes of the Latin American, what I wish to stress is their lack of originality. Human evil, it has been suggested, exhibits the traits of ordinariness, commonness, and banality; it is seldom unique and larger than life in its dimensions. With stereotypes, it is the same. Rather than reflecting original responses to unique situations, they have become part and parcel of day-in, day-out, humdrum existence; they are the ordinary creations of human nature at its most typical. With almost boring regularity they rest upon the distinction between what in the eyes of the would-be exploiters of other humans is the civilization of the former and the unmitigated naturalness (meaning savagery or barbarism) of the latter. Just as stereotypes become normal, routine, and taken for granted, so does the terrorism perpetrated in their name. Soon the terrorists become capable of remembering only those incidents that reinforce the stereotypes that in turn justify terrorism, and utterly incapable of heeding other instances that challenge the stereotypes and cast doubt on the moral acceptability of terrorism.

Stereotyping is by no means the exclusive habit of stronger groups that assert themselves in one way or another over weaker ones. Invariably, the weaker elements in asymmetrical relationships devise sweeping stereotypes with which to defame the stronger, not unlike the way some present-day Arabs distortedly depict the Jew. Similarly, in their generalized criticism of Americans during much of the past century and a half, Latin Americans have seemed blind to the fact that "differences in a population are often greater than the differences between populations." By their stereotyping, Latin Americans have also confirmed that "the most prevalent form of racism in the world in recent decades has been anti-Americanism."

Most especially, large numbers of Latin Americans, along with Africans set upon disparaging various nationalities of white imperialists, like to contrast their own spirituality and concern with "higher values" to the alleged cloddishness and calculating, cold-hearted materialism of the Caucasian Other. Throughout history, in fact, the tendency of underlings to contrast their spirituality with the base creatureliness of aggressors is just as much a constant as the imperialist's resort to contrasting his civilization to the colonial's primitivism. Someday, I trust, a comprehensive study will set forth the various facets of Latin American stereotyping of the North American. When it appears, the study will, I am confident, show that Latins have been just as bigoted, extreme, irrational, and self-serving in impugning the character of the gringo as North Americans have been in their collective character assassination of the generalized greaser. Undoubtedly it will also confirm that, as Mexico's grand old man of letters and Nobel laureate Octavio Paz has suggested, Latin Americans have been as divided in their assessments of norteamericanos as Yankees have been in their appraisals of the Latins with whom they share the hemisphere. According to Paz, his countrymen and their fellow Latin Americans feel an "unambivalent fascination" about the United States, "the enemy of our identity and the unavowed model of what we [want] to be." It is ambivalence on both sides of the Rio Grande that has saved stereotyping in the Americas from sinking to the levels it has reached elsewhere.

Latin American elites frequently have sought to define themselves and to strengthen their own sense of identity and peoplehood by contrasting themselves to the negative identity imputed, most of the time, to North Americans. Before Yankee-baiting became the preferred method for establishing identity, Latin elites bolstered self-awareness by reviling the inhabitants of sister republics along their borders, with whom they frequently engaged in armed hostilities. Furthermore, elites nourished a racism that contributed to white and whitish upper-class cohesiveness by disparaging the dark-skinned masses (Indian, black, mestizo, and mulatto) that comprised a majority of the population in almost all republics. In justifying their own power status, Latin elites tended to use the same sort of civilization-barbarism stereotyping whereby North Americans contrasted themselves to allegedly inferior peoples. All the while Latin America's privileged sectors expected that North Americans would go along with local Latin customs that dictated perpetuation of a gulf between the *gente decente* (decent people) and the dusky masses.

Disappointed in expectations of acceptance as equals by North Americans, frustrated because all too often they were lumped together with the unwashed herd by insensitive gringos, Latin America's *gente decente* responded with anti-American stereotyping. Often the intensity of their anti-Americanism bore a direct relationship to the strength of their disdain for their own lower classes with whom, they felt, gringos tended to lump them. Needless to say the *gente decente*'s anti-Americanism soared to new heights when, during the course of the twentieth century, various Americans (many of them the champions of blacks and Indians in their own country) began to side with the downtrodden elements of Latin society as they protested against ongoing exploitation.

NINETEENTH-CENTURY AMERICAN STEREOTYPING OF THE LATIN OTHER

Prior to the mid-nineteenth-century gold rush, early Anglo settlers in California, and even short-term visitors, distinguished between the cultured, gracious, hospitable ranch owners and the rabble. The prosperous *Californios* (original Hispanic occupants) they referred to as Spanish, and the ragged, dirty masses they designated Mexicans. That this division had long-lasting consequences is suggested by what passed for a joke still in circulation in the 1990s. Question: When does a Mexican become a Spaniard? Answer: When he marries your daughter.

The Anglo ability to distinguish between worthies and unworthies, which initially delighted upper-sector *Californios*, fell victim to the huge influx of fortune-hunting immigrants arriving on the scene just as the second half of the nineteenth century began. Rough, tumultuous hordes of Anglo gold-seekers arrived in the region, and so did scruffy hordes of Latin American adventurers from as far away as Chile and Argentina. Before long the first group branded all those in the second (together with Orientals afflicted by gold fever) as wild and depraved. Next, the Anglos extended their pejorative evaluations to the old-line, property-owning *Californios*. All the more did these persons of substance cease to be Spanish and become Mexican when Anglos embarked upon wholesale procedures to strip them of their old political powers along with their property. To justify such stripping, racist stereotyping proved highly useful.

Lumping all Latin Americans together and tarring them with the same brush was not confined to America's roughneck elements. With notable exceptions, influential men of affairs and letters shared in the tendency to see all Latin Americans as little removed from barbarism. In his most widely read novel (*The Yemassee*, published in 1839) William Gilmore Simms, "the greatest story-teller the Old South produced," pontificated that when a higher race encountered a lower, the great danger was that the higher would sink to the level of the lower. Southerners, and Americans in general, contrasting themselves to ordinary mortals, assumed that when *they* met inferior races they did not sink. But, when it came to Latin Americans, the civilized cities had clearly begun their descent into the surrounding morass of barbarism.

In his 1858 account of travels in Mexico, an American writer captured the prevailing mood of his countrymen when he criticized the upper classes for having succumbed to the "passionate and emotional" and "lighthearted" approach to life that also characterized the masses. Nor did the social polish of Latin upper classes fool William Gilpin toward the end of the century. An enormously influential soldier, politician, visionary writer, and prophet par excellence of the Anglo American's mission to uplift the world, Gilpin had Latin America partially in mind when in 1890 he disparaged societies that had "grown to be polished and enervated without emerging from semi-savage barbarism."

Emerson encapsulated the prevailing national wisdom of his age—and subsequent ages as well—when he declared: "All great men come out of the middle classes." Already in the age of Emerson Americans had begun to conclude that the trouble with Latin America lay in the absence of a middle class. The area to their south seemed populated by profligate elites and a vast herd of rambunctious wastrels. Unlike their counterparts in Europe, members of an emergent U.S. middle class did not have to struggle against an established aristocracy or fret over the risks posed by a large marginalized class. But, they shared the antiaristocratic bias and also the suspiciousness of shiftless lower classes that characterized Europe's rising bourgeoisie. This bias and suspiciousness inevitably poisoned their attitudes toward the sort of people who, in their imagination at least, populated Latin America.

Above all, American middle-class men esteemed the so-called manly qualities, as opposed to feminine weakness and emotionalism and childish fecklessness and fantasizing. Qualities that Americans admired, they consistently failed to find among Latin Americans. The appraisals that led a mid-twentieth-century U.S. diplomat to dismiss Dominicans already flourished at least a century earlier in the attitudes of Americans toward Latin Americans in general. "The longer you worked with Dominicans, the more you . . . disliked the weakness of the men, and, searching for explanations, you noticed how pampered are the infant males in Dominican families, how undisciplined the schoolboy males, how feckless the teenage males, and how vain and proud and sometimes absurd the adult males. They were not men, many of them, only spoiled brats grown up." Even some Latin Americans have concurred in the gringo diplomat's appraisal and have applied it more broadly than just to Dominicans. I remember an ambitious, upwardly mobile Venezuelan student whom I knew in the mid-1960s. He assured me that the pampered permissiveness in which the upper-class male children were raised in his country turned them into weak, self-indulgent, effeminate *animalitos* (little animals).

About the time of the American Revolution, Patrick Henry, "with wonder in his voice," proclaimed to an audience: "We are in a state of nature." If Americans had started in a state of nature, already in the early nineteenth century they had begun to take inordinate pride in overcoming and defying nature. Even their democracy, which had become the object of their smug satisfaction, seemed to attest to their ability to triumph over nature; for many Americans, among them Edgar Allan Poe, recognized that democracy, being a "system nowhere observable in nature," emerged only out of the ability to transcend nature. Latin Americans, in contrast, seemed incapable of progressing toward democracy or anything else worthwhile precisely because they simply could not get the upper hand over nature—either within or without.

An observer in California in 1848, shortly before it became a part of the United States, saw only an indolent Hispanic and Indian people. In California, he averred, "nature [was] doing everything, man [was] doing nothing." One year later another American commented on the widespread conviction among his countrymen that *Californios* grew "as the trees, with the form and character that Nature gives them." About a decade later, a U.S. traveler to Brazil noted that there "nature has done everything . . . but as yet man has done next to nothing." So, while Americans had started in but shortly emerged out of a state of nature, Latin Americans remained in the original state.

The first Latin Americans that significant numbers of Americans encountered resided in territory that ultimately became a part of the United States—among them the already-mentioned *Californios*. Historian Francis Parkman when engaged in research for his classic study *The Oregon Trail* (1849) encountered a group of Mexicans from New Mexico on the banks of the Missouri River. Here is how he describes the scene: "On the muddy shore stood some thirty or forty dark, slavish-looking Spaniards, gazing stupidly out from beneath their broad hats." Crossing the river he encountered a boat in which "the rowers, swarthy, ignoble Mexicans, turned their brutish faces upward to look, as I reached the bank." A while later, Parkman came upon some "squalid Mexicans, with their broad hats and their vile faces overgrown with hair." About the time Parkman encountered the Hispanic occupants of New Mexico, who obviously impressed him as animal-like, fur trapper Rufus Sage visited Taos. Here is his impression of its Mexican residents: "There are no people on the whole continent of America, whether civilized or uncivilized, with one or two exceptions, more miserable in condition or despicable in morals than the mongrel race inhabiting New Mexico." Another trapper found the Mexicans in his part of the country "depraved, indolent, untrustworthy, dishonest, cowardly, servile, ignorant, superstitious, and dirty"—among other undesirable traits. An American army officer on duty in the Texas–New Mexico region believed that the Indians he encountered were actually superior to the Mexicans. These latter, allegedly, "were content if they could satisfy their animal wants."

The French-born Jean-Baptiste Lamy, appointed first as bishop (1853) and later as archbishop (1875) of Santa Fe (on whose life Willa Cather based her enduringly popular novel *Death Comes for the Archbishop* [1927]), inclined sympathetically toward his Mexican-origin wards, in a paternalistic and condescending way. Toward the end of his life, though, even he revealed certain prejudices common among native-born Americans. "Our Mexican population" he wrote, "has quite a sad future. Very few of them will be able to follow modern progress. They cannot be compared to the Americans in the way of intellectual liveliness, ordinary skills, and industry. . . . The morals, manners, and customs of our unfortunate people are quite different from those of Americans." He concluded that men of progressive spirit would have trouble understanding the spirit of "our Mexican population," for it "is almost too primitive."

A traveler from Connecticut who journeyed through Texas in the mid-1850s concluded that his countrymen would find it difficult "to harmoniously associate with the bigoted, childish, and passionate Mexicans" who comprised a good part of the state's populace. Reporting on the California scene in the early years after the gold rush, an editorial writer for the *National Intelligencer* assured his readers that the Hispanic portion of the inhabitants "are a thieving, cowardly, dancing, lewd people, and generally indolent and faithless." Another witness to life in California at this time commented on the coarseness and lasciviousness of the Mexicans as well as their "degraded tone of manners." A generation or so later, even the tolerant Californian Josiah Royce (1855–1916), who gained renown as a Harvard professor of philosophy, described his native state's Spanish Americans as "an essentially amoral and childlike people" who could scarcely be held morally accountable for their actions.

When Americans began to arrive in some number in Mexico during the latter part of the nineteenth century, many felt compelled to scale the heights of Popocatépetl. "Climbing and trekking became a kind of mania among them. Hardly would a party return with stories of its climb up Popo, before another individual reported the exploits of his party's climb." Scaling Popo became for Americans a way to manifest their concern for physical fitness, a concern that rested on the values of self-control and of the muscular Christianity by then deeply embedded in Anglo American culture. At the same time, the American mania for conquering Popocatépetl served as a reproach to Mexicans, who showed absolutely no interest in this pastime because they had no cult of muscular Christianity and evidenced scant concern for physical fitness as an end in itself. People without interest in disciplining their own bodies so as to be able to assert human mastery over nature lacked, so far as the American climbers were concerned, the basic prerequisites of civilization.

The relatively few Americans who journeyed farther south than Mexico in the nineteenth century often found little more to praise than their compatriots who had encountered the Latins of Mexico or the American Southwest. To many of the women who accompanied the Forty-Niners as they made their way to California across Panama's isthmus, Panamanians were swarthy-visaged, often half-naked racial mongrels, as repulsive in their features as in their actions. When in the proximity of the natives' stench, women had to hold their noses and keep cologne handy. According to one lady traveler, "The natives were so impetuous

and excitable that it was almost impossible to do anything with them." Their cus-
tomary "tempestuousness was further aggravated by their tendency to drink,
gamble, and fight," another lady averred. These judgments were rendered in
1849 and 1850. A few years later, in 1856, some other women made the Panama
crossing and to their enormous relief discovered that safety was now assured "by
a sizeable contingent of U.S. Marines. Like the U.S. Cavalry stationed throughout the American West, the Marines guarded the intrusive immigrants from the
. . . native people." Thus were Panamanians equated with the savage Indian
tribes of North America whose animality could be kept in check only through
Uncle Sam's organized military might.

    Those Americans who ventured still farther south generally recorded impres-
sions of the natives no more flattering than those of travelers in Mexico or Central America. U.S. naval officers charged with defending their country's neutral
rights during the Latin American struggle for independence from Spain and Portugal (1810–1824) often sailed as far south as Chile and Peru. What impressed
them most was the pervasive lawlessness, the disregard for personal property
rights, the venality of public officials, and the evasion of financial obligations by
virtually all the natives. Naval officers also expressed disgust for the pagan superstitions that allegedly characterized the local practice of religion. Latins
could also strike the American observer as intellectually underdeveloped. Typically, a U.S. minister resident to the Republic of Ecuador commented on the
beauty of upper-class women, who seemed largely free from the taint of race
mixture. But, even among these females, the minister complained, "faces very
generally lack the expression which intellectuality alone can give."

    What Americans thought of Latin American men could be even more unflat-
tering, as some of the material already presented indicates. What lay at the heart
of the trouble with Latin American males as perceived by the gringo? Perhaps F.
Scott Fitzgerald without intending to hints at an answer in his marvelous 1920
short story "The Ice Palace." Fitzgerald deals directly here with some of the cultural differences that led to a virtually unbridgeable gulf between North and
South within the United States. In some ways, though, his probing of attitudes is
just as applicable to the chasm between Americans and Latin Americans. At one
point in the story Harry, the northerner, shocks the southerner Sally Carroll, to
whom he is at the time affianced, when he says: "I'm sorry, dear . . . but you
know what I think of them [southern men]. They're sort of—sort of degenerates.
. . . They've lived so long down there with all the colored people that they've
gotten lazy and shiftless."

    Up to now I have used the scattergun approach in pointing to evidence of
North American disdain for the Latin American, owing to the latter's alleged
stagnation in a state of nature. Next (and there will be some overlapping here),
I focus on some of the specific traits that purportedly attested to the Latin American's incompatibility with civilization.

SEX AND ALCOHOL, AND LATIN AMERICAN PRIMITIVISM

For Victorian-age Americans, middle-class respectability came increasingly to be associated with control over the sexuality that aristocrats and riffraff alike ostensibly indulged all too freely. Sublimation of sexual desire emerged as the hallmark of bourgeois civilization, whereas sexual abandon became the sure indication of atavism. In his 1906 book *The Future in America*, English writer H. G. Wells cast his eyes overseas and found many qualities to admire in Americans. They had, he opined, shaped "an intensely moral land" by curbing all lusts save one, the lust of acquisition. In an era of industrial revolution and some of the most dramatic conquests over nature and its resources in all the annals of history, it seemed fitting, at least to self-admiring Americans, that by their very lust for acquisition they could tame all other lusts.

Control over the libido was by no means a new quest for Americans when they enlisted in its cause in the nineteenth century. Some truth inheres in the popular image of seventeenth-century Puritan attitudes toward sexuality. For example, Puritans did indeed arrest, fine, and even whip married couples whose first child had arrived too soon. If anything, though, concern with mastering sexual excesses had sharpened by the mid-nineteenth century as the remnants of Calvinist fatalism gave way to entrepreneurial faith in the self-made man whose self-control would yield treasure in this life and the next. Just as Americans became obsessive about improving the body so as to guarantee physical health, so they turned relentlessly to self-discipline as a means to economic and spiritual well-being. For many of them, at least to judge by their words, sexual self-control seemed the source of every other form of self-control.

Among men's and women's reform societies appearing early in the nineteenth century were those dedicated to seeking "social regeneration through sexual purification." The women's societies might seem especially hostile "to the licentious and predatory male," but men could sometimes be as zealous as women reformers in seeking to banish licentious conduct. Indeed, manliness came to be associated with sexual self-control. Theodore Roosevelt was by no means unusual in priding himself on an abundance of both virtues. Honoring manliness in himself and others, Roosevelt also exulted in his sexual continence. "Thank Heaven, I am at least perfectly pure," Roosevelt confided to his diary in 1878 when at the age of twenty he speculated on a future wife. "Two years later, by then engaged, he again 'thanked Heaven' and rejoiced that he could tell his fiancee 'everything I have ever done.'"

For the businessmen intent upon building America's economic foundations, thrift seemed a cardinal virtue; and thrift meant establishing strict control over spending—both dollars and sperm. Economic and sexual self-control, ostensibly, went hand in hand. Roosevelt, with the patrician's contempt for the businessman, saw national strength and grandeur in far more than economic criteria. Just as much as with the businessman, though, Roosevelt's goals—including the military strength and the requisite power to discipline and uplift pauper classes and nations—demanded the kind of manliness and virility equated with stoic self-control, cold showers, and the stiff upper lip. Very possibly the more Americans proved incapable of living by the standards of continence, the more they reviled the Others who did not pay even lip service to the ideal and overtly indulged in "loose" life-styles.

Nineteenth-century defenders of American middle-class respectability assumed that excess spending of male sperm was bad both for the nation's economy and its morality. Beyond that, excessive sexual activity whether channeled into intercourse or masturbation resulted in race degeneracy, a gradual sinking into weakness, effeminacy, and—ultimately—barbarism. The antisex crusader Anthony Comstock (1844–1915) staunchly opposed birth control because it would encourage lust, which he saw as the basis of most evils that beset society. "Lust defiles the body, debauches the imagination, corrupts the mind, deadens the will, destroys the memory, sears the conscience, hardens the heart, and damns the soul." Impure and libidinous acts and even thoughts "unnerve the arm, and steal away the elastic step"; they "create rakes and libertines in society—skeletons in many a household. The family is polluted, home desecrated, and each generation born into the world is more and more cursed by the inherited weakness, the harvest of this seed-sowing."

John Harvey Kellogg (1852–1943), who eventually founded the food company that bears his name, agreed on all counts with Comstock, as did Sylvester Graham (1794–1851), whose name would be attached to a highly popular cracker. Both Kellogg and Graham sought to devise foods and diets for Americans that would curb the sexual appetite. According to Kellogg, "The reproductive act is the most exhausting of all vital acts. Its effect upon the undeveloped person is to retard growth, weaken the constitution, and dwarf the intellect." To Kellogg's litany of sexuality's evils, Graham added this wisdom: "It were better for you not to exceed in the [annual] frequency of your [sexual] indulgences the number of months in the year; and you cannot exceed the number of weeks in the year, without impairing your constitutional powers, shortening your lives, and increasing your liability to disease and suffering; if indeed, you do not thereby actually induce disease of the worst and most painful kind; and at the same time transmit to your offspring an impaired constitution, with strong and unhappy predisposition." Graham concluded that by abusing the sex organs through overindulgence of "instinctive appetites," man became "a living volcano of unclean propensities and passions. . . . He sinks himself in degeneracy, below the brutes."

As they concerned themselves with stamping out sexual excesses among the male members of respectable, middle-class society, Americans also worried about the sexuality of women. Frequently both women and men bandied about notions of the moral superiority of women. Invariably, the morally superior woman was a Madonna rather than an Eve, one who took no pleasure in the sexual act and accepted it only as a duty that must be stoically fulfilled in order to speed the propagation of society's better elements. Sometimes male obstetricians even intervened surgically to guarantee woman's indifference to sex by assaulting the clitoris. And, in fortifying both men and women psychologically against temptations of the flesh, conjuring up the unwholesome, sensuous Other proved helpful, or at least so it was assumed.

Nineteenth-century European imperialists divided humanity "into an Occident and an Orient, the latter being the sphere" of illicit sex and "fleshly delights." Europeans also divided the world into North and South spheres. Far to the south lay Africans, oversexed and not fully human; less far southward resided the Spaniards, Portuguese, and Italians, worthier than Africans but vitiated by their propensity for "un manly" conduct. Americans tended to place the libidinous Other either in the West (Indians, Latin Americans, and the debauched elements of white society) or in the South. Within their own country, the South was home not only to the mythically lustful black but to sexually uninhibited white upper-class males as well as profligate white trash. Especially as the tide of abolitionist fervor rose, northerners eroticized the entire South, picturing it as one "great brothel." Southern males, whether black, white upper-class, or white lower-class, afforded proof that "man reduced to a pure state of nature is not a Noble Savage but a neolithic satyr." Early in the twentieth century novelist Upton Sinclair, an antisouthern southerner and a sexual prude, still chose to depict the plantation of the slavery era, and even later, as a "house of shame, where black, half-naked girls, most of them harlots at heart, competed for sexual favors from the master (or anyone else readily available) and generally became pregnant by the time they reached age fifteen." In far less prudish manner, Mississippi's consummately great novelist William Faulkner developed this theme in such books as his 1936 classic *Absalom, Absalom!*

For many American northerners, the South lay also south of the border. The Other who occupied this South belonged both to morally dissolute classes (aristocracy and dependent peons) and to an inferior race. Both class and race shaped the Latin southerner as a lustful creature whose life-style challenged the accepted values of decent classes and races. As with Upton Sinclair's South, the Latin American South was dotted with plantation houses of shame where seminaked, dark-skinned sluts pranced about and competed for the honor of satisfying the master classes' animalistic urges. Corruption of this sort served to justify Americans in their imperialist designs on Latin America, just as Europeans found moral sanction for imperialism in the Dark Continent by envisioning Africans as creatures of unmitigated savagery and licentiousness, the two qualities being inseparable.

After spending some time in Latin America in the early 1890s, an American writer remarked that the Anglo Saxon "is a monogamous animal, while at any given moment the Latin's horizon is apt to be occupied by a petticoat or a succession of petticoats." In this instance, the writer dealt light-heartedly with character blemishes that had provoked stuffy self-righteousness from earlier observers of Latin American sexual mores. Here are the words that the author of an 1838 romance put in the mouth of a Texan addressing a Mexican army captain: "In point of chastity . . . the most important and influential qualification of Northern nations, we are infinitely superior to you—Lust is, with us, hateful and shameful; for you, it is a matter of indifference. *This* is the chief curse of the South; the leprosy which unnerves both body and mind. It is what caused the Roman empire to sink. . . . The Southern races must be renewed and the United States are the *officina gentium* for the new Continent."

Josiah Gregg (1806–1850), a nine-year resident in Mexico and author of the classic account of the early Santa Fe trade, sympathized with certain aspects of the culture he discovered south of the border; but he professed outrage at the pervasive licentiousness. For Mexicans, he charged, "the institution of marriage changes the legal rights of the parties, but it scarcely affects their moral obligations. It is looked upon as a convenient cloak for irregularities." In his 1857 book *El Gringo*, W. W. H. Davis registered full accord with Gregg. Among Mexicans, he averred, marriage served "as a cloak to hide numerous irregularities" engaged in by both partners. While married men "support a wife and mistress at the same time," Davis added, "too frequently the wife also has her male friend." In Davis's estimation, three-quarters of the married population among Mexicans went in for adultery.

In trying to account for alleged lack of sexual restraint among Latin Americans, Americans sometimes drew on their knowledge of Indian culture. The "fact" that Indians conducted themselves like "brute beasts," flaunted the ties and obligations of marriage, and gave free rein to sexual appetites originated, according to some Caucasian Americans, in aboriginal child-rearing practices, especially the custom of "allowing the wild freedom and nudity of children." This custom not only gave rise to sexual abandon as children matured but also induced generalized social disorder and undermined respect for all restraint. In general, Americans took the nudity of Indians as sure proof that they were barbaric, and the pawns of their passions. A similar line of reasoning consigned Latin Americans to barbarism.

In a book he published in 1838, a Yankee traveler to Colombia registered shock over the fact that children, especially of the abundant poor classes, ran about naked. Susan Shelby Magoffin traveled the Santa Fe Trail in the 1840s and also spent some time in northern Mexico. An intelligent and tolerant observer, she responded positively to many aspects of Mexican culture, observing at one point: "What a polite people these Mexicans are, altho' they are looked upon as a half barbarous set by the generality of [American] people." Nevertheless, she found it "repulsive to see the children running about perfectly naked." Nor could she calmly accept the state of nudity or near nudity in which women casually allowed themselves to be seen. She found it "truly shocking to my modesty" to encounter such sights while in the company of gentlemen and noted: "I am constrained to keep my veil drawn tightly over my face all the time to protect my blushes." Set against the prevailing standards of her time, Magoffin's comments are significant.

[. . .] Nineteenth-century values in America equated modesty with culture, civilization, and Christianity. Those who lacked modesty, allegedly, had attained the moral development only of children.

Certain men, of course, especially those of "low social station," might respond with frank fascination to the Latina's casualness toward nudity. At the outset of the Mexican War in 1846 when Gen. Zachary Taylor's army arrived on the Rio Grande, the soldiers realized at once "that the Mexican women were different. Standing on the river bank in early morning or evening, they gaped as the young women of Matamoros came down to the river, disrobed without hesitation or embarrassment, and plunged into the stream." Later on during the war one soldier observed of Mexican women: "Nearly all of them have well-developed, magnificent figures . . . [and] dress with as little clothing as you can well fancy." A "sharp-eyed Indianan" noted of the Mexican women: "Their bosoms were not compressed in stays . . . but heaved freely under the healthful influence of the genial sun and balmy air of the sunny south." Here were attractions indeed, but probably many an American soldier assured himself he would not want to marry one of these natural and uninhibited women, especially given the often-remarked tendency of Mexican and Latin women in general to surrender to obesity well before middle age—a reminder of the unpleasant consequences that befell women who let themselves go.

Some American male observers of Latin women liked nothing of what they saw. Gilbert Haven, an American preacher who spent a winter in Mexico in the 1850s, found the women, especially of the lower classes, ugly, their physical features reflecting their debauched morals. One explanation as to why most women remained single was the fee the clergy charged to administer the wedding rites. The underlying explanation, though, according to Haven, was that debauchery and fornication resided "in their blood. There was no seeming sense of shame . . . no modesty."

An American geologist visiting Cuba and Puerto Rico in 1898 noted that the women had little regard for marriage, and this accounted for the fact that 40 percent of all births were illegitimate. He did not blame the situation so much on the basic immorality of the Caribbean women as on the worthlessness of the men: What right-thinking woman would accept marriage to one of them? Still the notion that debauchery and fornication lived in the blood of Latin American women persisted. Indeed, the image of Latin America as one extended brothel seemed deeply engraved in the minds of many Americans. In the 1850s an American official wrote that standards of female chastity were deplorably low among the Mexican populace of New Mexico, where "the virtuous are far outnumbered by the vicious. Prostitution is carried out to a fearful extent; and it is quite common for parents to sell their daughters for money to gratify the lust of the purchaser." Both in New Mexico and Mexico, American soldiers seemed to believe that the majority of women were "primarily prostitutes."

Early in the twentieth century women members of some forty interdenominational missionary societies felt a special need to convert Latin American women to Protestantism so as to rescue them from prevailingly low standards of morality that led so many to take to prostitution. And, when the white-slave panic "reached its unaccountably hysterical peak in . . . 1913," the common assumption was that an American girl who disappeared (injected by the needle of some white-slave trafficker) "would wake up, helpless, in the brothels of Rio or Constantinople." Thus were Latin Americans and Turks lumped together as the worst offenders against sexual purity.

While some stereotypes may have remained constant, others have changed. No longer prevalent is the nineteenth-century conviction that smoking indicated a woman's uninhibited sexuality and probably her ready availability. Many a nineteenth-century American who traveled south of the border registered amazement not only at female immodesty but at the fact that women of all classes smoked—publicly and unabashedly. In appraising women, American males tended to agree with John Harvey Kellogg's assessment that smokers were likely to be addicted to sexual practices "still more filthy." A Yankee visitor to Colombia in the 1830s took female smoking as a sure indication of lack of willpower: if addicted to nicotine, it followed they were addicted to depravity in general. A woman visitor to Chile in the 1860s recorded her disgust not only with female but also male use of tobacco. The fact that Chilean men smoked provided a tip-off as to their "loose . . . notions of morality." [. . .]

Together with uninhibited sexuality and free indulgence in nicotine, excessive use of spices and condiments, of caffeine and chocolate struck many nineteenth-century North Americans as indicators of moral depravity bordering on barbarism. The "stimulant," though, that produced by far the worst effects on character and that undermined all of civilization's restraints when used to excess was alcohol. By what Americans believed to be pervasive alcohol addiction, Latin Americans dulled their intellectual capacity, loosened restraints on passions and instincts, and dropped out of the march toward progress. Americans themselves when their Republic was young had succumbed to alcohol addiction at an uncommonly high rate. Unlike Latin Americans, however, Americans liked to believe that they, or at least the decent elements among them, had overcome an addiction that consigned its sufferers to a state of nature.

Between the Revolution through which they gained independence and approximately the first quarter of the nineteenth century, American per capita consumption of alcohol registered an all-time high, as W. R. Rorabaugh documents in his book *The Alcoholic Republic*. Since then, consumption per capita has never come close to matching the early, heroic proportions of alcoholic intake. Helping to curb alcohol consumption was the rise of middle-class values of respectability. Increasingly, abstemiousness in drinking habits emerged as the recognized prerequisite for the "selfcommand, prudence and fortitude, and a strict control of the passions and appetites . . . [required] to maintain the empire of reason over sense." Freedom itself demanded the constant exercise of self-control through which humans liberated themselves from animalistic impulses. Out of self-denial issued independence, both from sin and from economic want.

By 1831, Rorabaugh has discovered, "the American Temperance Society reported more than 2,200 local organizations with more than 170,000 members; in 1834, 7,000 groups with 1,250,000 members." Together with men's and especially women's reform societies, Protestant ministers spearheaded the temperance movement, persuaded that salvation, and with it economic success, came only to those who withstood the temptations of demon rum. In the combined secular-religious campaign against alcohol abuse, Americans could draw cautionary tales from the experience of Native Americans. By their inability to withstand the temptations of alcohol, these children of nature blighted whatever potential they might once have had to advance to the civilized state. Chingachgook, Cooper's once noble red man of the Leatherstocking Tales, came in his besotted old age to embody for Americans of the respectable classes a frightening symbol of decadence.

Increasingly satisfied that ability to curb the intake of spirits evidenced not only religious but also social and even racial superiority, Americans grew increasingly censorious as they became acquainted with Latin American drinking habits—real and imagined; and remember that for most Americans initial contacts with Latin Americans got under way just as the zeal for temperance asserted itself in the northern republic. Americans who observed Mexicans in Texas, New Mexico, and California in the first half of the nineteenth century invariably commented on their addiction to drink—an addiction that men and women allegedly shared equally. Among the many Americans complaining about drunkenness as they crossed the border into Mexico itself was artist Thomas Moran. The natives delighted in filling themselves with pulque, and the more they drank, he complained, the more they voiced anti-American sentiments—sentiments that they emphasized by vulgar gestures. The same minister resident in Ecuador quoted earlier as he complained about the lack of intellectuality in the expression of upper-class women, attributed to alcoholism the "ugly, stupid, simpering look" that distinguished the country's Indian women. With utmost distaste, he observed that "the ruling passion of Indian women and men for drink" led them to "bacchanalian orgies." An

American traveler who made it all the way to isolated Paraguay toward the end of the nineteenth century commented on the lack of ambition that character-ized its inhabitants. It did not occur to them to improve their circumstances, for with a bit of food, ample liquor, and "some cigars to smoke all day," they had all they wanted of life. An earlier traveler had scorned Bolivians, in part because of their drinking habits and addiction to coca-leaf chewing, but he had found the Chileans more to his liking. Perhaps because of the prevalence of white blood among them, he surmised, they seemed relatively free from alco-hol addiction.

Few Americans traveled to Latin America, or even to the Hispanic Southwest. For impressions of their Latin neighbors, most Americans relied largely on travel accounts published by their more adventurous or wealthier compatriots. From these accounts they gleaned the impression that Latin Americans were largely Indian in racial composition and overwhelmingly in thrall to alcoholic spirits—even as North America's "savages." What is more, they learned from censorious travelers that the Catholic church, instead of fighting demon rum, as did North America's Protestant denominations, actually encouraged alcohol con-sumption as a means of honoring innumerable saints on their feast days. . . . The expression "Rum, Romanism, and Rebellion," coined by a Protestant clergyman during the political campaign of 1884, cast aspersions on the character of Irish Americans. But long before the Irish issue entered U.S. politics, many Americas had concluded that the true lair of rum and Romanism (or pulque and popish-ness) lay in South America, and that these two devilish forces contributed to an-other curse—chronic rebellion. The unholy trinity's power pretty much proved that Latin Americans were refractory to civilization.

II

THE MONROE DOCTRINE AND
ORIGINS OF U.S. EXPANSIONISM

Few individuals reflected on the Monroe Doctrine when it first came into being in 1823. Drafted by Secretary of State John Quincy Adams, the doctrine conveyed the preoccupation of the United States at a time when the future of the newly independent Latin American republics was far from certain. With the final battle of independence in 1824, it seemed clear that Spaniards would no longer be welcome in the region. The troubling issue for leaders in the United States involved the possible designs of other European powers, especially the British. The doctrine was intended to show that the United States would not look favorably on any European power's attempt to recolonize the new, weak nations of Latin America. The British feared the "Holy Alliance," made up of Austria, Prussia, and Russia, might have designs on Latin America. France was seen as yet another potential threat, and the United States—having concluded a major war with the British less than nine years earlier—could not trust the former mother country. The Monroe Doctrine, then, represented the U.S. attempt to define and broaden its political and economic sovereignty in the hemisphere.

The Monroe Doctrine would become increasingly useful to the United States, especially in the period after 1850 when economic and territorial expansion were key U.S. objectives in Latin America, particularly in Mexico and the Caribbean. Some argued that the Monroe Doctrine became nothing more than an argument in favor of U.S. intervention in the area and that its original goal (to keep out Europeans) had in fact become a sinister tool of exploitation. Others argued that the United States had become champion and protector of the Latin American nations and pointed to the similarities that bound the United States to Latin America (i.e., constitutional and political structures in Latin America modeled after the U.S. Constitution, strong presidentialism, and increasing levels of trade between the United States and Latin American nations).

The Monroe Doctrine became a topic of debate, especially after 1898 when the United Stated emerged as an imperialist power by forestalling Cuba's independence while helping to expel the Spanish, once and for all, from the Western Hemisphere. U.S. economic and military power in the region was underscored by passage of the Platt Amendment, named for U.S. Senator Orville H. Platt. The amendment became law on March 2 1901, and essentially allowed U.S. economic, political, and military intervention in Cuba to ensure order and stability. In 1903 the United States moved to secure land for the construction of an interoceanic canal; this occurred at the expense of the republic of Colombia, a nation that was winding down from civil war (the War of a Thousand Days) and that could therefore do nothing to stop U.S. wishes under the leadership of the irascible and expansionistic Theodore Roosevelt.

The writings of Dexter Perkins, Elihu Root, and Gaston Nerval represent the wide range of debate sparked by the Monroe Doctrine. Dexter Perkins was the first American to carefully study the doctrine from a scholarly perspective. He published his findings in two volumes and, although he was not quite willing to disavow the doctrine, he understood the doctrine as a source of inter-American tensions and misunderstanding. Perkins challenged the traditional assumption that the Monroe Doctrine helped to prevent a unified Holy Alliance attack against Latin America in the early 1820s. His work is also seminal because for the first time he carefully considered the reception of the Monroe Doctrine in various Latin American countries.

Elihu Root, as secretary of state under Roosevelt, was a clear and unwavering champion of the doctrine; his speech in 1914 (excerpted in chapter 7) represents the official State Department view of the doctrine at a critical period in U.S. history — 1914 was the year the Panama Canal opened for shipping and Europeans fired the opening salvos in what would become World War I. Root was convinced that the Monroe Doctrine had become more important than ever by 1914 and should be defended at all costs against critics who claimed it was little more than a doctrine of intervention and oppression.

Bolivian diplomat and intellectual Gaston Nerval takes quite a different approach to the Monroe Doctrine. He claimed in 1934 that the doctrine had outlived its usefulness and declared it "dead" and ready to be autopsied. This conclusion was drawn following a scathing criticism of the doctrine; Nerval shows how the Monroe Doctrine actually led to increased instability rather than stability in the Latin American region, particularly the Caribbean. His remarks came at a time when the United States had committed its foreign policy in Latin America toward promoting the Good Neighbor plan whereby cooperation and mutual support would define U.S.–Latin American relations in a spirit of pan-Americanism. Nerval stated that the Monroe Doctrine could only fracture any attempt at hemispheric solidarity.

Taken together, the four chapters in this part represent widely diverse interpretations of one doctrine. The three authors arrive at their conclusions based on divergent careers and opinions over a twenty-year period, suggesting the intensity, contradictions, and confusion surrounding the origins, application, and meaning of the Monroe Doctrine. We have also included the complete text of the Platt Amendment, as chapter 6. Students will be able to evaluate the amendment and place it within the historical context in which it belongs. Although it appeared seventy-eight years after the Monroe Doctrine, some of the central issues and preoccupations of the Platt Amendment demonstrate the important continuities of U.S. policy toward Latin America.

5

The Monroe Doctrine, 1823–1826

Dexter Perkins

Dexter Perkins broke new ground in 1927 with the publication of The Monroe Doctrine, 1823–1826. *A professor of history at the University of Rochester, Perkins contended for the first time since the issuance of the Monroe Doctrine in 1823 that the American continents were not really in jeopardy of recolonization by a European Holy Alliance attack after the wars of Latin American independence (1810–1824). For its time, Perkins's work was an important revisionist interpretation of the Monroe Doctrine because it departed significantly from standard, uncritical scholarship that emphasized an assumed European proclivity to control America politically, militarily, and economically. The British, particularly in Latin America, found that economic penetration could be readily achieved without political domination in the postindependence period. Perkins's work still stands as an exhaustively researched study of European intentions and priorities in Latin America in the early nineteenth century. He also debated, in a critical fashion, the reception of the doctrine in various Latin American countries; thus he was one of the first authors to think globally and critically about the Monroe Doctrine.*

The famous declaration of December 2, 1823, which has come to be known as the Monroe Doctrine, had a dual origin and a dual purpose. On the one hand, it was the result of the advance of Russia on the northwest coast of America, and was designed to serve as a protest against Russian expansion. Referring to this question of the northwest, President Monroe laid down the principle in his message to Congress that "the American continents, by the free and independent condition which they have assumed and maintain, are henceforth not to be considered as subjects for future colonization by any European powers." On the other hand, the message was provoked by the fear of European intervention in South America to restore to Spain her revolted colonies, and was intended to give warning of the hostility of the United States to any such intervention. "With the governments [that is, the Spanish American republics] who have declared their independence, and maintained it," wrote the President, "and whose independence we have, on great consideration and just principles, acknowledged, we could not view any interposition for the purpose of oppressing them, or controlling in any other manner their destiny, by any European power, in any other light than as the manifestation of an unfriendly disposition toward the United States."

Of these two aspects of the message, it is no doubt the second which involves the more interesting and important questions. How far did the manifesto of December 2, 1823, actually check European designs on the New World? How great was its immediate influence? Did it lower or raise American prestige? Did it arouse resentment or command respect? These are only some of the more significant questions that suggest themselves in connection with the message in its South American aspects. An examination of the Monroe Doctrine in the days of its origin must inevitably concern itself preponderantly with just these questions.

But, on the other hand, the non-colonization principle must not be neglected. It has a high importance in and of itself. It is indeed the most important *principle* connected with the Declaration of 1823. The pregnant sentence directed against Russia was to have a wide influence as time went on. It was to play a role of ever-increasing importance. From it were to be deduced many of the corollaries of the Monroe Doctrine, and on it has been based more than one state paper of large significance. It is a matter of great interest, therefore, to study its origins, to understand its logic, and to analyze the effect which it produced at the time of its enunciation. [. . .]

The revolt of the Spanish American colonies followed hard upon the Napoleonic conquest of Spain. From the very beginning, the sympathies of the United States appear to have been engaged upon the side of the revolutionists. American sentiment was distinctly favorable to a movement for independence which had at least a superficial resemblance to that of 1776, and which could easily be regarded as an effort to throw off an odious tyranny and establish throughout the greater part of the New World the blessings of republican government. Fellow feeling in a struggle for liberty and independence was an essential element in forming the policy of the United States with regard to South America.

It was indeed, to all appearances, a far more important element than any hope of material gain. In the formative period of this country's relations with the states of South America, certainly down to 1822, there is little evidence of the working of economic interest. In the absence of exact statistics for much of the period, and in view of the paucity of references to trade with the Spanish colonies, it is difficult to speak with precision. But certain general observations may safely be made. In the first place, the trade with Cuba and with Spain itself was far more important than the trade with the new republics of the South. A diplomatic policy favorable to the South American states might jeopardize or even sacrifice commercial interests superior to those which it would promote. If economic reasons were to be regarded as shaping political developments, there were more reasons for a cautious than for an active line of policy. In the second place, there was not, as in the case of Great Britain, any powerful pressure from the commercial classes in favor of colonial independence. The evidence on this point is partly negative, it is true, but it is negative evidence of the strongest kind. One can hardly imagine that the existence of such pressure would pass unnoticed in the debates in Congress, and in such contemporary records as the diary and writings of Adams, and the correspondence of Monroe. But it is not necessary to depend upon this fact alone. Statistics indicate that as late as 1821 only 2.3 percent of American exports and 1.6 percent of American imports were South American in destination or origin. In March of the same year Adams could tell Henry Clay that he had little expectation of any commercial advantages from the recognition of new states. And even later, in 1823, the Secretary of State speaks of commercial development as a matter of hope for the future rather than a present accomplishment. That hope may, of course, have counted for something from the beginning. But, all things considered, it seems highly probable that political sympathy, not economic self-interest, lay at the root of American policy so far as it revealed itself as favorable to the new states of South America.

From the very beginnings of the South American struggle this sympathy asserts itself. As early as 1810, the American government, then headed by Madison, sent agents to South America—Joel R. Poinsett to La Plata and Chile, and Robert Lowry to Venezuela. At the end of 1811, James Monroe, then Secretary of State, thought seriously of raising the question of the recognition of the new states, and of exerting American influence in Europe to secure like action from the principal European powers. He also entered into informal relations with agents from at least one of the revolted provinces. And in Congress, at the same time, in response to the sympathetic language of the President's message, a resolution was passed, expressing a friendly solicitude in the welfare of these communities, and a readiness, when they should become nations by a just exercise of their rights, to unite with the Executive in establishing such relations with them as might be necessary. Thus, very early in the course of the colonial struggle, the general bent of American policy was made plain.

But it was some time before the South American question became a matter of really first-rate importance. In the years 1810 to 1815, the prime concern of the administration at Washington lay in the preservation of American neutral rights, and, from 1812 to 1814, in the prosecution of the war with Great Britain. Moreover, the course of events in the overseas dominions of Spain was for some time hardly favorable to the revolutionists. In 1814 and 1815, indeed, it seemed entirely possible that the revolutionary movements might be snuffed out. In the north, in Venezuela and Colombia, the army of the Spanish general, Morillo, won victory on victory, and drove the leader of the revolutionists, Bolívar, into exile. In the south, in Chile, Osorio reestablished the power of the mother country, and in Buenos Aires the struggles of contending factions weakened the new government that had been set up. Under such circumstances, prudence would have dictated a policy of reserve on the part of the United States, even if its government had not been preoccupied with other and more pressing matters.

With the year 1817, however, a change takes place in the status of the colonial question. In the case of one, at any rate, of the new states, the struggle was virtually over. The republic of La Plata had declared its independence and successfully maintained it, so that not a Spanish soldier remained upon its territory; even more, it had dispatched its general, San Martin, across the Andes, and with the victory of Chacabuca, taken a great step toward the final liberation of Chile. Perhaps as a result of these developments, interest in favor of the recognition of the new state began to develop in the United States; there were numerous newspaper articles in the summer of 1817, notably the discussions of Lautaro in the Richmond *Enquirer*; and the affairs of South America became a matter of debate both in the councils of the administration and in the halls of Congress.

It is interesting, in the light of later events, to examine these developments. So far as the administration was concerned, the point especially to be emphasized is the warm sympathy of the President himself with the South American cause. There has been a tendency in some quarters, in connection with the evolution of the Monroe Doctrine, to ascribe a very slight importance to the views of the very man who promulgated it. Mr. Monroe has been pictured as "slow-moving and lethargic," as prodded forward only by the more vigorous mind and more determined will of John Quincy Adams, his Secretary of State. But as a matter of fact, Monroe was at all times quite as much interested in the colonial cause, and in as full sympathy with it, as Adams. From the beginning of his presidency, he showed his concern with regard to it. As early as May, 1817, some months before Adams took office, the President had determined upon a mission of inquiry to the provinces of La Plata, and as early as October he questioned his cabinet on the expediency of recognizing the government of that region. He raised the problem again in the succeeding May, even suggesting the possibility of sending an armed force to the coast of South America, to protect American commerce, "and to countenance the patriots." His views, it is true, were to be overruled or modified by his advisers. But his interest in positive action was very real, and is quite consistent with the character of the man whose flaming sympathy with the French republicanism had been so obvious in his earlier career.

Adams, on the other hand, expressed a very conservative view of the South American question. He was swayed by no theoretical devotion to republicanism, and had no particular confidence in the capacity of the new states for self-government. In a letter to Alexander Hill Everett, written in December, 1817, he expressed in some detail his doubts as to the similarity of the South and North American revolutions, and as to the whole trend of revolutionary activities. Long afterwards, as late as March, 1821, he told Henry Clay that he saw no prospects that the new states would establish free or liberal institutions of government. "They are," he declared, "not likely to promote the spirit either of freedom or order by their example. They have not the first elements of good or free government. Arbitrary power, military and ecclesiastical, was stamped upon their education, upon their habits, and upon all of their institutions. . . . I had little expectation," Adams added, "of any beneficial result to this country from any future connection with them, political or commercial."

Observations such as these do not, of course, indicate a fundamental antagonism to the movement of independence in South America. So great a lover of liberty, so theoretical a republican, as Thomas Jefferson, is to be found expressing much the same view. But Adams's interest in the new states was not based on any doctrinaire notions or theories of government. He wished them well, as he told Clay, because they were contending for independence. He wished them well because he hated colonialism in all its guises. But he was not the man to be swept off his feet by enthusiasm, or by the superficial resemblance of South American institutions to those of the United States. In the cabinet meeting of October 30, 1817, he opposed the recognition of La Plata with his usual definiteness. And in the discussions of the next year, he counselled caution in dealing with the whole problem. Far from advancing beyond the ground taken by the President, he exercised a restraining influence upon his chief. At no time can it fairly be said that he outstripped Monroe in zeal for the welfare of the new republics. [. . .]

The message of President Monroe was published in the United States on December 2, 1823, and was naturally, before many weeks had gone by, republished in the newspapers of Europe and of Spanish America. It will be interesting to examine the impression which it produced in all these instances, the reception which was accorded it in the press and among public men, and the interpretation which was put upon its resounding phrases.

As to the message in the United States, it is hardly necessary to say that in the majority of instances it was received with great cordiality, not to say enthusiasm. The American people, notwithstanding their frequently manifested devotion to peace, have never been any more averse to a "strong" foreign policy than the rest of the world. For months, for years, one might say, the press had been pouring scorn on the institutions and policies of Europe. The President's declaration, with its eulogy of American principles and its solemn warning to the autocrats of the Old World, could hardly fail to be a popular document.

The message [wrote Addington to Canning] seems to have been received with acclamation throughout the United States. . . . The explicit and manly tone, especially, with which the President has treated the subject of European interference in the affairs of this Hemisphere with a view to the subjugation of those territories which have emancipated themselves from European domination, has evidently found in every bosom a chord which vibrates in strict unison with the sentiments so conveyed. They have been echoed from one end of the union to the other. It would indeed be difficult, in a country composed of elements so various, and liable on all subjects to opinions so conflicting, to find more perfect unanimity than has been displayed on every side on this particular point.

The language of Addington seems in the main to be borne out by the general tone of the newspaper comment on the message. Almost without exception the press of the country rallied behind the President, and praised the sentiments which he had promulgated to the world. Almost without exception, too, they took the portentous language of the President's declaration at its face value. Only one newspaper out of a score which I have examined was really skeptical of the grave danger which menaced the United States. The rest seem to have taken the peril for granted. They took for granted, too, the ability of the country to repel any threat which might be offered. The self-confident nationalism of the "era of good feeling" is nowhere better illustrated than in the reaction to Monroe's manifesto. The idea that there could be any doubt about the capacity of the government to make good its words in action was hardly suggested. Barring an occasional appeal for increased military preparation, there was, in the public press, no hint of any kind that the United States was not ready to meet the Holy Alliance in its designs, and successfully oppose them. [. . .]

There was, also, perhaps, a reluctance to believe that the situation was as perilous as Monroe's words implied. It is a significant and interesting fact, illustrating the attitude of Congress toward the message, that, in the debate on a bill for the construction of additional sloops of war, the danger of a struggle over South America was not once mentioned; and the bill itself never came to a vote in the House. There were, of course, members of Congress who took the danger of intervention seriously. This appears clearly enough from the debate on Webster's resolution for the recognition of the Greeks in the first weeks of 1824. But nothing in the Annals of Congress makes it seem likely that the majority of the legislators responded very militantly to the militant mood of Monroe, or were much afraid of European intervention. In the House the only action taken was a request for further information on the whole South American question; and when this was answered by the President with a statement that he possessed "no information on that subject, not known to Congress, which" could "be disclosed without injury to the public good," the result was, to all appearances, to discourage any further consideration of the problem. In the Senate there was, so far as the Annals reveal, no discussion at all of the foreign policy sketched out in the message. In the increasingly cautious attitude of the administration in the later months of 1824, there may be traced, perhaps, something of the reluctance of the legislative body to approve the vigorous language of the Chief Executive.

As to the attitude of public men, outside the national legislature, it is difficult to judge. Only a few isolated examples of comment seem to have been preserved to us. Madison declared that the message could "do nothing but good." John Marshall gave more cautious adhesion in the declaration that we "cannot look on the present state of the world with indifference." At least two state legislatures passed resolutions commendatory of the President's stand.

To judge from these meager examples, the favorable reaction of the press found its counterpart in the reaction of those individual politicians or statesmen who had no direct responsibility to make Monroe's words good. It was only in Congress that a salutatory reserve tempered the enthusiasm which the President's declaration might have been expected to arouse. In the rest of the country, the general impression of the message appears to have been wholly an agreeable one.

So much for the reaction to Monroe's message to the United States. How was it received in those countries in whose interest it was promulgated? In order to answer this question, it is desirable to understand the circumstances, looked at from the Spanish American point of view, which prevailed at the moment of the President's manifesto.

In the first place, it is worth observing that the directors of the policy of the new states had none of the sources of information which made such a deep impression upon Monroe and his advisers. [. . .] It is not likely that the confidences of George Canning to Richard Rush, the British minister's warning of a projected congress on the South American question, which played so large a part in the debates of the cabinet at Washington, had any counterpart in the relations of the representatives of the new republics with the British or American government. In the voluminous correspondence of Santander and Bolívar, in the collection of diplomatic dispatches known as the *Diplomacia Mexicana*, there is no hint of any such confidence. There is no allusion to it in the diplomatic dispatches of our ministers. The Polignac interview, directly affecting in the most positive manner the fate of the new states, and vitally related to British policy, was made known to no South American government, as we have seen, before the end of 1823. If Canning chose so long to withhold information on a matter of such importance, it is entirely unlikely that he had talked with the South American agents in London as to the plans of the Continental Allies. Nor was there any sound reason why, so long as British policy remained in its formative stage, he should have done so.

In view of these circumstances, it is unlikely that anywhere in South America was there so definite a conviction of impending danger as there was in the mind of Monroe. And in certain instances, at any rate, there was a very distinct tendency to minimize the peril with which the new states were threatened. Perhaps

the most striking example of this temper is to be found in the attitude of Don
Bernadino Rivadavia, the Minister of Foreign Affairs for Buenos Aires. In July,
1823, Rivadavia had signed a treaty with the commissioners sent out by the constitutional government of Spain, and throughout the fall of 1823 he was working through commissioners sent to the other South American states to bring the
whole colonial struggle to a conclusion. The collapse of the liberal cause in the
Spanish Peninsula forced him to surrender these hopes, but he was not on that
account perturbed as to the possibility of European intervention. In the middle
of December, he declared improbable any interference on the part of the Holy
Allies. A fuller expression of his views is to be found in the important circular
sent on February 5, 1824, before the arrival of the message, to the representatives of Buenos Aires in the other republics of South America. In this circular, it
is true, Rivadavia speaks of the necessity of solidarity, and gives assurances of
the support of Buenos Aires, in case of European action, but at the same time he
distinctly discounts the danger. The impotence of Spain, he writes, has always
made it unlikely that the Holy Allies would seek to restore her authority in a
campaign 2,000 leagues removed from Europe; there would be no assurance of
success, and still less that Ferdinand VII could retain his ancient dominions were
he once put in possession of them. The chances were that the European powers
would seek rather to make their political views prevail by negotiation than to in-
terpose by force of arms.

The views of Rivadavia are in measure reproduced by another Spanish American Foreign Minister, Don Lucas Alamán, [sic] of Mexico, one of the most conspicuous figures in the revolutionary history of that republic. In his report to
Congress of November 1, 1823, Alamán, though admitting the possibility of intervention, indicated that such intervention was not likely to be attempted.

In Chile, on the other hand, there was more apprehension. As early as December 4, 1823, the Chilean legislative body proposed the sending of a joint
Chilean, Colombian, and Peruvian mission to England and the United States, to
urge recognition and seek to persuade the two AngloSaxon governments to
protest against the attitude of the Holy Alliance, "which was casting its eyes" on
South America. It recommended such action on December 4 to the Supreme Director, and again on January 7 and February 9. A few days later instructions were
drawn up for the Chilean member of this mission. The envoy was never sent, and
the deliberation with which the whole matter was treated may serve to indicate
that, though there was apprehension, there was not very serious fear of immediate intervention; but the danger at any rate was one which justified the taking of
countervailing measures.

In the case of Colombia, there are evidences of a considerable degree of anxiety. The historian Restrepo, himself a great witness of the events of 1823 and
1824, declares that there was great excitement along the littoral, and a genuine
fear that France would intervene in favor of Spain. Martial law was proclaimed

in some of the coast provinces. The Vice-President, Santander, in direction of Colombian affairs during Bolívar's absence in Peru, had proposed to the American agent, Todd, as early as June, 1823, an alliance to ward off the threatened danger, and in November he wrote to the Liberator about the designs of France in terms of apprehension. At the end of December the Colombian Foreign Minister, Gual, approached the newly arrived American minister, Anderson, with new suggestions of a more intimate connection between the two states. All these facts taken together suggest that the Colombian government was quite fearful of European action.

The attitude of Bolívar, who, in the period with which this chapter deals, was engaged in the liberation of Peru, is less easily defined. The tone of his correspondence is rather contradictory, depending perhaps in part upon the moods of his extremely volatile nature. Writing to Heres, the Peruvian Foreign Minister, at the end of December, he asserted flatly that France would do nothing as to South America. To Santander, on March 10, while still apparently without the reassurance of Monroe's message or encouraging tidings from the Old World, he expressed himself in the same strain. "This fear [of yours]" he declared, "does not appear to me to be justified; since no situation can persuade me that France will enter upon plans hostile to the New World, after respecting our neutrality in days of calamity." Finally, on March 21, the Liberator wrote to Sucre, "I do not believe at all in the League between France and Spain. We have documents that prove the contrary." But on the other hand there are two letters of a very different tenor in January. In neither of these does he flatly predict intervention; but the temper of both is distinctly one of alarm. Balancing these contrary views, it is perhaps to be indicated that Bolívar, while not free from doubts, was by no means as apprehensive as the government at Bogotá. [. . .]

In the case of Mexico, the first allusion to the message is to be found in the *Aquila Mexicana* for February 12, 1824. This, however, is a mere report from "a person who left New Orleans on the fifteenth of last month," to the effect that Monroe had taken his stand against the reconquest of the colonies. The language of the President was not published until February 26, and then only a short extract, by a writer who was obviously much more interested in the prospects of British recognition than he was in the attitude of the United States. Of the impression which it produced, in the immediate sense, we have virtually no knowledge. There was no American minister at Mexico City to describe, as did Rush from London, its enthusiastic reception; nor is the declaration mentioned in the reports of the British agent, or in the papers of the French agent, Samouel, who was in Mexico in the early summer of 1824. What Mexican officialdom thought of it, it is difficult to say. There are, however, several facts that deserve to be indicated with regard to it. Early in December, Migoni, the Mexican agent in London, wrote definitely that Great Britain would prevent intervention; and only a little later a Mexican named Thomas Murphy transmitted to his government the account of an interview with Villele in which the friendly feelings of the French government were made clear. It was therefore not long after the arrival of the message before other facts were presented to the directors of Mexican policy which must sensibly have diminished its effect. This conclusion seems, in a measure, to be borne out by the circumstance that Alamán in his *Historia de México*, no less than in his report of January 11, 1825, to the Mexican Congress, gave a very subsidiary place to the Monroe Doctrine in describing the international situation of 1823 and 1824, and that other Mexican historians of the epoch took the same view. It is noteworthy, too, that the message finds no place in the public manifestoes and speeches of the Mexican President, Victoria.

On the other hand, too much should not be made of such facts. Jealousy of the United States, rather than indifference to the message, may have prompted all the silences as to Monroe's declaration, and it would be unfair to deduce from them that the message was speedily delegated to oblivion. [. . .] Mexican statesmen, in common with many others, were sufficiently interested in the President's pronouncement to make appeal to it in the years immediately following its enumeration. [. . .]

How [to] summarize the South American attitude toward the Doctrine? The temptation, on the basis of the facts just analyzed, might well be unduly to minimize the role of Monroe's message. From the exaggerated view of its significance common to the conventional historical narrative, it is easy to fall into a contrary error. That the attitude of the United States was regarded as of less importance than that of Great Britain must be frankly recognized. That the circumstances under which the President's manifesto was made known operated to diminish its effects is probable. That there was far less apprehension in most Spanish American capitals than in Washington, and therefore a cooler estimate of the importance of the U.S. attitude, is tolerably clear. But all these things taken together must not be pressed too far. Monroe's declaration was by no means disregarded. Nor was it, once observed, relegated to oblivion. It was almost everywhere assumed by South American statesmen that Monroe meant what he said, and that the aegis of North American protection had been extended over the new republics.

6

The Platt Amendment of 1901

On February 25, 1901, Senator Orville H. Platt introduced in Congress the famous amendment bearing his name. On March 2 the bill became law, and on June 12 a constitutional convention meeting in Havana to draft a constitution adopted the amendment by a majority of one as an annex to the Cuban Constitution of 1901. The constitution also provided for universal suffrage, separation of church and state, a popularly elected but all-powerful president who could be reelected for a second term, and a weakened senate and a chamber of deputies.

The distinguished black general of the war against Spain, Juan Gualberto Gómez, summarized the feelings of the more radical leaders: "The Platt Amendment has reduced the independence and sovereignty of the Cuban republic to a myth."

The Platt Amendment stipulated the following:

The President of the United States is hereby authorized to "leave the government and control of the island of Cuba to its people" so soon as a government shall have been established in said island under a constitution which, either as a part thereof or in an ordinance appended thereto, shall define the future relations of the United States with Cuba, substantially as follows:

I. That the government of Cuba shall never enter into any treaty or other compact with any foreign power or powers which will impair or tend to impair the independence of Cuba, nor in any manner authorize or permit any foreign power or powers to obtain by colonization or for military or naval purposes or otherwise, lodgement in or control over any portion of said island.

II. That said government shall not assume or contract any public debt, to pay the interest upon which, and to make reasonable sinking fund provision for the ultimate discharge of which the ordinary revenues of the island, after defraying the current expenses of government, shall be inadequate.

III. That the government of Cuba consents that the United States may exercise the right to intervene for the preservation of Cuban independence, the maintenance of a government adequate for the protection of life, property, and individual liberty, and for discharging the obligations with respect to Cuba imposed by the Treaty of Paris on the United States, now to be assumed and undertaken by the government of Cuba.

IV. That all acts of the United States in Cuba during its military occupancy thereof are ratified and validated, and all lawful rights acquired thereunder shall be maintained and protected.

V. That the government of Cuba will execute, and, as far as necessary, extend, the plans already devised or other plans to be mutually agreed upon, for the sanitation of the cities of the island, to the end that a recurrence of epidemic and infectious diseases may be prevented, thereby assuring protection to the people and commerce of Cuba, as well as to the commerce of the southern ports of the United States and the people residing therein.

VI. That the Isle of Pines shall be omitted from the proposed constitutional boundaries of Cuba, the title thereto being left to future adjustment by treaty.

VII. That to enable the United States to maintain the independence of Cuba, and to protect the people thereof, as well as for its defense, the government of Cuba will sell or lease to the United States lands necessary for coaling or naval stations at certain specified points, to be agreed upon with the President of the United States.

7

The Real Monroe Doctrine

Elihu Root

Elihu Root, born in 1845 in Clinton, New York, was a successful corporate lawyer before entering public service. He served as U.S. secretary of war from 1899 to 1904 and was the principal architect of what later became known as the Platt Amendment (1901), which officially bound the United States and Cuba for thirty-three years. Article three of the amendment gave the United States the right to intervene in Cuba to maintain "stability." Root served as secretary of state under President Theodore Roosevelt from 1905 to 1909 and won the Nobel Peace Prize in 1912. Two years later he gave the address reprinted here, in which he argues for the continued and vigorous application of the doctrine, stating that the declaration "has grown continually a more vital and insistent rule of conduct for each succeeding generation of Americans" (p. 430).

The year this speech was delivered, 1914, is of critical importance in understanding Root's preoccupations. That year is remembered for the opening of the Panama Canal and the breakdown of order in Europe, which culminated in World War I in August. Root states, "It is plain that the building of the Panama Canal greatly accentuates the practical necessity of the Monroe Doctrine as it applies to all the territory surrounding the Caribbean or near the Bay of Panama" (p. 440). Thus the author's spirited defense of the Monroe Doctrine in 1914 should be framed within the context of the challenges posed by the opening of the Panama Canal and the international meltdown that resulted in world war.

We are all familiar with President Monroe's famous message of December 2, 1823.

> The occasion has been judged proper for asserting, as a principle in which the rights and interests of the United States are involved, that the American Continents, by the free and independent condition which they have assumed and

maintain, are henceforth not to be considered as subjects for future colonization by any European Powers. [. . .]

In the wars of the European Powers in matters relating to themselves we have never taken any part, nor does it comport with our policy to do so. It is only when our rights are invaded or seriously menaced that we resent injuries or make preparation for our defense. With the movements in this hemisphere we are of necessity more immediately connected and by causes which must be obvious to all enlightened and impartial observers.

We owe it, therefore, to candor, and to the amicable relations existing between the United States and those Powers, to declare that we should consider any attempt on their part to extend their system to any portion of this hemisphere as dangerous to our peace and safety. With the existing colonies or dependencies of any European Power we have not interfered and shall not interfere. But with the governments who have declared their independence and maintained it, and whose independence we have on great consideration and on just principles, acknowledged, we could not view any interposition for the purpose of oppressing them, or controlling in any other manner, their destiny, by any European Power, in any other light than as the manifestation of an unfriendly disposition toward the United States. In the war between these new governments and Spain we declared our neutrality at the time of their recognition, and to this we have adhered and shall continue to adhere, provided no change shall occur which, in the judgment of the competent authorities of this government, shall make a corresponding change on the part of the United States indispensable to their security. [. . .]

It is impossible that the allied Powers should extend their political system to any portion of either continent without endangering our peace and happiness; nor can any one believe that our southern brethren, if left to themselves, would adopt it of their own accord. It is equally impossible, therefore, that we should behold such interposition, in any form, with indifference.

The occasion for these declarations is a familiar story—The revolt of the Spanish provinces in America which Spain, unaided, was plainly unable to reduce to their former condition of dependence; the reaction against liberalism in Europe which followed the downfall of Napoleon and the restoration of the Bourbons to the throne of France; the formation of the Holy Alliance; the agreement of its members at the Conferences of Aix la Chapelle and Laybach and Verona for the insurance of monarchy against revolution; the restoration of Ferdinand the Seventh to the throne of Spain by the armed power of France pursuant to this agreement; the purpose of the Alliance to follow the restoration of monarchy in Spain by the restoration of that monarchy's control over its colonies in the New World; the claims both of Russia and of Great Britain to rights of colonization on the Northwest coast; the proposals of Mr. Canning to Richard Rush for a joint declaration of principles by England and the United States adverse to the interference of any other European Power in the contest between Spain and her former colonies; the serious question raised by this proposal as to the effect of a joint declaration upon the American policy of avoiding entangling alliances.

The form and phrasing of President Monroe's message were adapted to meet these conditions. The statements made were intended to carry specific information to the members of the Holy Alliance that an attempt by any of them to coerce the new states of South America would be not a simple expedition against weak and disunited colonies, but the much more difficult and expensive task of dealing with the formidable maritime power of the United States as well as the opposition of England, and they were intended to carry to Russia and incidentally to England the idea that rights to territory in the New World must thenceforth rest upon the existing titles, and that the United States would dispute any attempt to create rights to territory by future occupation.

It is undoubtedly true that the specific occasions for the declaration of Monroe no longer exist. The Holy Alliance long ago disappeared. The nations of Europe no longer contemplate the vindication of monarchical principles in the territory of the New World. France, the most active of the Allies, is herself a republic. No nation longer asserts the right of colonization in America. The general establishment of diplomatic relations between the Powers of Europe and the American republics, if not already universal, became so when, pursuant to the formal assent of the Powers, all the American republics were received into the Second Conference at The Hague and joined in the conventions there made, upon the footing of equal sovereignty, entitled to have their territory and independence respected under that law of nations which formerly existed for Europe alone.

The declaration, however, did more than deal with the specific occasion which called it forth. It was intended to declare a general principle for the future, and this is plain not merely from the generality of the terms used but from the discussions out of which they arose and from the understanding of the men who took part in the making and of their successors.

When Jefferson was consulted by President Monroe before the message was sent he replied:

> The question presented by the letters you have sent me is the most momentous which has ever been offered to my contemplation since that of independence. That made us a nation; this sets our compass and points the course which we are to steer through the ocean of time opening on us. And never could we embark upon it under circumstances more auspicious. Our first and fundamental maxim should be, never to entangle ourselves in the broils of Europe; our second, never to suffer Europe to intermeddle with cisatlantic affairs. [. . .]

As the particular occasions which called it forth have slipped back into history, the declaration itself, instead of being handed over to the historian, has grown continually a more vital and insistent rule of conduct for each succeeding generation of Americans. Never for a moment have the responsible and instructed statesmen in charge of the foreign affairs of the United States failed to consider themselves bound to insist upon its policy. Never once has the public opinion of the people of the United States failed to support every just application of it as new occasion has arisen. Almost every President and Secretary of State has restated the doctrine with vigor and emphasis in the discussion of the diplomatic affairs of his day. The governments of Europe have gradually come to realize that the existence of the policy which Monroe declared is a stubborn and continuing fact to be recognized in their controversies with American countries. We have seen Spain, France, England, Germany, with admirable good sense and good temper, explaining beforehand to the United States that they intended no permanent occupation of territory, in the controversy with Mexico forty years after the declaration, and in the controversy with Venezuela eighty years after. In 1903 the Duke of Devonshire declared "Great Britain accepts the Monroe Doctrine unreservedly." Mr. Hay coupled the Monroe Doctrine and the Golden Rule as cardinal guides of American diplomacy. Twice within very recent years the whole treaty-making power of the United States has given its formal approval to the policy by the reservations in the signature and in the ratification of the arbitration conventions of The Hague Conferences, expressed in these words by the Senate resolution agreeing to ratification of the convention of 1907:

> Nothing contained in this convention shall be so construed as to require the United States of America to depart from its traditional policy of not intruding upon, interfering with, or entangling itself in the political questions of policy or internal administration of any foreign state, nor shall anything contained in the said convention be construed to imply a relinquishment by the United States of its traditional attitude towards purely American questions.

It seems fair to assume that a policy with such a history as this has some continuing and substantial reason underlying it; that it is not outworn or meaningless or a purely formal relic of the past, and it seems worth while to consider carefully what the doctrine is and what it is not. No one ever pretended that Mr. Monroe was declaring a rule of international law or that the doctrine which he declared has become international law. It is a declaration of the United States that certain acts would be injurious to the peace and safety of the United States and that the United States would regard them as unfriendly. The declaration does not say what the course of the United States will be in case such acts are done. That is left to be determined in each particular instance. [. . .]

It is doubtless true that in the adherence of the American people to the original declaration there was a great element of sentiment and of sympathy for the people of South America who were struggling for freedom, and it has been a source of great satisfaction to the United States that the course which it took in 1823 concurrently with the action of Great Britain played so great a part in assuring the right of self-government to the countries of South America. Yet it is to be observed that in reference to the South American governments, as in all other respects, the international right upon which the declaration expressly rests is not sentiment or sympathy or a claim to dictate what kind of government any other country shall have, but the safety of the United States. It is because the new governments cannot be overthrown by the Allied Powers "without endangering our peace and happiness"; that "the United States cannot behold such interposition in any form with indifference."

We frequently see statements that the doctrine has been changed or enlarged; that there is a new or different doctrine since Monroe's time. They are mistaken. There has been no change. One apparent extension of the statement of Monroe was made by President Polk in his messages of 1845 and 1848, when he included the acquisition of territory by a European Power through cession as dangerous to the safety of the United States. It was really but stating a corollary to the doctrine of 1823 and asserting the same right of self-protection against the other American states as well as against Europe.

This corollary has been so long and uniformly agreed to by the Government and the people of the United States that it may fairly be regarded as being now a part of the doctrine. But, all assertions to the contrary notwithstanding, there has been no other change or enlargement of the Monroe Doctrine since it was first promulgated. It must be remembered that not everything said or written by Secretaries of State or even by Presidents constitutes a national policy or can enlarge or modify or diminish a national policy.

It is the substance of the thing to which the nation holds and that is and always has been that the safety of the United States demands that American territory shall remain American. The Monroe Doctrine does not assert or imply or involve any right on the part of the United States to impair or control the independent sovereignty of any American state. In the lives of nations as of individuals, there are many rights unquestioned and universally conceded. The assertion of any particular right must be considered, not as excluding all others but as coincident with all others which are not inconsistent. The fundamental principle of international law is the principle of independent sovereignty. Upon that all other rules of international law rest. That is the chief and necessary protection of the weak against the power of the strong. Observance of that is the necessary condition to the peace and order of the civilized world. By the declaration of that principle the common judgment of civilization awards to the smallest and weakest state the liberty to control its own affairs without interference from any other Power, however great.

The Monroe Doctrine does not infringe upon that right. It asserts the right. The declaration of Monroe was that the rights and interests of the United States were involved in maintaining a condition, and the condition to be maintained was the independence of all the American countries. It is "the free and independent condition which they have assumed and maintained" which is declared to render them not subject to future colonization. It is "the governments who have declared their independence and maintained it and whose independence we have on great consideration and on just principles acknowledged" that are not to be interfered with. When Mr. Canning's proposals for a joint declaration were under consideration by the Cabinet in the month before the famous message was sent, John Quincy Adams, who played the major part in forming the policy, declared the basis of it in these words:

> Considering the South Americans as independent nations, they themselves and no other nation had the right to dispose of their condition. We have no right to dispose of them either alone or in conjunction with other nations. Neither have any other nations the right of disposing of them without their consent. [. . .]

It happens, however, that the United States is very much bigger and more powerful than most of the other American republics. And when a very great and powerful state makes demands upon a very small and weak state it is difficult to avoid a feeling that there is an assumption of superior authority involved in the assertion of superior power, even though the demand be based solely upon the right of equal against equal. An examination of the various controversies which the United States has had with other American Powers will disclose the fact that in every case the rights asserted were rights not of superiority but of equality. Of course it cannot be claimed that great and powerful states shall forego their just rights against smaller and less powerful states. The responsibilities of sovereignty attach to the weak as well as to the strong, and a claim to exemption from those responsibilities would imply not equality but inferiority. The most that can be said concerning a question between a powerful state and a weak one is that the great state ought to be especially considerate and gentle in the assertion and maintenance of its position; ought always to base its acts not upon a superiority of force, but upon reason and law; and ought to assert no rights against a small state because of its weakness which it would not assert against a great state notwithstanding its power. But in all this the Monroe Doctrine is not concerned at all.

The scope of the doctrine is strictly limited. It concerns itself only with the occupation of territory in the New World to the subversion or exclusion of a preexisting American government. It has not otherwise any relation to the affairs of either American or European states. In good conduct or bad, observance of rights or violations of them, agreement or controversy, injury or reprisal, coercion or war, the United States finds no warrant in the Monroe Doctrine for interference. [. . .]

Since the Monroe Doctrine is a declaration based upon this nation's right of self-protection, it cannot be transmuted into a joint or common declaration by American states or any number of them. If Chile or Argentina or Brazil were to contribute the weight of her influence toward a similar end, the right upon which that nation would rest its declaration would be its own safety, not the safety of the United States. Chile would declare what was necessary for the safety of Chile. Argentina would declare what was necessary for the safety of Argentina. Brazil, what was necessary for the safety of Brazil. Each nation would act for itself and in its own right and it would be impossible to go beyond that except by more or less offensive and defensive alliances. Of course such alliances are not to be considered.

It is plain that the building of the Panama Canal greatly accentuates the practical necessity of the Monroe Doctrine as it applies to all the territory surrounding the Caribbean or near the Bay of Panama. The plainest lessons of history and the universal judgment of all responsible students of the subject concur in teaching that the potential command of the route to and from the Canal must rest with the United States and that the vital interests of the nation forbid that such command shall pass into other hands. Certainly no nation which has acquiesced in the British occupation of Egypt will dispute this proposition. Undoubtedly as one passes to the south and the distance from the Caribbean increases, the necessity of maintaining the rule of Monroe becomes less immediate and apparent. But who is competent to draw the line? Who will say, "To this point the rule of Monroe should apply; beyond this point, it should not?" Who will say that a new national force created beyond any line that he can draw will stay beyond it and will not in the long course of time extend itself indefinitely?

The danger to be apprehended from the immediate proximity of hostile forces was not the sole consideration leading to the declaration. The need to separate the influences determining the development and relation of states in the New World from the influences operating in Europe played an even greater part. The familiar paragraphs of Washington's Farewell Address upon this subject were not rhetoric. They were intensely practical rules of conduct for the future guidance of the country.

> Europe has a set of primary interests, which to us have none, or a very remote relation. Hence, she must be engaged in frequent controversies, the causes of which are essentially foreign to our concerns. Hence, therefore, it must be unwise in us to implicate ourselves, by artificial ties, in the ordinary vicissitudes of her politics, or the ordinary combinations and collisions of her friendships or enmities. Our detached and distant situation invites and enables us to pursue a different course.

It was the same instinct which led Jefferson, in the letter to Monroe already quoted, to say:

> Our first and fundamental maxim should be, never to entangle ourselves in the broils of Europe; our second, never to suffer Europe to intermeddle with cisatlantic affairs.

The concurrence of Washington and Hamilton and Jefferson in the declaration of this principle of action entitles it to great respect. They recalled the long period during which every war waged in Europe between European Powers and arising from European causes of quarrel was waged also in the New World. English and French and Spanish and Dutch killed and harried each other in America, not because of quarrels between the settlers in America but because of quarrels between the European Powers having dominion over them. Separation of influences as absolute and complete as possible was the remedy which the wisest of Americans agreed upon. It was one of the primary purposes of Monroe's declaration to insist upon this separation, and to accomplish it he drew the line at the water's edge. The problem of national protection in the distant future is one not to be solved by the first impressions of the casual observer, but only by profound study of the forces which, in the long life of nations, work out results. In this case the results of such a study by the best men of the formative period of the United States are supported by the instincts of the American democracy holding steadily in one direction for almost a century. The problem has not changed essentially. If the declaration of Monroe was right when the message was sent, it is right now. South America is no more distant today than it was then. The tremendous armaments and international jealousies of Europe afford little assurance to those who think we may now abandon the separatist policy of Washington. That South American states have become too strong for colonization or occupation is cause for satisfaction. That Europe has no purpose or wish to colonize American territory is most gratifying. These facts may make it improbable that it will be necessary to apply the Monroe Doctrine in the southern parts of South America; but they furnish no reason whatever for retracting or denying or abandoning a declaration of public policy, just and reasonable when it was made, and which, if occasion for its application shall arise in the future, will still be just and reasonable.

8

Autopsy of the Monroe Doctrine: The Strange Story of Inter-American Relations

Gaston Nerval [Raúl Díez de Medina]

Gaston Nerval [pseudonym for Raúl Díez de Medina], a Latin American diplomat, not only challenged the importance of the Monroe Doctrine in history but claimed that the document itself should be relegated to the trash bin of history. His views stand in stark contrast to those of Elihu Root published twenty years earlier. Nerval writes in his 1934 Autopsy of the Monroe Doctrine: The Strange Story of Inter-American Relations *how "the Monroe Doctrine has become the greatest cause of misunderstanding between them [the United States and Latin America]." It is hardly coincidental that Nerval's book was published one year after Franklin Delano Roosevelt assumed the presidency of the United States. FDR's election signified a shift in U.S. policy toward Latin America, especially with the announcement of his Good Neighbor Policy in 1933. Nerval calls for more international action rather than the unilateral policies that always seemed favored by Washington. His criticism of the Monroe Doctrine represents the sentiments of many Latin American intellectuals at the time and can be seen as representing one end of the spectrum of debate concerning the doctrine; Root is at the other extreme, and Dexter Perkins falls somewhere between the two.*

The "New Deal" in Pan-Americanism which was inaugurated by President Franklin D. Roosevelt in 1933 required the abandonment of the Monroe Doctrine, in the opinion of the Bolivian diplomat and journalist Raul Diez de Medina (b. 1909–), who wrote his indictment of the Doctrine under the pseudonym Gaston Nerval. He served in the Bolivian legation in Washington in 1930.

*   *   *

The Monroe Doctrine, as interpreted by the successors of President Monroe, has been the paramount feature of the Latin-American policy of the United States. It has been invoked to account for every action of this country in its relations with the Southern Hemisphere. It has been, maliciously or innocently, transformed, time and again, to fit the different situations and support the United States in each separate emergency.

Because of that, the Monroe Doctrine is inexorably linked with the fate of inter-American relationships. In the eyes of Anglo-Saxon Americans, the Monroe Doctrine justifies all the aggressive policies of the past. In the eyes of Latin Americans, it is the pretext for them.

We have seen that most of the theories and practices employed by the United States in Latin America, and officially or tacitly admitted as justified under imaginary powers of an ever-changing Monroe Doctrine, not only have disregarded the law of nations, but have also been the source of bitter controversies, resentment, and suspicion between Anglo-Saxon and Latin in the Western Hemisphere. The various phases of United States hegemony and of United States intervention in Latin America—territorial expansion, *paramount interest, Manifest Destiny,* overlordship, intervention in foreign affairs, intervention on behalf of Europe, intervention for policing purposes, the policy of the *big stick, dollar diplomacy,* etc.—must, then, be eliminated before any real program for Pan-American harmony is attempted.

But the mere discontinuance of such practices is not enough. As a matter of fact, the trend of the Latin-American policy of the State Department, for the past few years, has been one of gradual drifting away from the much discredited practices of yesterday. But, who is to guarantee to the Latin Americans, made extremely skeptical by contradictions and unkept promises in the past, that this improvement is more than a temporary one? Who is to guarantee to them that the abuses apparently disavowed are not to be again indulged in the future, under some new interpretation, or a revived one, of the multiheaded *shibboleth* which, for over 100 years, has furnished an excuse for every inexcusable act of the United States in Latin America?

The only way to eliminate completely the ground for suspicion and the resentment today prevailing—a condition essential to the success of any Pan-American scheme—is to discard the *shibboleth* itself. The only way to assure the Latin Americans that the unfortunate theories and practices of the past will have no repetition—and thus regain their lost good will—is to abandon the instrument which has served to foster them; to give up, once [and] for all, the fictitious and self-imposed rights successively "discovered" with each new interpretation of the Monroe Doctrine. The only way is to renounce the Doctrine itself which, rightly or wrongly, is so intimately associated with those practices and the peculiar theories which originated them.

Nor is it enough to state, at this eleventh hour, that the Monroe Doctrine really had little to do with such things as *have been* committed in its name, after the things have been committed and the Doctrine *has been* given and accepted for their explanation. High State Department officials have tried this, recently, in a vain attempt to vindicate the Doctrine, even though this attempt amounted to a disavowal of the past policies. They have advocated a return to the original Monroe Doctrine, probably to avoid responsibility for the changes and distortions wrought by their predecessors. But this can help only slightly. Individual declarations or pledges of good intentions for the future cannot change overnight the impression which 100 years of an elastic, capricious, ever-changing Monroe Doctrine, 100 years of the *modern Monroe Doctrine*, have created not only in Latin America, and in the United States, but throughout the world.

The only way to end all the misunderstanding and the resentment aroused by this much-abused Monroe Doctrine, and by the strange things which have been done in its name, is to drop the Doctrine itself; and not to drop only the modern versions of it—under which such things were possible—but the original Doctrine as well, whence the misinterpretations and misuses sprang. No amount of explaining or repentance will suffice to restore confidence in the old Doctrine, even if deprived of all the corollaries and malformations added by Monroe's successors. Besides, we have seen that even the merits of the original Monroe Doctrine have been grossly exaggerated.

*   *   *

With this in mind, let us outline, then, a three-point program. . . .

POINT NUMBER ONE: ABANDONMENT OF THE MONROE DOCTRINE

The necessity, and the urgency, of discarding the Monroe Doctrine, worn-out, misunderstood, and distorted beyond recognition, may be best emphasized by listing the ten different counts of this *indictment* of the Doctrine. [. . .]

1. The Monroe Doctrine was not intended for the benefit of the Latin American republics.
2. The original results and merits of the Monroe Doctrine have been grossly exaggerated.
3. The Monroe Doctrine is worn-out and useless.
4. The Monroe Doctrine is a unilateral, egoistic policy, and exclusively of the United States.

5. The Monroe Doctrine did not create Pan-Americanism, but, on the contrary, it arrested the Bolivarian Pan-Americanism of equal rights and mutual obligations.
6. The Monroe Doctrine has been violated and disregarded by the European powers against which it was directed, with the knowledge and, at times, the connivance of the United States.
7. The Monroe Doctrine has been distorted to serve as an instrument of the hegemony of the United States in the Western Hemisphere.
8. The Monroe Doctrine has been misinterpreted and abused to serve as a cloak for the intervention of the United States in Latin America.
9. The Monroe Doctrine has been misconstrued and misused to serve as the tool of United States imperialism in the Caribbean area.
10. The Monroe Doctrine is in conflict with all the modern peace machinery of the world and the present trends of international relations.

POINT NUMBER TWO: SUBSTITUTION OF A PAN-AMERICAN DOCTRINE OF JOINT RESPONSIBILITY

To take care of the problems of protection and joint action in case of anarchy, a Pan-American doctrine should be adopted by all the American states which would transfer the self-appointed powers until now held by the United States, alone, to a continental organization which would have in mind the rights of all, instead of the privilege of one.

Three steps can facilitate this:

A) Calling of a Pan-American conference, in which the chief problems involved in the political and economic relations of the United States with the Latin-American countries would be frankly discussed, the United States formally renouncing whatever privileges it has appropriated to itself under the Monroe Doctrine. It goes without saying that the kind of Pan-American conferences we have been having for the past forty years—which correspond faithfully to the kind of Pan-Americanism represented today by the *Pan American Union*, the Pan-Americanism of *recommendations*, diplomatic flirting, and bouquets of flowers—would not do at all.

*   *   *

B) Adoption by all the American states of the good principles involved in the original Monroe Doctrine, that is, the principles of opposition to non-

American colonization of American territory and opposition to non-American interference with American governments for the purpose of oppressing or controlling them. This could be done jointly or separately, either by each American government issuing a declaration to that effect. . . . or, better still, though greater obstacles inhere in this method, by signing a *continental pact of self-defense* in case of non-American aggression, just as Bolivar, the Liberator, planned. This would not be a mere internationalization or continentalization of the original Monroe Doctrine, as most of its advocates call it, both here and in Latin America, because, as we have seen, the original Monroe Doctrine was not advanced for the purpose of serving as a guarantee of mutual defense. It would really be an entirely new thing, establishing in a contractual form the guarantee which early Latin-American leaders thought, erroneously, the Monroe Doctrine gave them. It would, in fact, be more the enactment of the *Bolivarian doctrine* than the continentalization of the Monroe Doctrine. But it would serve better than anything else the only laudable principle which could have justified the Monroe Doctrine if the Doctrine had adhered strictly to it, and only to it, instead of refusing to sanction it for fear of foreign commitments and "entanglements," namely, the principle of *contractual continental self-defense.*

C) Devising and adopting, by all the American states, of a *Pan-American Doctrine of Joint Responsibility*, that is, one which would give all of them a voice in the solution of any controversies arising out of the problem of protection of foreign lives in any one of them where internal anarchy had completely destroyed any semblance of local government. This doctrine would provide for the respect of the sovereignty and independence of the weakest as well as the strongest of the American republics, and for the consultation of all the American governments before any action, any *joint action* for purely humanitarian purposes, could be undertaken in any country where civil war had plunged the foreign, as well as the native population, into chaos and anarchy. This doctrine would proscribe hegemony and over-lordship of any one of the nation members of the American family. It would proscribe the sort of intervention which we have witnessed in the past and which constitutes, today, the greatest barrier to Pan-American harmony. It would take the *big stick* out of the hands of Uncle Sam, who has certainly shown himself incapable of using it wisely, and it would place it in the hands of the *international community*, in this case, the American community of nations, the only one entitled to brandish it, to be used reluctantly and solely in extreme emergencies.

POINT NUMBER THREE: ORGANIZATION OF AMERICAN PEACE

The logical complement of the steps suggested, and a necessary complement if the friendship and cooperation of the American republics are to be established on solid ground, should be the effective organization of international peace in the Western Hemisphere.

*   *   *

III

FROM TR TO FDR: INTERVENTIONISM
AND THE GOOD NEIGHBOR POLICY

This part focuses on the period from roughly 1898, with the onset and conclusion of the Spanish-American War, through the Good Neighbor policy of the 1930s and 1940s. The chapters in this part, all from the perspective of U.S. diplomatic historians, represent three distinct interpretations of U.S. policy in Latin America during the first half of the twentieth century.

The United States as Empire became a reality by mid-1898, when the U.S. military won the Spanish-American War and began administering territories in the Caribbean that once belonged to Spain. Puerto Rico and Cuba fell under U.S. domination, and in the Pacific, Guam and the Philippines would become part of the U.S. sphere though the fighting in the Philippines dragged on for years at a cost of thousands of lives. Lester D. Langley's chapter in this part of the book deals with the difficulties of building American-style society in the Caribbean, and focuses on the work of Brigadier General Leonard Wood, a physician and Governor of Santiago de Cuba from 1898 to 1902. The chapter deals with the complexities, ambiguities, and cultural misunderstandings that led to a less than optimal U.S. occupation. The U.S. military forces left Cuba by 1902, but returned in 1906, and a few times after that, and Cuba's fortunes were directly tied to the United States until the 1959 Revolution.

In November 1903 Panama's Revolution for Independence was directly connected to Theodore Roosevelt's aggressive Caribbean policies—i.e., the policy of the "big stick": Caribbean and Central American nations were invited to behave, or else receive the wrath of the U.S. military. At that time, construction of a canal across Central America was seen as vital to U.S. security and commercial interests. The Colombian Senate, citing national sovereignty concerns, rejected the Hay-Herrán Treaty (January 1903), which would have allowed the United States to construct a canal over territory that before November 1903 had belonged to Colombia. Historian Samuel Flagg Bemis, one of the earliest U.S.

diplomatic historians who focused on Latin America, enthusiastically supported U.S. policy in the region, which he referred to as "the Panama Policy": this policy, based on "self-interested benevolence," was thought of as a rational, logical expression of U.S. power in a region where (according to the historians of the time) rationality was sorely lacking. Bemis focused on political and diplomatic considerations, and failed to consider profit as a motivator in the Panama Policy. Later revisionist historians would examine U.S. policy from a more "market driven" perspective.

Roosevelt's ideology concerning Latin America was formulated into policy through the Roosevelt Corollary to the Monroe Doctrine (1904). This was, essentially, a doctrine of intervention. Given that the United States had successfully used force in the region between 1898 and 1903, the president believed that military force was the most efficacious manner of affecting "positive" change in the region. He announced to the world in 1904 that a "civilized nation" might need to intervene in nations wracked by "chronic wrongdoing." The terms were clearly established, and Roosevelt's Corollary to the Monroe Doctrine led to multiple interventions between 1904 and the beginning of the Great Depression in Latin America. One such intervention involved a brief but unpopular invasion of Mexico on April 21, 1914, at Veracruz. In this section of our book, readers will find excerpts from President Woodrow Wilson's address to Congress when he defined the "crisis" in Mexico (ostensibly concerning little more than military honor) before committing U.S. troops to a military operation that cost around two hundred lives and came at the height of the decade-long Mexican Revolution (1910–1920).

The realities of World War I and changes in the global economy resulting largely from the conflict created U.S. prosperity followed by collapse. That collapse, generally referred to as "The Great Depression," began in October 1929. Raw materials and markets were significant features of the U.S. interest in Latin America during this period, but decades of military and political intervention had greatly strained U.S.–Latin American relations. The Policy of the Good Neighbor, generally associated with the presidency of Franklin Delano Roosevelt (1933–1945), sought to redirect tensions and mistrust within the hemisphere. The policy was also guided by economic and political realities that forced Roosevelt to form alliances and partnerships with Latin American nations. Bryce Wood writes of the Good Neighbor plan and its emergence as policy during the late 1920s and 1930s. He emphasizes the complexity of factors, issues, and interests involved in policy making and does not hesitate to question U.S. motives in policy formulation.

Taken together, the three chapters in this section and President Wilson's speech help to explain U.S. policy as it applied mostly to the Caribbean and Central America during the first half of the twentieth century. The three authors provide radically distinct interpretations of U.S. policy shaped by both the time period in which they wrote and the material on which they chose to focus.

9

Leonard Wood and the White Man's Burden

Lester D. Langley

In 1983, Historian Lester D. Langley published The Banana *Wars: United States Intervention in the Caribbean, 1898–1934. That book presented U.S. policy in the Caribbean basin as a long series of military interventions designed to impart U.S. objectives in the region. Cuba, of course, was the first "test case": the 1898 intervention was designed, ostensibly, to promote Cuban "independence"; the reality, as Langley points out, involved military and political control of the island, and the author focuses on the case of Brigadier General Leonard Wood, Governor of Santiago, whose writings, work, and objectives on the island framed the cultural and historic chasm separating the distinct development of Cuba and the United States.*

Almost exactly two months after the declaration of war against Spain in 1898, the United States launched a military invasion of Spanish Cuba.

Still flushed with pride over Admiral George Dewey's tremendous victory over the Spanish at Manila Bay on May 1, the American people expectantly awaited an equally glorious triumph in Spain's New World empire. Their perspective of the Cuban rebellion, shaped by exaggerated tales of Spanish wickedness and Cuban resourcefulness, almost unquestioningly followed the accounts of the sometimes rabidly pro-Cuban press and the propaganda dispensed by the Cuban juntas scattered along the east and Gulf coasts. The war on the island, the president had solemnly declared, had by spring 1898 deteriorated into a gruesome spectacle that shook America's moral sensibilities, and it was our humanitarian duty to end it. A conquering army of a republican nation would be dispatched to complete the campaign begun by the Cuban rebels: to destroy the four-hundred-year Spanish empire on the island and, because Congress had declared we were waging a war of liberation and not of conquest, to lay the foundation for a new republic.

The army that landed in eastern Cuba in June 1898 was typically American in its makeup of volunteers and a small cadre of career officers. It had no experience in tropical war. Its officers were either aging veterans from the Indian campaigns or thrill seekers like Theodore Roosevelt. Its leader was a three-hundred-pound, gout-ridden brigadier general, William Rufus Shafter, whom Roosevelt considered "criminally incompetent." The secretary of war, Russell Alger, a well-intentioned but irascible Michigan politician, was incapable of directing the war with the chaotic bureaucracy of the War Department. Alger quarreled so incessantly with the commanding general of the army, Nelson A. Miles, that President McKinley eventually bypassed both and directed the war himself.

The mission of this army was the defeat of Spain and Spanish authority on the island of Cuba, not the expansion of American territorial domain. But it would become in the course of the war an army for empire. Its troops would storm El Caney and San Juan Hill, take Puerto Rico, and pacify Manila. A meager contingent of 25,000 before the war, the American army would expand rapidly into a mighty force of 100,000 in the summer of 1898, 70,000 serving outside the continental United States, 30,000 in the Philippines on the other side of the globe. At war's end its commanding officers found themselves in the uncommon role of colonial administrators in Cuba, Puerto Rico, and the Philippines. And in August 1898 President William McKinley would at last find the perfect administrator for this empire in Elihu Root, a corporation lawyer who became secretary of war after Alger became involved in a bitter political fight in his home state and was compelled to resign.[1]

The war brought impressive victories—Manila Bay, San Juan Hill, Santiago—but it also taught painful realities. One of the first myths shattered was the pre-war image of craven Spaniard and noble Cuban. American troops landing at Daiquirí for the great assault against the Spaniards expected to be greeted wildly by their Cuban allies. Instead they were met by a ragtag guerrilla force, unkempt in appearance and darker in color than the drawings of Cuban rebels in New York newspapers. These wretches were less interested in camaraderie and battle tactics than in American rations. The Americans fed them but grew irritated when they refused to fight according to preconceived American notions of valiant warriors. This harsh judgment was in part explained by their tatterdemalion appearance. Grover Flint, who wrote a popular account of his wartime experience (*Marching with Gómez*, 1898), attributed Cuban dishevelment to sacrifice, but many others, including Theodore Roosevelt, simply believed that Cubans would be of little use in a fight.[2] American soldiers were similarly shocked when a Cuban squad, which had captured a Spanish spy, decapitated its prisoner.

If Cubans were inferior, as American soldiers came to believe, then it easily followed that Spaniards were superior—at least superior to Cubans. When Sherwood Anderson wrote that Spaniards had "dark cruel eyes" he imagined himself dispatching some evildoer in the glory of war and expressed a common prewar sentiment. But Americans serving in Cuba soon discovered that Spaniards could fight and fight bravely. At Las Guásimas the Rough Riders, who had landed contested at Daiquirí, encountered stubborn resistance and suffered seventy casualties. El Caney and San Juan Hill, probably the two most fiercely fought land battles of the campaign, swept away all notions of Spanish incompetence or cowardice in American minds. "No men of any nationality," Roosevelt said in a rare tribute to the Hispanic, "could have done better." When a group of American seamen tried to block the passageway to Santiago harbor, where the Spanish fleet was moored, by sinking an old collier in the channel, they were captured by one of Admiral Pascual Cervera's gunboats. The American commanders despaired of their fate but soon received a reassuring message from Cervera himself stating that all were well and would be fairly treated. Of this gesture Captain Robley D. ("Fighting Bob") Evans observed: "Never [have I witnessed] a more courteous thing done in war."[3]

The second reality for which neither the War Department nor the army was prepared was the condition of the battlefield. Most Americans who went to Cuba had some vague knowledge about the island's climate and terrain—after all, the rebellion had been covered in detail by the large eastern newspapers—but they greatly underestimated the exacting toll tropical climate can take on men and matériel. Troops were either inadequately supplied or provided with useless equipment. And their medical treatment became a national scandal. Men could be ordered to march in step, but officers were hard pressed to convince the individual soldier that drinking water must be boiled, latrines constructed, and drainage channels dug. By midsummer, in the stifling heat and malarial atmosphere, the army that had won a rousing victory at El Caney and San Juan Hill had been devastated by sickness. In one regiment—that of the unforgettable Private Charles Post—almost half of the nine hundred men were incapacitated. One by one the buglers came down sick, and there was no one to blow reveille or taps.[4] Elsewhere, the toll of diseased and disabled rose to alarming heights. When the Spanish surrendered Santiago, it was estimated, 90 percent of American soldiers were unable to continue fighting. The deposed secretary of war confirmed this grim statistic in his account of the war; 90 percent of American troops disembarking in New York, wrote Alger, were either ill or convalescent.[5]

Whatever the cost of the war to American soldiers, the physical toll on Cuba and its people was much greater. The years of struggle against Spanish rule and Spain's punitive retaliation had exacted a terrible price. Cuba had lost a tenth of its population, the census of 1899 revealed, a loss explained for the most part by rebel casualties and the harshness of Spain's counterrevolutionary measure, the *reconcentrado* program. The civilian population of the revolutionary eastern provinces had been herded into fortified towns in the garrisoned west, where they had died of starvation and neglect. More ominous was the terrible sacrifice of Cuba's children: In 1899, in a population of 1.5 million, the island counted only 131,000 children four years old and under, 226,000 between five and nine.

Neither countryside nor town had been spared in the devastation. The acreage farmed plummeted to 0.9 million from the 1.3 million acres tilled in 1895. Some provinces, such as Havana and Matanzas, had been severely damaged; Pinar del Rio, the westernmost province, cultivated more farmland in 1899 than in 1895, but its towns had been systematically burned in Antonio Maceo's western campaign. Where land was being farmed in 1899, hopelessly entangled laws made sale, transfer, or purchase difficult. Many of the large sugar plantations had been burned or could not operate; in Matanzas, center of Cuban sugar production in the nineteenth century, there were 434 mills in 1894, but five years later there were only 62. A similar precipitous drop in the number of mills occurred in other provinces.[6] Two-thirds of the island's wealth had been destroyed.

In June 1898 the American army had arrived as invader of Spanish domain; in the course of the war it had become conqueror of Cuba. Now, in 1899, despite a prewar congressional resolution disavowing any intention of annexing Cuban soil, American troops constituted an army of occupation.

In the debate over intervention, McKinley had declared his opposition to formal recognition of the Cuban republic. Thus, at war's end, the Cuban revolutionary junta, which had called for a free united Cuba in 1895, could rejoice in Spain's departure but faced an American army that intended to remain until the island was, in the official pronouncement, "pacified." During the war the people of Oriente province had elected a provisional government, composed mostly of rebel officers who organized an executive council, assessed taxes, and obtained supplies for the rebel army. Outside Oriente, however, the provisional government exercised little influence and was virtually ignored by the Americans. Its president, Bartolomé Masó, urged cooperation with the United States in the hope of obtaining American recognition. But the American government was of the view that Cubans were disunited. When the vice president of the provisional government, Domingo Méndez Capote, arrived in Washington in May 1898 to ascertain American policy, he learned that Cuban and Spanish conservatives were already pressing the Americans to remain after the Spanish surrender. McKinley's intentions were likewise known from his special message to Congress: "To secure in the island the establishment of a stable government, capable of maintaining order and observing its international obligations insuring peace and tranquility and the security of its citizens as well as our own."[7] The genesis of the Platt Amendment of 1901, defining Cuba's "special relationship" to the United States, had appeared.

After the Spanish surrender, the War Department created a Division of Cuba and divided the island into seven military departments, corresponding to old Spanish jurisdictions; in mid-1899 it consolidated these into four—the city of Havana, Havana province and Pinar del Río, Matanzas and Santa Clara, Santiago and Puerto Principe, each headed by an American general. Inevitably there were allusions to the Reconstruction Acts dividing the South into five military districts after the Civil War. (One of the governors in Cuba was Fitzhugh Lee, a southerner, formerly American consul general in Havana.)

The most capable of the military governors was probably William Ludlow, governor of Havana, an engineer who was sufficiently incensed at the wretched condition of the city that he advocated an American occupation "for a generation." But the departmental commander with the best political connections was Brigadier General Leonard Wood, a physician and career soldier, governor in Santiago, who instituted a regime of cleanliness in the city and meted out public whippings to citizens who violated sanitary regulations. Wood wrote detailed and perceptive reports on Cuban conditions for the secretary of war; his letters to the most influential of his friends, Theodore Roosevelt, were filled with savage comments on American mismanagement. One of Wood's aides published in the *North American Review* an equally strident condemnation of army misrule.

The commanding officer of these opinionated and occasionally troublesome proconsuls was Major General John R. Brooke, a Union hero at Gettysburg and, in 1898, commander of the First Corps. In December 1898, while Cuban and American civilians quarreled about the island's future, McKinley appointed Brooke military governor but failed to give him precise instructions about American policy. The result was that Brooke ran the military government on a day-to-day basis, taking care of immediate problems by the most expedient course. He reestablished the civilian bureaucracy, reopened schools, collected revenue, and ordered the streets cleaned. In most cities the Spanish bureaucracy had ceased to function. In Havana, for example, the Spanish city officials had stopped burying the dead—leaving corpses in the street—and had stripped public offices of furniture and supplies. His relief measures probably kept the population from starving.[8]

But he failed to appreciate, as did Leonard Wood, that the American presence in Cuba was as much political as military. Brooke might dispense food to starving Cubans or reopen the schools, but he made the mistake of reappointing Spaniards to their old positions in the bureaucracy, thus angering the Cubans who had fought not only for an independent Cuba but also for political office in the new republic. By the summer of 1899 criticism of the military governor was widespread, even among his subordinates. Root had already become dissatisfied with Brooke's perfunctory reports; he was much impressed with the stern regimen of Wood in Santiago. In the backstairs gossip of the McKinley administration, Brooke's cause was severely damaged, and Brooke hurt himself by censuring Wood for refusing to share the revenues of Santiago with the other provincial commanders.

McKinley remained customarily aloof in this bickering, but by the end of the year it was obvious that the campaign against Brooke (which Brooke called "malicious and wicked") had worked. In December 1899 the president named

Wood military governor of Cuba and instructed him to prepare the Cubans for independence.[9]

The official goal may have been the preparation of Cuba for independence, but Wood had uncommonly broad authority to accomplish that task. He was, wrote his biographer, "practically a free agent." Ecstatically optimistic about his task, he declared to the press a few weeks after his appointment that "success in Cuba is so easy that it would be a crime to fail."[10]

But governing in Santiago, where he ruled as virtual master over conquered Spaniard and war-weary Cuban, and ruling an entire country from Havana were quite different matters. He had already learned not to make Brooke's mistake of retaining the old Spanish bureaucracy. Cubans who took their places in the governmental machinery run by Wood now had a place, if not a sinecure. The problem was a gaggle of former rebel generals and political aspirants demanding more reward and power than Wood or the United States was willing to give. Maximo Gómez, the old Dominican, was offered what amounted to a sinecure for his acquiescence in behalf of the military government and haughtily refused. Most of the Cuban generals cynically believed that the American government intended to annex the island, despite the Teller Amendment and McKinley's—and Wood's—public disclaimers. The Cubans argued for universal manhood suffrage; Wood wanted an electoral code based on property holding as a requirement for suffrage. When General Rius Rivera, who served in the military government, proposed a plan for immediate independence, Wood peremptorily rejected it, and the Cuban resigned.

Wood attributed much of Cuban obstinacy to the long years of Spanish rule and Cuban inexperience in democracy:

> The great mass of public opinion [Wood wrote McKinley] is perfectly inert; especially is this true among the professional classes. The passive inactivity of one hundred and fifty years has settled over them and it is hard to get them out of old ruts and old grooves. . . .
>
> For three months I have had commissions at work on laws, taxation, electoral law, etc., and after all this time the only result is the adoption of practically the original plans submitted by the Americans to the commissions as working models. . . . The people . . . know they are not ready for self-government and those who are honest make no attempt to disguise the fact. We are going ahead as fast as we can, but we are dealing with a race that has been going down for a hundred years and into which we have to infuse new life, new principles and new methods of doing things. This is not the work of a day or of a year, but of a longer period. We are much hampered by the lack of practical experience on the part of the really influential men and much tact has to be used to steer and divert them without offending and causing pain.[11]

Wood was already demonstrating the "practical" approach to nation building. He arose each morning at 5:30 and began a day of furious routine, signing directives, giving orders, hearing complaints, and undertaking inspections of schools, hospitals, road construction, and public projects. He would even investigate the routine operation of a municipal court. He ran the military government like an efficient plantation owner with a show of southern charm for his Cuban wards coupled with a Yankee sense of organization and efficiency. He dined with the Cuban social elite and conversed with the lowliest *guajiro* (rural dweller) in the countryside. For sheer intensity of commitment, Wood was unmatched by any Cuban executive until Fidel Castro. Cubans who remembered the old three-hour workdays under the Spanish now had to adjust to Wood's bureaucratic regime of 9:00 to 11:00, 12:00 to 5:00, six days a week. Wood's office ran on a twenty-four hour schedule, with the day-to-day business supervised by Frank Steinhart, who later became U.S. consul and in 1908 took over Havana Electric Railway.

The American military in Cuba was, by 1901, a skeletal force, its numbers drastically reduced since Wood became military governor in December 1899. Following the war, the Americans had paid off the Cuban rebels (at roughly seventy-five dollars per man) and created a Rural Guard, presumably apolitical, that undertook the task of policing the countryside and maintaining order in the towns. Though American officers occasionally mediated disputes, American soldiers still in Cuba did little police work. An army of occupation, Wood believed, increased Cuban apprehensiveness about American intentions.

When Wood stepped down in May 1902 Cuba was not militarily occupied in the same way as, say, Germany after 1945, but it had already felt the imprint of American ways and techniques, expressed through a military regime and a stern-minded physician turned professional soldier. Mindful of the biblical injunctions on cleanliness, Wood had proceeded to sanitize the island's towns by strict regulations on garbage disposal (the Habaneras had always thrown their refuse in front of the house), paving of streets, and whitewashing of public places. Wood was convinced that filth explained Cuba's epidemics of yellow fever, though an eccentric Cuban scientist (of Scottish ancestry), Dr. Carlos Findlay, argued correctly that the culprit was the mosquito. Wood's vigorous sanitary campaign nonetheless probably helped to control another Cuban scourge, typhoid.

Preparation of Cuba for independence meant, of course, an educational system worthy of a young republic. Brooke and Wood had inherited a Spanish educational structure that had 541 primary schools and 400 private academies, most of them run by clerics. Brooke used the Spanish model, but Wood wanted the Cubans to have a "practical" education in civics, history, science, and vocational training. The model curriculum, written by an officer on the governor's staff, was patterned on the "Ohio Plan" and emphasized preparation for citizenship and the acquisition of skills or the learning of a trade. Hispanic tradition was intentionally denigrated. The texts were translations of American books (modified to Cuban conditions), and the Cuban teachers, before entering their classes of six-to-fourteen-year-old students, were themselves drilled in American credos of instruction. School boards and superintendents, as in the United States, supervised the curriculum and instruction. At the head of Cuba's new educational system stood Alexis Frye, a driven pedagogue who frantically converted old barracks, warehouses, and unoccupied dwellings into 3,000 schools, with 3,500 instructors and 130,000 students. Wood and Frye had a falling-out over the inclusion of what Wood called "radical" methods in class instruction, but their collective energies inspired what seemed to be a great educational experiment. Yet the enthusiasm did not survive, and an investigation in 1906 showed that school population had actually dropped to 1899 levels.[12]

One concern, more than any other, dominated Leonard Wood's thoughts during his governorship of Cuba, and that was the future of the Cuban-American relationship. To him the solution to what some commentators called "our Cuban problem" was not military but political. America had promised not to annex Cuba but had dispatched a conquering army to its shores; it had annexed Puerto Rico and promptly begun demonstrating toward its Caribbean possession a salutary neglect. It had annexed the Philippines but had to wage a grisly military campaign against Filipinos in a guerrilla war that left some Americans, such as Mark Twain, who had supported the Cuban intervention, with feelings of remorse and even revulsion at American practice.

Within a year of Wood's appointment, the Cuban political system took democratic forms. The governor permitted the creation of political parties—three quickly appeared—and participation in local elections. In November 1900 the constitutional convention began its deliberations. From the outset the delegates seemed anxious about the future of the island's relations with the United States. When McKinley or Root or Wood spoke of Cuba, their comments were laced with references to its "special importance" or "strategic position" in the American geopolitical scheme. Cuba was vital and vulnerable—vulnerable to European machinations, a nineteenth-century American fear now made even more obvious by Germany's naval aspirations in the West Indies, and vulnerable within from political inexperience and financial uncertainty. By removing Spanish authority, Root argued, the United States had become responsible for stable government in Cuba. The war against Spain had been a "moral" crusade, the preservation of Cuba's independence a matter of American self-interest.[13]

America's guarantee of Cuban independence thus became the central feature of the Cuban-American relationship, the formal criteria spelled out in the Platt Amendment, an attachment to the Army Appropriation Act of 1901. The amendment embodied Wood's and Root's prescription for Cuba. The republic must maintain a low public debt, so as to prevent financial calamity or misuse of funds; avoid violating American rights in its treaty relations with other nations; grant the United States the right to intervene to protect American lives and property and enforce sanitary measures; and provide long-term naval leases to the United States.

When the Cuban convention got word of the Platt Amendment, a furious debate ensued as to American intentions. Cuban sovereignty was clearly violated, as the more radical delegates pointed out. A special commission delivered a formal protest to Wood, who castigated the group as ungrateful for American contributions to Cuba's welfare. Another delegation arrived in Washington to protest directly to McKinley and discovered that he had already signed the Platt Amendment into law. Even Henry Teller, whose name had been attached to the 1898 resolution forswearing any intention to annex Cuba, supported the amendment. Root himself, one of its coauthors, lavishly entertained the Cubans, then followed with a six-hour discussion about American rights under the Monroe Doctrine. The Platt Amendment would be narrowly interpreted, he told his guests, and Cuban sovereignty would not be violated.

The mollified Cubans returned to Havana with American reassurances and tried to modify the amendment before incorporating it into the Cuban Constitution, as the United States required. But Wood insisted that no alterations would be permitted and that American troops would remain until the amendment became a part of Cuba's fundamental law. Wood believed he understood the reason for Cuban fears. Cuban critics of the Platt Amendment, he wrote Root, "have attempted to make it appear that the intervention will take place at the whim of the officers occupying naval stations." The remark referred to the practice in which naval officers sometimes landed forces or even conducted negotiations without specific orders. The presumption in Wood's comment was that modern communication had made this practice unnecessary. "One thing you can be sure of," Wood concluded, "there will be no serious disturbance in Cuba."[14]

Wood went on to become governor of the Philippines, but he never achieved in that faraway American colony the triumphs that he had enjoyed as proconsul of Cuba. The army returned to Cuba in 1906 in a second tour of occupation, but Wood did not command it.

When American troops left Cuba in mid-1902, Theodore Roosevelt had been president for less than a year. He was to find new opportunities in the emerging Caribbean empire of the United States; to exploit them, he employed a military service with more experience than the army in policing the tropics—the navy.

10

Development of the Panama Policy in the Caribbean and Central America (1902–1936)

Samuel Flagg Bemis

Samuel Flagg Bemis's monumental landmark study of U.S. foreign policy, A
Diplomatic History of the United States, *first published in 1936, was viewed as
the most comprehensive work on the subject to that date. Bemis, who held the title of Farnum Professor of Diplomatic History at Yale, wrote sympathetically
and approvingly of U.S. foreign policy, particularly as that policy related to
Latin America. One of his later works,* The Latin American Policy of the United
States *(1943), focuses exclusively on U.S.–Latin American relations. The author
stressed strategic policy, diplomacy, and politics rather than economics as guiding U.S. diplomacy; his position was challenged by revisionists who interpreted
U.S. diplomacy largely from the perspective of profit and investment opportunities. This excerpt presents Bemis's interpretation of the negotiations leading to
the construction of the Panama Canal.*

[. . .] After nine months of negotiations the Secretary of State signed with the
Colombian Minister the famous Hay-Herrán treaty (January 22, 1903). This
treaty authorized the New Panama Canal Company (the reorganized French
company) to sell its properties to the United States, and granted the United
States full control over a strip across the Isthmus covering the canal site, six
miles wide. For this the United States promised to pay to Colombia $10,000,000
cash, and, beginning nine years after the exchange of ratifications, an annuity of
$250,000 gold. The money was the least of the great benefits to Colombia; the
real value of the treaty was that it would bring suddenly to Colombia, particularly to the Colombian state of Panama, the inestimable advantage of a highly
prosperous seat at the crossroads of one of the two greatest waterways of the
world. [. . .] This treaty was to come into effect when ratified according to the
laws of the respective countries, which meant, in this instance, by the Senate of
the United States and by the Senate of Colombia.

The Colombian Senate threw away this priceless advantage by failing to ratify the treaty. Those small-minded senators thought they might get more money
from both the United States and from the Panama Company. Their conduct ex-
asperated President Roosevelt greatly, but we must remember, we must remember most emphatically, that Colombia had a perfect sovereign right to refuse to
ratify the treaty, just as the United States had a perfect right to refuse to ratify
without amendments the first Hay-Pauncefote treaty, the early treaties for the
purchase of the Danish West Indies, or the Treaty of Versailles, to mention only
a few of those where the Senate has exercised its constitutional prerogative. That
Colombia, for whatever motives, according to its constitutional forms, allowed
for in the treaty itself, rejected the treaty, did not give the United States a right
to intervene within the internal affairs of that nation. Nor did the old treaty of
1846 give the United States any such right beyond that of guaranteeing the neutrality of the canal route; more especially, it expressly guaranteed the sovereignty of New Granada (the earlier name for that republic) over the Isthmus.

The President was at first undecided what step to take after the Colombian
Senate's rejection; whether to take up Nicaragua, or "in some shape or way to
interfere when it becomes necessary so as to secure the Panama route without
further dealing with the foolish and homicidal corruptionists of Bogotá."[1] A
trusted adviser presented a confidential memorandum to this effect: that if
Colombia should reject the Hay-Herrán treaty, then the old treaty of 1846—the
one which had guaranteed so "positively and efficaciously" the sovereignty of
New Granada—could be interpreted to cover intervention in Panama to prevent
interruption of the transit by domestic disturbances, as well as to protect Colombian sovereignty and the neutrality of the canal route against attack by an outside power. He pointed out that the United States had repeatedly landed troops
to protect the canal route against riots and insurrectionary disturbances (he did
not cite instances where the United States had intervened to the advantage of in-
surrectionists and secessionists). [. . .]

Again, the New Panama Canal Company stepped into the situation. Mr.
Philippe Bunau-Varilla, who once had been the chief engineer of the company
on the Isthmus, hurried from Paris to the United States. He and a New York
lawyer who was counsel for the French company organized a revolution in the
state of Panama, working through the employees of the Panama Railroad Company, a subsidiary. Bunau-Varilla also had conferences with Professor John Bas-
sett Moore, Secretary Hay, and President Roosevelt, who became well aware of
the imminence of a revolution for the independence of Panama. No evidence has
been presented to show that these high officials of the United States directly con-
spired with the plotters, but they certainly did nothing to discourage a movement
which presented itself for their convenience. The President ordered the Department of the Navy to hold warships within striking distance of the Panama tran-

sit, on both sides. On November 2, orders went out to the commanders of these vessels to proceed to Panama and to "maintain free and uninterrupted transit," even to the extent of using armed force to occupy the route and to prevent Colombian troops being landed. Bunau-Varilla and his fellow conspirators [. . .] guessed that the United States would use its naval forces to prevent Colombian troops from being landed to put down the insurrection and prevent the secession of Panama. This is exactly what happened when the revolution occurred, as planned, on November 3, 1903. It was the formal statement of the U.S. Government to Colombia (November 11, 1903), that it would oppose the landing of Colombian troops to suppress the insurrection, which is the touchstone of the whole affair. That guaranteed the success of the insurrection; in effect it completed it. The United States had promptly recognized the *de facto* government, November 6, and on November 18 signed a treaty with the plenipotentiary of the Republic of Panama, none other than the Frenchman Bunau-Varilla. *Ipso facto* the treaty acknowledged the independence of Panama. The European powers also quickly recognized the new state. The Latin American republics (except Colombia) followed promptly (March, 1904) in greeting the full-fledged independence of a new sister republic.

The treaty conferred upon the United States the right to build the canal, fortify it, and to possess the canal zone, ten miles wide from Colon to Panama, "as if it were sovereign." For this Panama received $10,000,000 in gold coin, plus an annuity of $250,000 "in like gold coin," beginning nine years after ratification. The first article of the treaty stated: "The United States guarantees and will maintain the independence of the Republic of Panama." Other articles gave to the United States the use, occupation, and control (subject to indemnification for private owners) of any other lands and waters necessary and convenient for the construction and maintenance of the canal, the right to intervene for its maintenance and protection, and the right of eminent domain within the limits of the cities of Panama and Colon and adjacent territories and waters. This, of course, made Panama a protectorate.

President Roosevelt immediately set in motion the work of construction and fortification of the canal. It opened its locks to the commerce and the warships of the world on terms of entire equality (so long as the United States remained a neutral) in 1914. In office and out of office, Theodore Roosevelt throughout the remainder of his life defended his intervention in Panama. The verdict of history must be summed up in his own frank words: "I took Panama."[2] With patience, diplomacy could have secured control of a canal route in a more creditable way without the use of force. The episode antagonized Latin America. Public opinion there began to brand the sponsor-nation of the Monroe Doctrine with the accusation of conquest in that part of the world which it professed to have liberated from European interference. It has taken much diplomacy and a generation of time to soften away this stigma.

Despite the confidence of the President in the rectitude of his proceeding, the United States later pursued with Colombia a sort of conscience-stricken diplomacy. Even during President Roosevelt's Administration, Secretary of State Root arranged three companion treaties intended to satisfy Colombian grievances: a treaty between Colombia and Panama which recognized the independence of that republic and agreed to a boundary, with certain privileges in the use of the proposed canal; a treaty between the United States and Colombia which transferred to Colombia the first ten installments of Panama's annuity; and a treaty between the United States and Panama which sanctioned these changes and started the annuity five years earlier than required by the treaty of 1903. Popular opposition in Colombia led to the rejection of this settlement. Negotiations continued. Under Woodrow Wilson's Administration Secretary of State Bryan signed a treaty with Colombia (April 6, 1914) by which the United States expressed "sincere regret that anything should have occurred to interrupt or mar the relations of cordial friendship that had so long subsisted between the two governments." It also agreed to pay $25,000,000 indemnity, and to allow to Colombia and her citizens the same treatment as the United States and its citizens in the use of the canal; Colombia in turn recognized the independence of Panama, with a specified boundary. The opposition of ex-President Roosevelt, who vigorously denounced it as a "blackmail treaty," was sufficient to prevent its ratification by the Senate during his lifetime. After he died, his friend Senator Henry Cabot Lodge, chairman of the Committee on Foreign Relations, supported a treaty (ratified in 1921 by a vote of 69–19) which paid the indemnity but omitted the apology. Colombian threats to refuse petroleum concessions to American capitalists seem to have been a decisive influence on Senator Lodge and his colleagues who previously had opposed paying any indemnity. This settlement closed the affair but it took time to wipe out the rankle.

11

An Address to Congress on the Mexican Crisis (April 20, 1914)

Woodrow Wilson

Historian Arthur S. Link, who died in 1998, dedicated much of his life to editing, organizing, and publishing the papers of President Woodrow Wilson. The following text is that of the speech delivered to the U.S. Congress on April 20, 1914—one day before U.S. troops invaded Veracruz, Mexico's east coast port city. Mexico, struggling through one of its most difficult periods in modern history at the time of the U.S. landing, was humiliated by the invasion and suffered casualties of about two hundred dead and wounded. Wilson's rhetoric is consistent with the record of U.S. attitudes toward Latin America during this period: the Platt Amendment, Roosevelt's Corollary to the Monroe Doctrine (1904), and Wilson's speech calling for armed intervention in Mexico reflect a tendency to view Latin America as unstable and in need of heavy-handed guidance from the north.

Gentlemen of the Congress: It is my duty to call your attention to a situation which has arisen in our dealings with General Victoriano Huerta at Mexico City which calls for action, and to ask your advice and cooperation in acting upon it. On the ninth of April a paymaster of the U.S.S. *Dolphin* landed at the Iturbide Bridge landing at Tampico with a whaleboat and boat's crew to take off certain supplies needed by his ship, and while engaged in loading the boat was arrested by an officer and squad of men of the army of General Huerta. Neither the paymaster nor anyone of the boat's crew was armed. Two of the men were in the boat when the arrest took place and were obliged to leave it and submit to be taken into custody, notwithstanding the fact that the boat carried, both at her bow and at her stern, the flag of the United States. The officer who made the arrest was proceeding up one of the streets of the town with his prisoners when met by an officer of higher authority, who ordered him to return to the landing and await orders; and within an hour and a half from the time of the arrest orders were received from the commander of the Huertista forces at Tampico for the release of the paymaster and his men. The release was followed by apologies from the commander and later by an expression of regret by General Huerta himself. General Huerta urged that martial law obtained at the time at Tampico; that orders had been issued that no one should be allowed to land at the Iturbide Bridge; and, even if they had been, the only justifiable course open to the local authorities would have been to request the paymaster and his crew to withdraw and to lodge a protest with the commanding officer of the fleet. Admiral Mayo regarded the arrest as so serious an affront that he was not satisfied with the apologies offered but demanded that the flag of the United States be saluted with special ceremony by the military commander of the port.

The incident cannot be regarded as a trivial one, especially as two of the men arrested were taken from the boat itself—that is to say, from the territory of the United States; but had it stood by itself it might have been attributed to the ignorance or arrogance of a single officer. Unfortunately, it was not an isolated case. A series of incidents have recently occurred which cannot but create the impression that the representatives of General Huerta were willing to go out of their way to show disregard for the dignity and rights of this government and felt perfectly safe in doing what they pleased, making free to show in many ways their irritation and contempt. A few days after the incident at Tampico an orderly from the U.S.S. *Minnesota* was arrested at Vera Cruz while ashore in uniform to obtain the ship's mail and was for a time thrown in jail. An official dispatch from this government to its embassy at Mexico City was withheld by the authorities of the telegraphic service until peremptorily demanded by our Chargé d'Affaires in person. So far as I can learn, such wrongs and annoyances have been suffered to occur only against representatives of the United States. I have heard of no complaints from the other governments of similar treatment. Subsequent explanations and formal apologies did not and could not alter the popular impression, which it is possible it had been the object of the Huertista authorities to create, that the Government of the United States was being singled out, and might be singled out with impunity, for slights and affronts in retaliation for its refusal to recognize the pretensions of General Huerta to be regarded as the constitutional provisional President of the Republic of Mexico.

The manifest danger of such a situation was that such offences might grow from bad to worse until something happened of so gross and intolerable a sort as to lead directly and inevitably to armed conflict. It was necessary that the apologies of General Huerta and his representatives should go much further, that they should be such as to attract the attention of the whole population to their significance, and such as to impress upon General Huerta himself the necessity of seeing to it that no further occasion for explanations and professed regrets should arise. I, therefore, felt it my duty to sustain Admiral Mayo in the whole of his demand and to insist that the flag of the United States should be saluted in such a way as to indicate a new spirit and attitude on the part of the Huertistas.

Such a salute General Huerta has refused, and I have come to ask your approval and support in the course I now purpose to pursue.

This Government can, I earnestly hope, in no circumstances be forced into war with the people of Mexico. Mexico is torn by civil strife. If we are to accept the tests of its own constitution, it has no government. General Huerta has set his power up in the City of Mexico, such as it is, without right and by methods for which there can be no justification. Only part of the country is under his control. If armed conflict should unhappily come as a result of his attitude of personal resentment towards this government, we should be fighting only General Huerta and those who adhere to him and give him their support, and our object would be only to restore to the people of the distracted republic the opportunity to set up again their own laws and their own government.

But I earnestly hope that war is not now in question. I believe that I speak for the American people when I say that we do not desire to control in any degree the affairs of our sister republic. Our feeling for the people of Mexico is one of deep and genuine friendship, and everything that we have so far done or refrained from doing has proceeded from our desire to help them, not to hinder or embarrass them. We would not wish even to exercise the good offices of friendship without their welcome and consent. The people of Mexico are entitled to settle their own domestic affairs in their own way, and we sincerely desire to respect their right. The present situation need have none of the grave implications of interference if we deal with it promptly, firmly, and wisely.

No doubt I could do what is necessary in the circumstances to enforce respect for our government without recourse to the Congress, and yet not exceed my constitutional powers as President; but I do not wish to act in a matter possibly of so grave consequence except in close reference and cooperation with both the Senate and the House. I, therefore, come to ask your approval that I should use the armed forces of the United States in such ways and to such extent as may be necessary to obtain from General Huerta and his adherents the fullest recognition of the rights and dignity of the United States, even amidst the distressing conditions now unhappily obtaining in Mexico.

There can in what we do be no thought of aggression or of selfish aggrandizement. We seek to maintain the dignity and authority of the United States only because we wish always to keep our great influence unimpaired for the uses of liberty, both in the United States and wherever else it may be employed for the benefit of mankind.

12

The Making of the Good Neighbor Policy

Bryce Wood

In 1961 Bryce Wood published The Making of the Good Neighbor Policy, *an important study of the origins of the policy and a critical evaluation of its effects. A later work by the same author,* The Dismantling of the Good Neighbor Policy, *stressed the intersecting factors that contributed to the eventual collapse of the policy. Wood, a diplomatic historian born in 1908 who taught at Columbia University and Swarthmore College, cogently evaluates and criticizes the decision-making processes surrounding the origins of the policy. He is far more critical than Bemis of U.S. policy in Latin America, but like Bemis, Wood relies heavily and almost exclusively on State Department and other U.S. government documentation to build his arguments. Wood's more micro analysis of one specific U.S. policy was innovative for its time and is still considered a model of scholarship. His work led to more in-depth research on U.S. policy and its effects in Latin America.*

ORIGINS OF THE GOOD NEIGHBOR POLICY

During World War II the Good Neighbor policy came to be regarded with general satisfaction in the United States. Some fairly good-natured controversy, however, has arisen over the assignment of credit for the origination of that policy.

Herbert Hoover, after reviewing Latin American relationships during his administration, declared:

> As a result of these policies, carried on throughout my administration, the interventions which had been the source of so much bitterness and fear in Latin America were ended. We established a good will in Latin America not hitherto known for many years, under the specific term "Good Neighbor."

Hoover renewed this assertion in supporting the Good Neighbor policy against the attack upon it made in 1943 by Senator Hugh Butler. On this same occasion, however, prominent members of the Republican party cited Elihu Root and Charles Evans Hughes as originators of the Good Neighbor policy, and they were correct in recalling that the phrase "Good Neighbor" had been used by these statesmen. If the employment of a phrase were equivalent to the founding of a policy, credit might have been given to the Mexican commissioners who negotiated the Treaty of Guadalupe Hidalgo, establishing peace between Mexico and the United States in 1848, and who were apparently responsible for the inclusion, in the preamble, of the statement that the treaty should "assure the concord, harmony, and mutual confidence wherein the two peoples should live, as good neighbors."

The fundatory declarations of Hoover have been supported by an agreement of scholars, a group hazardous to engage, especially when surrounded by multifloral verbiage and cloaked in a rising myth. The myth is that the Good Neighbor policy, commonly associated with the administrations of Roosevelt, was actually Hoover's creation.

The agreement offers several varying but congruent judgments that may be arranged in order of the strength of their support for Hooverian claims. One view refers to "Hoover's Good Neighbor policy" and declares that, in its essentials, "the Good Neighbor policy had its roots in the Hoover administration; Roosevelt only adopted and expanded it." Others are: "Taken with other features of the Hoover-Stimson Latin American policy, it [the Clark Memorandum] warrants the assertion that those two statesmen laid the basis of the 'Good Neighbor policy' of the 1930s." "In fact, the Good Neighbor policy was born under Hoover, though it was baptized and came to maturity under Roosevelt." "Herbert Hoover completed the foundations for Franklin D. Roosevelt's Good Neighbor policy."

An appraisal of the degree to which these claims may be valid requires a review of some features of Hoover's policy and of the early approach of Roosevelt to Latin America.

After the Havana Conference of 1928, the government of the United States began, in a neighborly spirit, to take certain initiatives toward Latin America. The first move was ceremonial. In that year, between his election and his inauguration, Hoover visited ten countries in Central and South America, "for the purpose of paying friendly calls upon our neighbors to the south." Hoover encountered some evidence of hostility in the form of demonstrations in certain countries, but he was courteously received by the officials of the ten countries he visited from Honduras to Chile, Argentina, and Brazil. The press was less hospitable in some countries than in others. Before Hoover left the United States on November 19, 1928, an editorial in *El Mercurio* (Santiago, Chile) of November 12 warned him that "in South America the Republican [party] is considered more frankly imperialistic than the Democratic party"; the paper hoped that the tour might make Hoover realize that "imperialism is damaging to the United States: it enrages the countries that suffer from it directly and creates jealously, lack of confidence, mistrust, and animosity in all the others." However, in Guayaquil [Ecuador] *El Telégrafo* on December 4 said that Hoover's visit had been welcomed "because of the important and spontaneous declarations he made for the welfare of Ecuador and Latin America, and in support of international morality, as well as for his favorable statements concerning aid by the United States capitalists in the development of Ecuadorian industries." Personally, Hoover made a good impression on those who saw and talked with him, and a sympathetic response was enhanced by the presence of Mrs. Hoover.

One incident occurred during the trip that had an immediate bearing on policy and was the cause of some embarrassment to Hoover. He was quoted by *La Epoca* (Buenos Aires) on December 18 as saying in an interview with President Hipolito Irigoyen of Argentina that "in future the United States government would never intervene in the internal affairs of other countries, but would respect their sovereignty." The paper suggested that Hoover had implied that he was not in accord with the policy followed by Coolidge. Secretary of State Kellogg inquired of Ambassador Robert Woods Bliss in Argentina about the editorial and asked whether Hoover intended to issue a statement on the subject. Bliss replied that Hoover had not stated that he disagreed with Coolidge's policy; he had said that both he and Coolidge were opposed to intervention. The Ambassador had been authorized by Hoover to make a statement to the Argentine press, but he had thought it best not to call attention to the matter by starting a controversy. Bliss added that he had talked with Irigoyen, who had agreed that Hoover had not made the statements attributed to him by *La Epoca*; the incident seems to have been no more than an effort by an enterprising journalist to create a stir.

On the question of intervention, Hoover said publicly (*New York Times*, December 17, 1928) that "the fear of some persons concerning supposed intervention ideas of the United States are unfounded. The facts are gradually demonstrating more clearly and more fully that in my country there prevails no policy of intervention, despite any appearances of such an intention." This statement was greeted with satisfaction in Latin America; it found a mixed reception in the United States where the president-elect was thought by some to have prematurely commented on a question of foreign policy.

An interesting feature of the many speeches made by Hoover on his trip was his frequent reference to "Good Neighbors." He said, for example: "We have a desire to maintain not only the cordial relations of governments with each other but the relations of *good neighbors*."

In the area of active policy, it is a matter of record that the Hoover administration did not intervene in Cuba, and although it was unable to escape criticism for keeping Marines in Nicaragua for four years, it withdrew them when it considered that obligations undertaken following the Coolidge intervention were discharged. Further, Hoover and Stimson adopted a policy that did not attempt to make use of non-recognition as a method of unseating Latin American governments.

In the declaratory sphere of policy, Hoover stated publicly that "it ought not to be the policy of the United States to intervene *by force* to secure or maintain contracts between our citizens and foreign states or their citizens. Confidence in that attitude is the only basis upon which the economic cooperation of our citizens can be welcomed abroad. It is the only basis that prevents cupidity encroaching upon the weakness of nations—but, far more than this, it is the true expression of the moral rectitude of the United States." [. . .]

On the other hand, Hoover labored under several serious disabilities in trying to develop good will in Latin America. In the first place, he was the leader of the Republican party, and "in Latin America the idea has been rather widespread that imperialist tendencies have had their most effective interpreters among the Republicans, while it has been understood that the Democrats have been generally opposed to imperialism." It is an interesting phenomenon that, despite Wilson's interventions in Haiti, Mexico, and Santo Domingo, the Democratic party was generally regarded with greater good will than the Republican party. This attitude may be due to the linking of the latter with intervention or at least "interposition" to protect United States investors abroad, and by the difference in the public statements of the leaders of the two parties. The Republicans were identified with such catch phrases as "the big stick," "dollar diplomacy," and "I took Panama." The Democrats, despite Wilson's interventions, had avoided being labeled with easily remembered phrases resented by Latin Americans.

The Republican party's unpopularity in Latin America might have been gradually reduced by Hoover had he been able to carry his policy through a second term, but four years was too short a time to overcome this handicap, particularly when it was aggravated by the continuation of the Nicaraguan intervention. Moreover, Hoover's term of office fell just between the Havana and Montevideo conferences of American states, so that he did not have an opportunity, such as Hull seized at Montevideo, to sign a pledge of nonintervention—an action that was in accord with Hoover's principles and practice.

Finally, the passage in 1930 of the Smoot-Hawley tariff, with Hoover's approval, aroused great antagonism in Latin America. *El Mundo* (Havana), February 18, 1936, declared that "insistent and ferocious protectionism had built a Chinese Wall between the United States and the republics of Central and South America."

A review of the development of Roosevelt's thinking about Latin America may begin with an article he was asked to write as a campaign document for *Foreign Affairs* in 1928. Roosevelt gave serious attention to the article, and he received assistance in its composition from Norman H. Davis and Sumner Welles. His frame of mind in approaching it may be glimpsed from a letter to Senator

Carter Glass: "Is it not time, in view of the Nicaraguan slaughter, to revive the Wilson Mobile speech and his invitation to other American republics to join with us in solving local difficulties?"

In the article, Roosevelt stated:

> The outside world views us with less good will today than at any previous period. This is serious unless we take the deliberate position that the people of the United States owe nothing to the rest of mankind and care nothing for the opinion of others so long as our seacoasts are impregnable and our pocketbooks are well filled.

Associating "dollar diplomacy" with the Republican party, he claimed that it had placed "money leadership ahead of moral leadership." Wilson, however, had restored "high moral purpose" to our international relationships.

Although praising Hughes's achievements at the Washington naval disarmament conference, he attacked the Republicans on other questions, and then turned to the subject of the Americas, "in many ways, most important of all." He admitted that the interventions in Haiti and the Dominican Republic, in the first of which he had played an important part, were "not another forward step," because little attention had been paid "to making the people there more capable of running their own governments." In Mexico, he reluctantly conceded that "we were better off" than in 1927, but he gave credit to Dwight Morrow and Charles Lindbergh. Elsewhere throughout the Americas, however, recent policy "has allowed a dislike and mistrust of long standing to grow into something like positive hate and fear."

Concerning intervention, Roosevelt felt that, if a Latin American country should in future need "a helping hand to bring back order and stability," it was neither the right nor the duty of the United States to extend its hand alone, but only in association with other American republics, and "in the name of the Americas." "Single-handed intervention by us in the internal affairs of other nations must end; with the cooperation of others we shall have more order in this hemisphere and less dislike."

Referring to the "nine gray years" since 1909, Roosevelt claimed there had been bungling in Nicaragua and a failure in the Tacna-Arica dispute, and the only success that he saw was in Hughes's staving off a hostile majority on the nonintervention resolution at the Havana conference in 1928. Linking good will in Latin America to increased trade, he called for the opening of a new chapter in relations with that area. If the spirit behind United States leadership were great, the United States could "regain the world's trust and friendship," move once more toward a reduction of armaments, and "for a time renounce the practice of arbitrary intervention in the home affairs of our neighbors. It is the spirit, sir, which matters."

Although this article was written as a campaign document, it is significant because it stated five themes that were dominant in the Latin American policy of his administration: (1) a deep concern for securing good will in Latin America; (2) the idea that good will would increase trade; (3) a favorable attitude toward working in association with Latin American states; (4) hostility to "arbitrary intervention" in the domestic affairs of Latin American countries; and (5) emphasis on "the spirit" of United States policy.

The remote and immediate origins of the Good Neighbor policy in the thinking of Roosevelt were described by the President himself in 1942. He was asked by his Secretary, Stephen Early, to dictate about five hundred words on the origin of the Good Neighbor policy for use by Vice-President Henry A. Wallace in a speech accepting for Roosevelt an award from *The Churchman*. The President dictated the following statement, which is quoted here in full since it has received little attention:

The origin of the Good Neighbor Policy dates back to a day in the President's life when, as Assistant Secretary of the Navy at the beginning of the first Wilson Administration, the United States realized that Mexico had become critical. President Wilson decided that the insult to the American Flag at Tampico was more than this country could tolerate, in view of the unfriendly and undemocratic Administration then in power in Mexico. The Fleet was ordered to take Vera Cruz, which United States forces occupied for several months. History may show that this whole episode was realistically necessary but the fact remains that many were killed on both sides and the bad feeling throughout Latin America created by this action lasted for a generation. The President has always believed that the germ of the Good Neighbor Policy originated in his mind at that time.

In 1915 the atrocious conditions in the Republic of Haiti, ending with the brutal murder and cutting up of the President of Haiti, was causing unrest in other parts of the Caribbean, including Cuba, Santo Domingo, and Jamaica. The United States, under a policy which had lasted for many years, restored order both in Haiti and in Santo Domingo by sending Marines there and by occupying both Republics for a long period.

In all of these operations, President Roosevelt was impressed with the great emphasis placed on trade and finance in lieu of an approach from the standpoint of the right of self-determination and the use of a quarantine system for the restoration of order rather than the use of force in occupations. After he left Washington at that time, the President saw a rebirth of dollar diplomacy and the occupation of Nicaragua.

Soon after he became Governor of New York the terrible depression, starting in this country, spread all over the world, including Central and South America, and during the next four years most of our discussions with Latin America were still largely based on dollar diplomacy. This was accentuated by the fact that during the period from 1925 to 1930 New York banks, aided by the trips of Professor Kemmerer to various Republics, forced on most of these Republics unnecessary loans at exorbitant interest rates and huge commission fees.

The President, therefore, began to visualize a wholly new attitude toward other American Republics based on an honest and sincere desire, first, to remove from their minds all fear of American aggression—territorial or financial—and, second, to take them into a kind of hemispheric partnership in which no Republic would obtain undue advantage.

After the President's election in the autumn of 1932, he discussed this subject with Senator Hull, Senator Robinson, and with a number of others.

In February, 1933, he began to formulate his Inaugural Address. In a discussion of the Address with Professor Moley he drew the analogy between the relations of the American Republics and the relations between a citizen in a small community with his own neighbors and said, "What we need in a small community is the man who is a good neighbor to the people he associates with every day." The use of the words "Good Neighbor" was seized by Professor Moley as just the right term, and the President put it into his first draft of the First Inaugural.

This significant document shows signs of being hastily dictated and may not have been read by Roosevelt afterward. Among its interesting features are the linking of the origins of his conception of the Good Neighbor policy to the Vera Cruz incident and the definition of the two aims of the new policy—to banish the fear of territorial or financial aggression by the United States, and to form "a kind of hemispheric partnership." It is also of interest that, in 1942, when asked by Early to write about the Good Neighbor policy, Roosevelt not only accepted the invitation and himself applied the phrase only to Latin America, but stated that its immediate origin in the first inaugural address was to be found in a discussion about the American republics. In that address, the policy of the Good Neighbor was related to the whole "field of foreign policy" and, at first, Roosevelt hoped that this declaration might find a response throughout the world. However, in Europe there was no affirmative response from Germany or Italy, and in Asia Japan remained unmoved. It was with Latin America that the policy quickly became identified, and it is therefore understandable that Roosevelt in 1942 should emphasize the Latin American origins of the policy ideas as well as of the phrase itself.

IV

COLD WAR ARRIVES IN LATIN AMERICA

Even before the Cold War, the United States viewed revolutionary processes and governments with suspicion. The U.S. intervention in the Mexican Revolution (1910–1920), as exemplified by the scheming of Ambassador Henry Lane Wilson, the seizure of Veracruz, and the border crossing by General John J. Pershing, demonstrates a strong U.S. inclination to control revolutionary processes so they would never endanger U.S. interests in the region. Even governments that were not necessarily revolutionary but were simply reform-minded or just antiestablishment sparked concern in Washington. Maintaining the status quo against revisionist forces, either by intervention or through direct support of reactionary dictatorships, was the goal of U.S. policy. If change could not be managed or contained, the process would be subverted or manipulated to protect U.S. interests.

By 1945, as U.S.-Soviet relations began to deteriorate, Washington began to look with suspicion at some political movements in the region that were calling for reform and structural democratization. As Roger Trask explains, soon after the end of the Second World War, the United States began to view Latin America through the prism of the Cold War. The security imperative was at the top of U.S. concerns while Latin America sought to focus Washington's attention on the need for political and economic reform. The rhetoric and main preoccupations of the United States and Latin America grew as far apart as the asymmetries in power that defined the north-south relationship.

Security took precedence over all considerations, including democracy and development. One option was to support pro-U.S. regimes regardless of their track record on democracy and good governance. This position was taken first by the State Department's George Kennan, author of the "containment" doctrine, after a visit to Latin America in 1950. He suggested that the United States could not support democracy at the expense of its own security in a region of the world that demonstrated "no cultural inclination" toward democratic rule. Washington policymakers remained suspicious of "reformers" in the region, believing there was a communist sympathizer behind every social democrat.

It was not long before it became clear that U.S. policy was a self-fulfilling prophecy. Reactionary governments in the region, many supported by Washington, created the conditions that bred polarization, radicalism, violence, and ultimately, revolutionary movements. By the early 1950s, the United States faced several revolutionary challenges. Again, any regime that pronounced itself nationalist or reformist ran the danger of a confrontation with the United States. This was the case when the Eisenhower administration faced revolutionary governments in Bolivia (1952), Guatemala (1953–1954), and Cuba (1959). In all three countries, President Eisenhower and virulently anticommunist Secretary of State John Foster Dulles suspected communist influence. In Bolivia, after an initial period of concern, the United States chose cooperation over conflict. Washington's conciliatory policy, however, was kindled by a concomitant approach taken by the Bolivian government, which moved quickly to allay U.S. fears toward the revolution's leadership and intentions. Rather than undermine it, Washington worked to strengthen the regime by offering aid and technical assistance once it was convinced the National Revolutionary Movement (MNR) did not threaten U.S. economic and strategic interests. In the chapter in this section on the Bolivian case, Cole Blasier demonstrates that in addition to conciliatory actions taken by Bolivia, the positive role played by ambassadors and political leaders in the United States and Bolivia was critical in avoiding polarization of relations.

In Guatemala and Cuba, however, the results were rather different. In Guatemala, as Stephen Schlesinger and Stephen Kinzer point out in their classic work, the United States immediately opted to take the antagonistic path, although not so much because of communist infiltration (which was the official justification) but because of measures taken by the reformist government of Jacobo Arbenz to expropriate property of the United Fruit Company. In this case there was little anyone in Washington or Guatemala City could do to change the Eisenhower administration's strong predisposition to overthrow the popularly elected government of Arbenz. Mollifying attempts by the Guatemalan government, particularly by Foreign Minister Guillermo Toriello, were futile. The Guatemala case demonstrates that polarization can be prevented only when both parties are willing to leave room for compromise.

In the chapter on U.S.-Cuba relations, Alan Luxenberg delves into the question of whether the United States pushed Castro into the arms of the Soviets. Here, as in Guatemala, the Eisenhower administration was openly suspicious of the revolutionary regime and its belief that communist elements dominated the July 26 movement of Fidel Castro. As in Guatemala, some scholars, such as

Morton Morley, have argued that Havana's decision to expropriate U.S. property was the most important reason for U.S. hostility and the attempt to overthrow the Castro regime. Luxenberg, however, maintains that polarization of relations and the radicalization or communization of the regime were inevitable. U.S. policy may have only accelerated the process, but Castro and Eisenhower were predisposed to lock heads. Conciliation and cooperation were never true possibilities for either party.

These three cases show that although the United States was always strongly inclined to view revolutionary movements and governments with suspicion, the circumstances, policies, and outcomes in each case were, in fact, very different. The Bolivian crisis ended without conflict because of the Bolivian government's willingness to allay fears in Washington, whereas in Guatemala the Arbenz regime's determined effort to nationalize United Fruit's vast holdings, even though it was willing to pay fair compensation, was enough to raise U.S. ire. In Cuba a third scenario presented itself in which neither Washington nor Havana had any intention of compromising. A close examination of each of *these* "revolutions" and their effects on the United States is critical to gain a comprehensive understanding of the contour of U.S.–Latin American relations in the Cold War 1950s.

13

The Impact of the Cold War on U.S.–Latin American Relations, 1945–1949

Roger R. Trask

U.S.–Latin American relations reached a zenith during World War II. Perhaps at no other time, even during the span of the Good Neighbor Policy, had relations been characterized by such strong, mutual interests and cooperation. However, as Roger Trask suggests in this reading, by 1945, when serious problems with the Soviet Union were apparent, the Cold War came to define the relationship in a new and problematic manner. Suddenly, interests and objectives began to diverge. As Latin America attempted to focus on political and economic issues, the United States became preoccupied by the security imperative. According to Trask, when countries in the Western Hemisphere met in the late 1940s to establish the new postwar inter-American system, Latin America hoped that a new mutual defense arrangement together with the 1948 Charter of the Organization of American States "would serve to promote both the economic development of Latin America and the 'containment' of the United States." The United States, however, only sought to create a system that would contain any new or emerging Communist threat while ensuring political and economic hegemony via the promotion of U.S.-style democracy. In the end, the asymmetries in power allowed the United States to shape the OAS Charter in ways that served its interests, often to the detriment of its southern neighbors. Trask argues that if the United States had responded to Latin America's concern for economic development, "relationships within the hemisphere would have been happier."

For at least three decades after the end of World War II, the "Cold War" was the pervasive feature of international politics. That it vitally affected and at times dominated the foreign policies of its major participants as well as the less powerful nations is clear. This chapter is an attempt to describe and to determine the impact of the early Cold War on U.S.–Latin American relations. It is not intended to be a comprehensive analysis of the Latin American policy of the

113

United States at the time; that subject would require a work of much greater scope.

It was clear by 1949 that Latin America was a Cold War arena, although not a central theater of action. By that time, there had emerged an inter-American collective defense treaty and a formal organization to implement it. Not until 1945, however, when serious problems with the Soviet Union were apparent, did U.S. policymakers begin to accept the need for such agreements. While both the Latin American nations and the United States favored a more formal structure for the inter-American system after World War II, they had different objectives. Increasingly after the war's end, the Cold War influenced policy decisions in Washington.

The reversal by the United States after 1945 of its position on universal versus regional organization is a case in point. During World War II, as planning for a postwar international organization proceeded, the United States, led by Secretary of State Cordell Hull, committed itself to the concept of international rather than regional organization. The Dumbarton Oaks talks in 1944 and the Yalta Protocol of 1945 made this clear.[1] Latin Americans, encouraged by the so-called Good Neighbor policy of the interwar period and close collaboration with the United Nations allies during the war, wanted to create an autonomous regional organization. While such a body might have defense functions, the Latin Americans hoped that a strong regional organization would serve to promote both the economic development of Latin America and the "containment" of the United States. Some Latin American nations, especially those north of the equator, strongly resented what they perceived to have been, especially after 1898, the heavy-handed hemispheric policy of the United States. They questioned whether the Good Neighbor policy represented substantive change in the political and economic objectives of the United States in the hemisphere.[2]

At both the Chapultepec and San Francisco conferences in 1945, the United States was hard pressed to preserve its commitment to the primacy of international organization as the Latin American nations demanded an autonomous hemispheric grouping. At Chapultepec (the Inter-American Conference on the Problems of War and Peace, Mexico City, 21 February to 8 March 1945), the conferees, after tough bargaining and considerable compromise, settled on the "Act of Chapultepec," which espoused the principle that an attack against one American state was an attack against all, requiring a collective response. It was also agreed that an inter-American mutual defense treaty would be negotiated later. Secretary of State Edward R. Stettinius, Jr., who headed the United States delegation, noted that the problem at Chapultepec ". . . was to harmonize the regional agreement with the proposed general international organization and yet overcome the fear of Latin American countries that Great Britain and especially the Soviet Union might interfere in inter-American affairs." Stettinius might have added that the Latin Americans were also worried about interference by the United States.[3]

At Chapultepec there was extensive discussion about postwar economic policy. Just before the conference, Mexican Foreign Minister Ezequiel Padilla expressed the Latin American view, as paraphrased by an embassy official: "The Minister feels that upon the solutions found for the economic problems of this hemisphere depends the reality of continental unity. He pointed out that people are no longer moved by pamphlets filled with high sounding principles and that the way to the heart of the masses is through raising the standard of living and bringing about the economic development of the countries of Latin America." But the innocuous economic agreement adopted at Chapultepec demonstrated the unwillingness of the Department of State to accept the kind of economic program, based mainly on U.S. assistance, that the Latin American countries wanted.[4]

At San Francisco (the United Nations Conference on International Organization, 25 April to 26 June 1945), reconciling regionalism and universalism was one of the most troublesome tasks, especially because of the Latin American position. The United States reluctantly accepted the compromise, to which the Latin Americans made substantive contributions, resulting in Articles Fifty-one and Fifty-two of the United Nations Charter, permitting regional organizations.[5] It should be noted that during this struggle some Latin American spokesmen frankly expressed their fears of the Soviet Union. Colombian Foreign Minister Alberto Lleras Camargo, worried about communist activities in the hemisphere, predicted that the next war would be between the United States and the Soviet Union. The defense of the hemisphere, Lleras Camargo argued, depended upon an autonomous inter-American system.[6] Secretary Stettinius found especially irritating the fact that Assistant Secretary of State Nelson A. Rockefeller and Senator Arthur H. Vandenberg, a U.S. delegate, partially supported the Latin American position. Only after Stettinius agreed to a conference for later in 1945 to draft an inter-American defense treaty did the Latin American countries accept the regional compromise.[7] Stettinius did not, perhaps, realize their significance at the time, but Articles Fifty-one and Fifty-two later provided a partial foundation for the regional response of the United States to the assumed threat of "international communism" and the Soviet Union.

The inter-American conference to which Stettinius consented at San Francisco did not meet until August 1947. The major reason for the delay was a serious controversy between Argentina and the United States. In 1947, when the United States adopted a conciliatory stand on Argentina, it was dictated at least in part by the exigencies of the Cold War and the by then pronounced interest of the United States in an inter-American mutual defense treaty.

During World War II, Argentina refused to join the United Nations coalition and collaborated with Germany. Pressured by the United States and some Latin American nations, Argentina finally broke relations with the Axis powers in January 1944, but still maintained sympathy for Germany. When General Edelmiro Farrell took over as president in Argentina's military regime late in February 1944, the United States refused to recognize him.[8] Excluded from the Chapultepec meetings a year later, Argentina soon accepted the conference's invitation to adhere to its Final Act and declared war on the Axis. Thereupon the State Department recognized the Farrell government and supported Argentina's successful bid for a seat at the San Francisco Conference, a stand that provoked a serious controversy between the Soviet Union and the United States.[9]

Spruille Braden, an experienced Latin American hand, went in May 1945 to represent the United States in Buenos Aires, where the dominant personality in the government was Vice President Juan Perón. While Perón promised to execute the Chapultepec requirement that all Axis influences be eliminated from his nation, Braden, virulently anti-Perón, expected instant compliance. Braden hated Perón's anti-U.S. rhetoric and actions and the "neurotic nationalism" of his government. Perón objected to Braden's outspoken opposition and otherwise undiplomatic conduct; the ambassador hoped that his efforts would result in Perón's ouster. Seemingly as a reward for his tough line on Argentina, Braden returned to Washington in September 1945, to become Assistant Secretary of State for American Republic Affairs.[10]

From Washington, Braden intensified his anti-Perón campaign. He played a major role in encouraging Uruguayan Foreign Minister Eduardo Rodríguez Larreta to propose that the nations of the hemisphere adopt a policy of collective intervention. Without specific reference to Argentina, Rodríguez Larreta stressed the threat to human rights and argued that ". . . nonintervention cannot be converted into a right to invoke one principle in order to be able to violate all other principles with immunity." Eventually most of the Latin American nations rejected the Rodríguez Larreta doctrine as a subversion of the sacred principle of nonintervention; Secretary of State James F. Byrnes instantly endorsed it. The Latin Americans indicated by their response that they were less concerned about Argentina than they were about preserving the principle of nonintervention.[11]

On 11 February 1946, two weeks before Argentine presidential elections in which Perón was a candidate, the State Department issued the famous "Blue Book," a documentary compilation shepherded by Braden, indicting Argentina for its relationship with Germany during World War II. Although the State Department denied it, the Blue Book was an effort to influence Argentine votes against Perón. Recognizing the role of Braden, Perón campaigned on the slogan "*Perón o Braden*" and won in an open and honest election. The other American republics criticized this blatant intervention and resented the refusal of the United States to participate in the planned inter-American conference because of its attitude toward Perón's government.[12]

Braden's successor in Argentina, George S. Messersmith, favored rapprochement; so did the U.S. military establishment, which wanted to implement a program of arms standardization in the hemisphere and favored conclusion of the inter-American defense treaty. Messersmith argued that Argentina was making satisfactory progress in eliminating Axis influence, while Braden in Washington stuck to his hard line, still hoping that Perón's government would collapse. Within a few months of his arrival in Buenos Aires in April 1946, Messersmith (known in the State Department as "Forty Page George") began to write long letters to President Truman, Secretary of State Byrnes, Undersecretary of State Dean Acheson, and others, accusing Braden of double-dealing and insisting that he be fired. Messersmith reinforced his argument by frequent reference to the threat of international communism and the Soviet Union in Argentina.[13] Tiring of this internecine struggle, Truman recalled Messersmith in June 1947, and eased Braden out of the State Department. Both retired from the Foreign Service. Truman announced that Argentine-U.S. relations had been normalized.[14]

During these years, Perón often voiced his conviction that a Soviet-U.S. war was inevitable, and asserted that when the war came Argentina would side with the United States.[15] There is no evidence to prove that this particular assertion influenced the Truman administration to soften its Argentine policy, but it does illustrate Perón's willingness to play upon Washington's growing concern with the Soviet threat. Perón wanted arms from the United States and he began to get them in 1947. He also wanted the much delayed inter-American conference to get under way. The U.S. accommodation with Perón in 1947 helped pave the way to negotiation of a hemisphere collective defense treaty, then seen in Washington as a component of the new "containment" policy.

The Rio Conference (the Inter-American Conference for the Maintenance of Continental Peace and Security), which convened on 15 August 1947, had as its major task the drafting of a mutual defense treaty. President Truman approved a U.S. treaty draft as early as December 1945, and there were several Latin American drafts as well.[16] The motives of the various American republics varied to a considerable extent. One of the principal Argentine delegates told the U.S. chargé in Buenos Aires just before the conference ". . . that Argentina wishes to cooperate with the U.S. to make [the] Conference a success, and that all other considerations must be subordinated to achieving harmoniously a completely united front against extra-hemisphere aggression, particularly against Russia." Assistant Secretary Braden observed that one of the main conference problems would be to secure ". . . provisions which will adequately cover acts or threats of aggression executed through subversive activities, but which will not take the form of an alliance directed against the Soviet Union nor provide grounds for depression of democratic political opposition by dictatorial governments." Braden evidently wanted an alliance against the Soviet Union that did not look like an alliance.[17]

Given the emphasis that many Latin American spokesmen at Rio gave to their economic needs, one gets the impression that the mutual defense treaty was a secondary concern, perhaps looked upon as something to trade to the United

States in return for economic assistance. Speaking at the inaugural session of the conference, Mexican Foreign Minister Jaime Torres Bodet stressed increased economic cooperation ". . . as the one way to provide [the] only sound basis for hemisphere peace."[18] Using words disappointing to the Latin Americans, President Truman explained the U.S. position in person at Rio:

> In so far as the economic problems common to the nations of North and South America are concerned, we have long been aware that much remains to be done. We have been obliged, in considering these questions, to differentiate between the urgent need for rehabilitation of war-shattered areas and the problems of development elsewhere. The problems of countries in this Hemisphere are different in nature and cannot be relieved by the same means and the same approaches which are in contemplation for Europe. Here [in Latin America] the need is for long term economic collaboration. This is a type of collaboration in which a much greater role falls to private citizens and groups than is the case in a program designed to aid European countries to recover from the destruction of war.[19]

Understandably, the Latin Americans did not react enthusiastically to President Truman's remarks.

The Inter-American Treaty of Reciprocal Assistance concluded at Rio has been described accurately by the British scholar of inter-American affairs, Gordon Connell-Smith, as ". . . the first of the 'Cold War pacts' and the forerunner of the North Atlantic treaty and others." The treaty incorporated the familiar principle that an attack against one American state was to be considered an attack against all. When such an event occurred, an inter-American organ of consultation (a foreign ministers' meeting, the Governing Board of the Pan American Union, or after 1948, the Council of the Organization of American States) would decide by a two-thirds majority what kind of collective assistance would be provided. The treaty listed recall of chiefs of missions, the breaking of diplomatic, consular, or economic relations, and the use of armed force as possible responses. Each state was obliged to cooperate, except that no nation would have to use armed force without its consent. The Rio Treaty included provisions coordinating it with the United Nations, but emphasized the right of individual or collective self-defense embodied in Article Fifty-one of the Charter.[20] In a speech after his return as a delegate at Rio, Senator Vandenberg noted the collective defense orientation of the new treaty and described it as "sunlight in a dark world." "Nothing that we have done," Vandenberg declared, "is aimed at any other enemies than war and aggression and injustice, the three deadly foes of civilized mankind. . . . If there be those who suspect us of ulterior motives, they will merely confess their own."[21] Vandenberg probably would have translated "war and aggression and injustice" as "Soviet Union and international communism." While the Rio Treaty cannot be explained exclusively as a product of the Cold War, it was interpreted within that context by many people, both in the United States and Latin America.

At the Ninth International Conference of American States, held at Bogotá, Colombia, from 30 March to 2 May 1948, the main task was drafting the Charter of the Organization of American States.[22] But the issue of international communism played an important role. A week before the conference began, the State Department Policy Planning Staff completed PPS-26, entitled "U.S. Policy Regarding Anti-Communist Measures Which Could be Planned and Carried Out Within the Inter-American System." The paper, anticipating the discussions at Bogotá, described communism in the Americas as a "potential danger" which for the time being could be handled on a country-by-country basis. International communism, however, was a "tool of the Kremlin" and ". . . a direct and major threat to the national security of the United States, and to that of all of the other American Republics. . . ." The paper recommended that the United States propose an anticommunist *resolution* strongly condemning international communism but not enter into an anticommunist *agreement* with the other American republics. PPS-26 also proposed various steps the State Department might take to combat communism, including a study of whether the United States should endeavor to have all communist parties in the hemisphere declared illegal. Significantly, the paper recommended assisting the American republics with economic development, since ". . . effective economic and social cooperation is a major weapon to combat Communist influence. . . ."[23]

On the day the Bogotá Conference began, the National Security Council Staff issued NSC 7, entitled "The Position of the United States with Respect to Soviet-Directed World Communism." "The ultimate objective of Soviet-directed world communism," the report stated, "is the domination of the world. To this end, Soviet-directed world communism employs against its victims in opportunistic coordination the complementary instruments of Soviet aggressive pressure from without and militant revolutionary subversion from within." Anticipating the more famous NSC 68 of April 1950, the report recommended that the United States ". . . take the lead in organizing a world-wide counter-offensive aimed at mobilizing and strengthening our own and anti-communist forces in the non-Soviet world, and at undermining the strength of the communist forces in the Soviet world."[24] The analysis and conclusions of NSC 7 and PPS-26, both completed on the eve of the Bogotá Conference, must have been in the mind of Secretary of State George C. Marshall, who headed the U.S. delegation, and perhaps other members of his group. Indeed, at the first meeting of delegation heads at Bogotá on 30 March, Marshall asked whether the conference agenda allowed discussion of ". . . foreign-inspired subversive activities directed against [the] institutions and peace and security of American Republics. . . ." The delegation heads responded affirmatively, although informal discussion during the next week indicated considerable difference of opinion.[25]

Before the conference started, Ambassador Willard S. Beaulac in Bogotá reported that "Communists and left wing Liberals" might try to sabotage the meeting.[26] In the midst of the conference, on 9 April, the opposition Liberal Party leader Jorge Eliecer Gaitán was assassinated on the street in Bogotá. Serious riots and widespread destruction ensued; the Capitolio, the seat of the Inter-American Conference, was severely damaged, and the conference itself was suspended. Eventually the conference resumed in a Bogotá school after the Colombian government suppressed the riots, in which some communists participated. During these events U.S. military planes evacuated some women and nonessential conference personnel to Panama. Secretary Marshall planned to move the whole conference to Panama if necessary, but urged that the meeting continue in Bogotá. In a dispatch to the State Department, Marshall summarized his speech to delegation heads the day after Gaitán's death: "I stated that it was not only important but imperative that [the] conference continue and that revolutionary movements here were not confined to Colombia but had world-wide implications."[27] Marshall saw the international communist conspiracy at work in Bogotá, even though the riots were essentially an emotional response to the death of a charismatic leader and communist participation was incidental. The disruption of the conference facilitated unanimous agreement on the anticommunist resolution favored by the United States and recommended in PPS-26. Resolution XXXII of the Final Act of Bogotá, entitled "The Preservation and Defense of Democracy in America," declared "that by its anti-democratic nature and its interventionist tendency, the political activity of international communism or any totalitarian doctrine is incompatible with the concept of American freedom. . . ." The resolution provided for the adoption by each nation in the inter-American system of ". . .measures necessary to eradicate and prevent activities directed, assisted, or instigated by foreign governments, organizations, or individuals. . ." and for the exchange of information on such activities.[28]

The most important result of the Bogotá Conference was the Charter of the Organization of American States. This provided an institutional framework for the inter-American system and machinery for implementation of the Rio pact. The Latin American delegates, still concerned about the political and economic dominance of the United States in the hemisphere, hoped that the OAS would lead to genuine equality of nations in the region and provide a framework for the economic development of the American republics. The United States, as events later would make clear, looked upon the OAS mainly as an agency for collective defense in the Americas; from this perspective, the new OAS was consistent with and a part of the containment policy.[29]

As on earlier occasions the Latin Americans at Bogotá hoped that the United States would agree to large-scale economic collaboration. They were aware that the United States was embarking on a major effort, the Marshall Plan, for the economic reconstruction of Europe, and they hoped for a concurrent program for Latin America. Some State Department officials, including Ambassador William

D. Pawley in Brazil, favored such a step. Before the Bogotá Conference, Pawley suggested to President Truman the creation of a $2,000,000,000 Western Hemisphere economic development program. He argued that the Truman Doctrine, the Marshall Plan, and aid to China ". . . compel us to seriously consider our position with reference to the countries in the Western Hemisphere. This is important not only in regard to healthy economic relations but also because we must at all costs maintain sound political relations with our neighbors to the south."[30] But Secretary Marshall, in his major address before the Bogotá conferees, said that it was ". . . beyond the capacity of the United States Government itself to finance more than a small portion of the vast development needed. The capital required through the years must come from private sources, both domestic and foreign. As the experience of the United States has shown, progress can be achieved best through individual effort and the use of private resources." The Economic Agreement of Bogotá fell far short of what the Latin Americans wanted and never received the requisite number of ratifications.[31]

What can one conclude on the basis of this survey of major events in U.S.–Latin American relations during the first Truman administration? Was the Cold War an important factor in the Latin American policy of the United States during these years? It seems to me that the Cold War must be considered a new, and progressively more important, influence between 1945 and 1949. When we recall the Latin American crises of later years—the Guatemala affair of 1954, Vice President Richard M. Nixon's perilous trip to Latin America in 1958, the contest with Fidel Castro's Cuba, including the Bay of Pigs fiasco of 1961 and the missile crisis of 1962, and the old-fashioned military intervention in the Dominican Republic in 1965—the events of the Truman years seem mild indeed. During this period, the United States maintained the time-honored ingredients of its hemispheric policy: concern for security, determination to maintain political and economic hegemony, and the promotion of its own brand of democracy. The emergence of the Cold War did not cause the United States to alter its traditional objectives in Latin America; but the contest with "international communism" and the Soviet Union, a major determinant of U.S. foreign policy after World War II, ultimately became a significant influence on the nation's Latin American policy. This contributed to the shift from opposition to strong regional organization—demonstrated at both Chapultepec and San Francisco in 1945—to enthusiasm about the Organization of American States. The U.S. endorsement of a mutual defense treaty at Rio in 1947, as well as later commitments in NATO, SEATO, and other pacts, must be considered within the context of the Cold War. In agreeing to the Rio Pact and the OAS, the United States consciously accepted a system that could be utilized later, as it indeed was used, to fight the Cold War in the hemisphere. Similarly, the reversal of the State Department's position on Perón's regime in Argentina, necessary before the Rio Conference could be held, was in part a policy response to the Cold War.

An important step that the United States might have taken during these years to encourage close hemispheric collaboration in the contest with the Soviet Union was cooperation in the establishment of a program of economic development for Latin America based on a large injection of U.S. public and private loan capital. After World War II, the Latin American governments considered this their greatest need and foremost objective. Had the United States cooperated, relationships within the hemisphere would have been happier. The Good Neighbor system, instead of declining from the nominally friendly relationships that existed in 1945, might have become a program of substance and mutual benefits. Among those benefits could have been the unity of the hemisphere in case of threats from the outside. If it was indeed necessary for the United States to unite the other American republics in an anticommunist coalition, the Truman administration refused to consider using the method most likely to attract Latin American support. There was no guarantee, of course, that Congress would have approved such a program had it been proposed, or if instituted that it would have had the economic results anticipated by either the United States or Latin America.[32]

It is certain that the Cold War was by no means the only determinant of the Latin American policy of the United States during the post–World War II era. The evidence presented in this chapter, however, does make clear that the Cold War must be taken into account, along with several other major factors that cannot be discussed in a short essay, in any analysis of U.S.–Latin American relations after 1945. In fact, historians studying the development of the containment policy during the Truman period ought to pay more attention to Latin America. Certainly the region was important; after all, the Rio Pact and the OAS were the prototypes for a host of later Cold War collective defense treaties and regional organizations.[33] They were among the earliest examples of the Truman administration's implementation of the containment policy. They deserve more attention than they have attracted thus far from non–Latin Americanist specialists on the Cold War.

14

Latin America as a Problem in U.S. Foreign Policy

George Kennan

In 1950 one of the best-known U.S. diplomats and foreign policy intellectuals of the Cold War, George Kennan, expressed, after a visit to Latin America, what became the basis of U.S. policy toward the region: if necessary, support repressive regimes to protect U.S. interests against communist subversion in Latin America and the Caribbean. As head of the State Department's Policy Planning Staff (PPS) from 1947 to 1950, Kennan noted the relative absence of Latin America in most of the discussion and reports issued by the PPS. Determined to fill this gap, he toured Latin America, visiting Mexico City, Caracas, Rio de Janeiro, Montevideo, Lima, and Panama. As stated in his memoirs, he "found the journey anything but pleasant"; in fact, in some instances he found Latin America to be "noisy" and "repulsive." Kennan was appalled by the region's congestion, noise, and climate. He was greeted in several cities by anti-U.S. demonstrations and cries of "go home," and in Brazil and Peru his likeness was burned in effigy by university students. What most appalled Kennan was the tremendous contrast between rich and poor and the opulent, arrogant luxury of Latin America's elite, which he believed was superficial, banal, and self-indulgent.

Upon his return, Kennan prepared a thirty-five-page report for Secretary of State Dean Acheson on his impressions of the region and its significance for U.S. security interests. In the report he emphasized that the region was doomed to chaos and uncertainty because of geography, history, and race. Kennan argued that Latin America's climate and geography, along with the historical legacy of destruction and crimes against native peoples by the Spaniards, did not lend themselves to political stability, democracy, and prosperity. In short, as Gaddis Smith, in his seminal work The Last Years of the Monroe Doctrine *(1994), stated, "In Latin America Kennan saw a political culture too weak and selfish to support a democracy strong enough to resist the superior determination and skill of the Communist enemy" (p. 70).*

Kennan recommended that to protect U.S. interests in the region, the United States must keep Latin America within its sphere of influence; additionally, if necessary to halt communist plans to convert Latin America into a region of hostility and trouble for the United States, "we must concede that harsh governmental measures of repression may be the only answer; that these measures may have to proceed from regimes whose origins and methods would not stand the test of American concepts of democratic procedures." This recommendation was inconsistent with Kennan's previous warning in his famous "long telegram" that the United States avoid "allow [ing] ourselves to become like those (i.e., USSR) with whom we are coping"(Smith, p. 69).

Kennan's prescription that the United States support repressive regimes against the spread of communism in the region was a postwar extension of and adaptation to the long-standing U.S. policy of "strategic denial" (i.e., denying extrahemispheric penetration). Gaddis Smith states that the memorandum put forth what he called the Kennan Corollary to the Monroe Doctrine—a cornerstone of U.S. Cold War policy.

[. . .] It seems to me unlikely that there could be any other region of the earth in which nature and human behavior could have combined to produce a more unhappy and hopeless background for the conduct of human life than in Latin America.

As for nature, one is struck at once with the way in which South America is the reverse of our own North America continent from the standpoint of its merits as a human habitat. [. . .]

South America [. . .] is wide and vast in those portions of it which are close to the equator and least suited to human habitation, and it is the temperate zone into which the continent narrows at its southern extremity, pinching off with a fateful abruptness the possibilities for a vigorous and hopeful development of human society. [. . .]

Against this unfavorable geographical background, which would have yielded only to the most progressive and happy of human approaches, humanity superimposed a series of events unfortunate and tragic almost beyond anything ever known in human history. The Spaniards came to Latin America as the bearers of a national and cultural development which was itself nearing its end; a development in which many of the more hopeful origins had already died and little was left but religious fanaticism, a burning, frustrated energy, and an addiction to the most merciless cruelty. To those portions of the New World where an Indian civilization was already in existence, they came like men from Mars: terrible, merciless conquerors—the bearers of some divine punishment—whose sympathy and understanding could never be enlisted for local traditions or institutions, and to whom the only possible relationship was one of tragic and total submission, involving the abandonment of all prior attachments and customs.

Human history, it seems to me, bears no record of anything more terrible ever having been done to entire peoples. The shock to the national consciousness was profound and irreparable. Here, something was violently broken which was essential to the hopeful development of human society; and the effects of that terrible rupture [were] destined to endure through the generations, to a point in time which we cannot yet clearly forsee. [. . .]

In these circumstances, the shadow of a tremendous helplessness and impotence falls today over most of the Latin American world. The handicaps to progress are written in human blood and in the tracings of geography; and in neither case are they readily susceptible of obliteration. They lie heavily across the path of all human progress; and the answers which people have suggested to them thus far have been feeble and unpromising.

[. . .] And, in the realm of individual personality, this subconscious recognition of the failure of group effort finds its expression in an exaggerated self-centeredness and egotism—in a pathetic urge to create the illusion of desperate courage, supreme cleverness, and a limitless virility where the more constructive virtues are so conspicuously lacking. [. . .]

Nevertheless, as things stand today, the activities of the communists represent our most serious problem in the area. They have progressed to a point where they must be regarded as an urgent, major problem; and a correct understanding of their significance is basic to an understanding of the other phases of our policy problems.

A correct appraisal of the significance of communist activities in the hemisphere is difficult to achieve, because it is beset with temptations to error on both sides: that is, both on overestimation and underestimation. It is true that most of the people who go by the name of "communist" in Latin America are a somewhat different species than in Europe. Their bond with Moscow is tenuous and indirect (proceeding, as a rule, through at least one other Latin American capital besides their own, and then through Paris). Many of them are little aware of its reality. For this reason, and because their Latin American character inclines them to individualism, to indiscipline, and to a personalized, rather than doctrinaire, approach to their responsibilities as communists, they sometimes have little resemblance to the highly disciplined communists of Europe, and are less conscious of their status as the tools of Moscow. The Moscow leaders, we may be sure, must view them with a mixture of amusement, contempt, and anxiety.

It is also true that in no Latin American country, with the possible exception of Guatemala, does there seem to be any serious likelihood that the communists might acquire the strength to come into power by majority opinion.

Finally, even though the communists should come to power in one of these countries, that would not be the end of the story. If such an experiment remained isolated—that is, if their power were restricted to a single country—they would hardly be a serious military threat to the hemisphere as a whole. In this case, their relations with ourselves and their Latin American neighbors would probably soon become unspeakable; and Moscow's problem of maintenance of dominant influence and control over them would immediately become immensely more difficult, as it always must in the case of communists who seize the reins of power in areas outside Moscow's sphere of immediate military domination.

All this gives us no justification for complacency about communist activities in this hemisphere. Here, as elsewhere, the inner core of the communist leadership is fanatical, disciplined, industrious, and armed with a series of organizational techniques which are absolutely first rate. Their aim is certainly not the acquisition of power by democratic means, and probably, in most instances, not even the acquisition of complete governmental power at all at this juncture, since this would saddle them with responsibility more hampering than helpful to their basic purposes. Their present aim, after all, is only the destruction of American influence in this part of the world, and the conversion of the Latin American peoples into a hotbed of hostility and trouble for the United States. And in this their activities tie into the formidable body of anti-American feeling already present in every one of the Latin American countries, without exception. It is in this fertile breeding ground that the communists broadcast their seeds of provocation and hatred and busily tend the plants which sprout in such vigor and profusion.

We should not over-rate the actual military significance of this state of affairs. But we must recognize that implicit in these communist activities is the possible wrecking of both of these relationships [. . .] as basic to Latin America's part in our global policies. The positions gained by the communists in Latin America are already sufficiently formidable to interfere extensively with the normal development of our normal peacetime relations on these continents; and I do not think it can be said that the situation in this respect is improving. If a war were to break out in present circumstances I think we must recognize that we would probably be faced at once with civil war, at best, and communist seizure of power, at worst, in a whole series of Latin American countries. And this, as indicated above, could not only disrupt political confidence in us on a world scale, but would force us to take violent action in order to assure raw material supplies and retention of strategic facilities in this part of the world—to the detriment of our long-term relationship with the Latin American people as a whole. [. . .]

[. . .] It seems to me, that the Monroe Doctrine was understood throughout at least a century of our history as barring precisely that which the communists are now attempting to achieve: namely, the introduction into this hemisphere under any guise or pretext whatsoever, of a political system hostile to ourselves and designed to make the Latin American countries pawns in the achievement of the power aspirations of regimes beyond the limits of this continent. The Doctrine was, to use Secretary of State Kellogg's words, "simply a doctrine of self-defense." And it is precisely the principle of self-defense which is involved today in our attitude toward communist activities in this hemisphere.

If this view is correct, then we cannot take an indulgent and complacent view of communist activities in the New World at this juncture without recognizing that this constitutes an historical turning-away from traditional U.S. policy in the hemisphere and without a deliberate decision on our part that the reasons which led our diplomatic predecessors to adhere so long and so stoutly to a given point of view are no longer substantial.

Unless people are prepared to prove that this is so, they must concede that diplomatic precedent obliges us to concern ourselves most seriously with communism in Latin America.

What do we do about it?

In this question as to what the United States can do to oppose and defeat communist penetration in the New World, we find ourselves back in the familiar general problem of communist activities in third countries: a problem which is still the subject of a great deal of confusion in a great many minds.

I think the first thing to remember is that whatever is done to achieve this purpose must be done for the most part by natives of the particular country concerned, either in its government or otherwise. The burden of this effort can never be carried directly by the representatives of a foreign government. Our representatives can contribute in many ways to the creation of incentives and possibilities for local resistance to communist pressures; but they cannot themselves be the bearers of that resistance. To look to them for anything of this sort is to do them injustice and to misdirect our energies.

Our problem, then, is to create, where such do not already exist, incentives which will impel the governments and societies of the Latin American countries to resist communist pressures, and to assist them and spur them on in their efforts, where the incentives are already present.

We cannot be too dogmatic about the methods by which local communists can be dealt with. These vary greatly, depending upon the vigor and efficacy of local concepts and traditions of self-government. Where such vigor and efficacy are relatively high, as in our own country, the body politic may be capable of bearing the virus of communism without permitting it to expand to dangerous proportions. This is undoubtedly the best solution of the communist problem, wherever the prerequisites exist. But where they do not exist, and where the concepts and traditions of popular government are too weak to absorb successfully the intensity of communist attack, then we must concede that harsh governmental measures of repression may be the only answer; that these measures may have to proceed from regimes whose origins and methods would not stand the test of American concepts of democratic procedure; and that such regimes and such methods may be preferable alternatives, and indeed the only alternatives, to further communist successes.

I am not saying that this will be the case everywhere; but I think it may very well be the case in certain places. And I would submit that it is very difficult for us, as outsiders, to pass moral judgment on these necessities and to constitute ourselves the arbiters of where one approach is suitable, and where the other should be used. We will have to learn to leave this primarily to the peoples concerned and to be satisfied if the results are on balance favorable to our purposes. For us, it should be sufficient if there is a recognition of communist penetration for the danger that it is, a will to repel that penetration and to throw off communist influence, and effective action in response to that will.

How can those things be created where they are today not present, or not present in adequate degree? They can be created, in the first place, by a heightened appreciation, on the part of the governments and peoples in the affected countries, of the nature of the communist movement, of the fictions by which it operates, and of the dangers which it involves for the Latin American countries themselves.

This is of course a question of winning of confidence not only with the Latin American governments but with important elements of society behind the governments, and of utilizing that confidence with a view to instilling a correct appreciation of these realities. All that is part of our existing policy and practice, though our techniques might be improved in many instances.

But I doubt whether this alone will be enough. People will not be inclined to believe that communist penetration bears serious dangers for them, as long as there are no tangible evidences in that direction; and, since communist activity appears at present to involve them in little more than an intensified, and not altogether displeasing, fever of anti-U.S. activities and pronouncements, there will, if the matter is allowed to rest here, be too much of that comfortable temporizing which is summed up in the attitude: "I can safely profess myself a sympathizer of communism; for if the communists win, I am then covered; and if the Americans win, they are such inoffensive nitwits that they will do nothing to me, anyway."

To counteract this comfortable stance, from which no one but the communists can profit, we must find ways of demonstrating that a high degree of communist penetration in a given Latin American society bears with it hardships and disadvantages which make it unacceptable, and which require that people do something about it.

Now this gets into dangerous and difficult waters, where we must proceed with utmost caution. Our policies in recent years have greatly circumscribed our possibilities for inflicting hardships. We have forfeited—and rightly so—the right and the intention of any form of military intervention. Except in extremity, any direct pressure brought to bear on Latin American countries in any internal issues where the detriment to U.S. interests is not direct and immediately demonstrable holds great dangers. Furthermore, many of the communist activities which we would like to see curbed are not ones for which the respective governments would admit to any real responsibility or any power of counteraction; and in many instances they will be ones with which our own Government professes itself unable or unwilling to deal when they manifest themselves in our own country.

In general, therefore, it would be wise for us to avoid putting direct pressure on Latin American governments with respect to communist activities, except where those activities have some highly direct and offensive relationship to American interests. Where this is not the case, we must resort to indirection.

There are other ways, however, by which it should be possible for the United States to create situations which bring home to governments and peoples in Latin American countries the disadvantages of an excessive vulnerability to communist influence. But this would require the development of new techniques, now largely non-existent, for making our displeasure felt in discreet and effective ways with the government and peoples of the area. [. . .]

CONCLUSIONS

To sum up, the following are the points which seem to me worth stressing with respect to the subject of communism in Latin America.

1. The danger lies less in the conquest of mass support than in the clever infiltration of key positions, governmental and otherwise, from which to sabotage relations between these countries and the United States;
2. The positions already gained by the communists in this manner are ones which could cause us acute embarrassment in case of war;
3. We have not yet, by and large, appreciated the full seriousness of this situation;
4. We should give intensified and unified study to the communist movement in Latin America with a view to getting a clear picture of its various ramifications and keeping ourselves currently abreast of its development; and
5. We should apply ourselves to the elaboration of techniques for coercive measures which can impress other governments with the danger of antagonizing us through excessive toleration of anti-American activities and would not yet be susceptible to exploitation by our enemies as constituting intervention or imperialism or illicit means of pressure. [. . .]

. . . [Those] North Americans who have questioned the democratic origins of Latin American civilization, who have allowed for the possibility that our own political institutions might be the product of a peculiar national experience, irrelevant to the development of other peoples, and who have been inclined to doubt the propriety or the usefulness of efforts to set themselves up in judgment on the political habits of others. [. . .]

This view was set forth in classical terms in [John Quincy] Adams's record of an oral statement which he made to Henry Clay in 1821. Speaking of the question whether this country should take an active part in the wars of independence of the South American countries, Adams stated the following:

> So far as they are contending for independence, I wish well to their cause; but I have not yet seen and do not now see any prospect that they will establish free or liberal institutions of government. They are not likely to promote the spirit either of freedom or order by their example. They have not the first elements of good or free government. Arbitrary power, military and ecclesiastical, is stamped upon their education, upon their habits, and upon all their institutions. Civil dissension is infused into all their seminal principles. War and mutual destruction are in every member of their organization, moral, political, and physical. I have little expectation of any beneficial result to this country from any future connection with them, political or commercial. We shall derive no improvement to our institutions by any communion with theirs. Nor is there any appearance of a disposition in them to take away any political lesson from us.

Since this issue still wracks our formulation of policy with respect to Latin America, and arises anew with almost every change of government which occurs in the hemisphere, I took particular occasion, during my trip, to examine into the problem.

I must say, in the light of these efforts, that I am at a loss to find any considerations which justify us in taking official attitudes based on distinctions of an internal political nature in other countries or departing in any way from the principle of formal disinterestedness in the domestic affairs of these countries.

The reasons for this are several.

In the first place, the experience we have had in the century and a quarter which have elapsed since Adams made his statement is surely enough to justify us today in the conclusion that democratic institutions, as we know them in our country, are *not* universally native to Latin America, and that the processes of government are destined to operate for a long time in the future, in many of these countries, in ways which are strange and uncongenial to ourselves. Nothing we do in the way of direct interference in Latin America is going to alter this situation materially, particularly for the better. Our best prospect of promoting throughout the New World institutions more similar to our own lies in the power of example, and solely in that power. Thus far, the force of example, while not inconsiderable, has not been great enough to overcome many of the natural impediments to more orderly forms of government. Whether this will change in the future is partly a matter of the developments of our own society. [. . .]

I question whether we should hold our own institutions up as remedies for the governmental problems of other peoples. A faith in the ultimate efficacy of our institutions for ourselves does *not* logically or necessarily involve a similar faith in their universal applicability. Our national experience is in most respects a unique one; and it is not only possible but something logically to be expected that the institutions flowing from that experience, and organically intertwined with it, should be largely irrelevant to the requirements of peoples whose national experience has been different. [. . .]

Finally, it is impossible for a government such as ours to strike official public attitudes about the domestic political complexion of other governments without assuming a certain responsibility with relation to political developments in the respective countries. An expression of moral approval of a given regime makes us, in the eyes of its people and of the world opinion, the guarantor of its continued good behavior. It calls upon us to have an answer if such a regime is charged by its internal opponents or its outside critics with slipping over from the primrose paths of "democracy" into the wicked ways of oppression and dictatorship. If, on the other hand, we voice moral condemnation of a regime, on grounds of its methods in either the assumption or the exercise of power, we imply the existence of some preferable alternative, of which we have knowledge and which we could name upon demand. Here again the world will eventually look to us for an answer, of a sort which we will not always be able to give. [. . .]

For all these reasons, I think it urgently desirable that there be enforced upon our entire official establishment a form of discipline which would cause its members to desist from all sorts of moralizing or public judgment about the internal quality or propriety of Latin American governments. In this, our representatives and officials should be taught to bear in mind that it is not necessary to "like" a government in order to refrain from having an official judgment on it. They should feel themselves under no compulsion to have any personal reaction other than a profound distaste toward regimes which they will scrupulously refrain from judging or criticizing in public and official statements. [. . .]

METHODS OF EXERTION OF U.S. INFLUENCE

It has been noted above that we have divested ourselves, through a series of multilateral undertakings, of the possibility of intervening by force, or on any basis of special right and privilege, in the domestic affairs of Latin American nations. At the same time the extent of our economic commitments within the hemisphere, together with the extent of anti-American activities being inspired there by the communists, means that it is essential to us to have a more effective system of techniques and instrumentalities than we now have whereby our influence can continue to be brought to bear on the Latin American countries. Obviously, these must exclude actual military intervention, or threats of such intervention, and the cruder forms of diplomatic pressure which can be exploited against us, psychologically and propagandistically, by the communists. How can this be done?

The answer lies in the fact that with most of the countries of this hemisphere there exists a multiplicity of relationships with the government or the citizens of the United States so great as to constitute in its entirety a formidable instrumentality of U.S. influence. This implies, however, the coordinated exploitation of all these relationships, by our Government, to the extent that our Government has the power to control them or affect them, with a view to seeing that their total impact is directed to specific ends. In other words, the views and interests of our Government can be given greater force and expression in our relations with Latin American countries only to the extent that we can achieve a coordinated exploitation of all the various possible facets of U.S. interests.

There will of course be many relationships of a private or semi-private nature binding our country and a given Latin American country which can be affected by our Government only partially, and often only in small degree. But there will be a few which cannot be affected at all. And if the total capacity of our Government were to be mobilized and applied for the purpose of affecting these relationships in a manner favorable to the purposes of our Government in its relations with a given country or countries, then a highly significant improvement could be affected in our ability to influence and control developments in the entire area to the south of us. [. . .]

GENERAL TONE OF OUR APPROACH TO LATIN AMERICA

This brings me to the question of the general stance which we and our representatives adopt toward the governments and peoples of Latin America; for here, too, I would plead for a somewhat greater relaxation, reserve, and detachment than we have shown in recent years.

It is important for us to keep before ourselves and the Latin American peoples at all times the reality of the thesis that we are a great power; that we are by and large much less in need of them than they are in need of us; that we are entirely prepared to leave to themselves those who evince no particular desire for the forms of collaboration that we have to offer; that the danger of a failure to exhaust the possibilities of our mutual relationship is always greater to them than to us; that we can afford to wait, patiently and good naturedly; and that we are more concerned to be respected than to be liked or understood.

If this posture might be described in terms of an imaginary statement coming from our representatives to them, I would word it as follows:

"We are a great nation, with world responsibilities, situated at your side. We promoted your independence, and protected it over more than a century, for reasons which were indeed ones of our own self-interest but which you should recognize as of vital importance and utility to yourselves. We have a selfish stake in the preservation of your national independence and integrity which you should recognize as being of greater significance and importance to yourselves than any altruistic assurances or treaty undertakings which we could possibly extend to you. We expect you, recognizing this, to realize, then, that in matters of war and peace and of state security—that is, in the ultimate matters—your interests lie with ours, for reasons wholly practical and geographic, having nothing particular to do with any cultural or ideological affinity; and you should be careful not to wander too far from our side. [. . .]

"And here it is not the outward manifestations of respect which most concern us, although symbols are important too, and may not be wholly ignored. It is rather—respect, as expressed in action and fact. You must realize that we are serious people. We feel that the role we are playing in the world is of importance to many peoples besides ourselves; and it is therefore not only our duty to ourselves but also to some extent the consciousness of our world responsibility which compels us to require of you that you treat us as serious people and listen carefully when we speak."

"We, on our part, are aware of the importance you attach to your independence and your sovereignty and your pride in yourselves as nations. We find that understandable and unexceptionable, and we are prepared to recognize it in full. But you must recognize, as we do, the proper limitations of this national feeling. It obliges us to a scrupulous regard for your national dignity and for the sanctity of your domestic affairs. But it does not oblige us to accord you unrequited favors or privileges of an economic or financial nature. It does not give you the right to take for granted in our relationship the continuation of any bonds or associations which are not of mutual advantage. We cannot for a moment admit that the withdrawal or denial of arrangements which prove not to be of mutual advantage constitutes in any way an injury or an offense against you, any more than it does against us."

"We hold out to you what perhaps no great power—no great power of our relative importance in world affairs—has ever held out to neighboring smaller powers: the most scrupulous respect for your sovereignty and independence, the willing renunciation of the use of force in our relations with you, the readiness to join with you at any time in a large variety of forms of collaboration which can be of benefit to us both. But you will appreciate that the payoff for this unprecedentedly favorable and tolerant attitude is that you do not make your countries the sources or the seats of dangerous intrigue against us, and that you recognize that relationships no longer governed by the sanction of armed force must find their sanction in mutual advantage and mutual acceptability."

"This is our program. We consider it a fair and generous one. We are not prepared to depart from it."

"If you do not like it, we can afford to wait. Meanwhile, the responsibility is on you if you forfeit its advantages."

"If you do understand and appreciate it and wish to accept it as the basis of our relationship, our hand is out to you for a measure of international collaboration which we feel can stand as a model for the future and as an example to those parts of the world still troubled by the spirit of aggression and world domination."

It is my feeling that if such an attitude were to dominate our entire official apparatus in Latin America, and if the excellent people whom we have serving in that area today, relying on the long-term logic of this attitude, were to take with a relaxed equanimity many of the things which now cause a sort of haunted anxiety and a whole series of cramped reactions, we would be better disposed to face the problems of the future in an area where those problems will always be multitudinous, complex, and unpleasant.

15

The Hovering Giant: U.S. Responses to Revolutionary Change in Latin America

Cole Blasier

The general contention that the United States has always been antagonistic toward revolutionary processes and governments does not ring true in the case of Bolivia and its 1952 revolution led by the National Revolutionary Movement (MNR). In this reading Cole Blasier illustrates how conciliatory and concessionary responses by the U.S. and Bolivian governments prevented a polarization of relations. Rather than allow rumors and allegations of communist influence in the MNR to dictate policy, the Eisenhower and Kennedy administrations opted to work closely with the governments of Presidents Victor Paz Estenssoro (1952–1956, 1960–1964) and Hernán Siles Suazo (1956–1960), providing aid, grants, financial and technical assistance, and political support against the more radical elements in the government associated with the tin miners. In return, the MNR toned down its nationalist rhetoric and provided fair compensation to nationalized U.S. mining interests. Open communication and fact-finding missions, such as one led by Milton Eisenhower whose objective assessment helped to calm fears of communist infiltration in Bolivia, contributed to a healthy and productive relationship. Both parties were clearly disposed to avoid polarization and enhance cooperation. In Bolivia, unlike Guatemala and Cuba, Eisenhower did not confuse nationalism and agrarian reform with communism. Unfortunately, rather than the rule, the Bolivian case became the exception in U.S. policy toward revolutionary governments in Latin America.

The Mexican [1910] and Bolivian [1952] Revolutions were alike in that during their reformist phases both were treated with hostility by U.S. officials. [. . .] [Francisco] Madero suffered from the intrigues of Ambassador Henry Lane Wilson, and [Gualberto] Villarroel [the Bolivian president] was subjected to critical pressures from leaders in Washington as well as from U.S. representatives in Bolivia. After Madero's murder in 1913 and the revolution's turn to the Left, the

Mexican revolutionaries were viewed sympathetically by the Wilson administration. Like Madero, Villarroel was murdered, but was followed by what could
be termed "counterrevolutionary" governments from 1946 until 1952. When urban insurrections led to the deepening of the revolutionary process in 1952,
Harry S. Truman was still president and the Democratic party, which had so
stubbornly opposed the participation of the Movimiento Revolucionario Na-
cionalista (MNR) in Villarroel's cabinet, was still in power. [. . .] The major responsibility for coping with the Bolivian Revolution devolved upon the new Republican administration under President Dwight D. Eisenhower since he
assumed office in January 1953, nine months after the MNR gained control of
the government and only weeks after the nationalization of the large tin mines.
Although the Eisenhower administration did not have a record of hostility toward the MNR, there were none of the signs of presidential sympathy for the
revolution that Woodrow Wilson had shown toward the Mexicans early in his
own term. The Bolivian Revolution unfolded rapidly under a new U.S. administration whose response was scarcely predictable.

The causes of that revolutionary upheaval were profoundly domestic. In the
1930s and 1940s the economic base of the old social system was crumbling as
the tin content of the ore gradually dropped lower and lower and Bolivia's share
in the world tin market declined. The ailing tin mines and immobility in other
economic sectors resulted in the deterioration of living conditions of the middle
and working classes. Meanwhile, discontent grew among miners and other
working class elements now being organized into trade unions.

New leaders who emerged in the late 1930s consolidated their political organizations and pressed harder their criticism of the old system which, since its
defeat in the Chaco War in 1935, was increasingly discredited. Reform-minded
military leaders, David Toro, German Busch, and Gualberto Villarroel, each
having seized the presidency, moved against the traditional leaders. [. . .] After
his [Villarroel's] assassination, the rapid succession of presidents and cabinet
ministers during the *sexenio* [six-year presidential term, 1946–1952] was a
symptom of the weaknesses of the traditional political parties and their growing
lack of popularity in the cities. The decline of the ruling groups, growing discontent in the cities, and revolutionary turmoil in the mines all combined in the
overthrow of the traditional parties in the 1952 insurrection and the deepening
of the revolutionary process.

While domestic causes were the source of the social upheaval in Bolivia, they
were still intimately linked in the public mind with foreign relations. Not only
did Bolivia depend on foreign markets—often controlled by foreign governments—for the sale of tin, but the large tin magnates lived abroad as well, and
profits flowed from the country to them. An aroused and frustrated nationalistic
leadership found it convenient, if not always accurate, to attribute many of Bolivia's ills to foreign origins.

In the months preceding the April 1952 insurrection, Bolivia was once again faced with chronic economic crises, for the foreign demand for tin and the resultant high prices generated by the Korean War fell off. In 1951 negotiations between the Bolivian mining companies and Stuart Symington of the Reconstruction Finance Corporation (RFC) had reached an impasse. Bolivian ores began to pile up in Chilean and Peruvian ports in October 1951. The U.S. State Department, concerned about the political repercussions of the impasse, was reportedly hopeful that the RFC, which came under new leadership in early 1952, would soon reach an agreement with the Bolivians. The crisis continued and the economic impact on Bolivia by the following March was described as disastrous, further depressing the already low standards of living. [. . .]

The breakdown in negotiations with the RFC on tin exports and the resultant popular discontent generated by the crisis facilitated the MNR's seizure of government, but the MNR was not inclined to have the revolution explained solely in terms of RFC intransigence on tin sales. [. . .] The impasse over tin sales, however, did pose an extremely serious problem for the new MNR government since negotiations could not be resumed, even if agreement were possible, until the United States recognized the new regime.

DELAYED RECOGNITION

Prospects for a cordial relationship between Washington and the new men in La Paz were not good in April 1952. The MNR leaders were the same men tagged as Nazis during World War II and forced out of the Villarroel government in 1944. Party leaders, who made no secret of Marxist influence on their party program, were strongly critical of U.S. imperialism. Communists had also supported MNR candidates in the 1951 elections, with or without the candidates' consent. The MNR's vaguely leftist program, including proposals for the nationalization of the tin mines, disturbed conservative circles in Washington aroused by the anti-Communist campaigns of Senator Joseph McCarthy.

The MNR, however, did have some points in its favor. [Victor] Paz Estenssoro, who had won a plurality in the 1951 elections, had a constitutional claim to the office. While strong on revolutionary rhetoric, the MNR, with its Right, Left, and Center factions, was not committed to a specific, detailed, and radical revolutionary program. The overthrow of the old regime in April 1952 was a primarily urban insurrection lasting only a few days and with relatively little loss of life; most of the revolutionary innovations were made many months later. The Bolivian Revolution had not yet taken place.

Having suffered through the ordeal of nonrecognition in 1944, the MNR leadership made a great effort from the very first moments after the insurrection triumphed on April 12, 1952, to calm U.S. fears and to pave the way for early recognition and, most important, continued U.S. purchases of tin. Within hours of becoming provisional president, Hernán Siles Suazo promised a peaceful government that would respect international agreements and private property. On April 16 the new foreign minister, Wálter Guevara Arze, formally requested U.S. recognition in a note to the American embassy. On his triumphant return from abroad after the MNR takeover, Paz Estenssoro assumed the presidency and reaffirmed the MNR's plans to nationalize the large tin mines. He was careful to point out that this would not be done hurriedly, expressing desire to reach an agreement about nationalization with the mine owners. Siles was quoted early in May as saying that the MNR was the last bulwark against communism and was independent of Moscow, Buenos Aires, and Washington. He went on to distinguish nationalization from confiscation and to express his desire for the friendship and understanding of the American government and people. [. . .]

The United States formally recognized the MNR government on June 1, 1952—some seven weeks after the MNR seized power—noting that the new government was in control of its national territory and had agreed to live up to its international obligations. Washington was quick to point out, however, that its recognition did not imply any judgment of Bolivian domestic problems; but, in fact, the State Department agreed to recognize the MNR government only after it had been assured that compensation would be paid for the expropriated mining properties.

The United States' grudging recognition of the Paz government eliminated a grave liability to the MNR regime and gave it a new lease on life.

Formal communications between Bolivia and the United States were resumed, and, most important, the Bolivians were able to reopen their direct appeals for a long-term contract to sell tin at favorable prices. Ambassador Edward Sparks, a career foreign service officer, arrived in La Paz on June 3, 1952, the day after recognition was granted, and thereafter played an important role in strengthening U.S. ties with the new government. In September the United States bought up all available Bolivian tin not yet contracted for sale.

COMMUNISM AND EXPROPRIATIONS

Recognition was essential to establishing formal channels of communication between the two governments and to facilitate trade relations. It did not, however, resolve profound issues that threatened to divide the new revolutionary Bolivian government and the United States. The first involved the ideological and international orientation of the new government, and the second, the government's treatment of foreign-owned property, particularly property belonging to North Americans. Resolution of these issues largely determined the initial U.S. response to the Bolivian Revolution.

The bitterest enemies of the new government charged the MNR with being Fascist and Communist, sometimes simultaneously. [. . .] As the years passed and the true record of the MNR became better known, these charges lost much of their force, even though the full facts with respect to the MNR and Germany did not become available until many years later. Washington attributed far less significance to charges of fascism in the 1950s than during the war when the Nazis dominated Western Europe.

Attempts to tag the MNR with the Communist label were a greater threat in the early 1950s when tension between the United States and the Soviet Union was great. Since Bolivia had virtually no direct political or economic relations with the USSR in 1952, about the only arena of possible Soviet influence was through the international Communist movement. The charge of communism against the MNR was based partly on the vague intellectual influence that Marxism had exercised over the MNR's programs and the new government's moves toward the Left.

Making the charge of communism stick was difficult, however, because several different groups which identified with the international Communist movement had long maintained an identity distinct from the MNR and had, in fact, been bitterly hostile to it. The Communist movement in Bolivia had long been weak and divided. [. . .] The Communists were not represented in the MNR command which led the uprising, and representatives of the Communist party as such did not hold any ministerial or comparable posts in the subsequent MNR governments. [. . .]

The MNR government undertook to dispel U.S. fears about communism from the outset. Ambassador Andrade insisted, "[Our government] is not Communist. We give assurances that it is not dominated by a foreign government." [. . .]

In a surprisingly prophetic statement, Paz Estenssoro made his position on the Soviet-American conflict clear as early as 1944 when he said: "Especially in the case of nations like Bolivia international policy has to be formulated considering geographic and economic factors. In the event of a conflict of interest between the Anglo-American group and Russia, I believe that Bolivia will have to gravitate, necessarily, to the Anglo-American orbit." [. . .]

The MNR government succeeded in convincing the Eisenhower administration that it was not Fascist, Communist, or pro-Soviet. In his book, *The Wine Is Bitter*, Milton Eisenhower, who visited Bolivia as a representative of the president, dealt with this question directly. In fact, he used the Bolivian example to show how politicians, the mass media, and business leaders sometimes tag governments or political parties as Communist "in good faith but without essential knowledge." He added: "Sometimes men with selfish interests knowingly make false statements which poison the American mind and enrage Latin Americans. [. . .] It is harmful in our own country and devastatingly hurtful throughout Latin America for us to carelessly or maliciously label as 'Communist' any internal efforts to achieve changes for the benefit of the masses of the people. [. . .] We should not confuse each move in Latin America toward socialization with Marxism, land reform with Communists, or even anti-Yankeeism with pro-Sovietism." [. . .] In fact, he went on to argue that "rapid peaceful social change is the only way to avert violent revolution in Bolivia; physical strife would be the surest way of giving the Communists control."

The second major issue, the treatment of foreign-owned property, dramatically came to public attention when the MNR government nationalized the three large tin mining companies in October 1952. Nationalization was a dangerous step since it jeopardized Bolivia's sales of tin abroad—the nation's largest single source of foreign exchange to cover food imports. Such imports constituted about one-quarter of the national diet. The crisis was further aggravated by a precipitous drop in tin prices. [. . .]

The MNR leaders committed the government to paying compensation for the expropriated mines and time and again reassured Washington that the nationalization decree was not directed against private property in general nor against foreign holders in particular. Agreements were reached with all three mining companies providing for compensation, the first with the Patino company in June 1953. As a gesture of its faith in private foreign investment, the MNR government subsequently entered into agreement with foreign companies such as that of Glen McCarthy to develop sulfur deposits and with Gulf and other companies to exploit oil deposits. [. . .]

EMERGENCY ASSISTANCE (1953–1956)

The MNR government's convincing reassurance on the Communist issue and nationalization laid a good foundation for collaboration but placed the U.S. government in a dilemma. The strategic U.S. stockpile of tin had grown large and the United States sought both to economize on the price and to lower the volume of minerals purchased. U.S. officials were also disinclined to keep open indefinitely the government-owned tin smelter built in Texas during World War II, which was especially equipped to refine Bolivia's low-grade ores. Yet Bolivia had cooperated with the United States during World War II when tin was in such short supply, and it continued to be the only reliable, although costly, source of tin in the Western Hemisphere. Bolivia was desperately dependent on the United States to buy a large part of its product, particularly those lowgrade ores which could not be easily processed in European smelters. Low prices on the world market, in addition to U.S. reluctance to continue purchasing ore at earlier levels, were having a disastrous impact on the Bolivian economy. It appeared unlikely that the existing government could survive if relief were not forthcoming. [. . .] The *New York Times* praised the Bolivian government for the settlement, for having resisted the blandishments of Perón, and for having kept "the Reds in check." The editorial urged that the United States not permit the government to collapse in spite of the size of the U.S. stockpile and favored a long-term tin contract for "political" reasons.

The response of the Department of State was not long in coming. In a press release on July 6, the department offered the Bolivians a one-year contract to buy tin ores at the world market price at the time of delivery. In addition, the department committed itself to doubling the amount of technical assistance and undertaking studies of possible joint efforts to solve the country's economic problems—a broad hint of economic assistance to come. The announcement came at a crucial time, on the eve of the arrival in La Paz of the president's brother, Milton Eisenhower, on his first official fact-finding trip to Latin America. The significance of the Milton Eisenhower visit was not that he set a new policy, but that he provided authoritative and influential confirmation of the department's earlier policy reflected in the July 6 press release and initiated action to implement that policy.

What Dr. Eisenhower saw and learned in Bolivia disposed him favorably toward the MNR government, and his personal assessment of the situation and his influence in the U.S. administration appear to have played a vital role in implementing a large, long-term program of U.S. economic assistance to Bolivia: "Bolivia was in real trouble when I arrived. The price of tin had fallen sharply and people were starving. President Paz Estenssoro urged me to have the United States send emergency food supplies. In response, I made my first call home and spoke to Secretary Dulles, asked him to ship surplus food to Bolivia if possible. We did." [. . .]

The U.S. emergency assistance to Bolivia was formalized in an exchange of letters between Presidents Paz Estenssoro and Eisenhower on October 1 and October 14, 1953, respectively. President Eisenhower authorized the following emergency assistance:

1. To make available $5 million of agricultural products from Commodity Credit Corporation Stocks under the Famine Relief Act.
2. To provide $4 million from Mutual Security Act funds for other essential commodities.
3. To more than double the technical assistance program.

President Eisenhower also referred to an earlier decision to purchase tin "at a time when this country [had] no immediate need for additional tin," because of the traditional U.S. friendship with Bolivia and an awareness of the security threat to the free world when free men suffered from hunger or other severe misfortunes. Both presidents emphasized the emergency and humanitarian nature of the assistance but linked it to the development of Bolivian agriculture and the diversification of the economy, heretofore excessively dependent on tin exports. [. . .] The United States insisted as a condition of granting economic assistance that the MNR government reach an agreement with the former owners of the tin mines regarding compensation.

[Assistant Secretary] Cabot was more explicit than the president about the security factors bearing on the U.S. decision. Not only did he express his belief in the sincerity of the MNR government's opposition to "Communist imperialism," but he went on to describe the "implacable challenge of communism" in the hemisphere:

> The true test of hemispheric solidarity, upon which our security so importantly depends, is our willingness to sink our differences and to cooperate with regimes pursuing a different course from ours to achieve common goals. [. . .] We are therefore cooperating with it, for history has often described the fate of those who have quarreled over nonessentials in the face of mortal peril.

No clearer statement than this is needed to show that the United States did not extend assistance to Bolivia solely as a humanitarian gesture toward a people faced with famine—such assistance was also justified as a means of contributing to the security of the United States.

The crucial decision to come to the assistance of the new revolutionary government was much facilitated by the work of the Bolivian ambassador in Washington, Victor Andrade. [. . .] Returning to the United States as ambassador in the 1950s, he developed a personal relationship with Milton Eisenhower before the latter went to Bolivia on his first official visit, briefing him thoroughly on the MNR as well as on the opposition's positions. Andrade played golf with President Eisenhower from time to time at the Burning Tree Golf Club, an informal access to the president denied most ambassadors. According to Andrade, his most effective argument with the president was that aid to Bolivia would show the world that Eisenhower was not a reactionary inflexible Republican and could support a revolution. [. . .] Meanwhile, the United States increased economic assistance from the $11 million authorized in 1953 to about $20 million in each of the following two years, making Bolivia one of only three Latin American countries to receive outright grants, as opposed to loans. [. . .]

The tendency to justify U.S. emergency assistance in Bolivia as support of a government "showing courage and resourcefulness in combating the Communist problem" [was] intensified. Henry Holland, then assistant secretary for inter-American affairs, defended the expenditure as a way of helping the Bolivian government "to counteract Communist pressure."

One result of U.S.-Bolivian collaboration was that it encouraged foreign interests to invest in Bolivia. Of special significance was the signing of an investment agreement by the two governments in La Paz on September 23, 1955. By June 30, 1964, some $20 million in foreign investment was insured against expropriation under the program and over 80 percent of this amount was in oil. [. . .] Foreign interest was further stimulated by the government corporation's quintupling of its Bolivian crude oil output between 1952 and 1961. Foreign companies later began to export oil, particularly Gulf Oil of Pittsburgh which made shipments by a pipeline to the Pacific port of Arica, Chile.

MONETARY STABILIZATION (1956–1960)

The next politically significant phase in U.S.-Bolivian relations was the political struggle over the economic stabilization program announced in December 1956. After the 1952 insurrection the government increasingly resorted to the printing presses to finance governmental operations, publicly owned economic enterprises, and to meet demands of groups on which it relied for support. The tin mines could not provide taxable surpluses, partly because of the declining yields of tin and foreign exchange and partly because the politically powerful miners' organization had taken over management of the mines, where featherbedding, high government subsidies, declining output, and wage increases prevailed. [. . .]

In the face of what appeared to be impending political and economic collapse, the MNR government appealed to the United States for assistance, but the cash support initially provided was swallowed up in government deficits, and U.S.-supplied commodities either found their way to the black market or were smuggled abroad. In the end, the United States made it clear that either the Bolivian government had to put its house in order or U.S. assistance would be cut off. As a result, the Bolivian government requested that the United States send a financial mission to assist in this housecleaning operation. [. . .] The International Monetary Fund, the U.S. Treasury, and the International Cooperation Administration established a $25 million fund to stabilize the exchange rate of the *boliviano*. [. . .]

The struggle over stabilization concerned more than the additional burden of checking inflation; it became a struggle for control of the MNR. The crisis was intense, with President Siles wondering whether he might end up like ex-President Villarroel, hanging from a lamppost in the Plaza Murillo, and [U.S.] insistence that aid would be cut off if the stabilization plan were not carried through.

In the face of U.S. pressure and apparently convinced of the validity of the plan, President Siles dramatically defended stabilization, first by going on a hunger strike in La Paz and later, by a courageous visit to the mines to confront personally the miners. [. . .] By August 1957 President Siles had broken the opposition to the stabilization program, and from that time and through the 1960s Bolivia has had one of the most stable currencies in South America. In an address to the Bolivian congress in August, President Siles said that the country had been "on the brink of civil war" and that the stabilization program "saved the country from disaster." As a result of this episode, U.S. policy became even more clearly identified with the right wing of the MNR. [. . .]

ECONOMIC DEVELOPMENT (1960–1964)

The MNR leadership was so deeply involved in the revolutionary changes introduced after the 1952 insurrection and in conducting defensive economic policies that it was not feasible to mount an economic development drive until the early 1960s. Economic development became the major objective of Paz Estenssoro during his second term (1960–1964). This corresponded with the presidency of John F. Kennedy and the beginning of the Alliance for Progress.

After the 1952 insurrection the tin mines, which were still Bolivia's principal industry and the major source of foreign exchange, were looked to as a means of financing capital imports for economic development. Tin seemed to hold the key to Bolivia's economic development, but as production plummeted, revenues from tin sales sank. Low yields of ore, the deterioration of mining equipment, and inefficient management and labor practices meant that the cost of production frequently exceeded the price tin brought on the world market. [. . .]

But the type of reforms which foreign experts felt were necessary in management-labor relations and labor practices constituted political dynamite. Because labor had control of management in the tin mines, many experts estimated that several thousand surplus workers were featherbedding. Employment in the big three tin mines rose from 24,000 miners in 1951 to 36,500 in 1956 and dropped to 27,000 in 1961. The mines produced, however, only 15,000 tons in 1961 as compared with 34,600 tons in 1949, produced by only slightly fewer workers (26,000). [. . .] Measures to correct these practices faced the stolid opposition of the tin miners, the very group which had been a major element in the insurrection bringing the MNR to power and which was perhaps the largest organized group behind the MNR.

Despite the need for heavy investments in mining equipment, the United States had refrained from providing economic assistance to publicly owned and managed mining and industrial activities. The impact of U.S. economic assistance was strictly limited because of the unwillingness to grant aid to the nationalized industries, tin and oil, which provided a major share of GNP [gross national product] and export earnings. Economic assistance for education, health, and agriculture was politically less controversial in the United States than the provision of funds from U.S. tax sources to support nationalized industries. [. . .]

Paz Estenssoro returned to Bolivia from his diplomatic post in London in the late 1950s and was elected president for a four-year term in 1960. Early in his term he tried to lead Bolivia out of economic stagnation and showed a willingness to assume the political risks that rapid economic development would entail. He sought the economic and social objectives for Bolivia which had been denied the MNR earlier, capitalizing on the new, more liberal economic assistance policy of the Alliance for Progress and the Kennedy administration. In a sense, the MNR's revolution had adopted objectives as early as 1952 which were very similar to those of the Alliance for Progress a decade later. Kennedy looked to Bolivia as a kind of model, and Paz counted on Kennedy for personal and official support.

In the meantime, the USSR had developed interest in Bolivia, and during his visit to the United Nations in 1960, [Nikita] Khrushchev dramatically offered Bolivia the funds for constructing its own tin smelter so the nation would no longer have to depend on U.S. and European smelters. In December of the same year a delegation from the Supreme Soviet visited La Paz and announced a Soviet offer of credits in the amount of $150 million for the government-owned petroleum corporation, road building, railroads, and other public works, as well as the smelter; but, despite pressure from the miners and other leftist groups, the government postponed a decision. The United States opposed acceptance of the Soviet offer; therefore, President Paz considered the Bolivian choice clear— partly because prospective U.S. assistance was far more than he expected from the Soviets. Faced with the Soviet bid, the United States overcame its reluctance to support the government-controlled mining corporation, COMIBOL, and the Plan Triangular was presented as the U.S. answer to the Soviet offer.

Formulated in early 1961 and implemented over the course of the succeeding years, the Plan Triangular was the initial motivating force of Bolivia's economic development plan for the 1960s. But achieving rapid economic development meant facing up to the tin problem and the political implications its solution involved. The plan sought to rehabilitate the tin mines by providing funds for investing in the exploration of new mineral deposits, for metallurgical work to increase the recovery rate, for replacement of materials and equipment, and for commissary supplies, elimination of surplus labor, and technical assistance.

All this involved administrative changes in COMIBOL, greater labor discipline in the mines, and other politically sensitive issues. The United States, the Federal Republic of Germany, and the Inter-American Bank together pledged more than $37 million to the plan under conditions specified in the agreement with the Bolivian government. Like the earlier stabilization program, the Plan Triangular linked the United States once again into direct conflict with the tin miners' union and their leader, Juan Lechín.

Not surprisingly, the tin miners bitterly resisted the required layoffs of thousands of excess workers, and Paz faced a crisis and confrontation with the miners led by Juan Lechín similar to that of former President Siles in the stabilization controversy. He rose to the occasion, as Siles had, meeting the strikes, demonstrations, and other agitation with persuasion and coercive countermeasures. [. . .]

Meanwhile, U.S. commitments to Bolivia rose slightly above the average of the late 1950s through 1961 and mounted sharply to more than double the earlier level in fiscal year 1964. Obligations in that year amounted to nearly $60 million under AID [Agency for International Development] programs.

THE U.S. IMPACT

The United States and Bolivia not only reconciled their most profound conflicts and maintained friendly relations after the 1952 revolution but worked more closely together than almost any two countries in the hemisphere. The United States became intimately involved not only in the formulation of Bolivian policy but in its implementation as well. [. . .]

In the later years of the MNR governments, the United States had immense influence in Bolivia. Ambassadors [Ben S.] Stephansky and [Douglas] Henderson traveled with President Paz and were widely acclaimed throughout the country. The U.S. official missions in Bolivia were huge. In 1959 the economic assistance mission reached a peak of 118 professional employees and then stabilized at about 70 persons in the early 1960s. U.S. missions were about half that size in larger countries like Chile and Colombia, and Brazil, which literally dwarfs Bolivia, had only a slightly larger economic mission. The U.S. aid program was involved in almost all major aspects of Bolivian life including agriculture, health, industry, and public administration. The United States provided a direct subsidy for almost one-third of the Bolivian central government's budget in 1957 and continued to do so at gradually declining levels for the MNR governments thereafter. Consider how much influence U.S. officials whose government was meeting part of the Bolivian payroll had!

From the beginning the U.S. influence tended to check the nature and extent of revolutionary change. U.S. insistence on compensation for expropriated mining properties and support of private ownership and control served to prevent nationalization beyond the three major tin mining groups. U.S. policies consistently sought to limit or decrease government participation in the economy, such as control over foreign exchange and management of extractive industries, and to promote expansion of the private sector. Enacted under U.S. influence, the petroleum code, the mining code, and other measures helped to improve the investment climate for foreign capital.

Stabilization in 1957 and the Plan Triangular in 1961, both conceived and implemented with U.S. support, brought the MNR government into head-on conflict with organized labor, especially with the tin miners. Although U.S. representatives may not have felt politically or personally friendly to the tin miners, it would be difficult to prove that U.S. policies were directed against organized labor as such. Even so, the effect of U.S. influence was to make the United States an ally of the MNR Center and Right and the enemy of the labor Left. Thus, the effort of U.S. policy was to bolster the position of the Bolivian middle classes against organized labor as reflected in the well-known and persisting U.S. antagonism toward Juan Lechín.

In fact, that antagonism was sufficiently great as to have been an important factor in Paz Estenssoro's decision to amend the constitution to permit him to run for reelection in 1964. As one of the top three or four leaders of the MNR, Juan Lechín was to have his "turn" at the presidency in 1964, or so at least ran much talk within the MNR. Aware that he had long been considered in the United States as the bête noire of the Bolivian Revolution, Lechín sought to establish himself in the good graces of the United States. He visited the United States and later paid a formal call on Chiang Kai-shek in Formosa. When Lechín failed to win U.S. support, Paz concluded that the only way to insure the continued flow of needed external resources from the United States and from the international agencies was to run for the presidency himself as the only candidate who could beat Lechín. [. . .]

U.S. per capita economic assistance to Bolivia from 1952 to 1964 averaged more than to any other country in the world. After the emergency assistance was granted, President Paz testified that his government "would not have lasted without North American aid." President Siles later said that the stabilization program saved Bolivia from "disaster."

The United States appears at times to have influenced Bolivian foreign policy in its favor. For example, while having its own rationale, Bolivia supported Secretary Dulles's anti-Communist resolution at Caracas in 1954 and broke relations with Cuba in 1964 to help insure continued U.S. support. Bolivia, however, also successfully sustained positions counter to U.S. policy such as voting against the expulsion of the Cuban government from the OAS [Organization of American States] in 1962 and initially refusing to break relations with Cuba in August 1963. Bolivia maintained diplomatic relations with the eastern European socialist countries such as Czechoslovakia, Hungary, and Yugoslavia.

Military assistance from the United States had also been important in the development of domestic politics in the late 1950s and 1960s. In order to counter the opposition of armed miners in the stabilization controversy, President Siles began rebuilding the armed forces in 1958 with U.S. military assistance. Paz Estenssoro intensified this process in the 1960s as internal opposition to him grew as well. It appeared that he was relying increasingly on the military to strengthen his hand in dealings with Juan Lechín who broke with him in his second term. In fact, the Bolivian armed forces, with U.S. military assistance and increased influence through U.S.-sponsored civic action programs, became so powerful that they were able to overthrow Paz in November 1964.

Certain U.S. military officers were close to the leaders of the coup, and the Pentagon and State Department may have been at odds over the issue. President Paz deeply felt the loss of President Kennedy at the time of his assassination and felt his relations with Washington were never the same again. However, the official U.S. position, as represented by Ambassador Douglas Henderson and the American embassy, supported Paz. Henderson appears to have done his best to bolster Paz as the head of a government which was heavily supported under the Alliance for Progress. In any case, the coup against Paz, and the fall of the MNR government to the military under the leadership of the vice president, General René Barrientos Ortuño, appear to have been primarily domestic matters.

16

Bitter Fruit: The Untold Story of the American Coup in Guatemala

Stephen Schlesinger and Stephen Kinzer

In this classic work on the 1954 U.S. intervention in Guatemala, Schlesinger and Kinzer provide a detailed analysis of the forces, actors, and circumstances that led to the overthrow of the reform-minded government of President Jacobo Arbenz by the U.S. government and its proxy, Guatemalan "liberator" Colonel Carlos Castillo Armas. The Eisenhower administration, reacting immediately and negatively to the reforms—particularly agrarian reform—labeled nationalism and reform as communism. In many ways the Bolivian revolution in 1952 was more revolutionary than that in Guatemala, yet the United States adopted a more conciliatory and cooperative policy toward the former while taking an extremely hostile approach toward the latter. As Schlesinger and Kinzer emphasize, the aggressive and "irrational" response to Arbenz's reforms perhaps had more to do with the expropriation of United Fruit Company properties than with any communist influence in the government: "The takeover of United Fruit land was probably the decisive factor pushing the Americans into action." The Eisenhower administration was staffed by individuals, such as Secretary of State John Foster Dulles and CIA Director Allen Dulles, who were either legal consultants for United Fruit or served on the company's board of directors. Thus the well-being of United Fruit drove U.S. policy, which helps to explain why Washington paid such intense attention to a few leftists in Guatemala when there were more communists in strategically more important countries like Brazil, Chile, and Costa Rica. The determination and arrogance of Secretary of State Dulles and Ambassador John Peurifoy, coupled with the weakness and indecisiveness of Arbenz and his government, made "Operation Success" (the Central Intelligence Agency operation to overthrow the Guatemalan government), despite serious problems with planning and operation, a victory the United States believed could be replicated in Cuba after Castro's rise to power.

The Arbenz government had embarked on a land reform program that included expropriation of some of the vast acreage belonging to the United Fruit Company. The land reform was not popular either in the company's Boston boardrooms or in Washington, where the firm had enormous influence. United Fruit controlled directly or indirectly nearly 40,000 jobs in Guatemala. Its investments in the country were valued at $60 million. It functioned as a state within a state, owning Guatemala's telephone and telegraph facilities, administering its only important Atlantic harbor, and monopolizing its banana export. The company's subsidiary, the International Railways of Central America (IRCA), owned 887 miles of railroad track in Guatemala, nearly every mile in the country.

The Eisenhower administration had taken action in early March 1954—weeks before the much-publicized Czech arms shipment—to give Guatemala a final warning of its displeasure over the land seizures. At the Tenth Inter-American Conference in Caracas, Venezuela, Secretary of State [John Foster] Dulles had exerted heavy pressure on Latin states to endorse a resolution condemning "Communist" infiltration in Latin America. It was directly aimed at Guatemala, though no nation was named. Only Guatemala voted in opposition to it, with two others abstaining in meek protest.

A show of diplomatic correctness and conciliation, even pleading, now seemed Guatemala's only hope in dealing with the United States. What made this tactic exceedingly difficult for the Guatemalans was the character of the formidable U.S. ambassador in their country. John Peurifoy, a prickly and heavy-handed diplomat, had been especially chosen to exert pressure on Arbenz and, if that failed, to overthrow him. [. . .]

Within days of his arrival in Guatemala in late 1953, Peurifoy had gone out of his way to lecture President Arbenz on his tolerance of Communists and to warn him that American-Guatemalan relations would remain strained so long as a single Communist remained on the public payroll. After that, Peurifoy and the President seldom spoke, though Peurifoy and Foreign Minister Toriello conferred regularly.

Arbenz now instructed Toriello to meet with Peurifoy about the invasion and appeal to him to defuse the crisis. At one o'clock in the afternoon that June 18 [1954], Jorge Toriello left the President's office. He told a dozen foreign correspondents and thirty local reporters waiting for him on the first floor of the Palace: "The battle of Guatemala has begun. We stand as one man against this criminal invasion. We will not take one backward step."

So far the United States had given no formal reaction to reports of the rebel invasion. The State Department remained strangely silent in Washington. There was an undisclosed reason for the Department's circumspection. What Arbenz and Toriello might have feared was true: the U.S. government was in fact the secret creator and sponsor of the "Liberation" movement.

That morning John Peurifoy arrived at his embassy office in an ebullient mood. The night before, he had told his staff: "Well, boys, tomorrow at this time we'll have ourselves a party." He knew that the invasion he had helped plan was underway, and he was eagerly anticipating its outcome. Peurifoy was a blunt, politically ambitious self-described "tough guy" from South Carolina sent to Guatemala with a single mission: to change the direction of the reformist government, no matter how. He had been unable to convince President Arbenz to cooperate, and now Arbenz was about to receive his just desserts. The dawn leafleting and the early radio reports of air attacks and troop movements reassured Peurifoy that the plan, called Operation Success, was working. He sat down and dictated a stream of dispatches to Washington reporting the play-by-play from Guatemala City. [. . .]

Around four that afternoon [June 18], Guatemala City's anxious quiet was shattered by the drone of two planes approaching from the south. The aircraft, P-47s never seen before in any Latin Air Force, drew close, dove, fired a few .50-caliber machine-gun rounds at houses near the Guardia de Honor barracks—one of five forts in the city—and dropped five-pound fragmentation bombs, creating a series of loud explosions. Apparently fulfilling the threat contained in the morning circulars, one plane swerved about and machine-gunned the National Palace. After scattering more propaganda broadsides, the two intruders swung away toward the Pacific Ocean, later strafing the port of San José. [. . .]

Peurifoy arrived at the Foreign Ministry around 7:30 P.M. Toriello had also called in the French ambassador and the British chargé d'affaires. Most of the talking was between Peurifoy and Toriello. The two men knew each other well; they had conferred frequently during the eight months since Peurifoy's arrival in the country, attempting without success to settle the issue of compensation for the property seized from the United Fruit Company under Guatemala's land reform act. United Fruit wanted about $16 million for the tracts; Guatemala offered United Fruit's own declared valuation for tax purposes—$627,572. The U.S. ambassador, in an unusual role, had acted as the company's representative in the negotiations with Guatemala.

Toriello began at once with the matter of that afternoon's air strikes. He asked all three envoys to inform their governments that two P-47 planes had attacked Guatemala City. Without looking at Peurifoy, he pointed out that "this type of plane is manufactured in the United States." Peurifoy became indignant—"I interposed," he wired Dulles, "that P-47 planes could be found in many countries, even Czechoslovakia and Russia." He ingenuously suggested to Toriello that the planes might not actually be hostile to Arbenz. When Toriello told him that the planes had hit the National Palace, Peurifoy demurred. "I . . . saw no machine-gunning of the Palace," he told Toriello. [. . .]

Ambassador Peurifoy remained in his office receiving periodic reports. He learned of an emergency decree by the Guatemalan government banning international air flights and forbidding anyone to leave the country. He tried several times to reach Foreign Minister Toriello to protest the denial of exit permits for U.S. residents, but Toriello was unavailable. He learned also that the Guatemalan Army had moved "most of [its] military forces" out of the city during the day (later accounts indicate that 500 troops were sent to Puerto Barrios and to Zacapa). He cabled the report to Secretary of State Dulles—who was anxiously following the unfolding of the "revolt" he had also helped plan—but warned Dulles: "Enormous rumors mostly false . . . are circulating."

That day the U.S. State Department finally issued a formal statement on the Guatemalan situation. It said:

> The department has been in touch with ambassador John E. Peurifoy at Guatemala City by telephone and telegraph and the Ambassador reports that all Americans there are well and safe. Mr. Peurifoy is keeping in constant touch with members of the United States community in Guatemala and has made strong representations to local authorities regarding their safety. [. . .]

At 9:15 Sunday evening [June 27], President Jacobo Arbenz addressed his countrymen by radio. How many actually heard his words is uncertain, because the transmission was partially jammed by the CIA and many Guatemalans were in any case tuned to the news broadcasts by the "Voice of Liberation." Arbenz's text was not allowed to be published in the newspapers for over a month. [. . .]

It was not yet midnight when President Jacobo Arbenz, forty-one years old, walked slowly down the steps of the opulent National Palace facing Guatemala's Central Park. As he left, he passed a member of his presidential guard, who asked where he was going. *"Me voy al frente,"* replied Arbenz. Thinking Arbenz meant literally, "I'm going to the front," the young guard protested immediately, fearing the pressure had caused his leader to break. "You can't do that," the guard protested. "You can't go to the front. Which troops will you lead?" Arbenz couldn't manage a smile, but repeated *"Me voy al frente"* and pointed through the side door of the Palace. Then the guard understood. Arbenz had used the phrase in its colloquial sense, meaning "I'm going across the street." The guard fell silent and watched the President slowly cross Sixth Avenue and open the door of the Mexican Embassy. [. . .]

At the end, Arbenz acted realistically: he had no support from any quarter except from those, like his Communist backers, who knew that his departure would doom them and their hopes for Guatemala. He realized that the pressure would never let up until he was gone. All that could be accomplished by his refusal to leave, he had concluded, would be an escalation of fighting, the loss of many lives, and his ultimate downfall. [. . .]

United Fruit had for years been the largest employer in Guatemala as well as the largest landowner and exporter, and during the 1930s its holdings and power increased even further. In 1936, the firm signed a ninety-nine-year agreement with President General Jorge Ubico to open a second plantation, this time on the Pacific coast at Tiquisate. Ubico granted the company the kind of concessions to which it had become accustomed: total exemption from internal taxation, duty-free importation of all necessary goods, and a guarantee of low wages. Ubico, in fact, insisted that laborers be paid a daily wage of no more than fifty cents in order to keep other Guatemalan workers from demanding better pay. Around the same time, the company's relationship with Minor Keith's International Railways of Central America (IRCA) was formalized. United Fruit effectively took over IRCA, which owned two *very* important properties: the only Atlantic port in the country, Puerto Barrios, and virtually every mile of railroad in Guatemala. (The IRCA brought another advantage: it did not have to pay any taxes to the government until 1954 under Arbenz.)

Thus United Fruit exercised enormous economic control over Guatemala. Any business seeking to export goods to the eastern or southern ports of the United States (or to Europe or Africa) had to use Puerto Barrios, and since the company owned the town and all its port facilities, it had nearly complete authority over the nation's international commerce. In addition, the only means of moving products to Puerto Barrios was the IRCA rail line, whose schedule and rate structure were also controlled by United Fruit. The Fruit Company's "great white fleet" of more than fifty freighters alone had regular access to Puerto Barrios, and the company's intimacy with successive Guatemalan strongmen allowed it numerous "side deals" such as running the telegraph service.

Most United Fruit employees lived on the banana plantations and had little if any reason ever to leave. But there was sporadic trouble among workers, who naturally resented the huge profits they could see being extracted from the country through their labor. In the 1920s the company forcibly broke up a spontaneous strike that erupted when management announced it would require a seven-day work week. [. . .]

In some senses, the Fruit Company was benevolent and paternal. Its workers enjoyed better conditions than most farm laborers in Guatemala. The company provided adequate housing and medical facilities and even established a school for employees' children. (Critics liked to charge that the Guatemalan people indirectly paid for this largesse many times over through uncollected taxes on United Fruit property and exports.) Most of the company's American overseers, however, were from the deep South and brought their racial attitudes with them; company policy required "all persons of color to give right of way to whites and remove their hats while talking to them." During the Ubico years [1931–1944], peasants, performing forced labor for plantation owners, were sometimes given small plots for their own use. United Fruit, with more fallow land than any other company or individual in the country, consistently refused to allow the same arrangements. In addition, *la frutera* (as the company was known in Guatemala) had always resolutely opposed the organization of independent labor unions among its employees.

When the government of Juan José Arévalo came to power in 1945, with its outspoken support for the peasantry and its determination to free Guatemala from the domination of foreign interests, United Fruit was a most obvious target. A series of strikes broke out during the late 1940s, with workers demanding better conditions and a wage of $1.50 per day. The company granted some concessions, though its oft-repeated charge that the political deck was stacked against it was partially belied when one major strike at the Tiquisate plantation was declared illegal by the labor court established under the 1947 Labor Code. (The Labor Code was a source of constant anger at United Fruit, which at one point had threatened to "withdraw from Guatemala" because the law promised "to seriously interfere with and possibly make impracticable the further growth of the company.") [. . .]

The view of Central America as a region to be kept "safe" for American corporations was naturally not shared by all the people who lived there. To many Guatemalans, United Fruit represented with perfect clarity the alliance of American government and business arrayed against their efforts to attain full economic independence. Alfonso Bauer Paiz, Minister of Labor and Economy under Arbenz, expressed the bitterness felt by many of his countrymen toward the giant multinational when he said: "All the achievements of the Company were made at the expense of the impoverishment of the country and by acquisitive practices. To protect its authority it had recourse to every method: political intervention, economic compulsion, contractual imposition, bribery, [and] tendentious propaganda, as suited its purposes of domination. The United Fruit Company is the principal enemy of the progress of Guatemala, of its democracy, and of every effort directed at its economic liberation."

The history of the company's operations in Guatemala, as one American historian [Cole Blasier] observed in a scholarly study, makes that view plausible:

> For many Guatemalans the United Fruit Company [UFCO] was the United States. . . . In the past, UFCO and its sister companies had bribed politicians, pressured governments, and intimidated opponents to gain extremely favorable concessions. To the Guatemalans it appeared that their country was being mercilessly exploited by foreign interests which took huge profits without making any significant contributions to the nation's welfare. In the eyes of many Guatemalans, the foreign corporations had to pay for their past crimes and for the years in which they had operated hand-in-hand with the Estrada Cabrera and Ubico dictatorships to exploit the Guatemalan people. . . . It is not difficult to see how [Guatemalans could believe] that their country was economically a captive of the U.S. corporations.

Thomas McCann, who spent twenty years working for United Fruit and then wrote a book about the company, summarized its half-century of prosperity in Guatemala succinctly:

Guatemala was chosen as the site for the company's earliest development activities at the turn of the century because a good portion of the country contained prime banana land and because at the time we entered Central America, Guatemala's government was the region's weakest, most corrupt, and most pliable. In short, the country offered an "ideal investment climate," and United Fruit's profits there flourished for fifty years. Then something went wrong: a man named Jacobo Arbenz became President.

As Arévalo left the presidency and was succeeded by Jacobo Arbenz, the Fruit Company, like the rest of Guatemala, foresaw that idealistic generalities might soon give way to forceful actions. From the outset, Arbenz made clear that he would place a priority on building a highway to the Atlantic in order to end the IRCA/United Fruit stranglehold on the nation's foreign trade; he also announced plans to build an electric power plant which would free the country from reliance on an American-owned facility which was then the only major generating outlet in the country.

In October 1951, just seven months after Arbenz took office, Walter Turnbull, a top executive of the Fruit Company, arrived in Guatemala from Boston to demand that the company's labor contract be extended in its existing form for three more years. He insisted further that Arbenz promise not to increase the very modest taxes being paid by United Fruit and that the company be protected against any possible devaluation of the Guatemalan currency. His tone reflected the long-standing attitude in the Boston office, based on decades of experience under dictators from Estrada Cabrera to Ubico, that the Fruit Company could expect to dictate terms as it pleased to the governments of the countries where it owned property.

Arbenz replied to Turnbull in a manner to which the Boston executive was not at all accustomed. For the contract to be extended, he said, the company would have to pledge respect for the laws and constitution of Guatemala and accept the government as the final arbiter in any disputes between labor and management. In addition, he proposed that the docks at Puerto Barrios be improved, that rail freight rates be reduced, that United Fruit begin paying export duties, and that the company consider paying compensation for the "exhaustion" of Guatemalan land. [. . .]

In March 1953, the ax of land reform fell on the company, never before the object of such a challenge. In two separate decrees, a total of 209,842 acres of uncultivated land on the Tiquisate plantation in the lush Escuintla area near the Pacific was expropriated. The *frutera* had always left large amounts of its land uncultivated (in 1953, 85 percent of its land was unused); only as many bananas were grown as could be sold abroad. The company claimed it needed the vast fallow lands as insurance against plant diseases that periodically ravaged its bananas, though critics said its reserves far exceeded its real requirements.

In compensation for the seized property, the government offered $627,572 in bonds, based on United Fruit's declared tax value of the land. United Fruit, like other large landowners, had historically undervalued its property in official declarations in order to reduce its already insignificant tax liability. But now that the declared value was being used to determine compensation, the company howled in protest. On April 20, 1954, a formal complaint was delivered to Guatemalan authorities, not by the Fruit Company but by the U.S. State Department, whose top officials, beginning with Secretary Dulles himself, had close ties to the company. The note demanded $15,854,849 in compensation for the Tiquisate land, declaring that the government offer "bears not the slightest resemblance to just evaluation." It based its claim on international law, which, it contended, required fair compensation for lands seized from foreigners despite domestic laws.

The amount offered by Guatemala averaged about $2.99 per acre, while the State Department wanted over $75 per acre; the company had paid $1.48 per acre when it bought the land nearly twenty years earlier. Foreign Minister Guillermo Toriello refused to accept the State Department note, branding it "another attempt to meddle in the internal affairs of Guatemala," and bitterly attacked the United Fruit/U.S. government coalition. [. . .]

In October 1953 and February 1954, the government ordered two more expropriations of uncultivated United Fruit land—this time on the Atlantic coast—bringing the total of disputed property to 386,901 acres. Guatemala offered about $500,000 to the company for its newest takeovers. Throughout this period, Guatemalan officials were in negotiation with the State Department for an overall solution to the dispute. But at the same time, a more momentous series of meetings in Washington, called largely at the urging of United Fruit and its powerful supporters in the government, considered how to end the process which had led Guatemala to these unprecedented actions. [. . .]

Indeed, the Fruit Company was at that moment working quietly but effectively to convince the American government that Arbenz was a threat to freedom and must be deposed. The company hired a corps of influential lobbyists and talented publicists to create a public and private climate in the United States favorable to Arbenz's overthrow. Working behind the scenes beginning in 1950, these men influenced and reshaped the attitudes of the American public toward Guatemala. In their hands the fate of Arbenz and his ambitious social reforms was being determined. [. . .]

United Fruit could also count on an especially receptive audience in the Eisenhower administration, particularly among the main players in the Guatemalan drama. John Foster Dulles had been a senior partner of the New York law firm of Sullivan and Cromwell, which did legal work for the international financial house J. Henry Schroder Banking Corporation. Schroder Bank was the key financial adviser to the International Railways of Central America (IRCA), which owned most of Guatemala's train lines. In 1936, the United Fruit Company, holding a small interest in IRCA, sought to take over the railroad company to ensure its power to set transportation rates, as well as to block the entry of any rival banana operation into Guatemala. Dulles, as general counsel to Schroder, handled the negotiations, arranging a cozy deal with United Fruit at the expense of his putative client, IRCA, and reaping a tidy profit for the Schroder Banking Corporation.

Allen Dulles also did legal work for Sullivan and Cromwell in the 1920s and 1930s, often helping his brother on Schroder bank matters. Soon he was appointed to the board of directors of the bank. Schroder, meantime, maintained a share of stock in IRCA; indeed, as late as 1954, the president of Schroder was himself on the board of the railroad company, even while it was controlled by United Fruit. The Schroder Bank was, coincidentally or not, a depository of secret CIA funds for covert operations.

Among other influential figures sympathetic to the company was John Moors Cabot, Assistant Secretary of State for Inter-American Affairs, whose family owned stock in United Fruit. His brother Thomas had served as president of the corporation in 1948. UN Ambassador Henry Cabot Lodge was a stockholder, too, and had been a vigorous public defender of United Fruit while a senator from Massachusetts. The wife of Edmund Whitman, the Fruit Company's public relations director, was Eisenhower's personal secretary, Anne Whitman. Undersecretary of State Bedell Smith was seeking an executive job with United Fruit while helping to plan the coup against Guatemala (he later was named to its board of directors). Robert Hill, ambassador to Costa Rica during the coup, was close to the Fruit Company hierarchy, having worked for Grace Shipping Lines, which had interests in Guatemala. In 1960, he also became a director of the corporation. Thus many of the significant figures behind the Guatemalan coup were intimately acquainted with high Fruit Company executives and naturally favored their views over those of a Central American government whose "Communism" they publicly abhorred and about which they knew little or nothing else.

American national security considerations were never compelling in the case of Guatemala. State Department analysts in late 1953 treated the influence of Communists as relatively trivial except insofar as they had Arbenz's ear. The much-publicized claim that Guatemala could become a base for a Soviet seizure of the Panama Canal was also difficult to sustain. Guatemala had no diplomatic or military links to Russia or any Eastern European country except for its occasional meetings with officials from Czechoslovakia, from whom Guatemala ultimately purchased a single arms shipment in cash. No serious evidence ever turned up after the coup establishing a secret tie to the Soviets. Furthermore, the country, which sits 800 miles from the Canal, at the time maintained only a tiny, nonfunctional air force with a range of barely 300 miles. Guatemala had only one airport capable of handling jets, and U.S. observers could watch it at all times.

The principal evidence offered by Americans to justify fears of subversion in Guatemala was the land reform program, particularly as it affected United Fruit.

Such writers as Daniel James of the New Leader warned that Communists would use the program as a steppingstone to take over Guatemala. Several U.S. congressmen saw a disturbing similarity between the nationalization of oil companies in Iran and the expropriations of Fruit Company land in Guatemala—though both were accomplished legally under local law. [. . .]

By the summer of 1953, the U.S. was moving toward a showdown. Pushing arguments for moderation aside, John Foster Dulles and his brother Allen—who in his memoirs referred to Arbenz as a "stooge" of the Russians—decided that the CIA would direct the strike. No further bungled attempts by local operatives would be tolerated. Given the blood ties between the chiefs of the State Department and the CIA, the final authorization for the mission did not take long. As Howard Hunt wrote: "A word from one [brother] to the other substituted for weeks of inter- and intra-agency debate."

17

Did Eisenhower Push Castro
into the Arms of the Soviets?

Alan Luxenberg

The questions addressed in this reading by Alan Luxenberg continue to haunt historians and political scientists interested in U.S.-Cuba relations. The U.S. role in the Cuban Revolution is critical in understanding the rise, consolidation, and longevity of the Castro regime. Luxenberg looks at both sides of the argument (which he calls the conservatives and liberals) and concludes that the "communization" of Cuba was largely inevitable. Although Eisenhower had authorized secret plans to undermine Castro and Castro was quietly planning to communize Cuba, neither was reacting to a perceived threat from the other. As Luxenberg states, "The hostility which Eisenhower and Castro bore for one another existed independent of any evidence that the other was a threat." Luxenberg also suggests that those who argue that the United States pushed Castro may have based their thesis on faulty chronological evidence. This chapter calls for a more realistic assessment of U.S. power and its ability to either "lose or push a country." As Luxenberg concludes, "To argue that Eisenhower 'lost' Cuba to communism is to expect our government to be both omniscient and omnipresent. Similarly, to argue that Eisenhower is responsible for Castro's behavior is to elevate without reason the impact which the United States can be expected to exert on the behavior of other nations and leaders." In other words, domestic forces are more important than external pressures in understanding political developments.

In re-evaluating the Eisenhower years, historians have more and more come to believe that [Dwight] Eisenhower was prudent, strong, and well-versed in international affairs. In response to this revisionism, however, there has arisen a growing literature highly critical of the Eisenhower administration's relations with the Third World. Driven by an obsessive fear of communism, it is said, Eisenhower positioned the United States against the tide of history, against the

159

movements for reform and social justice, creating enemies out of potential friends. He tied the United States to unpopular and unrepresentative governments which were inherently unstable, and which would inevitably be supplanted by regimes that would, precisely because of this history, take sides against the United States. As Robert McMahon put it:

> The Eisenhower administration grievously misunderstood and underestimated the most significant historical development of the mid-twentieth century—the force of Third World nationalism. . . . The Eisenhower administration insisted on viewing the Third World through the invariably distorting lens of a Cold War geopolitical strategy that saw the Kremlin as the principal instigator of global unrest. As a result, it often wound up simplifying complicated local and regional developments, confusing nationalism with communism, uniting the United States with inherently unstable and unrepresentative regimes, and wedding American interests to the status quo in areas undergoing fundamental social, political, and economic upheaval.

[. . .] The case of Cuba offers a unique opportunity to test McMahon's thesis. For different reasons, conservatives and liberals argue that U.S. policy in Cuba was a failure. From the conservative viewpoint, we "lost" Cuba to communism on Eisenhower's "watch"; from the liberal viewpoint, we tied ourselves to a corrupt dictator and antagonized his successor, eventually pushing him into the arms of the Communists. That we failed in Cuba is not a question; the question is how did we fail?

Shortly after the Cuban Revolution nearly thirty years ago, *New York Times* reporter Herbert Matthews wrote: "I doubt the historians will ever be able to agree on whether the Castro regime embraced communism willingly or was forced into a shotgun wedding." As one who gave a mighty boost to the revolution when he reported on the front page of the *Times* that Fidel Castro was alive and well in Sierra Maestra, and who thereafter forged a strong bond with Castro, Matthews argued that "Castro did not originally want to become tied up with the communists. . . . He was trapped in 1959–1960 by . . . the massive pressures against him from the United States policies."

To this day, analysts on the Left maintain that Castro was not originally a Communist but a nationalist who became a Communist in response to the unwarranted hostility of the Eisenhower administration to his revolution and to his regime. A key point in their argument, and an unassailable one, is that Castro was not a member of the Cuban Communist Party (CCP). Moreover, he had a long history of antagonistic relations with the Party.

Conservatives have long believed that the U.S. State Department actively facilitated the advent of communism in Cuba; the works of Earl E. T. Smith and Nathaniel Weyl are cited most frequently in this vein, but they appear not to be taken seriously—and mostly for good reason, since they suggest that from the beginning either Castro was a dyed-in-the wool Communist or the Soviets had a hand in the Cuban Revolution. Both assertions are patently untrue. Yet, after more than forty-five years of Communist rule under Castro, it is hard not to look askance at those who would still suggest that if only Eisenhower had been a bit more accommodating, Castro would have remained a democrat. No one rules so ruthlessly for so long because of the putative hostility of a U.S. president.

Other observers have concluded that Eisenhower and Castro are equally at fault. By their mutual distrust, they pushed each other in opposite directions, making confrontation inevitable. A little more compromise on both sides would have changed the course of history. Still others concede that Castro went his own way for his own reasons—well beyond the ability of Eisenhower or anyone else to influence. Nonetheless, they argue that Eisenhower's unnecessary hostility pushed Castro farther and faster than he would otherwise have gone and, even more significant, helped him consolidate popular support for his policies.

The evaluation of our response to the Castro regime remains of interest and significance and not only to historians, for similar questions tend to reappear again and again in new guises. Did the United States push Sandinistas into the arms of the Communists? Witness the new book by Robert Pastor—*Condemned to Repetition: The United States and Nicaragua*—in which it is suggested that the Carter and Reagan administrations are, in dealing with Nicaragua, merely repeating the mistakes of the Eisenhower and Kennedy administrations in dealing with Cuba. [. . .]

What lessons, then, can be gleaned from the Cuban case? Did Eisenhower push Castro into the arms of the Soviets? The answer to this question must be considered along three lines of analysis, each pertaining to a different period of time. To answer the question most directly, we must look at the events of 1959; we will see that the administration acted earnestly to cooperate while Castro remained decidedly unmoved and can be judged, in retrospect, to have been immovable. Castro's turn to the Communists was not a response to Eisenhower's hostility but a reflection of his own ambitious objectives in Latin America, his virulent anti-Americanism, his megalomania, Cuba's internal political dynamics, and the bipolar character of the world order.

But, given Castro's stubborn aversion to the United States, did we unintentionally help him consolidate support behind an anti-U.S. posture and solidify his ties to the Soviets? For the answer to that, we have to examine the events of 1960, when the administration turned on the pressure through the use of economic sanctions. The evidence so far suggests that economic sanctions may have been somewhat counterproductive but can hardly be seen as instrumental in determining Castro's political evolution.

Finally, did we help bring about a Castro in the first place by having stayed too long by [Fulgencio] Batista's side? For an answer to this question, we must turn to the events of 1958, and possibly earlier, where we will find that the United States, mostly through inattention, became too closely associated with the highly unpopular Batista regime and was unable to act quickly and decisively to replace him with a more palatable leader—but for reasons that can hardly be attributed to Eisenhower himself or to his administration.

EISENHOWER AND CASTRO: WHO PUSHED WHOM?

To be sure, Eisenhower was no fan of Castro's. In his memoirs, Eisenhower reported that Allen Dulles, Director of the Central Intelligence Agency, informed him in the final days of 1958 that "a Castro victory might not be in the best interests of the United States," for Communists and other extremists had penetrated the 26th of July Movement. Thus was triggered a frantic and unsuccessful search for "a third force" associated with neither Batista nor Castro.

Nonetheless, relations between the Eisenhower administration and the new Castro regime did not get off to such a bad start, as Wayne Smith hastens to remind us. Assigned to the position of Third Secretary in the U.S. Embassy in Havana, in July 1958, Smith wrote in his memoir, *The Closest of Enemies*, that the "relations between the United States and Cuba were rather good during the first half of 1959." Washington had promptly recognized the new government on January 7, and selected an ambassador with the experience and disposition to set Cuban-American relations right. In assessing the Cuban president and his cabinet, the staff of the U.S. Embassy cabled the U.S. State Department: "None of the members appear to be pro-Communist or anti-United States." [. . .]

What went wrong, or, more precisely, who pushed whom in which direction? Did Castro provoke the Eisenhower administration or was it the other way around? This question requires answers to still other questions. First, when did Castro turn Communist? Was Castro determined to communize Cuba and ally with the Soviets even before he assumed power? When did the Eisenhower administration's wait-and-see attitude shift to mortal hostility?

The argument over who pushed whom turns on the question of timing, in particular the comparisons of two dates: (1) the date when Eisenhower changed his views on Castro and (2) the date that Castro determined to communize Cuba. If it can be established that one event took place before the other, cause and effect are indicated but not definitively established. Any argument that has the chronology wrong, however, can be rejected definitively.

If Castro had not originally planned to communize Cuba but did so in response to "premature" hostility on the part of the United States, then the argument can be made that the United States drove Castro into the arms of the Soviet Union. For those who argue that Eisenhower did the pushing, the earlier it can be shown that Eisenhower shifted toward a policy of such hostility, the stronger their argument. [. . .]

Tad Szulc attempted to resolve the question once and for all in his book *Fidel: A Critical Portrait*. Noted for his reporting on the Bay of Pigs (for the *New York Times*), Szulc has been following Cuba for as long as Castro has been in power. Sympathetic to the "winds of revolution" that blew over Latin America in the 1950s—he wrote a book by that name—Szulc was no fan of Eisenhower's. If anything, Szulc is very much a fan of Castro's, but that did not keep him from establishing that Castro became a Communist rather earlier than people ordinarily assume, beginning with the secret alliance with the Communists made before he assumed power (in January 1959) and which involved running a secret government after he attained power. [. . .]

On the basis of numerous interviews with Castro and with those who were involved in running Castro's "secret government," Szulc reconstructed the story of Cuba's communization. Just before the triumph of the revolution, Castro began holding regular, and clandestine, meetings with leaders of the Communist Party, who also kept these meetings secret from their own party rank-and-file. Why all the secrecy? To prevent a repeat of Guatemala—where the CIA successfully directed a covert operation to oust Jacobo Arbenz—by denying Washington the pretext required to launch a similar operation. Che Guevara was among those who left Guatemala when Arbenz was ousted, and there can be no doubt that when he befriended Castro in Mexico in 1956, the lessons of Guatemala were well-taken into account. Also in on the secret government were the leading members of the "Left-wing" of the 26th of July Movement, including Raúl Castro and Ernesto (Che) Guevara. In an interview with Szulc, Communist Party Secretary Bias Roca recalled Castro's humorous remarks; "now we are the government and still we have to go on meeting illegally." [. . .]

Though it was not until December 1961 that Castro proclaimed himself a Marxist-Leninist, by Fall 1959 most observers, according to Wayne Smith, knew which way the wind was blowing: "Whatever the precise moment of Castro's decision, by October 1959 most of us in Havana recognized that he had made it. [. . .] By the end of the year, all of Cuba's moderate cabinet ministers were gone."

Evidence exists that Castro consciously dissembled. As Castro said in a speech in 1961, "Of course, if we stopped at the Pico Turquino [a height in the Sierra Maestra] when we were very weak and said 'We are Marxist-Leninists' we might not have been able to descend from the Pico Turquino to the plain." In a letter to a friend in 1954, Castro wrote, "Much guile and smiles for everyone. . . . There will be ample time to squash the cockroaches together." As Theodore Draper put it: "Castro has suggested that he could not have won power if he had given the Cuban people the slightest forewarning of what he has presented them with."

All this notwithstanding, in a review that appeared in *The New Republic*, K. S. Karol allowed as how the real revelation of Szulc's book was not the early plans for the communization of Cuba but the disclosure that Eisenhower had determined to topple Castro as early as March 1959—well before any serious observer had heretofore concluded that Castro was steering Cuba toward communism. Until Szulc's revelation, it had been widely believed that the plan to topple Castro was not set in motion until a year later, 17 March 1960.

Like Szulc, Karol is also a journalist who has been following Castro for the past twenty years, and whose own book on the subject, *Guerrillas in Power*, is a work of sensitivity and erudition. Indeed, a good portion of the book shows why the Communist Party was held in such low esteem by people who sought the overthrow of the corrupt tyrannies that ruled Cuba. Karol details the history of the Cuban Communist Party, particularly its collaboration with Batista. . . . Indeed, from the beginning right up until mid-1958, the Communist Party heartily opposed Castro's movement. In an August 1953 edition of *Hoy,* the Communist Party newspaper, Castro's attack on the Moncada Barracks was described as "a putschist attempt, a desperate form of adventurism, typical of petty bourgeois circles lacking in principle and implicated in gangsterism." [. . .]

Szulc's view is not quite the opposite of Karol's. One might characterize it as a middle-of-the-road view, for Szulc argues that just as Castro's turn toward communism was not the result of Eisenhower's premature hostility, neither was Eisenhower's hostility the result of any real evidence concerning the communization of Cuba. In other words, the hostility which Eisenhower and Castro bore for one another existed independent of any evidence that the other was a threat.

According to Szulc, Castro became a Communist while the Eisenhower administration was still accommodating him in public but planning his downfall in private. Eisenhower's hostility to Castro developed while Castro was publicly extolling the virtues of democracy but secretly planning to communize Cuba. Thus, Szulc argues, each leader was engaged in secret plots against the other while remaining in ignorance of the actions of the other—consequently, neither Castro nor Eisenhower was acting in response to the plans of the other. The collision was not, as Richard Fagen once argued, the result of "an interactive and self-supporting system of threat and counterthreat, misunderstanding and counter-misunderstanding, retaliation and counter-retaliation."

Nonetheless, Szulc provides the material for Karol to argue that Eisenhower's plan to bring about Castro's downfall preceded Castro's turn toward communism. All this hinges in the presumed March 1959 decision to overthrow Castro by the Eisenhower administration. This is the sole piece of evidence (cited throughout the book) presented by Szulc to substantiate the charge that Eisenhower's hostility to Castro preceded any sign of future Cuban communization; this is also the sole evidence on which Karol bases his broader charge that Eisenhower pushed Castro into the arms of the Soviets. That being the case, it must now be agreed that the argument is critically flawed: *the March 1959 decision never happened.* [. . .]

NIXON AND CASTRO: THE MYTH AND THE MEMO

Karol's review of the Szulc book is not the first time that Karol has suggested that Eisenhower's shift came earlier than March 1959. In his book *Guerrillas in Power*, K. S. Karol cites, as evidence of an early shift in policy from accommodation to hostility, [Richard] Nixon's assessment of Castro following their April 1959 meeting and Nixon's determination to overthrow the Castro regime. His source is the Nixon memoirs, *Six Crises*.

Referring to a memorandum he wrote following his meeting with Castro, Nixon recalled:

In it I stated flatly that I was convinced Castro was "either incredibly naive about Communism or under Communist discipline" and that we would have to deal with him accordingly. . . . My position was a minority one within the Administration and particularly so within the Latin America branch of the State Department. . . . Early in 1960, the position I had been advocating for nine months finally prevailed, and the CIA was given instructions to provide arms, ammunition, and training for Cubans who had fled the Castro regime.

From this statement alone, even if it were entirely accurate, it would be wrong to infer a shift in Eisenhower's policy, since Nixon himself says that his view was a minority view within the administration, but this is what Karol concluded:

Castro had a long meeting with Vice-President Nixon who, according to his own testimony, concluded that this man had to be removed from office. He accordingly drafted a memo to all departments concerned, recommending the training of Cuban exile commandos that would help to overthrow the new regime.

As it turns out, Nixon misrepresented his memo, recording a harsher judgment and policy recommendation than he in fact made. Found by Jefferey Safford in the Mike Mansfield files and reproduced in *Diplomatic History*, Nixon's appraisal was surprisingly even-handed, even somewhat sympathetic:

My own appraisal of him as a man is quite mixed. The one fact that we can be sure of is that he has those definable qualities which make him a leader of men. Whatever we may think of him he is going to be a great factor in the development of Cuba and very possibly Latin American affairs generally. He seems to be sincere; he is either incredibly naive about Communism or under Communist discipline — my guess is the former. . . . But because he has the power to lead . . . we have no choice but at least to try to orient him in the right direction.

Nixon's record of his memo appeared in the middle of a critique of the Kennedy campaign; he criticized Kennedy for making Cuba a campaign issue, particularly the alleged failure of the Eisenhower administration to deal with

Castro strongly enough. Nixon argued that Eisenhower had, in fact, been secretly preparing an invasion which Kennedy already knew about, and that Nixon
had been in the forefront in urging such an invasion. Ironically, Nixon's misrep-
resentation of his memo gave Karol reason to suggest that Eisenhower wrongly
pushed Castro toward communism. [. . .]

THE TURNING POINT: HERTER'S MEMORANDUM

Three new books—the Higgins volume [*The Perfect Failure: Kennedy, Eisenhower, and the CIA at the Bay of Pigs*], the Rabe volume [*Eisenhower and Latin
America: The Foreign Policy of Anticommunism*], and Morton Morley's *Imperial State and Revolution: The United States and Cuba, 1952–1986*—make use of
the latest documentation to establish that November 1959 is the time that the
Eisenhower administration began to contemplate ousting Castro. Higgins and
Rabe cite a November 5th memorandum from acting Secretary of State Christian Herter in which he recommended to Eisenhower that the United States encourage opposition to Castro, both inside and outside Cuba. "Four days later,"
Higgins wrote, "the President approved of the State Department's recommendation, and the United States was at last launched upon a still officially secret war
against Cuba." The way Higgins puts it is perhaps a bit strong, since Eisenhower
merely initialed a document that recommended not the ouster of Castro but the
encouragement of opposition to his present course.

Morley cites what is apparently an earlier version of the same memo—this one
dated 31 October 1959—which Morley characterizes as recommending "that
U.S. policy be directed toward achieving the revolution's demise 'by no later than
the end of 1960.'" Since it is part of Morley's overall thesis that U.S. policy was
far more coherent—and hegemonic—than is usually presented, he concludes by
suggesting that these documents "do much to demolish the myth of the State Department's 'reasonableness' and 'moderation' during this period." [. . .]

Despite Morley's assertion that the United States was dead-set against Castro
even before day one, the earliest date that either he, Higgins, or Rabe establish[es] for Eisenhower's turn away from Castro is November 1959, when time
enough had passed for serious observers to pronounce judgment on Castro and
treat him as an enemy. Even so, Ambassador Bonsai pushed successfully for a
conciliatory statement from the president as late as January 1960. At the same
time, the administration sought a rapprochement with the Havana regime
through the good offices of the Argentine Ambassador to Cuba. Neither peace
offering enjoyed a positive response.

It would appear, then, that Eisenhower waited until the evidence was in,
and that it was not Eisenhower who pushed Castro into the arms of the Sovi-

ets, but Castro who went willingly. As Rabe conceded, "U.S. actions probably influenced the pace of revolutionary change in Cuba more than its ultimate direction."

THE QUESTION OF SANCTIONS

Mainstream analysts, like Rabe, who have conceded that Castro went his way for his own reasons rather than in reaction to U.S. policies, nonetheless blame Eisenhower for the cementing of Cuba's ties to the Soviets. The most eloquent exponent of this view is Richard Welch, who argued that

> U.S. efforts at economic coercion in the summer of 1960 produced results antithetical to the goals of U.S. foreign policy. They strengthened rather than weakened Castro's political authority; they made it easier for the Russians to accept the application of their Cuban suitor; they enhanced the importance of Communist supplies and markets for the Cuban revolutionary regime.

Proponents of this view have thus moved the burden of argument from the events of 1959, where they have effectively conceded that Castro was up to no good from the start, to those of mid-1960 where they argue that, given Castro's antipathy to the United States, the administration chose the wrong strategy to oppose him.

Having decided in March 1959 to plan for Castro's downfall, the administration determined to place economic pressure on the regime. This it did beginning in July when Eisenhower reduced the annual sugar quota for Cuba to the level it had reached by July. Later, in October, Eisenhower placed an embargo on all goods to Cuba (save medical and other emergency supplies). The argument is that these acts forced Havana to turn more and more to the Soviet Union to meet its basic needs while helping to consolidate popular support for Castro within Cuba. Welch and others suggest that had we maintained a conciliatory posture, the Castro regime might not have placed so many of its eggs in the Soviet basket, and any attempt to do so would have triggered popular discontent. [. . .]

It is difficult to respond to this argument without the benefit of archival material from Cuba but it is easy to see how an over-reliance on U.S. archives naturally results in a predisposition to over-emphasize the U.S. role. Moreover, many analysts bespeak almost an ethnocentric view that Washington can accomplish virtually anything it wants; foreign actors have no autonomy whatsoever. By mid-1960 it is equally plausible to suggest that nothing less than a successful invasion could have changed the outcome in Cuba. This we will never know.

Nonetheless, various studies have shown that economic sanctions are notoriously ineffective in accomplishing their objectives, especially if the objective is to change the behavior of another state. The author of one case study concluded that sanctions pushed Cuba into the Communist world. "In the absence of the boycott," Donald Losman states, "it is quite likely that Castro's economic relations with these states would not have assumed significant proportions." But this conclusion is overdrawn, for Castro's political direction was already apparent before 1960, and his link to the Soviet Union was more a strategic necessity than an economic one.

WAS CASTRO A COMMUNIST?

If it was not the intransigence of the Eisenhower administration which pushed Castro in the direction of the Communists, what did? Wayne Smith, whose credibility cannot easily be assailed by Eisenhower's critics, argues that it was Castro's own foreign policy ambitions which triggered the shift. Seeing himself as the new Simón Bolívar, Castro sought nothing less than the liberation of Latin America and its consolidation under one leader—himself. Though the United States was accepting Castro's internal reforms, Castro's objectives meant that no matter how well the United States responded, he would oppose the United States in the global arena. Thus was a collision course inevitable.

Castro's trip to Washington, in April 1959, at the invitation of the American Society of Newspaper Editors stands out as a critical instance where U.S. offers of cooperation were met with aloofness. (The invitation itself was a sign that the U.S. elite viewed the Cuban Revolution rather sympathetically.) Morley, who otherwise takes the position that Eisenhower was hostile to Castro from the beginning, quotes Felipe Pazos, president of the Cuban National Bank, on the atmosphere of that visit to Washington: "the attitude of the U.S. at this pre-preliminary stage was that of a most willing lender."

It is true, of course, that Eisenhower chose not to receive Castro (leaving the task to Nixon and Herter), thereby signalling some displeasure with the Cuban leader—a result, according to Eisenhower, of his suspicions that Castro was in fact a Communist, and because of his disgust, as he put it, over the numerous executions of *batistianos*. Eisenhower's decision not to meet Castro was probably a mistake but hardly critical; in fact, it appears that Castro did not wish to be received by Eisenhower. [. . .]

In his memoir, former U.S. ambassador Earl Smith traced Castro's communism back to the Bogotá riots of 1948, though most other accounts believe that Castro's involvement in the *bogotazo* was incidental. Interestingly, in a memorandum dated 7 December 1957, Smith himself indicated that there was no evidence that Castro was a Communist—which suggests that Smith was doing a little revision by the time he got around to his memoir—when he wrote that "the Cuban Government accuses Castro of being a Communist, but has not produced evidence to substantiate the charge." [. . .]

In the June National Intelligence Estimate (NIE), the [CIA] addressed one key question explicitly, if cautiously: "We are unable to answer the simplified question 'Is Castro himself a Communist?'" But they concluded that Castro's regime was "deeply and increasingly influenced by the Communists," leaving no "prospect of democratic government under his regime. . . . [G]iven the mutuality of interest between the Castro regime and the Cuban Communists, it is difficult, and in most respects academic to try, to distinguish the policy and actions of the Castro regime from those which would be expected of a government under actual Communist control."

In the December estimate, they went a little further: "for the most practical purposes, the present Cuban Government can be regarded as Communist." That same month, an intelligence report from the U.S. State Department pursued the same line when it recognized that "a strongly anti-American and pro-Soviet but not avowedly Communist Government like Castro's serves the purposes of the Bloc far better than would an openly Communist regime." What is clear is that if Castro intended to communize Cuba from the very beginning, the best way to have gone about it was precisely the way Castro conducted himself—by criticizing the local Communist Party, by draping himself in the mantle of a democrat, and by appearing on *Meet the Press* (as Castro did in April 1959) to declare that "I am not a Communist."

What appears to have confused everyone is that Castro was not a card-carrying member of the Communist Party and, in fact, was opposed by the Party from the time of his attack on the Moncada Barracks until just before the revolution. Wayne Smith reported that "we found no credible evidence to indicate that Castro had links to the Communist Party or even had much sympathy for it." Nevertheless, it is not enough to suggest that just because an individual is not a member of the Communist Party that such a person cannot be an enemy of the United States. [. . .]

According to Ernesto Betancourt, Castro's registered representative in Washington in 1957–1958, ideology was never a serious interest of Castro; his only objective was to secure and retain power. Anti-Americanism was an instrument to achieve that objective. However, anti-Americanism placed Castro in jeopardy so long as he had no sponsor to back him up—hence his reliance on the Soviet Union. In other words, Castro's ties to the Soviets were a logical outgrowth of his hostility to the United States. There was nothing Washington could have done to prevent Castro's turn to the Soviets, for Castro needed, and used, his anti-Americanism to consolidate his power. [. . .]

EISENHOWER AND BATISTA

Even if it can be agreed that Eisenhower did not push Castro into the arms of the Communists, and even if the administration cannot be blamed for failing to discern in a timely way Castro's ultimate intentions, it is possible that Eisenhower does not fare so well in respect to a somewhat broader question: Did Eisenhower push Cuba into the arms of the Communists? The focus here is not on what Eisenhower did in response to Castro but what he did—or didn't do—in response to Batista.

Cuba's strongman from 1933 to 1944, Fulgencio Batista re-assumed power in a bloodless coup in March 1952, just months before an election that he was sure to lose. Though he had appointed Communists to his Cabinet during his previous reign, he was regarded as a stabilizing force by the Truman and Eisenhower administrations, who felt a strong regime was urgently needed to quell the rising tide of political violence, gangsterism, and corruption that pervaded Cuba at the time.

Castro's revolution was launched not long thereafter, on 26 July 1953—the date that gave Castro's movement its name—with a failed attack on military barracks. Castro was captured, imprisoned, and placed on trial. His speech at the trial—"History Will Absolve Me"—became his political manifesto, calling for free elections and restoration of the democratic constitution of 1940 (put in place by none other than Fulgencio Batista, in a previous incarnation). Less than two years later, he was granted amnesty and left for Mexico. [. . .]

Until 1957, Washington appeared to be far more consumed by questions of quotas and commerce between the United States and Cuba than by Cuba's growing political crisis. By all accounts, U.S. Ambassador Arthur Gardner (1954–1957) was a political ally and social partner of Batista's. Gardner's excessive closeness to Batista evidently became a matter of some concern to the U.S. administration, which replaced Gardner in mid-1957. Ambassador Earl E. T. Smith, like his predecessor, was a wealthy contributor to the Eisenhower campaign. If his mandate was to place some distance between Washington and Havana, he got off to a good start by openly criticizing a display of brutality which took place right in front of him. Over time, however, he too became identified with the regime.

In a surprisingly thoughtful memo—surprising only because the conventional histories paint a rather lurid picture of an ignorant ambassador—Smith identified the problem as between a corrupt, brutal regime on the one hand and a terrorist movement on the other. [. . .] Smith sought to secure from Batista a commitment to restore "constitutional guarantees" but sympathized with Batista's argument that he could not do that so easily so long as "terrorism and conspiracy threaten his Government." He therefore urged that the United States intensify efforts to bring about an agreement between the Cuban government and the responsible opposition for the holding of free elections. Even by today's standards, this is not an unreasonable or rigidly conservative stance. [. . .]

With the March 1958 arms embargo, the Eisenhower administration delivered a tremendous psychological blow to the Batista regime—and did so aware of the likelihood that this blow would be fatal. [. . .] In Ambassador Smith's view there was no doubt "that the decision by the State Department to suspend the shipment of arms to Cuba was the most effective step taken by the Department of State in bringing about the downfall of Batista." [. . .]

Rather late in the game, in December 1958, the Eisenhower administration began in earnest to seek some alternative to both Batista and Castro. "Batista must relinquish power," Secretary of State Christian Herter concluded in a memo to the president, dated 23 December 1958. So Eisenhower hoped for some democratic "third force" to appear, but the prospects of finding such a third force were small. As Hugh Thomas so skeptically put it: "Since 1959 the only real opponents of Castro of any quality have been men and women who were with him for a time, and certainly so in 1958, and might have been the most bitter opponents of the United States at the time." Some time in 1958, the forces of opposition coalesced around Castro. By the time the highest levels of the administration in the United States were paying attention, it was too late. [. . .]

In early December 1958, the United States sent William Pawley, businessman and sometime diplomat, to deliver a "personal," rather than a presidential, message to Batista: the suggestion was that Batista leave the country in order to make way for a military junta that would be as acceptable to Batista's critics as to Batista. Pawley was not persuasive, but the same message—had it been conveyed on behalf of the president of the United States—might have succeeded. Why the Eisenhower administration failed to take this step is not clear. Perhaps it was a failure of nerve. Later, on 14 December, Ambassador Smith informed Batista that he no longer enjoyed the support of the U.S. government.

THE UNIMPORTANCE OF LATIN AMERICA

Perhaps the greatest source of error in U.S. foreign policy comes from inattention. This is especially true in the case of Latin America, for Latin America has consistently been low on Washington's national security agenda, and not without good reason. The threat of Communist expansion was greatest, naturally, at the periphery of the Communist empire: Western Europe, the Far East, and the Middle East. Hence, these areas, rather than Latin America or Africa, commanded the greatest share of Washington's attention. That being the case, U.S. policy for Latin America was, in large part, the responsibility of the assistant secretary of state, his subordinates, and special presidential adviser Milton

Eisenhower. This arrangement rendered significant policy initiatives in the area as well-nigh impossible.

Only the imminent threat of communist penetration could vault Latin America onto the agenda of the president and his secretary of state—as happened with Guatemala in 1954. As for Cuba, it scarcely entered the consciousness of our highest officials until 1958, when it was probably too late to accomplish anything positive. [. . .]

FOR DICTATORS, A HANDSHAKE INSTEAD OF A KISS?

For Matthews as for others, the lesson of Cuba was simple: instead of raising a bulwark against communism, "dictators pave the way for the Communists." This was the lesson, certainly, that presidential candidate John Kennedy drew (he also criticized the administration for being too soft on Castro). It was also the lesson that the administration itself drew, however late.

Indeed, the administration began to take this lesson to heart even before the revolution in Cuba. Upon his return from a 1958 trip to Latin America that was marred by violent anti-U.S. demonstrations, Vice-President Nixon recommended that we differentiate between democrats and dictators, making clear our preference for the former. Give the democrats an *abrazo*, he urged, the dictators only a handshake. This motion was seconded by Milton Eisenhower upon his return that same year from a fact-finding mission (his second) to Latin America. In fact, Milton Eisenhower specifically urged that the United States withhold military assistance from dictators all over the world, though he did not appear to persuade other key people—for the simple reason that such a blanket policy would probably have created more crises than it would have resolved.

Nevertheless, the president himself averred, at a National Security Council (NSC) meeting in 1958, that "in the long run the United States must back democracies." In his memoirs, Eisenhower wrote: "after my brother Milton's investigations in Latin America, I became convinced we were making fundamental policy errors" because U.S. aid was going to support regimes which denied people basic human rights. Thereafter, he said, "special aid was to be extended only if recipient nations carried out social reforms which truly promoted economic and political democracy." From these sentiments emerged the inauguration of the Inter-American Development Bank (IDB) and related measures to spur social and economic reform. Upon this foundation was built John Kennedy's Alliance for Progress. [. . .]

In the case of Cuba, a critical part of the problem, perhaps an insoluble part, is that the possible replacement of Batista by a more democratically oriented individual would have required the attention and participation of the president and secretary of state *before the situation entered a period of crisis*. By the time the issue became sufficiently critical to merit attention of the president himself, it was probably too late for Washington to be effective in resolving the problem on terms favorable to the United States. Yet, for the president to spend time on an issue that is not critical means that he is not spending enough time on truly critical issues. He has only so much attention to give. [. . .]

It is useful to juxtapose the debate over U.S. relations with "friendly tyrants" with the debate over U.S. relations with radical regimes. In the case of the former, liberals, or regionalists, think we should use a stick to oust Right-wing authoritarian regimes; in the latter case, they think we should use carrots to wean the radical regime away from communism or immoderation. For conservatives or globalists, the exact reverse is the case: try to moderate the authoritarian but punish the Communist totalitarian. As Jeane Kirkpatrick argued in her classic article "Dictatorships and Double Standards," chances are we will be more successful in the long run with the Right-wing authoritarians. Even without a charismatic figure like Castro, chances are that the Batista regime would have come to an end sooner rather than later.

In the end, it is difficult to see how Eisenhower could have known in time that Batista should have been eased out, or how he could have known Castro's carefully hidden intentions. To argue, then, that Eisenhower "lost" Cuba to communism is to expect our government to be both omniscient and omnipresent. Similarly, to argue that Eisenhower is responsible for Castro's behavior is to elevate beyond reason the impact which the United States can be expected to exert on the behavior of other nations and leaders.

V

DEVELOPMENT AND CONFLICT IN U.S.–LATIN AMERICAN RELATIONS

Well before the Cuban Revolution, U.S. policy documents and actions demonstrated that the United States placed Latin America within the prism of the East-West conflict. Security took precedence over all considerations, including democracy and development, the latter being at the top of Latin America's agenda in the relationship with its northern neighbor. As the Guatemalan case demonstrates, democracy became the first fatality of U.S. Cold War policy in Latin America as the objective in Washington turned to blocking communist expansion. As George Kennan's 1950s memo (discussed in the previous section) indicated, political stability, even if it meant supporting dictators, had to take precedence over democracy and development.

In the area of development, the message of the Truman and Eisenhower administrations was disappointing to Latin Americans. In the late 1940s Latin America was in the throes of tremendous social, political, and economic change. Many reformist regimes sought to address the historical socioeconomic problems of the region such as poverty, income inequality, maldistribution of land, and social injustice. Latin America turned to the United States for help but that country had other, more pressing areas in which it wanted to spend its foreign aid. At the Bogotá Conference that created the Organization of American States in 1948, Latin Americans failed to receive a U.S. commitment for an economic assistance program akin to the European Marshall Plan. U.S. representatives at the meeting stated that rather than expecting U.S. aid, Latin America should open its economies to trade and investments to generate growth and development. No massive aid program was in the works for Latin America.

When John F. Kennedy became president in 1961, the administration changed course and designed a multi-billion-dollar assistance program that combined

U.S. foreign aid with support for democratic reform. The Kennedy administration believed there was a direct link between poverty and revolution. The principal objective was to prevent future revolutions such as the one in Cuba by assisting Latin America with its development needs. Although it was heralded as a dramatic shift in U.S. policy, the Alliance for Progress was nothing more than the administration's own approach to meeting the principal U.S. Cold War concerns—hemispheric security and anticommunism.

Jerome Levinson and Juan de Onís's book *The Alliance That Lost Its Way: A Critical Report on the Alliance for Progress* addresses some of the weaknesses and failures of the assistance program. The excerpt included here criticizes the "arrogance" of a Kennedy administration that believed the United States could resolve Latin America's historically entrenched socioeconomic problems by designing and implementing an assistance program. Moreover, the authors note the extent to which the United States misunderstood the roots of Latin America's development problems. In the end, rather than stabilizing the region, the Alliance for Progress accelerated a process of modernization that, as Samuel Huntington described in his classic 1968 work *Political Order in Changing Societies,* contributed to social chaos and instability. The absence or weakness of institutions and the inability of the state to adjust to and accommodate the "politicization of social forces" created an environment that led to "revolutionary conditions." In the face of such a threat the military, with the support of the Johnson and Nixon administrations, staged coups during the 1960s and 1970s. Ironically, then, Kennedy's Alliance for Progress helped to create the exact circumstances it was attempting to contain—social polarization, chaos, and military authoritarianism.

In the late 1970s and the 1980s three crises loomed that led to conflict and confrontation between the United States and Latin America. The first of these was financial. In the late 1960s Latin America began to borrow heavily to finance major infrastructure and development projects. This process—during the 1970s—was expanded and accelerated because of low interest rates and the international financial system's willingness to disburse capital to recycle widely available petrodollars. Rather than investing the loans in productive activities, much of the money went to consumption and corruption. When interest rates rose rapidly in the early 1980s, a recession hit the developed countries; Latin America found itself with an unprecedented debt service obligation and no way to pay. This crisis culminated with the Mexican moratorium and bailout of 1982. Throughout much of what Margaret Daly Hayes has called the "lost decade" of the 1980s, Latin America's standard of living fell precipitously.[1] The United States, arguing that the entire debt crisis was a simple liquidity problem, made no real effort until the late 1980s with the Brady Plan to assist Latin America with its huge financial burden. The debt crisis became a source of tremendous friction between Washington and Latin America, with many Latin

Americans arguing that the developed world was using debt to reassert its hegemony in the region by forcing a relationship of "dependence" on U.S. capital and markets.

Riordan Roett's chapter traces and examines the Latin American debt crisis, focusing on the many "plans" offered to resolve the situation. Roett also offers important insight into the interdependence entailed by the debt crisis. In other words, he links the debt servicing problem to the threat of a possible financial and economic crisis in the United States and Europe.

The second crisis during the 1980s that drove hemispheric relations to one of the lowest points of the Cold War involved Central America. President Ronald Reagan was determined to make Central America the new battleground of the Cold War, an area in which the Soviet Union would not be allowed to make any strategic headway. In Nicaragua the administration showcased the Reagan Doctrine—supporting anticommunist guerrillas (i.e., contras, from the Spanish *contra-revolucionario* [counterrevolutionary]) fighting a counterrevolutionary war against a Soviet-Cuban ally (the Sandinistas). In El Salvador and Guatemala the Reagan administration was determined to prevent friendly but politically vulnerable governments from falling to communism, in spite of the fact that those governments were often gross violators of human rights. The administration was clearly engrossed by and obsessed with Central America, paying little attention to other issues of import to Latin America—including the debt. Despite efforts by some Latin American countries, including the so-called Contadora Group (Colombia, Mexico, Panama, Venezuela) and its support alliance, to mitigate the impact of the Cold War in the region and Central Americans' own attempts to establish a peace process, Washington was determined to "make a stand" in the region (by supporting conflict) and to eliminate any last vestige of Soviet-Cuban influence in the region.

The chapter by Robert Pastor, a National Security Council official in the Carter administration, examines U.S.-Nicaraguan relations in the context of U.S. policy toward revolutionary processes and governments in Latin America. According to Pastor the United States repeated the same policy and therefore made the same mistakes. Rather than support the process of change to avoid polarization and anti-Americanism, U.S. policy achieved the opposite objective—that is, it adopted approaches that have contributed to, if not exacerbated, radicalism, polarization, and anti-Americanism. As Pastor has noted in other published work, Washington's policy toward Central America had more to do with reversing the decline of U.S. power in Latin America than with staving off a perceived threat to U.S. interests emanating from Central America.

The final crisis in hemispheric relations during the 1980s involved drug trafficking. This part includes an important chapter by Bruce M. Bagley and Juan G. Tokatlian, noted experts on drug trafficking and U.S. policy toward Latin America. The authors review U.S. drug policy in the 1980s and demonstrate its many flaws, specifically from the perspective of Washington's shortsighted and counterproductive supply-side approach. On a conceptual level, the authors note that U.S. policy was dominated by Cold War, realist assumptions inadequate for dealing with such a complex and interdependent problem. The George H. W. Bush administration's emphasis on repression and unilateralism, rather than co-operation and multilateralism, exacerbated the political, social, and economic consequences of drug trafficking in the Americas. Indeed, for Latin America, the 1980s is remembered as a lost decade because of missed opportunities and misguided policies from Washington.

18

The Alliance That Lost Its Way: A Critical Report on the Alliance for Progress

Jerome Levinson and Juan de Onís

In this 1970 critical analysis of President Kennedy's heralded Latin American policy, the authors assert that Washington's plan to seek security through development was doomed to fail because of the "overambitious idealism of its development goals and the pointless obsessiveness of its concern for security." This excerpt from Levinson and de Onís's acclaimed text on the Alliance for Progress cogently characterizes the weaknesses of this massive endeavor. Specifically, the authors suggest (contrary to the thinking of developmentalists like W. W. Rostow) that the United States could not simply contribute to the development of developing economies by channeling massive amounts of funds to those economies. Moreover, the notion that societal transformation combined with economic growth and development would lead to political stability and democracy was equally flawed. Levinson and de Onís note that the alliance's greatest short- coming was its inability to transform rigid and antiquated social structures and institutions that impeded the "trickling down" of development aid. Democracy and social reform needed to precede development if all groups, particularly the most marginal, were to benefit from Kennedy's program. This chapter begins with President Kennedy's announcement of the Alliance for Progress at the White House in 1961.

Address by John F. Kennedy at a White House reception for members of Congress and the diplomatic corps of the Latin American republics, March 13, 1961

[. . .] We meet together as firm and ancient friends, united by history and experi- ence and by our determination to advance the values of American civilization. For this New World of ours is not a mere accident of geography. Our nations are the product of a common struggle, the revolt from colonial rule. And our people share a common heritage, the quest for the dignity and the freedom of man. [. . .]

Throughout Latin America, a continent rich in resources and in the spiritual and cultural achievements of its people, millions of men and women suffer the daily degradations of poverty and hunger. They lack decent shelter or protection from disease. Their children are deprived of the education or the jobs which are the gateway to a better life. And each day the problems grow more urgent. Population growth is outpacing economic growth; low living standards are further endangered; and discontent—the discontent of a people who know that abundance and the tools of progress are at last within their reach—that discontent is growing. In the words of José Figueres, "once dormant peoples are struggling upward toward the sun, toward a better life."

If we are to meet a problem so staggering in its dimensions, our approach must itself be equally bold—an approach consistent with the majestic concept of Operation Pan America. Therefore I have called on all people of the hemisphere to join in a new Alliance for Progress—Alianza para Progreso—a vast cooperative effort, unparalleled in magnitude and nobility of purpose, to satisfy the basic needs of the American people for homes, work and land, health, and schools—*techo, trabajo, y tierra, salud y escuela.*

First, I propose that the American republics begin on a vast new ten-year plan for the Americas, a plan to transform the 1960s into a historic decade of democratic progress.

These ten years will be the years of maximum progress, maximum effort, the years when the greatest obstacles must be overcome, the years when the need for assistance will be the greatest.

And if we are successful, if our effort is bold enough and determined enough, the close of this decade will mark the beginning of a new era in the American experience. The living standards of every American family will be on the rise, basic education will be available to all, hunger will be a forgotten experience, the need for massive outside help will have passed, most nations will have entered a period of self-sustaining growth, and though there will be still much to do, every American republic will be the master of its own revolution and its own hope and progress.

Let me stress that only the most determined efforts of the American nations themselves can bring success to this effort. They and they alone can mobilize their resources, enlist the energies of their people, and modify their social patterns so that all, and not just a privileged few, share in the fruits of growth. If this effort is made, then outside assistance will give vital impetus to progress; without it, no amount of help will advance the welfare of the people. Thus if the countries of Latin America are ready to do their part, and I am sure they are, then I believe the United States, for its part, should help provide resources of a scope and magnitude sufficient to make this bold development plan a success—just as we helped to provide, against equal odds nearly, the resources adequate to help rebuild the economies of western Europe. For only an effort of towering dimensions can ensure fulfillment of our plan for a decade of progress.

Secondly, I will shortly request a ministerial meeting of the Inter-American Economic and Social Council, a meeting at which we can begin the massive planning effort which will be at the heart of the Alliance for Progress.

For if our Alliance is to succeed, each Latin nation must formulate long-range plans which establish targets and priorities, ensure monetary stability, establish the machinery for vital social change, stimulate private activity and initiative, and provide for a maximum national effort. These plans will be the foundation of our development effort, and the basis for the allocation of outside resources. [. . .]

Third, I have this evening signed a request to the Congress for $500 million as a first step in fulfilling the Act of Bogotá. This is the first large-scale inter-American effort, instituted by my predecessor, President Eisenhower, to attack the social barriers which block economic progress. The money will be used to combat illiteracy, improve the productivity and use of land, wipe out disease, attack archaic tax and land-tenure structures, provide educational opportunities, and offer a broad range of projects designed to make the benefits of increasing abundance available to all. We will begin to commit these funds as soon as they are appropriated.

Fourth, we must support all economic integration which is a genuine step toward larger markets and greater competitive opportunity. The fragmentation of Latin American economies is a serious barrier to industrial growth. Projects such as the Central American Common Market and free-trade areas of South America can help to remove these obstacles.

Fifth, the United States is ready to cooperate in serious, case-by-case examinations of commodity market problems. Frequent violent change in commodity prices seriously injures the economies of many Latin American countries, draining their resources and stultifying their growth. Together we must find practical methods of bringing an end to this pattern.

Sixth, we will immediately step up our Food for Peace emergency program, help establish food reserves in areas of recurrent drought, help provide school lunches for children, and offer feed grains for use in rural development. For hungry men and women cannot wait for economic discussions or diplomatic meetings—their need is urgent, and their hunger rests heavily on the conscience of their fellow men.

Seventh, [. . .] I invite Latin American scientists to work with us in new projects in fields such as medicine and agriculture, physics and astronomy, and desalinization, to help plan for regional research laboratories in these and other fields, and to strengthen cooperation between American universities and laboratories. [. . .]

Eighth, we must rapidly expand the training of those needed to man the economies of rapidly developing countries. This means expanded technical training programs, for which the Peace Corps, for example, will be available when needed. It also means assistance to Latin American universities, graduate schools, and research institutes. [. . .]

Ninth, we reaffirm our pledge to come to the defense of any American nation whose independence is endangered. As its confidence in the collective security system of the OAS [Organization of American States] spreads, it will be possible to devote to constructive use a major share of those resources now spent on the instruments of war. Even now, as the government of Chile has said, the time has come to take the first steps toward sensible limitation of arms. And the new generation of military leaders has shown an increasing awareness that armies cannot only defend their countries; they can, as we have learned through our own Corps of Engineers, help to build them.

Tenth, we invite our friends in Latin America to contribute to the enrichment of life and culture in the United States. We need teachers of your literature and history and tradition, opportunities for our young people to study in your universities, access to your music, your art, and the thought of your great philosophers. For we know we have much to learn. [. . .] With steps such as these, we propose to complete the revolution of the Americas, to build a hemisphere where all men can hope for a suitable standard of living, and all can live out their lives in dignity and in freedom. To achieve this goal political freedom must accompany material progress. Our Alliance for Progress is an alliance of free governments, and it must work to eliminate tyranny from a hemisphere in which it has no rightful place. Therefore let us express our special friendship to the people of Cuba and the Dominican Republic, and the hope they will soon rejoin the society of free men, uniting with us in common effort. This political freedom must be accompanied by social change. For unless necessary social reforms, including land and tax reform, are freely made—unless we broaden the opportunity for all of our people—unless the great mass of Americans share in increasing prosperity—then our alliance, our revolution, our dream, and our freedom will fail. But we call for social change by free men—change in the spirit of Washington and Jefferson, of Bolívar and San Martín and Martí—not change which seeks to impose on men tyrannies which we cast out a century and a half ago. Our motto is what it has always been: Progress, yes; tyranny, no—*progreso, sí; tiranía, no!* [. . .]¹

THE ALLIANCE: A PRELIMINARY AUDIT

The birth of the Alliance for Progress in 1961 marked a dramatic and fundamental reorientation of Washington's policy toward Latin America. Since World War II, Latin American officials had been appealing for a regional aid program of substantial proportions, an appeal that gathered strength and conviction with the success of the Marshall Plan in Europe. Washington, under Truman, had responded to these appeals by explaining, with a diplomat's tact and a lawyer's logic, that the purpose of the $27 billion in aid that the United States had supplied for the reconstruction of western Europe was primarily to meet the challenge of Soviet communism, but that the development needs of Latin America, where no such security threat was present, could be satisfied largely by private foreign capital, provided the region maintained a good investment climate.

Until shortly before the creation of the Alliance, U.S. public economic cooperation with Latin America was limited to financing exports of U.S. equipment, to long-term sales of agricultural commodities, and to a modest technical assistance program for demonstration and training in health, education, and agriculture. When development funds were mentioned, the Latin Americans were advised to get into line, along with other developing countries, for credits from the International Bank for Reconstruction and Development (IBRD); and they were told that balance-of-payments assistance was available from the International Monetary Fund (IMF).

But in the last years of the Eisenhower administration, Washington's attitude — avuncular, haughty, and parsimonious, mainly because the exigencies of the Cold War diverted its preoccupation and priorities elsewhere—began to change. The cause was clear. A wave of rebellions had swept out of power a number of military dictators whom the U.S. State Department had previously hailed as champions of anticommunist stability in Latin America. Not the least of these rebellions was Fidel Castro's stunning overthrow of the Cuban dictator Fulgencio Batista in 1959. At precisely that juncture the change in Washington became perceptible. The Eisenhower administration put up $350 million as the initial capital of the new Inter-American Development Bank; Congress authorized a $500 million fund for social investments in Latin America, such as low-cost housing, urban water-supply systems, credits to small farmers, and education; and the United States belatedly joined an international agreement to stabilize coffee prices. It was a good start, generous and positive when compared with the help that had been provided before, but modest and unassuming when compared with what was to come.

The fundamental change began when John F. Kennedy, at the very beginning of his administration, spoke in bold and heady terms of billion dollar aid for a decade of planned economic development and social reform in the hemisphere. His message proposing the Alliance for Progress was an invigorating mixture of compassion and hope, ambition and urgency, which quickened the hopes of millions throughout Latin America. Reformist political ideas, concepts of economic planning, and a host of other notions that had been confined to the fringes of inter-American discussions suddenly found wide audiences. The result was a striking improvement in the U.S. dialogue with the Latin Americans, particularly those whom the Kennedy administration identified as the agents of democratic change and social reform, and an almost euphoric belief in what they could achieve.

Many of these political leaders, economic planners, and intellectual innovators — described loosely as the "democratic left"—as well as younger, more radical exponents of revolutionary change, had risen to prominence in the Latin American rebellions of the late 1950s. The senior figures of the democratic left, President Rómulo Betancourt of Venezuela and President Alberto Lleras Camargo of Colombia, were essentially New Dealers in political outlook, and they fell in naturally with the New Frontier president in the White House. With these leaders, and the expectation that other modern and moderate political reformers would come forward throughout Latin America, the confident policymakers in the new administration of President Kennedy formulated in the Alliance for Progress a bold and comprehensive ideology of democratic development. It postulated not only rapid economic growth (the dominant goal of the Marshall Plan) and social reform (which has played a part in southeast

Asian development programs), but at the same time the strengthening of representative political democracy.

Cuba's growing allegiance to the Communist bloc helped to accelerate and shape the creation of the Alliance as a democratic alternative to Cuba's revolutionary socialist formula for development in Latin America. As its architects in Washington and throughout Latin America conceived it, support from the United States would enable the democratic left to bring about economic development and fundamental social change within a framework of representative political institutions.

If idealism was a strong element in the Alliance, so were overconfidence and even brashness. It was assumed, for instance, that Latin America's ruling classes would refrain from obstructing the process of democratic development, presumably on the grounds that, as President Kennedy said, "those who make peaceful revolution impossible will make violent revolution inevitable." And the United States would protect the process from Castro-inspired or supported disruption by providing counterinsurgency training and equipment for the Latin American military and maintaining or establishing CIA stations in each country.

THE QUANTITATIVE PROMISES

Yet the Charter of Punta del Este, which formally established the Alliance, sought to express the ideology of democratic development in terms of the Latin American reality. The charter enumerated certain objectives, some of them specific, which the Alliance was to achieve by 1970, and which can now be used as yardsticks against which to measure its performance.

The primary objective, on which all others were thought to hinge, was an economic growth rate of "not less than 2.5 percent per capita per year" in each Latin American country. Since the region's population growth rate remained at 3 percent a year (the charter contained no reference to the population question), production of goods and services would have had to increase at a rate of more than 5 percent a year to reach this target. [. . .]

The second objective was a more equitable distribution of national income, providing a fairer share of the projected increases to the poorer working class and peasants—the great majorities at the depressed base of the Latin American social structure. According to estimates for nine Latin American countries (including Argentina, Brazil, and Mexico), between 1960 and 1963 the wealthy upper 10 percent of the population received about 42 percent of national income while the poor bottom half received only 14 to 21 percent. A survey taken in 1968 shows little if any change in this structure of gross income inequality. Only Chile seems to have accomplished a significant redistribution of income in favor of the poor. [. . .]

Still another objective was fuller utilization of the region's natural and human resources in the form of increased industrialization and reduced unemployment. But although industrialization has advanced significantly in most Latin American countries, unemployment has not been reduced. According to estimates by the Economic Commission for Latin America (ECLA), the supply of jobs in relation to the size of the labor force has increased more slowly during this decade than during the 1950s, and unemployment, partly disguised as underemployment, has risen from 18 million persons in 1960 to 25 million now. [. . .] The Latin American economies—even those that are growing quite rapidly—are unable to absorb the growing contingents of young job seekers that enter the labor market each year.

The charter proposed "to raise greatly the level of agricultural productivity and output and to improve related storage, transportation, and marketing services." Advances have been made in the agricultural area, with Latin America's food production increasing by 4 percent annually, a step ahead of population growth, while investment in the modern commercial agricultural sector has been strong. But, according to the *Rockefeller Report*, "While overall food production is going up, food production per person, due to the population explosion, is estimated at 10 percent less than it was at the end of World War II. And each year there are eight million more mouths to feed."

The charter recommended agrarian reform, including, "where required," the transformation of "unjust structures of land tenure and use." But progress toward a more equitable structure of land tenure and rural income distribution has been very slow. Mexico, Venezuela, and Bolivia have moved ahead with pre-Alliance agrarian reform programs; Chile and Colombia have made real efforts; and Peru has begun to apply what appears on paper to be the most radical agrarian reform law since Cuba's. Other countries, including Brazil, haven't even tried. In the lifetime of the Alliance the number of peasants seeking land has grown more rapidly than the number of family lots provided by division of estates, colonization, and entitling of squatters.

In education the goal was "to eliminate adult illiteracy and by 1970 to assure, as a minimum, access to six years of primary education for each school-age child in Latin America." Unfortunately, the decade has seen no significant increase in adult literacy. To be sure, the percentage of children not enrolled in primary schools did decline from 52 percent to 43 percent between 1960 and 1967. But at the end of 1967 an estimated 27 million school-age children—about three-quarters of a million more than in 1960—were still receiving no formal education.

The health goals were to add five years to life expectancy, to halve the infant mortality rate, and, for this purpose, to provide potable water and sewage-disposal systems for not less than 70 percent of the urban and 50 percent of the rural population. In fact, life expectancy has been extended somewhat, the infant mortality rate has been somewhat reduced, and some water systems have been built, but the specific goals are still remote. [. . .]

The charter also called for economic integration ultimately taking the form of a Latin American common market, but:

> After more promising initial progress, economic integration in Latin America has reached a plateau from which further significant advances will require considerably more effort on the part of Latin American governments to take the action necessary to achieve stated objectives, as well as substantially more time than had been anticipated.

The first step toward achievement of all these objectives, was to be the formulation of national development programs on the principles of self-help and "the maximum use of domestic resources, taking into account the special conditions of each country," but including the "necessary structural reforms."

Specifically, the main economic burden of the development programs was to fall upon those in Latin America who could pay for them, through tax reforms "demanding more from those who have most." At the end of the decade, in Latin America as a whole, tax collections, primarily as a result of improved administrative techniques and organization rather than structural reforms, had increased in real terms by 35 percent since 1961. This increase is about the same as the region's cumulative growth of domestic product and thus is far from spectacular.

During the Alliance decade, domestic savings were to provide 80 percent of the capital for necessary investment. In fact, according to the Inter-American Committee on the Alliance for Progress (*Comité Interamericana de la Alianza para el Progreso*, or CIAP), domestic savings have financed 90 percent, largely because of a shortage of foreign investment.

In the charter the United States undertook for the first time to support Latin American development with a specific long-term financial commitment:

> A supply of capital from all external sources during the coming ten years of at least $20 billion [to] be made available to the Latin American countries with priority to the relatively less developed countries. The greater part of this sum should be in the form of public funds.

The charter failed to specify whether this figure was to be gross or net (after Latin American repayment on existing debt). Thus between 1961 and 1969 Latin America received over $18 billion from all external sources. However, more than half of its foreign long-term credits were offset by the cost of servicing past foreign loans, an outflow that continues to mount.

The charter made four references to foreign private investment. Though positive, they were brief and vague. The U.S. business community viewed their brevity as a rebuff by the Kennedy administration and their vagueness as a refusal to provide security against expropriation. Thus during the early years of the Alliance new U.S. private investment in Latin America declined considerably, and the business community sought security for existing investments from Congress, through, for example, the Hickenlooper Amendment. However, in 1964, with the Castro threat receding and Thomas Mann, known as a friend of business, in the State Department, U.S. investment in Latin American began to expand once again.

When the Alliance began, many Latin American countries were deeply in debt and virtually unable to meet their debt payments. A substantial amount of early Alliance lending went to refinance the existing debts. At the same time, the trend in U.S. private investment in the region has been toward Latin American-based manufacturing for local markets, generally increasing the region's imports of raw materials without increasing its exports. Thus Latin America's annual payments of principal and interest on loans, together with profit remittances by foreign investors, have been rising much more rapidly than exports. [. . .]

THE QUALITATIVE PERFORMANCE

But though the Alliance has not come close to most of its explicit objectives and specific targets, it has had some significant results. The decade has given Latin America a new development consciousness, which has permeated large segments of the population (including two of the region's most tradition-oriented institutions, the military and the church). Economic planning, particularly in Brazil, Colombia, and Chile, has reached an impressive level of sophistication, and throughout the hemisphere young, technically trained people are playing major roles in the key public-sector institutions. At the same time, the private sector contains a growing middle level of successful entrepreneurs and an increasing number of efficient industrial managers.

This new sophistication has been accompanied, in many cases, by a profound disillusionment with the Alliance, based in part on failure to reach the charter's targets. Viewed in retrospect, the targets themselves reflect not only the projections of the Latin American development experts but also the optimism with which the Kennedy administration (intentionally, although not cynically) had infused inter-American relations. But hindsight also shows that the problems of development are more difficult, and the political consequences of unfulfilled expectations more disastrous, than the authors of the charter ever anticipated.

The Alliance, defined as the record of inter-American relations in the past decade, provides additional justification for disillusionment. If it has succeeded in preventing any new Castro from coming to power in the hemisphere, it has done so by military means, failing conspicuously to advance the cause of the democratic left. The United States has intervened openly in the Dominican Republic and less obviously in Brazil and Guatemala to assist not the democratic left but the military and civilian forces of conservatism. In disputes between Latin American governments and U.S. corporations, the United States has applied economic pressures against the Latin American governments with a fine disregard for the disputed issues. Loan officials have consistently required that countries seeking financial assistance undertake monetary stabilization programs; they have not required programs of social reform. The U.S. Congress and the executive branch have restricted loan funds to purchases of U.S. goods (particularly those that are not competitively priced) and such other uses as are consistent with a favorable U.S. balance of payments.

These policies have raised serious doubts about both the U.S. commitment to democratic development in Latin America and the Alliance formula for attaining it. They have also given the left and the right in many Latin American countries a common cause: nationalistic opposition to what both regard as a dominating U.S. presence. This opposition has taken forms ranging from restrictions on the acquisition of local banks by U.S. banks to outright expropriation, and has given momentum to at least two successful military coups d'état. [. . .]

The spirit in which the U.S. Congress agreed to the creation of the Alliance was less one of compassion for Latin America's needy millions than fear of a spread of Castroism. Even when this fear was at its height, the Congress was less generous in its appropriation of funds than President Kennedy had wished. And as the urgency of the Castro threat diminished, so did the annual Alliance appropriation. At the same time, the priority and cost of the Vietnam War were rising. Preoccupied with Vietnam, the U.S. government has treated Latin America as either a means of shoring up the balance of payments or a potential site for revolutions that might endanger the "national security."

The United States has devoted the largest single portion of its regional aid during the past decade to the development program of authoritarian Brazil.[2] Such allocation may be consistent with the size and importance of Brazil, but it is inconsistent with the criteria for Alliance lending set forth in the charter. Although U.S. policy-makers have debated this issue at great length, they have usually resolved it by giving greater weight to a country's economic performance than to its political or social conditions in determining loan allocations.

Of course the United States has also supplied assistance to Latin American countries in which constitutional processes, accountability of public officials, electoral contests, and party debates have both contributed to the establishment of social reforms and proved compatible with good economic management. But the priority of economic considerations goes far to explain the difference between aims and achievements under the Alliance for Progress.

These considerations have traditionally dominated U.S. policy in Latin America. The Alliance was designed to break free of them. Its fate raises vital questions about the purposes and consequences of foreign development assistance for both donor and recipient. [. . .]

EPILOGUE: AFTER THE ALLIANCE

A decade of the Alliance for Progress has yielded more shattered hopes than solid accomplishment, more discord than harmony, more disillusionment than satisfaction. The progress has been halting, painful, and uneven, and the nations allied are discontented, restless, and tense. Without the Alliance the Latin American experience in the 1960s might have been even more turbulent. But the Alliance was unable to impose reconciliation on the fundamental conflicts it sought to overcome. It was a dramatic and noble crusade, deriving from excessive idealism and over-optimism, a momentum that was slowly but indisputably dissipated in encounters with harsh realities—economic, political, social.

To be sure, most proponents of the Alliance in the United States considered themselves hardheaded and realistic. They viewed stepped-up support by Washington for national development in Latin America not only as a constructive and generous gesture toward the developing republics of the south, but as an essential and reasonable means of protecting the vital security interest of the United States. As they conceived it, the Alliance could counteract the appeal of Castroism to Latin America's once docile masses of workers and peasants by offering them economic benefits and social reform within a democratic political framework. In retrospect, the program designed to kill two birds with one stone has hit neither squarely. It has not removed the danger of revolution and it has not brought significant economic, social, and political advancement to the poor of Latin America.

Some of the internal contradictions of the Alliance were apparent even at its birth. The Pentagon had little confidence in the ability of reformers to maintain political stability in Latin America. The U.S. business community pointed out that the emphasis on reform was likely to produce economic instability and a poor climate for U.S. investment. And a great deal of the original enthusiasm for the Alliance was lost once the Cuban missile crisis reduced the appeal of Castroism in Latin America and its ability to arouse fear in Washington. Within the first few years of the decade, the reformist elements in Latin America proved less effective than their supporters in the United States had hoped, and administration officials learned that development in Latin America was a far more complex, expensive, and far-reaching process than reconstruction had been in western Europe.

Conventional development assistance usually serves to accelerate the economic growth of the recipient country. The economic benefits will tend to follow the recipient country's existing pattern of income distribution; unless they are accompanied by social or political restructuring, they will go primarily to those who already hold wealth and power. The Alliance principle of distributing the benefits of economic growth throughout a society by means of social and political reforms was new to both development economists and loan officials in the United States. But experience soon showed them that social and political reforms were indeed destabilizing. Thus they gradually narrowed their focus to monetary stabilization and economic growth, in which they achieved significant advances, particularly toward the end of the decade. In education and agriculture they turned their efforts away from adult literacy and agrarian reform, to technical education and agricultural production. These changes reflect not only an increasing technocratic orientation but a shift of political concern from bettering the lives of the marginal masses to protecting the key elements of the core society. [. . .]

THE LESSONS OF THE ALLIANCE

What considerations, then, should shape future U.S. policy in the hemisphere? By and large, the major lesson of the Alliance is that the reach of the United States should not exceed its grasp. Between the overambitious idealism of its development goals and the pointless obsessiveness of its concern for security, the United States really undermined the Alliance before it could get started. When the security issue lost its urgency and when other problems arose to demand higher priority—the war in Vietnam, the need to defend the dollar, the pressure of protectionist lobbies, the domestic urban crisis—the Alliance was deflated and distorted. The resulting situation is the worst of both worlds. The people of the United States feel that their generosity has not been appreciated and, in view of both domestic inflation and pressing domestic needs, appear unwilling to do more, while Latin Americans generally resent the restrictions placed on use of the funds made available, as well as the patronizing attitude with which they were often provided. [. . .]

Another lesson of the Alliance is that a profound and perhaps very painful readjustment is taking place in Latin America, one that the United States may influence in minor ways but cannot begin to dominate or direct. Basic relationships—economic, political, and social—are being strained, broken down, rebuilt, and strained again, a process that must continue until it produces a new balance. In all likelihood, the upheaval that began before the Alliance but accelerated under it will become even more pronounced in the years ahead, so that further upheaval and experimentation and change will be the rule rather than the exception. Already various forms of authoritarian government have emerged; others are almost sure to follow. The United States, as a democracy dedicated to constitutional processes and civil liberties, cannot provide financial assistance to authoritarian regimes without calling its own political system into question. This limitation on policy may make an Alliance impossible, but it is a real and practical constraint that springs from the nature of democracy.

[. . .] The lesson that the Alliance has taught in this critical area is that the United States must learn to live with and expect change, and that its response should be flexible and measured rather than excessively rigid or tough. In fact, long before the Alliance, the United States learned that it could accommodate such revolutionary change; in both Mexico and Bolivia it accepted new property relationships without permanent damage to its own interests.

It is safe to predict that in the coming decade inter-American relationships will face fresh uncertainties and harsh tests that demand policies much more effective than those of the Alliance decade. Policy-makers must use greater realism and sophistication in both the making and the implementation of commitments. They must also deepen their awareness of and sensitivity to the internal conflicts afflicting the varied social classes of Latin America. And they must achieve a profound and sure understanding of just what constitutes the national interest of the United States in its relations with its sister republics.

19

Condemned to Repetition: The United States and Nicaragua

Robert Pastor

In this reading, Robert Pastor, director of Latin American affairs in the Carter Administration's National Security Council, offers a keen and unique analysis of U.S. policy toward Nicaragua in the 1970s and early 1980s. Although the chapter focuses on Nicaragua, Pastor makes important generalizations about and comparisons of U.S. policy toward revolutionary processes and governments— specifically in Cuba—to demonstrate Washington's inclination to repeat the same mistakes when it deals with revolutionary governments in Latin America. A pattern to U.S. policy evolves from, first, support of and later dissociation from a right-wing dictatorship (Batista and Somoza) to identification with the revolutionary goals and a search for a moderate third force to, finally, confrontation with the revolutionary regime. Pastor notes that U.S.-Nicaraguan relations did not occur in a vacuum. Other nations, particularly in Central America, supported the FSLN (Sandinistas) and sought to reduce what they believed was the polarizing and destabilizing presence and policy of the United States. Like the authors in the previous chapters, Pastor attempts to explore the domestic and international factors in the United States and Nicaragua that, as in most other revolutionary nations (except Bolivia), led to an inevitable confrontation between the United States and revolutionary governments.

REPEATING U.S. POLICY: SEVEN STAGES

With almost uncanny precision, U.S. policy toward Nicaragua passed through each of the seven stages of U.S.-Cuban relations twenty years before: from identification with the regime in 1974 to indirect war in 1982.

1. *Identification.* The power of Anastasio Somoza Garcia and his two sons rested first on their control of the Guard, second on a united Liberal Party, and third on their identification with the United States. The United States sometimes protested or rejected that identification, and in 1945, 1947–1948, 1963, and 1978–1979 tried to encourage Somoza to step down or not to seek reelection. Nevertheless, at critical periods during the Cold War and during the tenure of two U.S. Ambassadors, Thomas Whelan and Turner Shelton, the United States identified its interests with those of the Somoza family. It was a short-sighted policy in which the United States paid a heavy price.

2. *Distance and Dissociation.* In 1975, after the resignation of Richard Nixon and his Ambassador, the United States began to distance itself from Somoza. The Carter Administration withdrew U.S. support from Somoza, but it initially rejected the opposition's request to mediate because it wanted to separate itself from a past in which it had been the pivotal political actor in Nicaragua. It altered this preferred policy in September 1978, when it appeared that Somoza was trying to eliminate the moderate option and leave Nicaraguans and Americans with a simple but unacceptable choice between Somoza and the Communists. There was a consensus in the Administration that the longer Somoza remained in power the more likely it was that the Sandinistas would win a violent revolution. The issue became how to prevent that worst-case scenario without harming other interests.

    The United States reluctantly decided to mediate, but it did so in small steps that permitted policy makers to think that the change did not weaken the Administration's commitment to nonintervention and that it reinforced other principles, like regional cooperation. Carter's first decision was to support a Central American mediation effort, and when that failed, he insisted that U.S. mediation be undertaken within a multilateral framework under the auspices of the OAS [Organization of American States].

    To those inside and outside the Administration who had a different view of the appropriate U.S. role, each decision by the Administration was frustrating and inadequate. A more pragmatic perspective recommended that the United States force Somoza's departure. Although President Carter's aversion to mediation was overcome, he was reluctant to accept a unilateral strategy because he believed a multilateral approach was in the best long-term interests of the United States, and he would not approve overthrowing Somoza. Instead of forcing Somoza's resignation, the Carter Administration tried to negotiate the terms that would permit a free plebiscite. That effort failed, and the U.S. imposed sanctions against Somoza in February 1979.

3. *The Left Legitimized by the Middle.* Between February and July, the middle drifted toward the Sandinistas, as the United States had feared they would. Having failed to secure Somoza's resignation, the moderates in

Nicaragua despaired. They did not have the patience or the organization to wait; they thought the Sandinistas were more moderate than they actually were; and they ignored the United States and listened to Costa Rica, Panama, and Venezuela, all of whom had decided that the only way to displace Somoza was by helping the Sandinistas. Alfonso Robelo later explained that he joined the Junta of the Revolutionary Government "because the support of [Omar] Torrijos, Carlos Andrés Pérez, and [Rodrigo] Carazo [Odio] gave me confidence that it was the right thing to do."

The intrinsic weakness of a policy of distance and dissociation is that it ultimately depends on the blind man seeing the light. Having decided not to overthrow Somoza and having been unable to encourage his departure through sanctions, the United States lacked a policy during this period. All it could do was hope that the blind man, Somoza, would see. Instead, the blind man was struck by lightning. In the month of June, as the Sandinistas' "final offensive" gathered military equipment and assembled political support, the United States came to recognize that its nightmare was coming true.

4. *The Search for a Third Force.* The United States searched desperately for an Executive Committee of credible moderate leaders that would assume power after Somoza's departure and call for a cease-fire. That would have allowed time for the Guard to stabilize and for the Committee to negotiate a modus vivendi with the San José Junta [Sandinistas].

The strategy failed. After the sanctions, the U.S. Embassy in Managua had few officers to maintain contacts with the opposition. By the time that Ambassador Pezzullo arrived, the moderate opposition was embittered, and many had gone to San Jose and allied with the Junta. When the moderates were ready, Somoza was intransigent, and the United States did not move him; when Somoza was ready to go, and the United States was ready to facilitate a new government, most of the moderates were not. Those few who were prepared to consider an Executive Committee wanted unequivocal assurances from the United States.

Because of Latin America's growing support for the Junta, the widening insurrection in the country, and the atrocities committed by the Guard, Carter made his support conditional on multilateral cooperation, which did not materialize. The Executive Committee idea died. Working with other leaders in the region, the Administration negotiated a final arrangement that both precluded a bloodbath and permitted a relationship to be developed with the incoming Junta.

5. *Relating to the Revolution.* After the Sandinistas' victory, the Administration sought good relations. The United States tried to help the revolution, deny it an enemy, and hope the new government would become more pragmatic and less ideological. The relationship was awkward, but the Nicaraguan government showed it was not impervious to internal or to outside Western

influence. There were signs of arbitrariness and tyranny but also of political space; independent institutions were harassed, but permitted to exist and criticize; the government seemed willing to share some power, but not all of it; the Sandinistas were interested in diversifying their relations with Europeans and Latin Americans, but reserved their principal relationships with Cuba and the Soviet Union; there was enthusiastic support for health and education, but these services were delivered in a Marxist, anti-American package; and there was moral solidarity with other revolutionaries, but the FSLN (Sandinista National Liberation Front) restrained their impulse to provide material support.

6. *Distance and Negotiation*. In mid-November 1980, despite promises, the Nicaraguan government decided to provide massive aid to the Salvadoran rebels. On receiving the evidence in its last days, the Carter Administration suspended its aid to Nicaragua. The Reagan Administration entered office with a pledge to end aid and a perception that Nicaragua and Cuba were major threats to U.S. interests. Nonetheless, the Administration negotiated with the Nicaraguan government, which halted its arms transfers to the Salvadorans. For political and ideological reasons, the Reagan Administration did not resume aid.

A second round of negotiations tested the ability of two extremely resentful governments to reach an agreement on security issues. Neither side passed the test. The Reagan Administration then walked away from the bargaining table, convinced the Sandinistas were not serious. The Sandinistas did not read the United States any better; they were unaware that this was their last chance to negotiate peacefully with the Administration.

7. *Confrontation*. President Reagan's decision to support exiles whose goal was to overthrow the Nicaraguan regime was a fateful one, which led to a gradually deepening American commitment to the rebels and an escalation of the war. The watershed occurred on March 15, 1982, when the Sandinistas declared a state of emergency in response to military attacks by the contras and the disclosure of the U.S. covert program. Prior to that date, no important Nicaraguan leader, except [Edén] Pastora, had left the country for exile. Subsequently, there was a steady stream of moderate leaders joining the violent opposition. With the intensification of the war, the political space in Nicaragua grew smaller and the dependence on Cuba and the Soviet Union increased.

EXPLAINING U.S. POLICY

From identifying with a dictator to confronting a revolutionary government: How can we explain the evolution of U.S. policy toward Nicaragua? *Repetition.* U.S.

objectives toward Nicaragua in the twentieth century can be described succinctly as seeking to: (a) preclude the emergence of a regime that might be hostile to the United States and friendly to its adversary; (b) prevent instability from being exploited by a rival power; and (c) deter or preclude Nicaragua from interfering in its neighbors' affairs. These, of course, are classic security interests and explain the continuity of U.S. concern. U.S. policy makers focus on Nicaragua when they perceive a threat to one of these interests. Then, they pursue a fourth interest: (d) to promote peaceful change by economic and political development.

The cycle in U.S. policy between neglect of Nicaragua and panic when events seem to veer in an adverse direction, an often-described cycle, is merely a restatement of the security motive that drives or stalls U.S. policy. Primary U.S. interests in Nicaragua and the region do not stem from a desire to extract resources or to implant a political philosophy, although the history of U.S. policy in Central America is replete with examples of both, but from fear, a rather unseemly fear for such a large nation facing such a small one, but a fear nevertheless that a hostile group could come to power and ally with a rival of the United States. Some U.S. policy makers have exaggerated the threat; others have underestimated it; but few have denied it.

The security motive helps to explain why and when the United States became exercised about developments in Nicaragua, and it partially explains why the United States identified with Batista and Somoza and confronted the Cuban and Nicaraguan revolutionary governments. But it does not adequately explain why the United States dissociated itself from Batista and Somoza and why it initially respected the two revolutionary governments. Nor does it explain the repetitive pattern of U.S. policy. [. . .]

For that reason, "political character" or "style" might be better for referring to the political attitudes and beliefs that North Americans use to understand and approach local and international politics. In citing "national experience" as a source of U.S. foreign policy, I want to draw a concept broad enough to include style and character; my purpose is to visualize the source of U.S. foreign policy as relatively stable but also capable of adapting as the nation's perception of itself and the world changes.

In the case of Nicaragua, the question of why the United States "so often supports dictators" is easily answered: it mostly didn't. Most U.S. administrations were uncomfortable with the Somoza regime and particularly with its attempts to identify with the United States. When did the United States support him? President Nixon shared Somoza's fervently anticommunist view of the world, and others thought the Somozas [were] hardly the worst dictators in an area that appeared to have no aptitude for democracy. When the United States needed Nicaragua's support either for specific actions in Guatemala or Cuba or for a global objective, the United States subsumed its dislike for the regime. This, of course, is the tradition in international relations.

Given this tradition, what is most surprising in U.S. policy toward Nicaragua is not the moments when it has treated Somoza well but the historically longer-lasting periods of detachment from and distaste for the regime. Since Somoza took power in 1936, the United States has spent much less time debating whether to support him than it has trying to decide what to do about him. The explanation for this resides in the political character, values, and experience of the United States, which has always given more attention to the character and internal behavior of regimes than have most other nations.

North Americans identify with the "middle" abroad, meaning not just the middle class or businessmen but rather all people and groups in favor of gradual and peaceful change. In a 1974 poll, nearly three-fourths of the American people agreed that it was "morally wrong" to support military dictatorships even if that government provided military bases for the United States. Because North Americans dislike dictators, U.S. policy makers are generally defensive about charges of supporting them. For example, when Luis Somoza visited the United States in 1959 as Nicaragua's president, he was surprised and upset that the Administration "shied away" from him. The State Department was worried, according to an internal memorandum, that official contact with Somoza would confirm "accusations that the U.S. favors dictatorships."

When the "middle" delegitimizes a dictator, U.S. officials are compelled to follow the "middle." Even a conservative Administration cannot sustain a policy of supporting a dictator if the middle groups in that country have rejected him. That explains the distancing from both Batista and Somoza. It also explains why the Reagan Administration, which had originally embraced Philippine President Ferdinand Marcos and Haitian President Jean-Claude Duvalier, kept its distance when the middle openly opposed both leaders.

The United States is uncomfortable about supporting dictators but also about overthrowing them. In response to the question whether the United States should ever consider overthrowing a Latin American government, 63 percent of the American public said no; 24 percent said yes. For an American, elections are the natural "middle path" between dictators and revolutionaries. An election is often the last idea considered by people trying to remove a dictator, but it is generally the first thought of U.S. policy makers.

Some in Latin America believe that revolution is the only way to overcome the structural barriers that prevent social justice, but almost no North Americans believe that U.S. views are shaped by an eighteenth-century constitution that encourages incrementalism. Because class mobility is the norm in the United States, North Americans reject the Marxist premise that the class struggle is permanent.

Rather than accept permanent divisions, U.S. policy generally aims to bring groups together for dialogue. Typically, the U.S. government referred to the Junta in San José as the head of the Government of National *Reconciliation* while the Junta called it the Government of National *Reconstruction*. U.S. policy makers tend to reject the idea that there are no middle options. As long as there are two views, there has to be a middle option; the only question is whether the two sides can be moved to accept a compromise. U.S. policy consistently projected this aspect of its national experience onto Nicaragua. Even the Reagan Administration repeatedly pledged to suspend support for the contras if the Sandinistas agreed to a dialogue with the contras.

An important element in the U.S. political character is the tendency to mix principle, a vision of what the United States should do, and pragmatism, what it can do. The dislike for the Somoza regime reflected the principle; the occasional compromises, pragmatism. The president pronounces the principles: for Carter, it was nonintervention, human rights, and regional consultation; for Reagan, anticommunism and democracy. The president's advisers try to apply the principle to solve problems or crises, but sometimes a principle impedes a solution to the problem. In that case, the president maintains the principle until a stronger case can be made for modifying or discarding it. Those who do not share the vision or who see an easier way to solve a problem are frustrated. But the distinction between these two points should not obscure the facts that principle rests partly on a pragmatic cost-and-benefit calculation and that the pragmatic argument often has a strong moral basis.

An important debate during the Nicaragua crisis that illustrates this tension in the national style was whether to force Somoza's resignation. The pragmatic argument was very powerful: no one could force out Somoza but the United States; failure to do so would lead to a Sandinista victory. The analysis was accepted, and it proved correct. Yet the Administration did not follow the analysis to its logical conclusion. Why? There were five reasons: the threat, the principle, the consequences, the uncertainty, and the precedent.

First, Somoza was an indirect, not a direct threat to U.S. interests. The Administration disliked Somoza's regime, but the only threat that it posed was that its continuing in power increased the chance of a Sandinista military victory, which, it was believed, was more likely to threaten U.S. interests.

Second, the principle of nonintervention was a fundamental element of Carter's approach toward Latin America, but it was not sacrosanct. As Carter stated: "We have no inclination to interfere in the internal affairs of other nations unless our direct security interests are threatened." Because Somoza did not directly threaten those interests, the United States would not intervene. "Intervention" has been defined and interpreted in many different ways. The Carter Administration defined it narrowly to mean that the United States would not unilaterally overthrow a standing government. A collective effort was viewed differently.

A third reason for not overthrowing Somoza stemmed from a concern with the consequences of the action. If the United States had forced Somoza out, it would have had to assume responsibility for the consequences, which would almost certainly have been a period of great instability. It was also possible that the National Guard, which was so closely tied to Somoza, might collapse on his departure, leaving a clear path for the Sandinistas to come to power. In short, deposing Somoza could produce the very outcome the United States wanted to avoid. Moreover, the United States would probably have had to deepen its involvement in Nicaragua to keep the opposition from fragmenting and the Guard from either disintegrating or taking power.

A fourth reason was uncertainty and a lack of information. A nation, like an individual, infrequently takes undesirable actions unless it has no other choice. As late as one month before Somoza fled Nicaragua, the United States thought a "third force" could assume power because it was unaware that the Sandinistas had accumulated an arsenal and logistics network sufficient to defeat Somoza. Nor did the United States know that the FSLN's political support from Latin American democratic governments was so deep that it could preclude a third option. [. . .]

Fifth, the decision to force the resignation of a foreign head of state is, as U.S. Speaker of the House Jim Wright said, "extreme." Somoza was despised with good reason, but compared to several other military dictators in Latin America, like Pinochet of Chile, Videla of Argentina, Stroessner of Paraguay, or Castro of Cuba, he would hardly qualify as the most ruthless. If one started by overthrowing Somoza, then where would one stop?

In sum, the United States chose not to overthrow Somoza because of a national experience that seeks "middle options" abroad as well as at home and because of a mixture of principle and pragmatism, a tension that has long shaped U.S. foreign policy. What is most illuminating is how this reluctance to overthrow a right-wing dictator in the midst of a succession crisis also characterized the policies of Eisenhower and Kennedy in the Dominican Republic (1960–1961), Kennedy (1961–1963) and Reagan (1985–1986) in Haiti, and Reagan (1985–1986) in the Philippines. In every case, the president rejected the option of pushing out a rightist dictator. In the one case where an Administration did force out a dictator—[Ngo Dinh] Diem of South Vietnam—the Kennedy Administration soon regretted it.

The U.S. predilection for the "middle" explains both the desperate search for a "third force" as the succession crisis in Nicaragua reached a climax and the decision not to intervene when the United States finally recognized the strength of the rebels' support among moderates within the country and among legitimate democratic governments in the region. From the beginning to the end of the crisis, the "middle" unknowingly stimulated, guided, and defined the parameters of U.S. policy.

In relating to the Cuban and Nicaraguan revolutionary governments, the United States was initially sympathetic, but this changed as it began to realize that the revolutionaries viewed the United States as [the] enemy and acted on that perception. Judging by the statements of Congressional supporters as well as opponents of aid to the Sandinista government, the American people had a low threshold of tolerance for virulent criticism by leaders of small, neighboring nations like Nicaragua who were at the same time requesting aid. The United States slid toward confrontation because of a visceral reaction, but it confronted Nicaragua, as it had Cuba, only when it perceived that its security interests were affected. [. . .]

As the United States repeated the seven stages in its relationship with Nicaragua, it was guided by its national experience through a polarized terrain of unattractive options. It began its journey by dissociating itself from the dictator, then searched futilely for a middle option, then stumbled through a half-hearted attempt to relate to the revolution, and finally was drawn into an unproductive confrontation. At each step, the U.S. government sought a "middle path."

EXPLAINING CHANGE

In addition to the continuity and the repetition in U.S. policy toward Nicaragua, one can also see important policy changes over time. Choices were made from a wide range of options and instruments, from trying to stabilize a dictator to trying to destabilize him, from aiding the military to assisting economic development. When faced with the prospect of Somoza taking power or being reelected, the Administration of Franklin Roosevelt remained silent, that of Harry Truman broke diplomatic relations, and that of Richard Nixon helped him secure another term. When faced with a leftist Sandinista regime, Jimmy Carter lobbied Congress to provide it [with] economic aid, and Ronald Reagan lobbied Congress to provide its enemies [with] weapons.

The United States is motivated by security concerns, but its choices of how, when, and in what ways to respond to a threat require a richer explanation. Within the parameters of the interests and values of the United States, Presidents have considerable latitude in deciding how much attention and priority to give to a particular interest or value. Each Administration's policies reflect a reaction to its predecessor and an independent judgment about which U.S. interests matter most.

Moreover, a new Administration, particularly one that represents a different party from its predecessor, tends at the beginning to overstate differences with its predecessor in order to justify its mandate for change. William Howard Taft condemned the "big stick" of Theodore Roosevelt and announced "dollar diplomacy," which in turn was criticized by Woodrow Wilson, who offered a ringing defense of liberty and democracy. Similarly, Jimmy Carter criticized the covert acts to destabilize governments by his predecessors and identified his Administration with human rights, and Ronald Reagan rebuked Carter for opening the Caribbean to Communism and enunciated a doctrine aimed at overturning leftist governments. [. . .]

Perhaps the most important single variable explaining why policies change and why Administrations choose different policies is an Administration's perception of the nature and intensity of the threat that the United States faces. The more distant the threat the more likely an Administration will adhere to its initial principles; the more immediate the threat the more likely the Administration's policy will evolve. As the Cuban and Nicaraguan crises reached a climax, the Eisenhower and the Carter Administrations began contemplating options—such as forcing the dictator's resignation—that they had rejected before.

Threat perception not only explains changes during a single Administration, it also helps to explain the differences between Administrations. Although the Carter Administration was unlikely to have maintained a good relationship with the Sandinista government after finding evidence of its arms transfers to the Salvadoran guerrillas, it is inconceivable that it would have organized and supported a covert war, as Reagan did. The two Administrations had sharply divergent perceptions of the nature and intensity of the threat. To Reagan, the Sandinistas represented an immediate, grave, Soviet-inspired threat that was testing the will and jeopardizing the interests of the United States. His policies flowed from that definition. To Carter, the Sandinistas represented a Central American revolution; the United States should try to help it and contain it simultaneously.

In addition to a president's ideology and perception of threat, a third factor that is important in explaining why a policy changes is the period in which it occurs. The way policy makers perceive an issue like the Nicaraguan revolution is affected by the general swings in the public mood and by significant international events, such as the Iranian revolution or the Soviet invasion of Afghanistan.

Traumatic events like the Cuban or Nicaraguan revolutions also influence perceptions for a certain period of time. The pace and concern of U.S. policy makers quickens after such traumas. U.S. policy toward Haiti and the Dominican Republic from 1960 to 1964, for example, sought to avoid another Cuba; toward the Philippines and Chile in 1985–1986, "another Nicaragua." [. . .]

UNABLE TO RETREAT

This explains why the Sandinistas came to power, but it does not explain the radicalization of the revolution, which was not inevitable. Because of the Sandinistas' preconceptions of imperialism, the United States was limited in its ability to influence them positively. The most it could do was not make the situation worse. The Nicaraguan government wanted to diversify its relations, and thus the major opportunities for positive influence rested with Latin American and European governments. [. . .]

The process through which these two protagonists should find themselves on the precipice of a military confrontation was certainly foreseen. Both sides claimed they wanted to avoid confrontation, yet both contributed to it. Each had a fearful prophecy of the other that connected and came true. The suspicions that each harbored for the other led them to interpret the behavior of the other in the worst possible light. Therefore, each felt the need to take defensive measures, which were interpreted as provocations by the other side. This, in turn, led to deliberate provocations.

By 1983, the Reagan Administration deliberately sought to transfer legitimacy from the Sandinistas to the contras [the U.S.-supported counterrevolutionary force] and to isolate Nicaragua from the rest of Central and Latin America. To achieve this goal, moderate leaders in Nicaragua needed to leave and join the armed opposition outside the country. In four years, hardly a long time, U.S. policy had shifted from trying to avoid polarization in Nicaragua to promoting it. [. . .]

What of the Sandinista strategy? The Sandinistas viewed negotiations and tolerance of criticism as a sign of weakness. Either the government was unaware, or it did not care about the effect of its actions on the Congressional debate over funding the contras. At crucial points in the debate, in May 1985 and then in March and May 1986, the Nicaraguan government took actions that strengthened President Reagan's case for aid to the contras. Why? Because as Omar Cabezas, a Sandinista leader, explained: "The only thing they are debating in Washington is how and when to destroy us." Nicaraguan government radio echoed this point: "Nothing good will come from Congress. We must be prepared."

In short, both governments were insecure and distrusted each other so completely that they were unable to consider any way to influence the other except by force. Nicaragua's moderates, who were squeezed to the left during the revolution, were then squeezed to the right by both the Sandinistas and the Reagan Administration.

Philip Bonsai concludes his analysis of the Cuban revolution by suggesting: "A conviction that the United States would take care of the situation sapped the activism of much of the [moderate] opposition." Many Nicaraguan moderates also thought the United States "would take care" of the revolution, but by allying with the FSLN when Somoza was finally ready to leave, they made it difficult for the Carter Administration to assist a democratic transition. Later, by leaving Nicaragua to join the contras, the moderates made it easy for the Reagan Administration to polarize and radicalize the revolution.

20

The Debt Crisis and Economic Development

Riordan Roett

Riordan Roett, a noted scholar in the field of Latin American development and debt, summarizes the debt crisis of the 1980s and its deleterious effects on Latin American socioeconomic development. The plans developed by the industrial economies, particularly the United States, to solve the region's financial problems are also addressed. The debt crisis sparked what is commonly known as the "lost decade" of the 1980s when debt servicing, global recession, and a dramatic drop in export receipts led to the most severe socioeconomic crisis the region had seen since the 1930s. Roett shows the interdependence of the debt crisis, showing how the inability of Latin America to service its debt and purchase exports from industrial economies could threaten the financial and economic stability of the United States and Europe. In the end, much-needed macroeconomic adjustment in Latin America and concessionary plans by industrial economies to alleviate the debt burden helped to ease the regional and global effects of the debt crisis. As Roett points out, the U.S. move to open markets and facilitate investments in Latin America through free trade agreements and the Enterprise for the Americas Initiative developed by president George H. W. Bush helped to mitigate financial collapse and began a process that brought prosperity through economic integration and cooperation between the United States and Latin America.

When the debt crisis erupted in the summer of 1982, the "lost decade" began in Latin America and the Caribbean. The crisis management approach of the 1982 to 1988 period worked—barely. While Brazil did declare a formal moratorium in 1987, after the spectacular failure of its heterodox Cruzado Plan, other countries were pressured and encouraged to avoid taking the same step. Coordination between the private commercial banks, the U.S. Treasury, and the international financial institutions accomplished that task.

The crisis management approach was, however, just that—a stopgap measure, because the crisis did not abate. In 1988 two new administrations took Office: Carlos Salinas de Gortari in Mexico and George H. W. Bush in the United States. Salinas, an active participant in the economic recovery program instituted in 1982 by his predecessor, decided that a major renegotiation of the Mexican debt was urgent if further reform efforts were to be meaningful. The Bush administration, sensitive to the politics of U.S. relations with Mexico and convinced that a new policy was required, devised the Brady Plan, named for the new secretary of the treasury. As David Mulford, Brady's undersecretary for international affairs, has described it:

> The turning point came in the spring of 1989 when the U.S. Government . . . designed a plan to crack the problem. This strategy replaced the previous "new-money approach" by setting out a comprehensive plan based on the realities of the market. Policy reform by the debtor countries was still emphasized as the key for their recovery, but this time policy reform was supported by a comprehensive plan for restructuring and reducing debt with the support of official sources.

By mid-1992, twelve of the sixteen major debtor nations had achieved debt reduction by refinancing agreements with their commercial banks, accounting for 92 percent, or some $240 billion, of their outstanding commercial bank debt. Once completed, these agreements were expected to produce more than $50 billion in effective debt reduction, while lifting much more of the remaining burden from the debtors' backs through market-based collateralization.

In response to the debt reduction schemes of the Brady Plan approach, the fiscal adjustment and structural changes in the major Latin American economies have made Latin America, once again, an attractive investment alternative. One sign was the activity in the stock markets:

> Of the world's six top-performing stock markets last year, five were in Latin America . . . they were in Argentina, Colombia, Brazil, Mexico, and Chile. . . . Investors who for a decade were intimidated by Latin America's mountain of debt now are pouring more than $40 billion per year into the region, turning once sleepy stock markets there into money machines—and attracting back billions in flight capital. [. . .]

The lost decade has ended from an economic and financial viewpoint. What is now needed is a decade of investment in social measures to compensate for the severe drop in living standards, wages, and social services in the last ten years. Governments are beginning to understand the urgency, in this decade, of not repeating the mistakes of the past. Many are seeking to use the Brady Plan reforms to initiate sensible macroeconomic management and to address long-ignored social issues.

We will only know at the end of this decade if this approach was both economically feasible and politically possible. Government planners often find it more challenging to deal with broader economic adjustment processes than with the more micromanagement required to achieve successful social investment goals. But it is clear to most observers that the impressive economic turnaround will be consolidated only if the social sector receives as much attention. Failure to do so will inevitably result in political unrest with unforeseen consequences for the region. [. . .]

THE DEBT CRISIS IN PERSPECTIVE

As Pedro-Pablo Kuczynski has cogently summarized,

> There is no great mystery about the origins of the debt crisis in Latin America: first, and most important, an extremely high level of external debt, most of it at floating interest rates; second, the impact of a very large rise in international interest rates, mostly denominated in dollars at a time of a rising U.S. dollar, upon the service of this debt; third, an eventual, but not immediate, decline in export earnings due to a deep international recession; and, finally, as in most debt crises, a loss of confidence on the part of the lenders, who initially started to lend at shorter terms and eventually stopped altogether, precipitating the suspension of debt service.

During the 1950s and 1960s, the economies of Latin America and the Caribbean expanded. Growth was uneven, but the quality of life for millions of citizens improved. Income distribution remained badly skewed against the poor, but an expanding middle class offered new opportunities for mobility and inclusion in the modern sectors of the economy in many countries. The pattern slowed in the 1970s due to the heavy burden of oil import bills after the first petroleum crisis in 1973. It was also caused by slower growth in the industrial countries during the decade that reduced the demand for commodities exported by the developing nations.

Confronted with a decision to continue growing or introduce substantial cutbacks in spending, the region's governments opted for continued growth. To do so meant to borrow; hence, the massive public-sector deficits that burden the region today. While the private sector borrowed, it was overshadowed by governments and the state agencies that garnered the bulk of the new lending flows. Flush with petrodollars, the world's commercial bankers were willing and anxious to find new customers. Latin America and the Caribbean were a godsend for them. The assumption of the borrowers was that world economic conditions, while not good, would not further deteriorate, allowing them to service the new debt. Careless about details, the region's financial and political leaders did not understand the implications of borrowing from commercial banks at floating interest rates and relatively short maturities. As Barbara Stallings has commented,

> In the 1970s there was a peculiar combination of cooperation and competition among the banks. Cooperation arose because the large loans were syndicated. A

lead manager brought together a group of banks, which could number in the hundreds, and each took a piece of the loan and shared the risk.

Competition entered as the largest banks vied for the "mandate" to organize syndicates and obtain the front-end fees that were more lucrative than interest payments. Thus the lone investment banker traveling to a Latin American city in the 1920s in hopes of selling a $50 million loan was replaced by "pin-striped salesmen" [who] crowded each other in Intercontinental hotel lobbies and the reception rooms of finance ministers in order to offer $500 million. Also unlike the 1920s, U.S. banks were joined in the competitive fray by European and Japanese institutions as the 1970s moved on.

The shift to private commercial bank loans paralleled a drop in loans from industrial countries and from the international financial institutions. These loans generally had fixed interest rates and relatively long maturities. The 1970s also saw a drop in direct foreign investment in Latin America. The savings level dipped in the region, public deficits grew, and erratic exchange rate and interest rate policies affected growth levels.

In the 1990s, a decade that will see almost all of Latin America and the Caribbean governed by civilian, democratic regimes, it is crucial to remember that there were few such governments in the 1970s. On the continent, only Colombia and Venezuela were democratic in the 1970s. Military authoritarian regimes were still in their heyday. They eagerly turned to the international commercial banks to maintain the only credibility they possessed—the capacity to generate high levels of growth. The policy decision to borrow was made by a small group; without functioning parliaments, interest groups, and the free press to challenge their authority, it was easy to justify the new credits as necessary for growth and development. The situation was even worse if one considers whether or not the borrowed funds were invested or saved. The evidence strongly suggests that they were not saved but were spent on pharaonic megaprojects with limited utility for social development, were dispensed as pay-offs, evaporated amid old-fashioned corruption, or left the country as flight capital, never to be seen again.

The ship began to founder in the late 1970s. International oil prices tripled in 1979. The inauguration of Ronald Reagan in 1981 and the policies of his administration heightened the international economic crisis of 1980 to 1982 that produced unprecedented interest rate levels. Interest payments exploded for the Latin American countries. In the short run, they borrowed more to service the debt, but export earnings were dropping precipitously as demand dropped sharply in the developed world. The banks reacted poorly to the Malvinas/Falklands War in mid-1982; confidence was weakening that Latin America was sufficiently stable to continue to service its debt; and a state of war, unthinkable just months before, raised new fears of disruption in the region.

THE CRISIS ERUPTS

In response to the turbulence in the world economy, high interest rates, and diminished export earnings for the Third World, the commercial banks stopped lending in mid-1982. In August of that year, Mexico informed U.S. officials that it was almost out of foreign exchange reserves and could no longer service its debt. During the "Mexican weekend" of 13–15 August, the patchwork response that continues today was cobbled together by the U.S. government and international financial institutions.

Some observers believed that Mexico was an isolated case and that a package of international loans would be sufficient to tide it over. This belief was strengthened by the political nature of the debt announcement in Mexico; the Mexican leadership heralded the nationalization of the banking system and the reimposition of exchange controls by President José Lopez Portillo on 1 September. The international community was quickly disabused of this false impression in Toronto in September 1982. At the joint annual meeting of the IMF [International Monetary Fund] and the World Bank, it was suddenly clear that Brazil was the emperor without clothes. Within eight weeks of the Toronto meeting, where Brazil failed to negotiate significant new loans, it too sought a moratorium on the repayment of principal to its commercial bank creditors. Within weeks, the rest of Latin America, with the exception of Colombia, moved to reschedule its outstanding debt.

From the position of the industrial country governments, it was critical to avoid a breakdown of the international financial system. Key to any policy response was a continuation of interest payments by the debtors; otherwise the private commercial banking system would be in serious danger of collapse. Of particular concern to the U.S. Federal Reserve System and to the White House was the poor health of many of the major banking institutions in the United States. U.S. banks were saddled with bad loans in the housing, agricultural, and energy sectors. To be hit with a moratorium by Third World debtors would prove disastrous. Everything had to be done to maintain interest payments. [. . .]

STABILIZATION AND ADJUSTMENT

An immediate consequence of the 1982 to 1983 debt crisis was the necessity for programs of economic stabilization and adjustment. The IMF played a critical role in this process. As Werner Baer and Howard Handelman have written,

> All stabilization and adjustment programs require considerable economic sacrifice from much of the population. Such programs usually try to contain the forces that have produced inflation and to correct distortions that have grown out of the inflationary

process. Orthodox programs, favored by the International Monetary Fund (IMF) and by monetarist policymakers, involve some combination of currency devaluation, reduction of import controls, credit restrictions, reduction of government subsidies on basic consumer goods (including fuel and basic foods), higher prices for public utilities, freeing of prices, wage repression, reduction of public employment, and reduction of the fiscal deficit. These policies usually produce a slowdown of economic growth, or even a period of decline. Thus, stabilization confronts policymakers with the problem of how to allocate economic sacrifices. Should they be evenly shared by all socioeconomic groups, or should they be borne more heavily by specific sectors?

The answer, of course, is clear. The heaviest burden has been carried by the poorest segments of Latin America.

Government after government undertook IMF-monitored programs of adjustment and stabilization. The quickest way to achieve IMF goals, necessary for multilateral and private commercial bank credits, was to cut the social services budget. This was feasible in some countries because military governments could do so without fear of rebuke. Fledgling democracies did it with trepidation or postponed the inevitable for a year or two until forced to take the steps required to maintain their creditworthiness. From the perspective of the industrial world, the issue was whether or not the Latin American governments would "bite the bullet" and do as they were told—or react collectively.

LATIN AMERICA REACTS

The latter concern was a real one, from the position of the commercial banks and the industrial countries. As the frightening dimensions of the combined international economic crisis and the adjustment measures that were being demanded by the combined creditors became apparent to Latin American leaders, they reacted. President Osvaldo Hurtado of Ecuador wrote to the executive secretaries of the Economic Commission for Latin America and the Caribbean (ECLAC) and the Latin American Economic System (SELA) on 11 February 1983. The Ecuadoran chief executive requested the two entities to "prepare as soon as possible a set of proposals designed to develop the response capacity of Latin America and to consolidate its systems of cooperation."

The two organizations drafted a document entitled "The Bases for a Latin American Response to the International Economic Crisis" in May 1983. The document was discussed at a meeting in Quito that month and again in August when a decision was taken to convene a heads-of-government conference in January 1984 in Quito. [. . .]

In January 1984 at the heads-of-government meeting, a "Declaration of Quito" and a "Plan of Action" were approved. The declaration called for an immediate response from the creditor countries to ameliorate the dramatic fall in living standards and the economic and financial crisis that afflicted the region. It was widely noted that a democratic trend had begun in the region. Newly elected civilian regimes were desperate to find a solution both to the impossible situation they had inherited from their predecessors and the further worsening of the economic situation in the mid-1980s.

In May 1984 the presidents of Brazil, Colombia, Mexico, and Argentina issued a joint letter that dramatically called for help from the industrial countries. It was ignored. In June 1984 seven Latin American heads of state addressed an urgent letter to the Group of Seven, about to convene for their annual economic summit in London. The letter called for a "constructive dialogue among creditor and borrowing countries." The Latin Americans stated that it was impossible to imagine that their financial problems could be resolved only by "contacting banks or through the isolated participation of international financial organizations." Deflecting the Latin Americans' entreaty, the final communiqué of the London summit brusquely rejected the call for negotiations and offered "help" only if the Latin governments reduced their spending and worked to put their houses in order.

The growing frustration of the Latin American political leaders led to the organization of the Cartagena consensus group in June 1984. Speaking at the opening of the meeting, then president Belisario Betancur of Colombia stated: "Latin America's foreign debt service has become so burdensome that it threatens the very stability of the international monetary system and the survival of the democratic process in the various countries." The Cartagena conference strongly endorsed the Quito declaration and called for a response from the industrial countries. [. . .]

It was clear that the strategy of the industrial countries was one of buying time—of the containment of the crisis by dealing with one country at a time and avoiding any contamination of the rest while the worst case was dealt with. Thus, a series of emergency packages, bridge loans, and credits were implemented from 1982 through 1985. A drastic cutback in the living standards in the debtor countries was the other side of the coin, of course. Imports were severely cut by Latin America, and large trade surpluses were generated to pay the interest on the outstanding debt. Latin America by 1983 had become a capital exporter, an anomaly in the theoretical development literature. Latin American governments, desperate to retain access to the international financial community, particularly for critical revolving trade credits needed to support the export surplus program, accepted the creditors' scheme.

Why did Latin America's efforts to act collectively fail? There is no easy answer to this question. A number of reasons account for the politically ineffective strategy of the Latin American states. Many were new democracies and their leaders were uncertain how far they could go in pressing their case with the industrial countries. Any effective strategy would require the active involvement of both Mexico and Brazil, and one or the other was usually following its own strategy during the 1980s. The tactics of divide and conquer by the industrial countries were brilliant—from their perspective. The United States was given the lead in responding to Latin America and it was able to apply Paul Volker's quarantine scheme with great success. Latin America found that it had few allies in the industrial world, and the Third World was a sympathetic but ineffective ally in the debt struggle. As Richard Feinberg has written,

> The Latin American nations—individually or collectively—never really had their own debt strategy. . . . Whereas the creditors—public and private—overtly organized to coordinate strategies for managing old debts as well as for providing new loans under certain conditions, the debtors remained independent from each other. Individual debtors, too, failed to devise or articulate very clear strategies beyond seeking to remain current on interest payments, regain creditworthiness, and minimize the costs of refinancing.

Democracy also provided a surprising escape valve for the tensions in the Latin American countries. Contrary to many fears that the debt crisis would destroy fledgling democracies, they have survived the "lost decade" and have been able to convince their people of the need to work with, not against, the international financial community.

THE BAKER PLAN

By 1985, the industrial governments sensed a sharp increase in debt fatigue. At his inauguration in July 1985, President Alan Garcia declared that Peru would allocate no more than 10 percent of its annual export earnings to service the debt. A "Declaration of Lima," signed by the Latin American leaders attending the Peruvian ceremony, called on the industrial countries to accept coresponsibility for the debt crisis and to recognize the linkage between interest payments and export earnings. At the same meeting, the Support Group was created to assist the Central American Contadora process in Central America. Fidel Castro convened a widely reported but ineffective series of debt meetings in Havana in the summer of 1985. And at the UN General Assembly meeting in September 1985, Presidents José Sarney of Brazil and Alán García of Peru, among others, were sharply critical of the lack of response to the plight of the debtor countries.

Important political changes had taken place in Washington in the ensuing years, one of which was James Baker's transfer from the White House to the U.S. Treasury. As treasury secretary, Baker was now the Reagan administration's coordinator for a response to the debt crisis. The second Reagan administration, while virulently ideological in its Central American policy, was more benign on broader hemispheric issues. At the joint meeting of the IMF and the World Bank in Seoul in October 1985, the Baker Plan was announced. It had three components. The first called for continued adjustment among the debtor countries; the second stipulated that the private commercial banks would lend an additional $20 billion over a three-year period; and third, the World Bank and the Inter-American Development Bank would provide new loans totaling $9 billion over three years.

The Baker Plan made good headlines but it did little to address the debt burden. The economic summit in Tokyo in June 1986 laconically endorsed the Baker Plan but did not indicate any change of policy on the part of the industrial countries. At the Venice economic summit in June 1987, Baker announced an "enhancement" of the Baker Plan that he termed a "Menu of Options." The menu was a wish list of possible financial mechanisms for reducing Latin America's debt, ranging from debt-equity conversion schemes, to exit bonds, to project lending, to on-lending. But the menu failed to reduce the debt. [. . .]

The announcement of the menu had been preceded by a dramatic decision at Citicorp, the lead bank in the restructuring process and one of the major creditors of all the Latin American states, that it would allocate $3 billion to its loan loss reserve fund precisely to protect itself from bad Third World loans. The U.S. Treasury and the Federal Reserve supported the decision; other commercial banks in the United States did not, since a comparable move by them would be highly costly in terms of earnings and investor returns.

The year 1987 saw a series of initiatives that indicated no one had any new answers to the debt crisis. In September the conservative *Financial Times* of London questioned whether or not a bits-and-pieces approach was sufficient:

> The question is whether muddling through is still the best strategy or whether the governments of the developed countries should themselves provide resources to solve the problem. Muddling through is always easy, but is it enough? It is difficult to believe that the running sore of developing country debt will be healed without a willingness of major developed countries to contribute to the treatment.

That theme was echoed by the newly organized Group of Eight Latin American states that met in Acapulco, Mexico, for their first summit meeting in 1987. In the final document, they declared that

> The economic crisis undermines democracy in the region because it neutralises the legitimate efforts of our people to improve their living standards. It is contradictory that the same people who call for democracy also impose, in world economic relations, conditionality and adjustment schemes that compromise that very democracy, and which they themselves do not apply in correcting their own imbalances.

LATIN AMERICA ADJUSTS

Quietly, the democratic governments of Latin America had begun to realize in the middle of the lost decade that the old development models of the early post–World War II years were now inadequate. Some countries came to that realization sooner than others. Many viewed the dramatic reversal of Chile's economic fortunes in the mid-1980s with quiet admiration but often with the fear that it required an authoritarian regime to implement such drastic structural adjustment measures. The fact that the administration of Mexican president Miguel de la Madrid was beginning to do the same strengthened the apprehension. It was widely believed that the changes under way in Mexico were due to the pervasive influence of the Institutional Revolutionary Party (PRI) and its massive bureaucratic strength throughout the country.

The failure of the Cruzado Plan in Brazil in 1986 and the slow collapse of President Raúl Alfonsin's Austral Plan in Argentina further cautioned Latin America's leadership from embracing the siren call of deep adjustment. But by the late 1980s, a number of countries had adopted far-reaching goals of internal change. The economies of the region were being opened to new investment; privatization schemes were under way to transfer to the private sector inefficient and bloated state companies; it became widely recognized that the internal debt was in most countries as serious, if not more so, [as] the external debt. Exchange rate policies had to be adjusted, exports diversified, and interest rates stabilized.

Latin America's leaders understood that they remained highly vulnerable to exogenous developments and trends. But by the last years of the decade, muddling through was all that was available. [. . .]

Did Latin America receive many benefits from its adjustment in the mid-1980s? Very few. Indeed, the situation tightened in 1987 to 1988 as regional banks in the United States began to write off Latin American debt. The Bank of Boston, for example, announced in December 1987 that it would write off $200 million. It was widely understood that the bank had given up hope of repayment of that portion of its loan portfolio to the debtor countries. Other regional banks followed throughout 1988. [. . .]

By 1988 to 1989, the decade's crisis had abated. The industrial countries were occupied with East-West questions. There was the general impression, with the exception of Chile, Bolivia, and Mexico, and a few of the smaller Central American and Caribbean states, that Latin American governments were irresolute, disorganized, well-meaning perhaps, but unwilling to understand the major trends in the globalization of the world economy. If they were unable to understand the need to restructure in order to compete, there was little the industrial countries could or would do to help them. Democracy had survived. Elites had not brought back the billions of dollars of flight capital that would provide a comfortable cushion for efforts at renewed growth in the region. And efforts such as those of the Group of Eight, and other regional groups, were ineffective and incapable of backing up their desperation with any action that would be seen as threatening to the industrial countries.

That perception changed sharply in the United States at the end of the Reagan administration. The new government of Mexican president Carlos Salinas de Gortari, who took office in December 1988, made it clear in 1989 that continued restructuring without debt relief was unacceptable. The Salinas government's willingness to challenge the conventional wisdom of the 1980s regarding the debt strategy was matched in the United States by a growing concern with the bilateral relationship. A period of Mexico bashing in the mid-1980s had yielded to a realization that American foreign policy and security interests were deeply affected by events in Mexico. [. . .]

THE BRADY PLAN

The year 1988 was a slide year in the debt discussions. With the upcoming presidential election in the United States, it was clear that the Reagan administration would take no new action. Besides, Treasury Secretary Baker was deeply involved in running the campaign of then Vice President Bush. With the victory of the Bush-Quayle ticket in November 1988, the debt issue moved quickly. The president-elect met with Mexican president Salinas in Texas. It was "leaked" during the transition that the new American government would move beyond the Baker plan and the Menu of Options soon after the inauguration in January 1989.

Secretary of the Treasury Nicholas Brady announced what has been termed the Brady Plan in March 1989. It stressed voluntary debt reduction by the banks—writing off loans in negotiation with the developing countries—as well as new lending to help them pay off old loans and develop the means to produce more foreign exchange and put their debt burden behind them. The plan relies heavily on the IMF and the World Bank to lend money to those countries and undertake structural reform to help them cut back on their outstanding obligations. A total of $28.5 billion was originally put forward in support of the new program, $24 billion from the IMF and the World Bank and $4.5 billion from the government of Japan. The goal was to reduce interest outflows by $7 billion a year for three years, but it was quickly pointed out that the U.S. target would require $40 to $50 billion of new funds.

At first, the private commercial banking community, highly vulnerable to reduction of its Third World debt exposure, resisted. Throughout 1989 they signaled their fatigue with Third World debt. In September 1989 Manufacturers Hanover announced that it would add $950 million of a Japanese infusion of $1.4 billion of fresh capital to its loan loss reserve fund. Chase Manhattan followed with a decision to increase its loan loss reserve by $1.9 billion. J. P. Morgan stated that it would add $2 billion to its reserve, a step that left it with 100 percent of its medium- and long-term exposure to Third World debt fully covered. The Morgan message was loud and clear. It indicated that it was turning its back on the new lending component of the Brady Plan. Now that it was fully covered, it had the flexibility to do with its portfolio what it wanted, without the pressure to grant new loans so that the old ones could continue to be serviced.

A second obstacle was the inability of the United States to provide more public funding for debt reduction. The debate between the U.S. private commercial banks and the Bush administration was clear—and bitter. The banks urged the Bush administration to make more resources available to encourage them to undertake greater debt reduction and to provide guarantees for new loans. [. . .]

By the end of 1989, a brief power struggle erupted. The players were the banks, the Third World countries, and the governments of the industrial countries. The issue was clear. Would the U.S. government and the other industrial countries provide sufficient enhancements for the private commercial banks to proceed with debt reduction? The banks were challenging a deficit-ridden U.S. administration to make a massive financial contribution to allow debt reduction to move ahead. [. . .]

If a turning point can be identified that broke the logjam in 1990 to 1991, it was the Brady Plan negotiation between the banks and Mexico. The government of President Carlos Salinas de Gortari had inherited a difficult economic and political situation. While the initial reforms undertaken by his predecessor, Miguel de la Madrid, appeared promising, they had not yet restored confidence in the country's economy. The social fallout from the debt crisis in the 1980s had generated a strong, populist reaction to the Salinas candidacy. Only the indefatigable efforts of the ruling PRI, which has never lost a presidential election, guaranteed Salinas's hairline victory.

Salinas entered office with an excellent economic team, most of whom had worked with him in the 1980s in the de la Madrid government. Salinas was determined to continue the deepening of the reform process and to press immediately for international financial concessions to restore the creditworthiness of Mexico. That was essential, he reasoned, to begin to put the 1980s behind him and to begin to attract new direct foreign investment and capital flows. [. . .]

Throughout 1990, additional voices were raised to express misgivings about the Brady Plan. The Institute of International Finance (IIF) in Washington, a think tank that speaks on behalf of the commercial banks, stated in May that the plan has encouraged an "alarming increase in country arrears to commercial bank creditors." The IIF report blames the Brady initiative for engendering "a loss of discipline in the [international financial] system and the build-up of payments arrears to commercial banks and official agencies." The IIF concern reflects a related issue of growing concern in financial circles: the health of the private commercial banks. [. . .]

It was in mid- or late-1990 that the terms of reference about the Latin American debt changed. The stark reality confronting Latin America in the 1990s was summarized by ECLAC in late 1989:

> The economic crisis that has affected Latin America and the Caribbean during most of the 1980s persisted during the last year of the decade, as the average per capita product fell for the second year running, this time by 1%, while inflation averaged the unprecedented 1,000%. . . . The region's expanding trade surplus continued to be insufficient to cover the huge burden of debt service and only five Latin American and Caribbean countries managed to meet those commitments fully and timely in 1989.

ECLAC continues to report that the net resource transfer abroad in 1989 reached nearly $25 billion—the equivalent of almost 18 percent of the value of the region's export of goods and services and approximately 3 percent of its gross domestic product. If Mexico is excluded from these figures, the net resource transfer abroad in fact increased to nearly $23 billion, from less than $18 billion in 1988. The 1989 performance suggests that "most of the countries of the region seem now to be reaching the limits of their capacity for adjusting to external constraints, on the basis of their present structures of production." But just as ECLAC was issuing its pessimistic assessment, the international financial markets rediscovered Latin America. That rediscovery has changed the nature of the debate regarding regional debt in the 1990s.

THE ENTERPRISE FOR THE AMERICAS INITIATIVE [EAI]

An additional factor in the debt debate emerged in June 1990 with the announcement at the White House of the EAI. It was heralded as a "new partnership for trade, investment, and growth" in the Americas. It called for free and fair trade within the hemisphere; domestic and foreign investment, new capital flows, a reduction in debt burdens, and an improvement of the environment; and additional support for debt and debt-service reduction.

As reported one year later, the initiative was "a triumph of timing which promised rewards for the sort of reforms the Latin Americans had already begun." But the movement on specifics has been slow. Negotiations are under way on the North American Free Trade Agreement (NAFTA) with Mexico, Canada, and the United States seeking a new concept of North American trade. "Framework" agreements for freer trade have been signed with sixteen countries, as well as the southern common market of Argentina, Brazil, Paraguay, and Uruguay. Chile received the first enterprise debt reduction and investment package in 1991.

Progress has been made in raising the $1.5 billion from the United States and other industrial countries for the creation of an investment fund proposed by President Bush. The fund is intended partly to support privatization efforts.

The problem has been the U.S. Congress, which has vocally endorsed the program but has been slow to pass legislation necessary for further action. Of all the trade, food, and foreign aid credits the president wants to make available for debt reduction, only forgiveness on some of the food debt has been authorized. Bills granting reduction on the rest moved slowly through both Houses.

The most dramatic result of the initiative has been the enthusiasm of the Latin American governments. President Bush visited South America in December 1990 and received a warm and enthusiastic endorsement for the initiative. All the Latin heads of states, during their visits to Washington, have supported the program. Combined with the economic restructuring that continues throughout the hemisphere, it has changed the tone and the nature of the debate about U.S.–Latin American ties for the first time in decades.

21

Dope and Dogma: Explaining the Failure of U.S.–Latin American Drug Policies

Bruce M. Bagley and Juan G. Tokatlian

Bruce Bagley and Juan Tokatlian, two experts on drug trafficking in the Americas, attempt to conceptualize U.S. drug policy in the 1980s from the perspective of international relations theory. According to the authors, U.S. supply-side strategies have flowed directly from the core assumptions and internal logic of realist analyses of international political economy widely accepted by the U.S. public and foreign policy elites. U.S. supply-side policy has emphasized repression, unilateralism, militarization, and punitive acts against source countries in Latin America believed to be absent in the war against drugs. As a result of a lack of consensus and cooperation, the authors state that the U.S.-imposed antinarcotics strategy has lacked "legitimacy, credibility, and symmetry."

Bagley and Tokatlian suggest that U.S. policy has been counterproductive, particularly interdiction programs that raise "the cost of smuggling activities, thus increasing the profit incentives for other traffickers." Moreover, U.S. pressure on source countries to adopt repressive policies against drug traffickers created a crisis of governability, particularly in Colombia during the 1980s. The authors suggest a more pragmatic and flexible policy that takes into account the complex and interdependent international political economy of drug trafficking. Specifically, they suggest an approach that emphasizes multilateralism, consensus, and demand-side policies and funding as more effective in dealing with the profit incentive and violence associated with supply-side strategies. With such an approach, U.S. policy could obtain the legitimacy, credibility, and symmetry needed to harness cooperation in Latin America while effectively addressing the drug problem in the Americas.

The conceptualization of the "drug problem" in the United States and much of Latin America and the Caribbean underwent a dramatic transformation during the 1980s. At the outset of the decade, U.S. policymakers viewed drug trafficking and consumption primarily as criminal and public health issues. For their part, most Latin American and Caribbean officials either neglected these questions or saw them as basically American problems that would have to be resolved in the United States by U.S. authorities. As of 1990, however, there was apparently widespread consensus among both U.S. and Latin American leaders that drug production, smuggling, and abuse constituted significant threats to national security and societal well-being throughout the hemisphere. The combination of a complex set of international, regional, and country-specific factors produced this remarkable— albeit still tentative and uneasy—convergence of national perspectives.

[. . .] The central argument of the essay is that despite the emergence of a conceptual consensus around the definition of the drug phenomenon as a serious national security threat, U.S. efforts to "impose" an "antidrug" national security regime during the 1980s proved ineffective in halting drug cultivation, processing, and trafficking in the hemisphere because from the perspective of most Latin American and Caribbean leaders, the U.S.-inspired regime lacked legitimacy, credibility, and symmetry. To construct an operative international drug regime in the 1990s will require that the U.S. government abandon the coercive, punitive, and unilateral policies that have guided its antinarcotics strategy to date and replace them with a more cooperative, multilateral framework that takes into account the complex and multifaceted nature of both demand and supply within the interdependent political economy of the hemispheric drug trade.

DRUGS AND NATIONAL SECURITY: THE U.S. PERSPECTIVE

In the United States, the explosive surge in crack consumption, the accompanying increases in drug-related crimes in many American cities, and the attendant rise in U.S. media coverage of drug issues clearly fanned public awareness of and leadership concern with the country's drug epidemic. Unfolding events in Latin America also focused public attention on these topics. Among the most notable were the highly acclaimed arrest, extradition, and trial of Colombian drug lord Carlos Lehder; the detention and subsequent bribed release of another major Colombian trafficker, Jorge Luis Ochoa; the indictment of Panamanian strongman Manuel Antonio Noriega in U.S. federal court and his prolonged defiance of Washington; the "deportation-kidnapping" of Honduran cocaine boss, Juan Ramón Mata Ballesteros, and the ensuing anti-American riots in Honduras; the cold-blooded assassination of the Colombian attorney general, Carlos Mauro Hoyos, and hundreds of other Colombian government officials, judges, and political leaders by drug-syndicated consortium hit men; widely circulated rumors concerning Contra, Cuban, and Nicaraguan involvement in the trade; and repeated allegations of high-level drug corruption among Mexican, Caribbean, and Central and South American government officials.

Electoral rhetoric and press coverage unquestionably sensationalized the drug question during the 1980s. But the "hype" also reflected growing preoccupation in the United States with the heavy economic and social costs of expanding drug abuse at home and the intensifying challenges to U.S. interests abroad. By 1989 substance abuse in the U.S. work force (including both illegal drugs and alcohol) cost the U.S. economy an estimated $200 billion annually in lost production and productivity, job- and transportation-related accidents, and health care. Meanwhile, the enormous profits derived from the illicit trade fueled the growth of violent criminal organizations whose economic resources, political influence, and firepower gave them the wherewithal to destabilize, to intimidate, or, in some cases, to manipulate various national governments in the region.

Rising concern in the 1980s over the economic and social consequences of the drug "plague" at home and the growing power of the international drug rings abroad drove both the U.S. executive branch and Congress to regard narcotics trafficking as a national security problem. This perspective was strengthened by the fact that virtually all of the marijuana and cocaine and 40 percent of the heroin smuggled into the United States annually was cultivated and processed in Latin America and the Caribbean.

President Ronald Reagan declared "war" on drugs in February 1982 and pledged his administration to the task of curtailing America's burgeoning drug consumption. To accomplish this urgent national security objective, the federal government rapidly increased the resources available for antidrug efforts both at home and abroad, reaching $6.3 billion in fiscal year (FY) 1989. Strongly backing the president's war on drugs, bipartisan majorities in Congress enacted tougher drug legislation, broadened the U.S. military's role in the fight, funded intensified interdiction efforts at U.S. borders and overseas, and expanded U.S. antinarcotics initiatives in foreign source and transit countries. Over the course of Reagan's tenure, Washington consistently demonstrated its preference for supply-side over demand-side strategies via its allocation of an average of 70 percent of authorized funds to supply-oriented—versus only 30 percent for demand-oriented—programs.

Realism and Supply-Side Strategies

The underlying consensus on supply-side strategies in Washington's design and implementation of the war on drugs during the 1980s flowed directly from the core assumptions and internal logic of "realist" analyses of the international system— and of the U.S. role within it—widely accepted by U.S. foreign policy elites from both parties. At base, the realist paradigm posits an international system in which (1) nation-states are the key actors in international politics, (2) state policymaking elites (as rational actors) design and implement foreign policy, (3) national security interests always rank highest on national foreign policy agendas, and (4) threats to national security emanating from the international system warrant the use of the full range of national power resources (including force) to obtain desired responses from hostile or uncooperative nation-states: "self-help" is both a right and the ultimate recourse of every sovereign nation in defense of its national interests and security.

Parting from the premise that the international system is inherently anarchic and conflictual, the realists contended that hegemonic powers, such as the United States, had to accept responsibility for enforcing the international "rules of the game" and preserving order or run the risk that the international system might lapse into instability and interstate warfare. From this perspective, the United States not only had the right, but also the duty, to use its dominant leadership position and superior power capabilities to persuade or compel subordinate states to cooperate on issues such as the war on drugs, for failure to do so could endanger U.S. national security and, ultimately, the stability of the international system as a whole. Adoption of the realist interpretation, in effect, inexorably led to the supply-side strategy and unilateral escalation tactics advocated by President Reagan during the 1980s as central components of the U.S. antidrug campaign.

Realist analyses unquestionably inspired the successive antinarcotics bills passed by Congress during the 1980s. The new laws explicitly sought to provide the economic resources, personnel, administrative structures, and policy guidelines whose absence, insufficiency, or ambiguity their supporters believed had hobbled the Reagan administration's ability to carry out the war on drugs effectively. Notwithstanding Washington's perennial optimism, however, none of the various legislative initiatives approved over the decade were efficacious in resolving the nation's drug problems.

A serious flaw in the realist paradigm is the overly simplistic assumption that nation-states are always the primary actors in international politics, including the arena of international drug trafficking. In fact, multiple sub-national and transnational actors are involved in this international industry, most of whom operate outside, if not in direct defiance, of national authorities throughout the hemisphere. It is simply unrealistic to expect effective implementation of antinarcotics policies from many Latin American countries whose weak governments do not control their entire national territory; they do not have the power or resources to rein in, much less totally suppress, the well-financed, heavily armed, and ruthless drug mafias operating in their midst, no matter how insistent or painful U.S. efforts to persuade or punish become. [. . .] If the relatively powerful U.S. government has failed to destroy New York's famous "five families" despite a decades-long campaign to do so, can the comparatively much weaker governments of, for example, Colombia or Mexico be expected to do better?

Assertion of state control over the multiple transnational actors directly or indirectly involved in U.S.–Latin America drug trafficking networks is equally problematic in most cases. A variety of private, multinational, and commercial banks, as well as other international financial institutions, engage in illicit money-laundering activities, which few, if any, Latin American governments are equipped to regulate effectively. Similarly, state monitoring and law enforcement capabilities in most areas are generally insufficient to suppress the unauthorized importation of chemical precursors employed in cocaine-processing laboratories. In fact, even though U.S. businesses have supplied perhaps 90 percent of these inputs, until the enactment of the 1988 antidrug law, not even the U.S. government had seriously attempted to regulate the export of these basic chemical products. To believe that the institutionally weakened, financially strapped governments of Latin America and the Caribbean will be in a position to gain or maintain absolute control over these actors within the next decade is out of touch with reality. To sanction them for failing to do so is both hypocritical and counterproductive in the long run. By and large, Latin American governments do not merit sanctions; they need consistent and sustained help to strengthen state institutions and regulatory capabilities and to provide alternative economic opportunities for their populations.

In general, the realists' state-primacy assumption ignores, or gravely underestimates, the relative autonomy of the international market forces involved in the drug trade and the concomitant capacity of the drug traffickers to circumvent, adapt to, or defy state efforts to regulate or eradicate their illicit multimillion dollar industry. As long as the U.S. and other developed country markets for drugs remain profitable, suppliers will be motivated to find innovative ways to produce and smuggle narcotics to meet that demand and will be able to marshal the resources required to override whatever enforcement schemes Latin American states undertake.

The debt crisis and severe economic contractions that wracked most Latin American economies during the 1980s further complicated the situation by undermining state authority and reducing the monies available to implement antidrug programs. At the same time, the booming drug trade created employment opportunities and earned scarce foreign exchange in otherwise stagnant or declining national economies, thereby increasing the relative financial and political clout of the drug barons vis-à-vis traditional political and economic elites.

Equally revealing, even where U.S. interdiction efforts had positive results—as, for example, in reducing the flow of marijuana smuggled into the United States from Mexico during the 1970s—alternative sources of supply and transshipment quickly emerged to meet continuing demand. In practice, the decline in Mexican marijuana production was offset by a parallel boom in marijuana exports from Colombia. The subsequent success of the South Florida Task Force's mid-1980s interdiction campaign against marijuana and cocaine traffic from Colombia to Florida, in turn, stimulated a resurgence of Mexican marijuana cultivation and smuggling, along with a dispersion and proliferation of alternate smuggling routes through Mexico, Central America, the Caribbean, and the Pacific.

Meanwhile, behind the new non-tariff barriers created by Washington's intensified drug interdiction and overseas eradication programs, the profitability of domestic marijuana cultivation rose exponentially, thus providing additional incentives for U.S. producers to enter the market. Whereas in the early 1970s domestic U.S. cultivation accounted for only 1–2 percent of the marijuana trade, by 1989 U.S. growers were harvesting an estimated 4.5 thousand metric tons annually and had captured some 25 percent of total U.S. demand. [. . .] [In] the late 1970s innovative U.S. producers developed more potent, hybrid strains of cannabis, such as the now-famous *sinsemilla* variety grown in Hawaii and California, which more than doubled the potency of the average marijuana cigarette smoked by consumers in many parts of the United States.

Modification of the realists' state-primacy assumption to incorporate relevant subnational and transnational actors and market forces into the analyses in no way implies that nation-states are unimportant in international politics, even in the global drug trade. It means simply that state-state relations must be located and analyzed in the broader world economic and political contexts within which they take place. At the policy level, it means that to be credible and effective, U.S. narcotics control efforts abroad must be designed and carried out on the basis of more sophisticated assessments of the structure and dynamics of the international political economy of the drug trade and the extent and limits of individual Latin American governments' economic, technical, and enforcement capabilities vis-à-vis international drug trafficking organizations.

A second distortion or oversimplification present in the realist paradigm lies in its assumption that Latin American governing elites select and execute foreign policies intended to advance perfectly delineated and widely accepted national interests. In fact, national policymakers in several countries of the region must routinely operate without the luxury of fully elaborated conceptual schemes that define and prioritize their nations' vital interests. Furthermore, they often must cope with fragile political systems of tenuous legitimacy where viable consensus on basic national interests is difficult to attain. [. . .]

In many respects, Colombian policymakers in the 1980s confronted precisely such a "devil's dilemma" with regard to the issue of extradition of Colombian traffickers for prosecution in U.S. courts. On the one hand, the Colombian judicial system was manifestly incapable of bringing the country's most powerful drug lords to justice and U.S. pressures to extradite (often accompanied by implicit or explicit threats of sanctions) were intense. On the other hand, compliance aroused strong nationalist opposition, undercut system legitimacy, and provoked murderous reprisals against government officials by drug traffickers. Caught in these treacherous crosscurrents, Colombia's policymakers first refused to extradite, then yielded to U.S. pressures, subsequently procrastinated in the face of a withering campaign of mafia violence and intimidation, and then backed away from further compliance for more than two years only to renew it again after August 18, 1989, in the wake of a dramatic upsurge of narco-violence capped by the assassination of a leading Liberal presidential candidate, Senator Luis Carlos Galán.

A third faulty realist premise is that the U.S. foreign policy agenda (not to mention those of Latin American nation-states) is characterized by a clear hierarchy or prioritization of issues in which drug trafficking, because of its security implications, ranks at the top. In practice, the United States has a range of interests in Latin America; these often inhibited or diluted Washington's commitment to combating international drug trafficking during the 1980s. [. . .]

Predictably, the White House was in such instances harshly denounced for failing to pressure source and transit countries more vigorously. In the context of expanding interdependence and its attendant tensions, however, such trade-offs are inescapable facts of life; to ignore them altogether would be myopic and possibly counterproductive. As the major power in hemispheric affairs, the United States inevitably includes in its foreign policy agenda a range of interests that cannot always or easily be reconciled. But U.S. overseas antidrug policies have been driven more by short-run domestic political criteria, partisan posturing, and electoral cycles than by reasoned calculations of the costs and benefits for U.S. national interests abroad in the long term. [. . .]

A final misleading realist assumption is that the use of unilateral force or self-help—including retaliation and sanctions as well as direct intervention—are appropriate and potentially efficient policy instruments in the U.S. war on drugs abroad. In practice, several factors combined to reduce or negate the effectiveness of such policies in the 1980s. First, as noted above, many Latin American states were incapable of controlling their national territory or the powerful criminal drug organizations active within their boundaries; unilateral U.S. efforts to pressure them to do more or to castigate them for not doing enough did not and could not alter this reality.

Second, given the extensive U.S. economic and politico-strategic interests in most Latin American source and transit countries, threats of sanctions may inflict too much damage on other important U.S. interests. Mexico provides an excellent case in point. Despite deep dissatisfaction in the Reagan administration and in the U.S. Congress with Mexico's efforts to rein in drug trafficking, the U.S. executive branch consistently refused to decertify or directly sanction the Mexican government on grounds that such measures would reduce rather than improve cooperation with Mexico on drug issues and endanger other American goals in the process.

Extensive U.S.-Mexican interdependence seriously constrained Washington's ability to bring the full range of its overall power capabilities to bear against Mexico, and thus to compel fuller cooperation or compliance, for to do so inevitably would injure U.S. interests as well. Moreover, the outpouring of Mexican nationalism and anti-U.S. sentiment along with the legacy of tensions and frictions in U.S.-Mexican relations indicated that the costs of unilateral actions could not be valued in dollar terms alone.

The assumption that the U.S. armed forces could—if so ordered—interdict drug smuggling efficiently also reflected the realists' consistent overestimation of the efficacy of force as an instrument of policy. In fact, the U.S. military had neither the equipment nor the technical training required to undertake drug interdiction successfully. Despite the use of war analogies and the invocation of national security threats, the war on drugs is qualitatively different from the conventional wars that the U.S. military trained for traditionally. Drug trafficking does not involve the incursion into U.S. territory of large groups of easily detectable, hostile forces. On the contrary, drug smuggling is by definition a clandestine activity undertaken by individuals or small groups with the express intention of penetrating U.S. borders unseen and then disappearing without a trace. [. . .] Moreover, given the country's status as one of the preeminent trading nations in the world, the almost infinitely variable channels of entry available to traffickers, and the huge profits to be derived from drug trafficking, interdiction efforts—whether carried out by the military or any other U.S. agency—are inherently incapable of seizing more than a small percentage of the total flow of illicit drugs brought into the United States. Ironically, unless the nation's borders can be "sealed" completely, U.S. interdiction programs will at most marginally raise the cost of smuggling activities, thus increasing the profit incentives for other traffickers.

Realism and Reality

[. . .] War proclamations, bigger budgets, and more seizures, arrests, and convictions notwithstanding, at the end of President Reagan's watch, the U.S. government was still losing the war on virtually every front. Illicit drugs of all types—especially marijuana, cocaine, and heroin—were more readily available and generally cheaper in the United States in 1989 than they had been at the outset of the Reagan presidency in 1981. Drug use and abuse in U.S. society had increased dramatically over the 1980s and the U.S. drug market remained the biggest and most lucrative in the world. Drug-related crimes and violence had reached epidemic proportions in many U.S. cities, greatly exacerbated by the rapid spread of crack. The national public health system proved unable to cope with the surging demand for treatment and rehabilitation. Law enforcement agencies were overworked, under-funded, often outgunned, increasingly demoralized, and plagued with corruption. The nation's courts and prisons were overwhelmed by the influx of drug-related arrests, trials, and convictions. At the same time, the expanding economic and political power of the drug traffickers threatened, or already had compromised, the institutional integrity and political stability of several Latin American governments, thereby endangering important U.S. interests in the hemisphere. In addition, as a result of U.S. pressure on Latin leaders to "do more" to cooperate with the United States in the war on drugs, violent reprisals directed against government officials and public figures had intensified significantly, placing in doubt the survival of civilian, democratic regimes in various countries of the region.

DRUGS AND NATIONAL SECURITY: THE LATIN AMERICAN PERSPECTIVE

By the mid-1980s, political leaders and administration officials from Mexico to the Andean republics had gradually come to the conclusion that their state security was seriously threatened by the drug problem. To understand the forces behind this conceptual shift, it is necessary to examine how and why it occurred and who was responsible for it, as well as the scope and content of the new national security interpretation of the narcotics issue among the different governments of the region.

At least three factors converged to produce this "late" recognition of the drug problem as a national security priority for most Latin American states. First, the initial position embraced by most Latin American and Caribbean leaders had held that it was largely an American problem, thus justifying a passive approach to it on their part and leaving them vulnerable to the unchecked growth of drug abuse and powerful trafficking organizations in their own countries. On the one hand, they had argued that the insatiable U.S. appetite for drugs was the driving force behind the narcotics trade. On the other hand, they observed that the bulk of drug profits was realized (and invested) in the U.S. economy, which made the United States the key player in the international political economy of drug trafficking. In short, because the United States was seen as both the major consumer and the financial epicenter of this illegal industry, they concluded that the solution to the drug problem would have to come from Washington. [. . .]

Second, Latin America's self-defeating indifference gave the United States free rein to proceed unilaterally to produce a self-serving diagnosis of the drug problem couched in realist premises and to carry out a strategy to combat narcotics trafficking that ignored many of the central concerns of Latin Americans. For Washington, the origins of the drug problem were to be found on the supply side—in Latin America and Caribbean centers of cultivation, processing, and transshipment (diagnosis)—while the most appropriate policies for combating the trade were seen to be suppression at the source (strategy). In accord with this interpretation, after the inauguration of President Reagan in 1981, U.S. pressures on Latin America increased both quantitatively and qualitatively.

The very language of Reagan's war on drugs symbolically captured this tendency in U.S. antidrug policies; the same rhetoric has been invoked by the Bush administration. [. . .]

Third, as U.S. pressures on Latin America to cooperate more fully rose steadily over the decade, few if any Latin American nation-states devised their own alternative strategies to confront the drug issue. This absence of coherent, feasible, and broadly accepted solutions of Latin American origin, combined with the lack of sufficient state resources and the prevailing attitudes of permissiveness or social tolerance toward the narcotics business rooted in the economic benefits it generated, provided fertile ground for the expansion of the drug industry and the criminal rings that manage it. Moreover, virtually all Latin American countries placed other vital interests above the war on drugs as the key priorities of their domestic and foreign policy agendas (for instance, debt, economic growth, poverty, unemployment, income distribution, political violence, and democratic consolidation). [. . .]

THREAT AND TRANSFORMATION

A series of important symbolic events in both the United States and Latin America catalyzed the transformation of Latin American thinking on the narcotics question in the mid-1980s. First, the rhetoric of the war on drugs was formalized in April 1986, when President Reagan issued National Security Decision Directive 221 stating that drug trafficking constituted a lethal threat to U.S. security interests and authorizing an expanded role for the U.S. military in the antinarcotics fight. Second, the decision to move ahead with Operation Blast Furnace in Bolivia in July 1986, with the direct involvement of American troops, signaled that the U.S. government was increasingly disposed to militarize the fight against drugs in Latin America. Third, the emphasis on repression, criminalization, and penalization contained in the 1986 antidrug legislation passed by the U.S. Congress highlighted the trend toward escalation in the war on the international narcotics trade. In effect, the crystallization of a national security perspective on the drug problem in Washington left the governments in the hemisphere little option but to accept the U.S. lead.

In Latin America, the predominance of the hard-line stance in U.S. policymaking circles became, in and of itself, a major source of national insecurity for the governing elites of the region. In effect, compliance with the U.S. national security approach pushed some Latin American states to take up front-line positions in the war on drugs. Their intensification of narcotics control efforts, in turn, unleashed an unprecedented spiral of narco-violence against the state and of state counter-violence against the *narcos*. [. . .] But the rising levels of violence generated by both the progressive militarization of the U.S. antinarcotics strategy in Latin America and the bloody responses of the drug traffickers—along with accompanying paramilitary and guerrilla conflicts—set in motion a wave of drug-related crime and terrorism that directly threatened state security, most dramatically in Colombia and Peru. [. . .]

The alternative outcome—where instead of pursuing the fight against drug traffickers, government officials cooperated with them—was initially less violent, but ultimately no less threatening to both societal and state security. In cases such as the García Meza narcomilitary coup in Bolivia, the Namphy-Paul corrupt military clique in Haiti, or Noriega's military-run money-laundering and smuggling schemes in Panama, state institutions and democratic processes were subverted to the detriment of their nations' entire populations. Second-line states such as Bolivia, Jamaica, and Mexico—major source countries that did not suffer extensive drug violence in the 1980s—were nevertheless beset by increasing corruption and criminality that endangered state security at least indirectly and raised fears that they might be subjected to narco-violence in the future. This combination of present and potential dangers, along with growing U.S. pressures, prompted them to define the drug problem as a national security issue. Although more removed from drug corruption and violence, third-line states like Argentina, Brazil, Ecuador, Venezuela, and many Caribbean and Central American nations were also motivated to adopt, partially or totally, national security interpretations of the drug problem as preemptive measures to forestall possible "Colombianization." [. . .]

CONCEPTUAL CONSENSUS AND THE IMPOSITION OF AN ANTIDRUG NATIONAL SECURITY REGIME

At base, the U.S. insistence on the application of supply-side approaches and military escalation called upon the "source" and "transit" nations in Latin America and the Caribbean to bear the heaviest share of the costs in the fight against drugs. U.S. authorities relied on economic incentives and sanctions, political-diplomatic pressures and reprisals, and occasional resorts to direct military intervention (or the more subtle threat of force) to exact fuller cooperation from Latin American and Caribbean governments. In short, realist U.S. policymakers invoked American superior power resources to impose what may be labeled as an "antidrug national security" regime on the nations of the hemisphere, despite the often bitter criticisms voiced by political leaders throughout the region. Following Stephen Krasner, the term *regime* is defined here as "sets of implicit or explicit principles, norms, rules, and decision-making procedures around which actors' expectations converge in a given area of international relations." An "imposed" regime refers to one that lacks legitimacy, credibility, and symmetry. A regime lacks legitimacy when the nations that are expected to observe the "rules

of the game" established by the hegemonic power do not accept them as binding and try to avoid or circumvent the policy prescriptions and obligations laid
down. A regime lacks credibility when the strategies and tactics proffered are not
seen to be, at least potentially, efficacious in achieving the goals or objectives
posited. A regime lacks symmetry when the costs and benefits of maintaining it
are not viewed as fairly distributed among the parties involved.

Despite the emergence of a general consensus around the notion that international drug trafficking is a security threat for most, if not all, of the nations in the
hemisphere, there is ample evidence that U.S. efforts to impose an antidrug
national security regime throughout the 1980s failed to fulfill the three basic
requirements—legitimacy, credibility, and symmetry—needed for effective in-
stitutionalization. In 1990 the regime was not perceived as legitimate in much of
Latin America and the Caribbean because the roles assigned to various partici-
pating nations had not emerged from collective negotiations and agreements and
because the policy priorities that flowed from it were seen to be the product of
unilateral decisions by U.S. policymakers. It was not perceived as credible because the fundamental thrust of the U.S. narcotics policy focused mainly on
stopping drugs at their source in Latin America and the Caribbean while doing
little to address demand in the United States or to control the export of chemical
inputs, conventional arms trafficking, or money-laundering operations. It was
not perceived as symmetrical because it did not allocate equitably the burdens
involved in enforcing the rules of the game, especially in terms of the human,
institutional, and economic costs incurred by Latin American and Caribbean nations vis-à-vis those borne by the United States. [. . .]

To create the conditions for a consensual regime, it is essential that the U.S. administration first develop an alternative analysis of the international political
economy of drugs that takes into account the complex interdependent nature of
the transnational narcotics business. The roots of drug trafficking and consumption go deep into the economic, social, and political structures of both North
American and Latin American societies. Replacement of the inadequate realist
paradigm with a political economy perspective would require that both the demand and supply facets of the drug problem be addressed simultaneously. The
huge profits that stimulate production and trafficking and fuel the violence and
criminality associated with drug dealing must be eliminated or at least reduced
significantly. Otherwise, the logic of supply and demand within the interdependent international economy will inevitably reproduce the conditions that perpetuate drug trafficking, while stacking the deck against efforts by state authorities—
in developing and developed nations alike—to rein in the industry.

Second, the U.S. government must accept the need to establish cooperative, multilateral decision-making mechanisms in order to obtain a workable, consensus-
based regime. There will undoubtedly be glitches, frustrations, and backsliding in
these attempts, but over the long run, a consensual approach to the international

drug trade provides the only realistic hope for a concerted solution. A corollary to this transition from unilateralism to multilateralism is the need to undertake long-term institution-building efforts both nationally and internationally to improve regulatory and legal capabilities throughout the hemisphere. To be sustainable, such institution-building tasks will have to be coupled with renewed economic opportunities for the hundreds of thousands reliant on the drug industry in Latin America and the Caribbean. [. . .]

Third, to cope with the complex phenomena of demand and supply, the U.S. government must seek to delink national security from the larger set of issues— medical, health-related, social, economic, legal, political, environmental, and diplomatic—that are present within the multifaceted drug problem: there is not "one" problem but many. The narrow national security view limits the options and reduces the flexibility available to government authorities in the United States, Latin America, and the Caribbean to deal with the broad spectrum of issues they face. [. . .]

FROM REAGAN TO BUSH: CONTINUITY AND FAILURE

Although the Reagan administration and its domestic critics frequently differed on specific tactics during the 1980s, the general rationale of U.S. legislation in the drug area consistently reflected a broad consensus between the presidency and Congress that Washington could and should escalate the war effort on all fronts: harsher penalties for both consumption and trafficking; more resources, manpower, and equipment to combat traffickers; tougher law enforcement and interdiction programs domestically and internationally; and intensified political-diplomatic pressures on (or sanctions against) uncooperative source and transit country governments. There was also agreement that the U.S. armed forces and their counterparts in trafficking countries could and should assume key roles in the antidrug battles. [. . .]

Hard-liner dominance in this issue was evident in U.S. budgetary specifications contained in the Anti-Drug Act of 1986. Of the unprecedented $3.9 billion authorized by the U.S. Congress for the antinarcotics effort in FY 1987, three-quarters [was] earmarked for expanded law enforcement, interdiction, and eradication/ substitution programs (supply) versus approximately one-quarter for education, prevention, treatment, and rehabilitation (demand). In effect, the 1986 legislation maintained the same ratio between supply and demand strategies that the Reagan administration had established at the outset of the war on drugs.

In late October 1988, visibly frustrated by the lack of tangible progress in curbing drug production, trafficking, consumption, and related violence—and faced with intense public pressure to "do something" about the U.S. "drug plague" in advance of the November 1988 presidential election—the U.S.

Congress enacted a major new antidrug law: the Anti-Drug Abuse Act of 1988. While retaining the traditional emphasis on supply-side strategies typical of previous U.S. narcotics legislation, the 1988 law focused more explicitly on the demand side of the equation, earmarking 50 percent of federal funding in FY 1989 for domestic demand control and enforcement programs and projecting an increase to 60 percent (demand) versus 40 percent (supply) in FY 1990 and subsequent years.

The shift was not merely cosmetic nor simply a function of political posturing and election-year politicking, although those features were certainly present; it reflected deep disillusionment in the U.S. Congress with the ineffectual supply-side orientation of U.S. antidrug policies during the 1980s. In short, by late 1988 majorities in both houses of Congress had concluded that the current strategies and tactics were simply not getting the job done: the shift was driven by failure.

The heightened priority assigned to demand-side measures in the 1988 law suggested that a conceptual transition away from supply-side policies might be under way in Washington when President Bush assumed office in January 1989. The transition was, however, at best partial and incomplete. The 1988 law did not abandon supply-oriented programs; rather, it renewed or even increased authorized federal funding for these efforts while simultaneously opening a second front directed at demand reduction in the United States.

The Bush administration's record on resource allocations between demand and supply over the first two years in office continued to reflect a higher emphasis on supply control and interdiction than on demand reduction. In addition, beginning with his antidrugs rhetoric during the 1988 presidential campaign, through his inauguration promise that "this scourge will end" and the September 5, 1989, presentation of the new National Drug Strategy prepared by "Drug Czar" William Bennett, right up to the U.S. invasion of Panama on December 20, 1989, President Bush consistently escalated his war of words against drug use and trafficking, thereby raising public expectations of a quick fix to many of the most noxious aspects of the drug question. At the same time, his tough language resonated throughout Latin America and the Caribbean, increasing fears of growing unilateralism in U.S. narcotics control programs abroad.

The Bush administration also steadily expanded the involvement of the U.S. military in the war on drugs at home while stepping up pressure on Latin American governments to assign a greater role to their own armed forces in combating drug trafficking. The extent to which the Bush White House sought broader U.S. military participation in the domestic drug fight was clearly in evidence during Secretary of Defense Richard Cheney's September 19, 1989, statement indicating that "detecting and countering the production and trafficking of illegal drugs is a high-priority national security mission" for the Pentagon. During 1989–1990, funding for the military's antidrug activities was increased substantially and its role was widened: for example, U.S. Navy cooperation with the U.S. Coast Guard in interdiction programs on the high seas, U.S. National Guard participation in patrol activities on the U.S.-Mexican border, U.S. Air Force collaboration with U.S. Customs in aerial service, the military intervention in Panama to oust General Noriega, and the ill-fated deployment of the U.S. fleet off the Colombian coast without Bogotá's permission. Other signs of militarization were found in the construction of Vietnam-style fire bases for DEA [Drug Enforcement Administration] operations in Peru's Alto Huallaga valley. [. . .]

The emphasis on militarization in the Bush administration's international drug policies was nowhere more evident than in the highly publicized "Andean Strategy" announced in September 1989. In the first phase of this initiative—the $65 million emergency aid package sent to Colombia in late September—the U.S. government delivered primarily conventional military equipment, even though the Barco administration had requested intelligence-gathering devices and technical assistance for the severely debilitated Colombian judicial system. The second phase—the budgetary proposal of $261 million for Bolivia, Colombia, and Peru during the first year of the Andean Strategy—contemplated almost exclusively military and police aid. Likewise, the overall Andean plan's projected expenditures of $2.2 billion over the next five fiscal years (1991–1995) also emphasized military assistance over funding for development, health, and social issues and institution building.

At the February 15, 1990, Cartagena Summit attended by President George Bush, Colombia's Virgilio Barco, Peru's Alán García and Bolivia's Jaime Paz Zamora, Bush diplomatically downplayed the military dimensions of U.S. strategy to avoid serious controversy at the meeting while admitting that U.S. demand was a basic factor in the booming international drug trade. Within a few weeks, however, the cordiality and optimism observed at this historic and symbolically important summit began to fade when the U.S. Navy seized two Colombian freighters within the two-hundred-mile international limit without previous approval of the Colombian authorities.

CONCLUSION

The decade of the 1980s witnessed intense pressure on the part of the U.S. government to install an antidrug national security regime in the hemisphere. These efforts failed because Washington did not establish a legitimate, credible, and symmetrical framework capable of coping with the multiple problems presented by international drug production, smuggling, and use.

Notwithstanding some hopeful signs in the 1988 U.S. antinarcotics legislation and in the Bush administration's greater focus on demand-side issues, however, in practice U.S. policy priorities and actions during the first two years of the

Bush presidency constituted a reaffirmation of the traditional realist-security approach with its concomitant emphasis on militarization of U.S. antinarcotics policies at home and abroad. In our view, such attempts to return to the flawed strategies and tactics of the past decade are doomed to failure. Only by modifying both American conceptual premises and postulates (from realism to an interdependent political economy framework) and strategy (from militaristic unilateralism to multilateral and cooperative initiatives) will it be possible for the nations of the hemisphere, in the North and South alike, to make real progress in the fight against drugs. By progress, we do not mean total victory or a drug-free society, but rather movement toward the more modest and realistic goal of effective containment of the negative economic, social, and political consequences of the U.S.–Latin American drug trade in all its dimensions.

VI

LATIN AMERICA AND THE UNITED STATES: FROM THE 1990s TO POST-9/11

The end of the Cold War in 1989 signified a dramatic change and turning point in U.S.–Latin American relations. For the first time, except for a brief period in the 1920s and early 1930s, the United States felt that its security interests in Latin America were safe from extra-hemispheric threats. Previous threats from the Holy Alliance, Great Britain, and France in the nineteenth century, imperial and Nazi Germany during the first forty-five years of the twentieth century, or the Soviet Union during the Cold War, so strongly dominated the structure, issues, and debate involving U.S.–Latin American relations that as the new era of the 1990s loomed, a unique opportunity emerged to restructure, reformulate, and adapt to the changing environment.

During the 1990s the administrations of George H. W. Bush and Bill Clinton worked in a determined fashion to shift hemispheric relations. President Bush scaled back the confrontational posture of his predecessor's rhetoric and policy toward Latin America and pushed to the forefront issues that sought to promote peace, stability, and economic growth in the region. For example, the Enterprise for the Americas (EAI) and the North American Free Trade Agreement (NAFTA) negotiations became the cornerstone of President Bush's Latin American policy: both policies sought the expansion of trade and investments by encouraging Latin American to continue its economic reforms. However, as the contributions by Michael LaRosa and Lance R. Ingwersen and by Wesley Ingwersen and Laura Ávila point out in relation to immigration and the environment, respectively, very little attention was devoted to these contentious issues when considering strategies to build free trade and cooperation between the United States and Latin America. Nevertheless, President Bush's fresh approach helped establish the foundations to promote reciprocity and a spirit of mutual respect and cooperation in the hemisphere.

The Clinton administration in its Presidential Decision Directive (PDD) 28, "U.S. Policy toward Latin America and the Caribbean," outlined the key elements of U.S. policy: Clinton's policy objectives included protecting and promoting democracy, promoting economic reform and integration, encouraging sustainable development, and fighting drug trafficking. The administration's message of cooperation, consensus, and consolidating a "convergence of interests and values" expanded and deepened much of what the previous administration had accomplished. Disagreements and unmet expectations still characterized Clinton's Latin American policy, but it was undeniable that even on the issue of the environment and immigration, Washington had moved beyond simple rhetoric, albeit for some there was still much to do, as the readings in this section suggest.

George W. Bush's inauguration as president in January 2001 energized a renewed U.S. focus on Latin America. During the course of the 2000 campaign and in the months after assuming office, the president made it clear that the number one priority of his administration's foreign policy was Latin America. He hoped to expand and deepen much of what his predecessors had left unfinished: His particular interest involved trade and Bush hoped that his legacy for U.S.–Latin American relations would be to build a permanent Free Trade of the Americas Association (FTAA). However, the tragic events of 9/11 dramatically shifted U.S. foreign policy toward terrorism and the Middle East, much to the detriment of U.S. interests in Latin America, as pointed out in the readings from Michael Shifter, Jorge G. Castañeda and Arturo Valenzuela. The broad U.S. policy agenda that defined administration policy toward the region in the first few months, quickly narrowed to focus on security matters. Once again, Washington returned to the period when it looked at the Latin American region through the exclusive prism of national security. Gradually, as Washington disengaged, Latin America's governance challenges grew—poverty, violence, corruption, and inequality weakened the legitimacy and effectiveness of democratic institutions in the region.

In his contribution, Jorge Castañeda, former Mexican foreign minister, asserts that U.S. neglect in Latin America will come at a cost to U.S. interests and Latin American stability and prosperity. As challenges mount against democratic rule, U.S. security interests are threatened. Michael Shifter, Program Director and Senior Fellow at the Inter-American Dialogue in Washington, D.C., argues that opportunities for deepening a common hemispheric agenda—begun by president George H. W. Bush—were completely squandered after 9/11. More importantly, Shifter notes that unilateralism in U.S. foreign policy has considerably weakened the spirit of mutual cooperation that had been building for over a decade in hemispheric relations. Finally, Arturo Valenzuela of Georgetown University alludes to the growing dangers of anti-Americanism in Latin America and insists that Washington needs to move beyond the narrow agenda of security and free trade to address Latin America's social and economic ills. The three readings also focus on the poor handling of several crises in the region (i.e., Argentina and Venezuela) as an indication of the administration's inability or unwillingness to understand the serious challenges and opportunities the region offers U.S. strategic interests.

Meanwhile, the Latin American public has grown increasingly dissatisfied with the results of democratic rule and economic neoliberalism. The target of the discontent has been the United States and globalization along with elected governments, which are perceived as corrupt and incompetent. For many in the region, FTAA was to be the answer to all of the region's socioeconomic problems. However, as Luisa Angrisani points out in her analysis, not only has free trade not delivered Latin America from social and economic despair, but, as Washington has focused its energies on the Middle East, free trade negotiations have stalled. The vacuum created by a perceived U.S. indifference has challenged Latin America to look inward—toward broadening and deepening economic and diplomatic ties within the region. Angrisani suggests that this development might not bode well for U.S. leadership in the region. Meanwhile, other key hemispheric issues such as immigration and the environment—discussed in chapters 23 and 26, respectively—not only remain unresolved but, in fact, have been largely unaddressed. As of this writing, the immigration issue is back on the front burner, but a clear, satisfactory immigration policy is unlikely to emerge anytime in the near future.

Finally, Professor Richard L. Harris of California State University, Monterey Bay, argues that progressive movements in Latin America have failed to provide an alternative to globalization and the failed policies of neoliberalism. Although some organizations have provided counterproposals, none have received much traction or enough support to mobilize social groups across the region. Professor Harris identifies the accomplishments of some groups in Brazil and Mexico, but their efforts have not generated widespread appeal outside their national borders. All the readings in this section clearly indicate that U.S.–Latin American relations in the post-9/11 period are replete with frustration and uncertainty. The expectations that many in the hemisphere had with the fall of the Berlin Wall were frustrated by the consequences of the collapse of New York's Twin Towers.

22

More Latin, Less America?
Creating a Free Trade Area of the Americas

Luisa Angrisani

President George W. Bush, upon assuming the presidency in January 2001, was unequivocal in his determination to shift the focus of U.S. foreign policy to Latin America. The administration decided that stronger ties to the region could result from negotiations leading to a Free Trade Area of the Americas (FTAA). The FTAA was to be the answer to the region's political and economic woes— poverty, unemployment, weak political institutions, and economic stagnation. However, as Luisa Angrisani points out, September 11 dramatically shifted the administration's priorities toward "devoting all its energies to the Middle East while essentially turning it back on its closest neighbors." Thus, free trade negotiations stalled and U.S.–Latin American relations entered their worst period since the end of the Cold War. Rather than complaining, Angrisani notes that Latin American countries turned inward—to Latin America—in order to broaden and deepen economic/diplomatic ties within the region. Brazil and Mexico have worked deliberately to strengthen economic and political influence in their subregions, in the Mercosur countries and Central America, respectively. The relative U.S. absence has created a vacuum that others are filling. Meanwhile, Washington's leadership role in the region diminishes.

Shortly after becoming president, George W. Bush embarked on a campaign to expand the North American Free Trade Area (NAFTA) to encompass thirty-four nations in the Western Hemisphere, spanning from Canada in the north to Argentina and Chile in the south. The new trade bloc—the Free Trade Area of the Americas (FTAA)—would include over 800 million consumers and a total economy of some $13 trillion. Bush repeatedly stated that the free trade area would strengthen democracy, promote economic integration, and bring peace and prosperity to Latin America, all of which the president, speaking at the Third Summit of the Americas in April 2001 in Québec City, described as vital to U.S. national interests.

Though grand plans of uniting the Americas have been around for some time (Simón Bolívar was the first to come up with the idea), negotiations always faltered on fears that stronger, more economically diverse nations would take control and subvert the sovereignty and national identity of smaller countries. This concern, the old core-periphery argument, was a standard part of all talks on integration issues and was generally invoked against the United States whenever Washington touched on the subject (as the elder President Bush did in 1990). Those countries in favor of free trade with the United States, like Chile, preferred tailored bilateral accords anyway and therefore had no pressing desire to advance regional pan-American integration.

After taking office, George W. Bush was able to allay these fears and rally support for the FTAA. At the Third Summit of the Americas, delegates from thirty-four countries (every Western Hemisphere country except Cuba) agreed to set January 2005 as the deadline for finalizing negotiations. Heralded as an unprecedented agreement, the FTAA was to be the answer to the region's economic woes. The free movement of goods, technology, and labor was proposed as the solution to Latin America's increasing levels of poverty, unemployment, and economic stagnation. And to sweeten the deal, the United States was offering up a bevy of substantial perks, including a promise to put on the table all issues, such as those U.S. policies that are viewed negatively in Latin America and the eventual elimination of all tariffs (though this would not have to take place until 2015). Even so, getting all thirty-four countries to agree, despite very vocal critics, was a miraculous feat.

What happened? Since April 2001, talks have stalled, and the core-periphery arguments have returned in a new light and with a new slant—and returned with a vengeance. The old cries to close off trade avenues and implement import substitution policies have been left behind. The region today is rallying for free trade, but without relying on the United States to be the sponsor of such initiatives.

The defining moment in U.S.–Latin American relations came on September 11, 2001, after which the United States opted to devote all its energies to the Middle East while essentially turning its back on its closest neighbors.[1] Though the state of affairs following the terrorist attacks could perhaps not have been anticipated, the effects of the U.S. response were eminently predictable. It pulled all attention away from Latin America and polarized the region rather than building a solid coalition grounded in a common purpose. Coupled with a series of unforgivable mistakes—the Treasury Department's diplomatic gaffes with regard to Argentina's economic crisis (which many insist only exacerbated Argentina's problems), the State Department's failure to condemn the coup that briefly ousted Hugo Chávez in Venezuela, and the Bush Administration's disparaging remarks about Brazil's 2002 presidential elections—America's policy shift cast the United States in an increasingly negative light.

Spurned countries decided they did not need the United States to help them out of their troubles (Argentina and Brazil), nor did they need to support the United States in its overseas adventures (Chile and Mexico). The war in Iraq widened the divide in relations between the United States and its southern neighbors, and the fallout since the end of the war has only made matters worse. Latin Americans are ever more skeptical of the self-appointed U.S. role as the champion of democracy. Serious questions abound regarding the validity of the war—whether weapons of mass destruction ever existed and what U.S. intentions really were—and the perception of the Bush Administration as bordering on tyrannical has gained much more currency in the region.

Neglecting its once most-favored neighbors will ultimately have steep consequences for the Bush Administration. Politically, the United States will face more open dissension in the international arena. Economically, the United States may end up missing the biggest trade opportunity in its history.

COURTING THE LOCALS

Part of understanding the damage of the fall involves realizing what heights we had reached before it. The decision to create the FTAA was a major step in cementing U.S. influence in Latin America. President Bush highlighted his interest in strengthening ties by making direct overtures to regional leaders—his first official presidential trip was to visit Mexican President Vicente Fox at his ranch in Guanajuato, breaking the tradition of honoring Canada with a president's first visit. In addition to the usual promises to increase trade and improve ties across borders, the president touched on the one topic that had been taboo in U.S. politics for decades: legalizing the status of Mexican immigrants. Though most observers knew that an immigration accord would be difficult to pass through Congress—probably even impossible—the willingness of the Bush Administration to at least address the issue was heartening to Fox, the underdog who was able to break the Institutional Revolutionary Party's (PRI) seventy-one-year monopoly on power and the darling of both domestic and international political analysts. The political outsider and savvy businessman was making moves for Mexico, becoming friendly with the United States and taking on issues that resonated with the average Mexican: jobs, immigration, and social improvements.

Talks on immigration issues were decidedly over after the September 11 attacks. U.S. legislators, heeding the calls of their constituencies, formed a united front on such matters. Far from discussing amnesty for illegal immigrants, they discussed laws to increase vigilance on the border under the rubric of homeland security. The domestic price for Vicente Fox was steep. He and his advisers could no longer flaunt their close relationship with the Bush Administration when dealing with the Mexican legislature, as it had now been transformed into a liability. In the buildup to the war in Iraq, Fox became painfully aware that in order to salvage his domestic political bargaining power, he would have to make a bold break with Bush. Fox thus announced that Mexico would support a "compromise solution" and not a U.S.-sponsored invasion. The decision shocked the Bush Administration, which had counted on Mexican support in the UN Security Council. Instead, the Bush Administration saw its close neighbor and second-largest trading partner side with France, the embodiment of an ungrateful ally in the eyes of the United States. Newspaper editorials highlighting Mexico's allegiance with France frightened the Fox Administration and galvanized the feeling that the Fox-Bush friendship was, for all intents and purposes, over.

A similar situation occurred in U.S.-Chile relations. Having witnessed Chile's failure to secure free trade agreements with both the first Bush Administration in the early 1990s and the Clinton Administration several years later, skeptics were wary that any progress would be made with the second Bush Administration. After two years of negotiations, the skeptics were proven wrong, as U.S. Trade Representative Robert Zoellick announced in December 2002 that negotiations for the U.S.-Chile Free Trade Agreement were complete. Ratification and implementation, which were expected to take place quickly, instead stalled on Chile's decision not to support the war in Iraq at the UN Security Council.

Chile's ties to the United States put it between a rock and a hard place: choosing to seek a bilateral trade agreement with the United States had driven a wedge between Chile and its South American neighbors. Brazil and Argentina had long courted Chile to join the Southern Cone Common Market (known as Mercosur) in an attempt to form a united front—of sorts—in South America. Chile faced a difficult choice. On the one hand, it could ally with a trading bloc in which individual states always subverted agreed tariff limits by issuing decrees and granting preferential treatment to their domestic industry at the expense of their trading partners. On the other hand, it could follow a trade policy that would result in assured access to the holy grail of markets, the United States.

This was an unenviable position in which to be, but, ultimately, Chile's President Ricardo Lagos opted for the United States. It was a move that Mercosur members (Argentina, Brazil, Paraguay, and Uruguay) would not soon forget. Chile gained notoriety in the region for having chosen not to join the Mercosur club, and when relations with the United States soured over Iraq, it paid dearly in the local media. The Lagos Administration opposed the war, as did most other Latin American nations, but its opposition was especially detrimental to the U.S. campaign for support because Chile, like Mexico, had a seat on the UN Security Council. Although President Lagos tried to reassure business interests that his opposition to the war would not negatively impact the trade agreement, it became obvious that it would. The treaty's ratification was inexplicably delayed, and Mercosur members secretly gloated.

Chile realized it would need some insurance if the United States decided to delay ratification indefinitely. Sensing that the tide was turning in Latin American politics because of the newfound success of left-leaning politicians in many countries, Lagos decided to be proactive. Visits to neighboring countries and favorable commentary in the local press were part of his campaign. Though Lagos will not be able to cobble together his own coalition, he will be able to garner enough goodwill to restart talks to join Mercosur, something that will further weaken America's bargaining power.

CHANGING OF THE GUARD

An obvious leadership vacuum opened up when the United States turned its attention away from the region. Faced with a rapidly disintegrating trade scenario, several regional players decided to take matters into their own hands by beginning a discussion of regional integration. From Vicente Fox, principal U.S. trade partner, to Fidel Castro, principal U.S. irritator, the region's leaders all agree the time is ripe to begin a process of increased integration—even if they clearly disagree about its ultimate shape. In separate attempts to carve out their spheres of influence, Mexico and Brazil began negotiating new agreements and enhancing old ones to secure leadership roles in the emerging debate over regional economic integration. Their moves to fill the newly opened power vacuum have caused the United States to take notice. Furthermore, if the situation in the Middle East takes a significant turn for the worse, the United States will have to take action if it is to retain some negotiating power among its neighbors to the south.

Brazil has emerged as the most problematic actor with regard to U.S. influence in Latin America. After a tense electoral period in December 2002, Luiz Inácio da Silva, a left-leaning former labor leader known locally as Lula, secured the presidency with a substantial popular mandate. Immediately thereafter, he set out on a tour of his country to visit and show concern for the poorest segment of the Brazilian population. His "Zero Hunger" program, which provides food subsidies, was launched with surprising bipartisan support, thus securing Lula's image as a concerned politician and social reformer. Following that triumph, he set out on a regional trip to rally support for increased economic integration and home-grown solutions to the region's social ills. His whistle-stop tour included visits to Mercosur partners Argentina, Uruguay, and Paraguay, and to several members of the Andean Community (made up of Bolivia, Colombia, Ecuador, Peru, and Venezuela), as well as to Chile. Lula's oft-repeated mantra of a stronger, united South America was very well received, but it conveniently left several actors out of the picture—NAFTA in general and the United States and Mexico in particular.

Lula's efforts to win support for a South American free trade area have centered on convincing his neighbors of the inequality inherent in U.S. trade policies. He has on several occasions voiced his opposition to U.S. policies that are detrimental to South America: namely, U.S. farm subsidies and the early 2002 imposition of steel tariffs. Despite U.S. promises that these issues will be addressed in the context of the FTAA, Lula remains unconvinced—particularly because of the powers of "fast track" authority, which were granted to President Bush by the U.S. Congress in 2001. Fast track authority allows the president to proceed rapidly with trade negotiations, eliminating much of the bureaucracy and facilitating talks. However, fast track authority also imposes harsh restrictions on the administration's ability to negotiate more open trade in certain product categories. Not surprisingly, these categories include textiles, steel, and agriculture—the most heavily protected product areas in the United States and the areas in which Brazil and several other Latin American nations have substantial comparative advantages.

The recently passed 2002 Farm Bill is a perfect case in point. Though farm subsidies are limited under the terms of the Uruguay Round Trade Agreement, the powerful U.S. agricultural lobby, in a bid to reap the highest possible benefit for a small number of domestic producers, has expertly molded the legislation. Under this bill, U.S. farmers will receive subsidies averaging $19.53 billion annually for the 2002–2007 period—a substantial increase from the $15.27 billion average annual payment in the previous Farm Bill (that covered the years 1996–2001). But perhaps the most disturbing aspect of the Farm Bill is how it directly flies in the face of previous agreements that were intended to "level the playing field" with the developing world.[2] Since commodity production is a major part of the developing world's economy, such subsidies only create a more uneven playing field.

Steel tariffs are another example. The 30 percent tariff on steel imports imposed by Congress was intended to grant relief to America's ailing domestic steel industry. It effectively insulated domestic producers from their foreign competitors and disproportionately affected Brazilian steel exports. Prior to the imposition of steel tariffs, Brazil had a favorable balance of trade with the United States. Conditions now, however, are decidedly less favorable. The United States claims that these issues can be resolved once FTAA negotiations get under way, but Lula and many other leaders in Latin America would rather apply pressure now than wait until the FTAA is created. (The WTO ruled in July that the steel tariffs violate global trade rules. The United States is appealing the decision.)

Lula's strategy to combat U.S. protectionism focuses on expanding Mercosur to include Chile and Bolivia as full members, as well as including the rest of the Andean Community. His keen understanding of Mercosur's potential as an engine of unification was evident at the group's June 2003 meeting in Asuncion,

Paraguay. The Brazilian contingent presented a comprehensive plan made up of five programs: the political, social, and cultural program; the customs union program; the common market program; the new integration program; and the border integration program. Each program highlights the current situation and what steps Mercosur can take as an integrated body to redress issues and problems.

The goals include improving democratic institutions, limiting corruption, and improving social conditions. (Lula has already become the champion of the poor in Brazil and wants to expand his constituency to include the poor of Mercosur as well.) In addition, the plan seeks to strengthen the customs union and expand the common market by including new partners and negotiating trade agreements with the European Union, India, South Africa, and South Korea. The joint statement issued at the end of the meeting reiterated Mercosur's commitment to the development of democracy, the protection of human rights, and a multilateral approach to international conflict through the United Nations and the Security Council—a not-so-subtle indication of the group's hesitancy regarding U.S.-led conflict resolution. In addition, the statement outlines that negotiations with the Andean Community will be completed by the end of 2003.

Before other countries can be included, however, the original members must iron out their difficulties and harden their commitment to the common market—with "common" being the operative word. Both Brazil and Argentina have often approached tariff policy with an eye toward protecting their own industrial sectors. When common policy did not suit their individual needs they issued domestic decrees that did, often at the expense of the trading bloc.

Without a resolution to this problem, a policy of South American economic integration would not be worth the paper on which it was printed. At the June Mercosur meeting, Lula deftly handled this issue of unilateral backsliding from common policy. For now, Argentina's cheap imports of capital goods will be tolerated, as will Brazil's imports of chemicals. But these waivers are to be eliminated in 2004. In an appeal to the smaller members, Uruguay and Paraguay, Lula stressed the need to have a directly-elected parliament in place by 2006 that will hold sway over common policies. A joint monetary institute that would work toward the creation of a common currency is also to be in place by 2006. In addition, the June resolution announced that bidders on government contracts would no longer receive special treatment from their home governments—something that had been on the table for some time but on which little consensus could be reached. These concessions produced one very positive effect: Uruguay committed itself to negotiating trade agreements solely as part of Mercosur, forgoing bilateral treaties. This proved a critical step toward greater integration, for Uruguay had often threatened economic unilateralism in response to such movements by Brazil and Argentina.

The trading bloc stands to gain greatly from including new members. Trade agreements between Mercosur and Peru are under way and should be completed by the end of this year (2003). Venezuelan President Hugo Chávez attended the June meeting as a precursor to the start of negotiations with Mercosur, and that pact should also be completed by year-end. (Though Peru and Venezuela are both members of the Andean Community, they are interested in completing individual treaties with Mercosur as quickly as possible. These treaties would be similar to a larger treaty encompassing the entire Andean Community, but they would likely come into effect before a Mercosur-Andean Community treaty.)

Mexico has emerged as another regional leader willing to take the place of the United States in negotiating trade talks, but it is at a certain disadvantage (much more so than Brazil) because of its location and its historical allegiance to the United States. In the international sphere, Mexico's fortunes have been tied to the United States and not to the rest of Latin America because of NAFTA. Evidence of this can be seen in the fact that Mexico's recent bond issues have been successful, while other Latin American bond issues have been cancelled because of skyrocketing risk ratings. Mexico's links to the United States served it well when relations were good: It was able to place all sorts of issues on the international market, but this success was based solely on its relationship with the United States. Once it soured, Mexico, rather than drift alone, opted to return to its roots and reestablish links to Latin America for better or for worse.

Originally one of the main proponents of the FTAA, Mexico has since turned to its much-neglected neighbors to the south in an effort to form its own coalition. After successfully completing negotiations with the Northern Triangle—the area made up of El Salvador, Guatemala, and Honduras—Mexico is now negotiating a free trade agreement with all of Central America. President Fox has campaigned hard to gather a following for the Plan Puebla Panama, the free trade area that would unite the region from Mexico in the north to Panama in the south. Fox hopes that a larger Mexican presence in the region will bring that country back into the Latin American fold after a long, self-imposed hiatus.

Trade talks are going well so far. The Northern Triangle agreement provides both Mexico and the Central American countries with substantial trade benefits. The best part of the agreement, however, is the message it sends: namely, that a free trade area can be achieved, with positive benefits, without U.S. sponsorship. The agreement includes provisions that spur infrastructure improvements for entire countries, such as an interconnected highway network and electricity grid, rather than improvements solely for areas in which international companies are situated. Though domestic opposition to some aspects of the trade agreements have been disruptive, the potential for sparking development and growth is great.

There is a danger that, in flexing its trade negotiation muscles, Mexico will run up against Brazil—and Brazil is a formidable power. The region's largest and most populous country is centrally located and has much to gain from being the directing force in the region. Mexico will continue to be held back by the impression, prevalent in Latin America, that Mexico has only turned to the south because it was spurned by the United States. And even Mexico's supposed partners in the trade game, the Central American countries, are hedging their bets. They have embarked on trade talks with the United States to create CAFTA (the Central American Free Trade Agreement), just in case things with Mexico do not pan out.

WHAT'S A FADING GIANT TO DO?

Latin American leaders have accepted that the positive effects of free trade outweigh the negative, but they are aware they cannot depend on the United States to take the lead in these matters. As the possibility of non–U.S.-centered regional trade areas become more of a reality, the United States will have to reengage in talks or risk being left out of the loop. And in this regard, it appears that a slight shift in focus is taking place.

In a somewhat surprising move, the Bush Administration announced that it would sign the U.S.-Chile free trade agreement in June 2003 despite numerous delays brought on by Chile's decision not to support the U.S. intervention in Iraq. U.S. Trade Representative Robert Zoellick signed the agreement in Miami with little fanfare. Generally, signing such agreements is cause for celebration and a visit to the White House, but not this time. Though the United States might not have really wanted to sign the trade agreement, officials realized that their position in the region was being compromised because of it. In an attempt to reinsert itself in regional trade circles, the administration consented to sign the agreement, but relations with Chile remain strained. The House of Representatives ratified it on July 23, and the Senate followed suit on July 31.

In addition to signing the agreement, Zoellick traveled to Argentina and Brazil on a goodwill mission. His goal was to convince Nestor Kirchner in Argentina and Lula in Brazil that the United States is still keen on creating the FTAA. He received a cool reception. No commitments were made, but the lines of communication have been reopened. In late June 2003, Lula traveled to Washington for a visit with President Bush, making him the first Latin American leader to do so since the Iraq war. The meeting went well, despite fears that the two leaders would find little common ground. Though Lula did state that he was interested in re-starting FTAA talks, he did not, however, offer a specific date for doing so.

The U.S. absence has left a vacuum that others want to fill, and unless some moves are made quickly, America's leadership role in the region will be greatly diminished. The United States would be particularly wise to appease Brazil's concerns if it wishes to smooth relations between the two countries and continue its push for the FTAA. Putting agricultural subsidies and steel tariffs on the negotiating agenda, in earnest, would be the most obvious way to do so.

Another sticking point is Washington's proposal to impose stringent intellectual property rights that would far exceed requirements set by the World Trade Organization. U.S. negotiators are seeking to limit the ability of nations to issue compulsory licenses, which allow the local production of generic versions whether or not the patent holder approves. Brazil, which successfully gained WTO approval to continue the practice, has long been a supporter of compulsory licensing, for it provides cheaper versions of necessary medicines. Additionally, the United States should scale back calls for unlimited access to Latin American markets for services and make concessions on nontariff barriers that the United States regularly imposes, such as phytosanitary controls.

Though domestic lobbies make it difficult to scale back on some unfair trade practices, the United States as a whole risks losing much more than these individual sectors gain. Though concessions will ultimately have to be granted by all sides, advancing a hemisphere-wide trade agreement should be a top priority for the Bush Administration. Losing markets—and allies—is far too costly in these uncertain times.

> Do not think that this is a matter of your liberty or your slavery. It also concerns the loss of the empire and the danger from the hatred you have incurred in its exercise. It is no longer possible to step down [from the empire]; . . . you hold it, so to speak, like a tyranny. While it may have been unjust to acquire, it is now dangerous to let go of it.
>
> —Pericles's final speech to the Athenians
> Thucydides, *The Peloponnesian War*, 2.63.1–2

23

U.S. Immigration Policies in Historic Context: A Latin American Case Study

Michael LaRosa and Lance R. Ingwersen

The United States has always been a place of attraction for Latin American citizens who have arrived to escape political tensions, economic difficulties, and warfare. Until 1929, the United States held an essentially "open door" policy with respect to Latin American immigration. The following chapter surveys U.S. immigration policy, focusing on policies directed at Latin Americans. The chapter concentrates on the period from the 1980s to the present, but documents a long history of changing political, social, and economic landscapes that has shaped immigration policy. The essay demonstrates the complexity of immigration policy, and suggests that debate over policy options is likely to continue in the immediate and distant future. This chapter is especially pertinent today, as calls for immigration reform are once again commanding the attention of leaders in Washington and making headlines in the press.

> "From the earliest days of our history, this land has been a refuge for the oppressed, and it is proper that we now, as descendents of refugees and immigrants, continue our long humanitarian tradition of helping those who are forced to flee to maintain their lives as individual, self-sufficient human beings in freedom, self-respect, dignity, and health."
>
> —President John F. Kennedy

Immigration policy in the United States has historically been formulated in response to changing attitudes and significant events that alter public sentiment. Wars, economic crises, and periods of public paranoia have been followed by anti-immigration waves in the United States; in contrast, people tend not to discuss immigration policy during periods of economic prosperity and peace. This chapter will focus on the recent immigration debate in the United States, emphasizing the period since 1986, while placing immigration policies and patterns from Latin America in the context of U.S. history.

The terrorist attacks on 9/11 changed the contour of U.S. history, and laid the groundwork for a renewed discussion of the role of "the other" in U.S. society. Americans began once again to focus on the question of "American identity," and suddenly, men from Middle Eastern countries generated suspicion for many citizens of the United States. Many Middle Easterners—particularly those who had overstayed student, travel, or other visas, or had some sort of criminal record—were quietly detained and deported. Passage of the "Patriot Act" and the creation of a new Department of Homeland Security helped Americans believe that the government was "doing something" to stop future terrorist attacks. By October 2001, the United States was at war in Afghanistan, taking down the Taliban. Seventeen months later, the United States declared war on Iraq for reasons that, as of this writing, are not entirely clear. The first "American" casualty of the war was Marine Corporal José Gutiérrez, age twenty-two, who lived as an orphan on the streets of Guatemala before coming to the United States in 1995 by walking and jumping freight trains. He lived in Lomita, California, joined the U.S. Marines, and died in Iraq on 21 March 2003; he was not an American citizen at the time of his death, but was awarded citizenship posthumously. Gutiérrez, among many others, paid the ultimate price in serving and protecting the United States. His tragic story also serves as a microcosm of the many significant contributions immigrants have made through the course of U.S. history; the U.S. economy and culture are dependent on immigrants, and our nation has prospered thanks in large measure to immigrants' energy, talents, and willingness to work for low wages, usually performing unpleasant work.

According to statistics from 2004, there are about thirty-six million foreign-born persons living in the United States. This number does not include approximately eleven million persons living in the United States without legal documentation. Of all undocumented persons residing in the United States, about 60 percent are from Mexico—the country that shares a 2,000-mile border with the United States. Naturally, then, any discussion of immigration, immigration reform, and policies must take into consideration the unique, historic border that links together the United States and Mexico, the first world and the developing world, a predominantly Anglo/Protestant Culture and a Hispanic/Catholic culture.

The story begins in 1846 when the United States invaded Mexico, seized the capital city, and annexed, via the 1848 Treaty of Guadalupe Hidalgo, 51 percent of Mexican territory. That territory comprises present-day Texas, Arizona, New Mexico, California, Utah, and Colorado. Some Mexican citizens who lived in important cities, such as El Paso and San Antonio, headed south after 1848, crossing a border that had in fact crossed them. Others stayed, establishing a significant Hispanic presence in the United States over 150 years ago. Some of the traditional Hispanic families in the Southwest, specifically in south Texas and southern New Mexico, trace their ancestry back to this period of warfare, social change, and political upheaval.

Fifty years later, the 1898 short war with Spain, the so-called Spanish-American War, whereby the United States took control of the final vestiges of the Spanish overseas empire—i.e., Cuba, Puerto Rico, Guam, and the Philippines (after several years of intense, bloody conflict)—dramatically impacted patterns of immigration from the Caribbean. Puerto Rico became a "self-governing Commonwealth in Association with the United States," and Puerto Ricans have been U.S. citizens since 1917. Cuba's story is quite different; diplomatic relations between Cuba and the United States were ended in January 1961, after Fidel Castro's 1959 Socialist Revolution. Current U.S.-Cuba policy is an eerie reminder of the Cold War, and Cubans who escape Castro's island nation—and arrive to the U.S. shore, touching land with at least one foot—are granted political asylum.

Between 1910 and 1920, the first major political and social revolution of the twentieth century occurred in Mexico. The Mexican Revolution resulted in the deaths of about 1.5 million Mexican citizens and displaced about one million more, most of whom traveled north to the United States. They settled in the cities and towns along the border and moved into southern California, Arizona, New Mexico, and Texas, establishing a presence that remains visible today. There, they worked in agriculture and construction at a time when population density in the "West" was extremely low, and workers were needed to harvest and construct the infrastructure for the cities that would emerge: Houston, El Paso, Las Cruces, Tucson, Phoenix, San Diego, and Los Angeles all benefited from this free flow of skilled and inexpensive labor.

The First World War coincided with the Mexican Revolution, and at the conclusion of the world conflict, the United States underwent a period of heightened anti-immigration sentiment. The mood of the country was decidedly "isolationist," as evidenced by the U.S. refusal to sign on to Woodrow Wilson's League of Nations. Reflecting growing fears from the 1917 Russian "Red" Revolution, the U.S. Congress passed the "Emergency Immigration Act" of 1921, which restricted immigration from belligerent countries (primarily Germany, Italy, and Russia). This Emergency Act was formulated into the Immigration Act of 1924 and passed during the administration of Calvin Coolidge. This legislation set "quotas" for immigrants entering the United States; quotas were set at 2 percent of the total of any given nation's residents in the United States, as reported in the 1890 Census. By using the 1890 Census, the U.S. government was clearly interested in excluding Italians, Russians, and Bulgarians. Initially, the legislation failed to include guidelines for the Western Hemisphere, reflecting the fact that, in the early 1920s, Latin American immigration was hardly perceived as a "threat" to any segment of U.S. society or culture.

In October 1929, the stock market and banking collapse cost millions of Americans their life savings and plunged the economy into a deep, prolonged depression. Unemployment levels in the United States that reached 40 percent during the worst years of the Great Depression had a lasting impact on immigrants from Mexico and other parts of Latin America. A new "anti-immigrant wave" hit the United States and, according to one author, "More than 500,000 [Mexicans] were forcibly deported during the 1930s, among them many who were U.S. citizens."[1]

Toward the end of the 1930s, the United States was facing new challenges, namely, preparation for a Second World War. The United States would not officially enter the conflict until after the Japanese attack at Pearl Harbor in December 1941, but the country, in 1939, began restructuring industry toward wartime production. This meant, of course, the need for increased numbers of seasonal agricultural laborers in the South, Southwest, and West; citizens from Mexico would meet this need via a new program, agreed to by the U.S. and Mexican governments, known as the *bracero* program. The program began in 1942 and lasted until 1964. About five million migrants came to the United States via formal, temporary contracts that stipulated their length of stay, working conditions, and wages, and that guaranteed housing, good working conditions, and decent food (*braceros'* daily wage was set at the local rate, and those workers engaged in "piece work" were to receive no less than thirty cents per hour). Board was deducted from the *bracero* wage at $1.75 per day, and workers understood that 10 percent of all earnings would be repatriated, via banks in the United States, to savings accounts in Mexico as a sort of "forced savings" program. Much of this money (estimated at about 150 million dollars) was never paid out to the *bracero* workers.

But the program did represent a spirit of cooperation between the United States and Mexico at a time of international crisis. Mexican laborers, then, contributed to the stability and efficacy of the U.S. agricultural sector during the war, and Mexican Americans distinguished themselves as soldiers in the U.S. army. According to Juan González, "more than 375,000 Mexican Americans saw active duty in the U.S. armed forces, many in critical combat roles."[2] Mexican pilots flew missions in the South Pacific in support of the Allied effort, and Mexican raw materials including petroleum, minerals, and agricultural products helped the Allies defeat the Axis powers by 1945.

Discrimination against Mexicans and African Americans after the war demonstrated a glaring contradiction in U.S. society. How could Mexican Americans and African Americans be treated as "second-class citizens" after they contributed so bravely to the war effort—to the preservation of democracy—and died in the struggle against fascism/racism in Hitler's Europe? Postwar prosperity in the 1950s and 1960s contributed to the formulation of a new social consciousness in the United States. An increased push for more equal rights and opportunities culminated in the landmark civil rights legislation of 1964. And from this early 1960s spirit of fighting against discrimination, admitting past mistakes, and using the power of the federal government to "correct" past abuses, the U.S. Senate passed the Immigration and Nationality Act Amendments on 3 October 1965. This legislation abolished the 1924 quota system, which was deemed discriminatory. After 1965, 170,000 people from the Eastern Hemisphere and 120,000 from the Western Hemisphere were allowed to enter the United States per year. For the first time in over forty years, immigrants were selected based on their skills rather than their country of origin. Most of the votes in the Senate against this legislation came from racist Southerners, who fought feverishly against civil rights legislation and immigration reforms that would permit entry to persons from underdeveloped countries (i.e., Asians and Latin Americans).

After 1965, the next major immigration reform act that directly affected Latin American immigration to the United States was the Immigration Reform and Control Act (IRCA), passed during the presidency of Ronald Reagan in 1986. This legislation granted legal immigration status to some 2.7 million "unauthorized" individuals (mostly agricultural workers living in the Southwest United States originating from Central American countries and Mexico) and sought to penalize employers who knowingly hired undocumented immigrants. Of course, this law spurred an overnight cottage industry in false documentation—fake (but passable) documents could be produced for employers, who by taking only a cursory glance, covered themselves from prosecution under the law. The 1986 legislation did not stop the flow of undocumented immigrants as it was intended to do. Failure to adequately enforce the employer provisions of the legislation did little to prevent the hiring of undocumented workers, and U.S. policy in Central America actually exacerbated the migratory flow. In fact, a few years earlier—during the final days of the Carter Administration—the 1980 Refuge Act was passed in response largely to the influx of Central American immigrants fleeing from their war-torn homelands. The Refuge Act declared that anyone could apply for political asylum if they could demonstrate a "well-founded fear of persecution" based on race, religion, or political/social organization membership.

The passage of the IRCA legislation of 1986 can be understood as a Republican president caving to pressure from his own party to "do something" about increasing flows of poor immigrants from Mexico and Central America. Americans were loath to realize that U.S. policy in El Salvador, Guatemala, and Nicaragua contributed significantly to the mass exodus from those countries. Ronald Reagan's obsession with Central America derailed, and nearly destroyed, his presidency: Secret operations conducted out of the basement of the White House funded Nicaraguan *contrarevolucionarios* (*contras*) who battled the Marxist Sandinista Government of Nicaragua against the wishes of Congress, which by 1986 had placed limits on the amount of funding the *contras* could receive. Reagan referred to the *contras* as "freedom-fighters" for their staunch anticommunist positions. Their critics called them thugs, or terrorists.

The 1986 IRCA legislation was ineffective at stopping or curbing migratory flows: Latin Americans continued to arrive as scorched earth tactics in Guatemala, El Salvador, and Nicaragua destroyed crops and left behind tens of thousands of corpses. By November 1990, reflecting the chaos of Central America, the U.S. Congress was forced to grant Temporary Protected Status (TPS) to Salvadorans, Guatemalans, and Nicaraguans who argued that they would more than likely be killed due to the violence and instability in Central America should they return to their homeland. Since the United States was financing at least one side in each Central American conflict, the petition could not be ignored in Washington.

The 1986 reform, rather than ending immigration from Mexico and Central America, actually encouraged lawlessness, as people created fake documents and employers learned to look the other way. The decade of the 1980s is generally referred to as the "lost decade" in Latin America. Debt, inflation, economic stagnation, and "negative social development" characterized the entire region. This decade was particularly cruel for Mexico because in the middle of the decade, on 19 September 1985, a massive earthquake struck the capital, killing some 8,000 citizens and leveling vast sectors of the city. It would take years, and billions of dollars, to rebuild the city. By the end of Miguel de la Madrid's term as president of Mexico (1982–1988), Mexico's foreign debt was estimated at 105 billion dollars and the annual rate of inflation was running over 159 percent.[3] Given the severity of the economic crisis at home, Mexicans headed north, and U.S. federal legislation, such as the Immigration Reform and Control Act of 1986, did not stop them.

The early 1990s were marked by political change in the United States, as the Democratic Party took back the White House after twelve years of Republican rule. However, the Clinton administration's immigration policy did not differ dramatically from President George H. W. Bush's. During the first year of his presidency, Clinton focused his energy on passing NAFTA, the North American Free Trade Agreement. The president's thinking reflected the so-called Washington Consensus, which posited that uniform standards of finance, banking, and trade—directed by the World Bank, the International Monetary Fund, and Inter-American Development Bank—should be strictly applied in Latin America. The Consensus also encouraged a reduction in trade barriers and the privatization of government-controlled entities in Latin America such as utilities, airlines, mines, etc. NAFTA was passed in the fall of 1993 with bitter opposition from some manufacturing sectors in the United States and U.S. labor unions. These groups predicted that passage of NAFTA would lead to a downward drag on U.S. wages. Environmental groups in the United States worried about lax environmental standards in Mexico, and others in the United States criticized the treaty because it would—in terms of trade and finance—treat Mexico as an "equal partner." The thought of Mexicans as being equal to Americans created some degree of tension and historic dissonance among the more conservative, traditionalist, and/or racist elements of the U.S. population. Simply put, this notion did not square with many Americans' conception of how the world "should" work. Texas billionaire businessman Ross Perot famously predicted that the treaty would create a "giant sucking sound" as jobs and energy moved from the industrial United States to Mexico.

Perot's prediction was based on some clear facts: Beginning in 1965, Mexico's border industrialization program was created as a way to stimulate trade and manufacturing along the U.S.-Mexican border and to take advantage of the proximity to the U.S. market. By 1993, some 2,000 plants (mostly U.S.-owned) operated in Mexico along a 2,000-mile swath extending from the Pacific Ocean to the Gulf of Mexico. Close to half a million workers were employed in these plants, called *maquilas*. Just four years after NAFTA went into effect, about a million Mexicans were employed in these plants. The rapid growth of *maquilas* has actually accelerated the pace of migration (both legal and undocumented) to the United States; people generally migrate in "stages," and a first step in the process often includes a brief stay in the border cities of Reynosa, Juárez, or Tijuana. The *maquila* plants, which predominantly employ young women who have migrated from the central valley of Mexico or other densely populated regions, have not been able to absorb the entire supply of Mexican laborers. Those without work in the border towns can either return home or cross to the United States in search of work.

NAFTA went into effect on 1 January 1994 and began eliminating barriers to free trade such as tariffs and value-added taxes on goods and financial transactions between Canada, the United States, and Mexico. However, the trade agreement—purposefully—never allowed this freedom of movement for humans. In the minds of many U.S. leaders, NAFTA—an economic policy—would generate some spillover effects on immigration flows as well. By promoting job creation in Mexico and generating wealth in all three NAFTA nations, NAFTA, in theory, would discourage future labor flows from Mexico to the United States. Trickle-down economics, a remnant of the Reagan era, mandated that the overall increase in continental wealth would wend its way, eventually, to the average Mexican. Mexico, many Americans thought, would have more jobs to absorb the growing supply of labor. And in some respects, NAFTA functioned as it was intended to. It helped drive up corporate profits, and provided work for many in the *maquila* industry, but the jobs were tightly regulated factory jobs that paid the Mexican minimum wage. Though *maquila* workers can earn between eight and ten dollars a day, unions are virtually nonexistent and strongly discouraged from organizing, and life in the poor neighborhoods of these border cities is grim. For the majority in Mexico, NAFTA did not improve living conditions and standards. Trickle-down rarely occurs in Latin America.

The response to implementation of NAFTA took the world by surprise. On 1 January 1994, a group calling itself the EZLN (or Zapatista Army of National Liberation) made international headlines when peasants in the south of Mexico demanded protection against the provisions of NAFTA. They asked, via their charismatic spokesman, "Sub Comandante Marcos," how poor, indigenous farmers in the southernmost region of the country would compete against giant nationally subsidized U.S. agribusinesses. They vowed to fight in the name of the early twentieth-century revolutionary leader, Emiliano Zapata, who struggled for his peoples' right to *tierra y libertad*—land and liberty. The world saw in early January the desperate conditions in which many lived in the south of Mexico—a region where only 20 percent of the homes had electricity, 50 percent of the homes had dirt floors and twenty-eight out of one hundred children never graduated from the first grade.

The year 1994 went from bad to worse in Mexico: In March, the hand-picked successor to President Carlos Salinas, Luis Donaldo Colosio, was assassinated, and by the end of the year, the Mexican economy was in a transparent free fall, culminating in a stock market collapse in early 1995. President Bill Clinton engineered a bailout of about 40 billion dollars for Mexico, because, under NAFTA, a hemorrhaging Mexican economy could only have negative effects on the new "free trade zone" and serve as a strong impetus for many to migrate north. The southern peasant rebellions, the political assassinations, and the economic collapse tended to validate the arguments of those who fought against NAFTA. The events of 1994 and 1995 certainly contributed to growing migration from Mexico to the United States.

By the early 1990s, anti-immigration sentiment (which meant, essentially, anti-Mexican) in the United States had grown more intense. The downturn of the California economy in the early 1990s was blamed on poor Mexican immigrants. The fact is, however, that cuts in defense spending after the 1989 fall of the Berlin Wall and readjustments in the American economy meant fewer available high-paying, white collar and middle-class jobs in Southern California. At the same time, U.S. investment in Mexico increased exponentially—to 91 billion dollars by 1997—and this heavy investment along with increased U.S.-Mexican trade (from about 13 billion dollars in 1986 to 50 billion on the eve of NAFTA) translated into dislocation in the United States. This reality caused some leading scholars to contend that "the industrial heartland of North America [had been] unceremoniously uprooted from America's Midwest to Mexico's northern border."[4] Entire factories moved out of the United States and many jobs were lost in the industrial Midwest. But California's woes in the early part of the 1990s had more to do with domestic issues: shrinking defense spending, the new "postindustrial" economy, and an aversion, in California and elsewhere, to growing revenues through taxation; poor Mexican immigrants simply served as an easy target for public frustrations.

Historically, during times of significant social tension, economic crises, or wars, segments of the U.S. population will lash out against immigrants. This happened during the late nineteenth century and early twentieth century with legislation that all but prohibited the Chinese from immigrating to the United States. Japanese Americans were rounded up and interred during the Second World War; Russians became the focus of a mob mentality that gripped the nation during the 1950s Red Scare and Congressional un-American Activities Committee Hearings, under Senator McCarthy. With the collapse of Soviet-style communism in the late 1980s, people in the United States began to lash out at Mexican immigrants. The most notorious and glaring example of U.S. anti-Mexican hysteria can be found in the passage of the 1994 California Proposition 187, the so-called Save Our State ballot initiative.

Proposition 187 sought to deprive undocumented immigrants of their rights to public schooling, nonemergency health care, and public welfare benefits. By trying to demonize elementary school children (referring to them as "illegal aliens"), the initiative ultimately failed. Teachers refused to act as immigration police. Physicians quickly reminded the voters of California that their professional responsibilities required them to take the Hippocratic Oath, which superseded any and all ballot initiatives. Physicians made it clear that they would continue to treat sick people who arrived at their hospitals, regardless of immigration status, ability to pay, race, religion, etc.

The courts struck down Proposition 187, citing that individual states did not have the right to deny social services, education, or other federally funded programs; had California implemented the proposition, the state would have lost up to 16 billion dollars in federal education aid and grants. The proposition was officially declared dead in July 1999, nearly five years after being passed by 59 percent of California's voters.

Immigration was not a significant national issue in the presidential election of 2000; the economy was growing and was able to absorb both documented and undocumented labor. People crossed the border to work for, on average, 278 dollars per week versus thirty-one dollars in Mexico. Undocumented immigrants were moving beyond the traditional points of attraction (California and Texas), and heading to states where demand for agricultural labor, construction work, and work in poultry plants was high. Thus, the population of Hispanics (predominantly Mexicans) has grown rapidly in the past five to ten years in Alabama, Arkansas, Georgia, North Carolina, South Carolina, and Tennessee. North Carolina, for example, one of the fastest-growing states in the country, has seen a dramatic increase in jobs in the construction sector, in the food service industry, and at poultry processing plants—job sectors that tend to hire undocumented workers.

Presidential candidate George W. Bush learned a valuable lesson by 2000: he saw what happened to the politicians in California who supported Proposition 187, and he winced at Pat Buchanan's angry, exaggerated, militaristic rhetoric on immigration during his failed 1996 presidential campaign. Candidate Bush declared himself a "compassionate conservative" and said he would enforce existing immigration laws if elected, but made it clear that he had no intentions of deploying the military to the Mexican border. As governor of Texas, candidate Bush understood the need for inclusive, nonstrident language when discussing immigration in the United States. In fact, after being appointed president by the U.S. Supreme Court in December 2000, Mr. Bush cultivated a friendly relationship with Mexico's president, Vicente Fox, a conservative, devoutly Roman Catholic businessman who won the presidency in 2000 as a non-PRI outsider.[5] Fox visited Washington in September 2001—this was the first official "state visit" hosted by President Bush. President Fox addressed Congress and was eager to discuss a new proposal that would reframe immigration "politics" between the two nations. Immigration reform discussion began in earnest some months earlier, in February 2001, when President Bush visited Mexico and Mr. Fox initiated an aggressive agenda that included bilateral negotiations on immigration, recognition of the two countries' mutual and intertwined histories, and an open discussion of a guest worker program for Mexicans engaged in seasonal work in U.S. agriculture.

Immediately before the 9/11 attacks, Latin America was primed to finally become a significant partner and area of interest to the United States. Talks were progressing on establishing the FTAA (Free Trade Agreement of the Americas). Presidents Bush and Fox had engaged in cordial talks concerning a guest worker program between the United States and Mexico. Fox's visit and address before the U.S. Congress on 7 September 2001, generated bi-national enthusiasm. Americans and Mexicans alike were anxious to see cooperation, open dialogue, and mutual respect among the leaders of the United States and Mexico, in contrast to the misguided policy recommendations and angry anti-Mexican rhetoric of the recent past. However, four days after Fox's Congressional address, nineteen terrorists crashed four commercial aircraft inside the United States, an act that changed the perspective of the Bush administration and U.S. history. After 9/11, history would repeat itself regarding U.S.–Latin America relations: Latin America, as in the past, would be relegated to the back burner in U.S. foreign policy making.

In 2004, Samuel Huntington, a renowned Harvard political theorist, drew much criticism when he wrote a politically charged article titled "The Hispanic Challenge" in the March–April 2004 issue of *Foreign Policy*. Huntington argued that the remarkable increase in Spanish-speaking immigrants from Latin America was dividing the United States. He warned that "the cultural divide between

Hispanics and Anglos could replace the racial division between blacks and whites as the most serious cleavage in U.S. society."[6]

During the 2004 presidential campaign, President Bush announced his intention to reinitiate talks for a guest worker program with Mexico; thus, the immigration debate was rekindled in Washington. Soon thereafter, two significant events renewed public interest in immigration and suggested that immigration discourse would be more highly charged than ever before. Latin America reentered the U.S. frame of reference for the first time since 9/11, but not in a way that pleased most Latin Americans.

Proposition 200 in Arizona and the Minutemen Project marked a return to the anti-immigrant backlash of the mid-1990s. More specifically, Proposition 200 reintroduced the subject of unauthorized immigration. During the 1990s several measures were undertaken to tighten border security in California. Operation Gatekeeper was a federally funded project that erected fences and lights, and increased the number of border patrol agents with the goal of reducing and discouraging the movement of undocumented persons. These measures failed in that they simply redirected the flow of immigrants from California to the deserts of Arizona. Proposition 200, approved by the voters of Arizona on Election Day, 2004, attempts to prevent undocumented immigrants from receiving public benefits and criminalizes the actions of state and local government officials who do not report undocumented individuals. The passage of Proposition 200 in Arizona exacerbated a growing wave of anti-immigrant sentiment nationwide. For example, in October 2004, the Minutemen Project was undertaken. Its purpose was to send armed, untrained, and unqualified paramilitaries to patrol sections of the Arizona-Mexico border. The organization's name is meant to conjure up images from history of the brave individuals who fought in the American Revolutionary War against the British in the late eighteenth century.

The effects of Proposition 200 have been significant and widespread. Similar legislation has begun to appear in numerous states throughout the United States, and since April 2005, more than forty extremist, radical anti-immigrant vigilante groups like the Minutemen have organized in twelve states. Recently, "Real ID" legislation passed the U.S. Congress, essentially preventing undocumented immigrants from obtaining driver's licenses and thus making it very difficult for them to be contributing and productive community members. The Real ID language was tacked on to the Emergency Supplemental Wartime Appropriations Act that approved billions of additional dollars to help fund the wars in Iraq and Afghanistan while providing funds for victims of the 2004 Asian tsunami.

In addition to armed vigilante groups, other seemingly nonviolent groups and coalitions have emerged in the past few years to publicize anti-immigrant platforms through the use of politically charged rhetoric and denigrating terminology. Citizens Against Government Waste is asking for contributions to help stem the "tidal wave of illegal aliens" while U.S. English, Inc. warns individuals to beware that "our American way of life is being undermined by the spread of foreign languages"; they advise vigilance and a commitment to preventing multilingualism "while we still have a chance to take back our country."

The anti-immigrant backlash has not been the exclusive purview of extremist groups and vigilantes. Professor Huntington's recent book, *Who Are We?* saturated classrooms and academic circles throughout the United States, and added academic veneer to a growing fear of the "other" in American society. In the book, the author presents Latin American immigration as threatening the American way of life and American identity. Latin Americans, he claims, do not assimilate into American society, either linguistically or geographically. He suggests that Anglo and Hispanic cultures are fundamentally different; they are unable to coexist in harmony, which results in a "cultural clash" that will continue to grow and divide the United States. Critics of Huntington have focused on the author's xenophobic tone. José Luis Valdés-Ugalde and Leonardo Curzio have asserted that Huntington's work is racist toward Mexicans (a group the author singles out among Latin American immigrants).[7] Others have noted how Huntington presents the immigration "problem" as though it were occurring in a dichotomous world, where national identities are static and prevailing norms and attitudes never change.

As if immigrants arriving to and living in the United States were not facing enough barriers from anti-immigrant groups and policies, the rhetoric of "terrorism" has now been connected to the immigration debate. The thousands of miles of border shared between the United States and Canada and the United States and Mexico are now being watched as potential springboards of terrorist activity. Law enforcement is focusing more on immigrant groups as potential terrorists, adding to the complexity and difficulty of immigrant reception in the United States. The rhetorical connection established between terrorism and unauthorized immigration has prompted a heated debate in Washington regarding immigration reform. Some believe that increased border security (i.e., more agents, more money spent on technology to help discover undocumented immigrants) is the best method for securing our borders and reducing unauthorized immigration. Others feel that a more holistic approach is necessary, providing pathways to legalization for the undocumented. As of this writing, several legislative proposals are currently in the public domain. In the Senate, the Secure America and Orderly Immigration Act of 2005, is sponsored by Senators Edward M. Kennedy (D-MA) and John McCain (R-AZ). This bill would provide a comprehensive approach to immigration reform, calling for measures to increase border security and promote family reunification, while providing pathways for new legal immigration and legalization of undocumented immigrants. Senators John Cornyn (R-TX) and John Kyl (R-AZ) take a distinctly different approach. Their proposal, the Comprehensive Enforcement and Immigration Reform Act, would give state and local police increased powers to enforce federal immigration laws, and stipulates an expedited "removal" process, while failing to provide legal pathway toward permanent citizenship and worker protections. Under this legislation, all undocumented workers would be forced to leave the United States for their country of origin; they could reenter the United States via some sort of temporary worker program. It is highly unlikely, though, that eleven million people will return to their countries of origin should this legislation pass, and the effects on the U.S. economy of such a mass exodus would be severe. Undocumented individuals comprise over half (58 percent) of the agricultural labor force in the United States and just under 25 percent in private household services.[8] A 2005 *New York Times* article highlighted another staggering statistic: Undocumented immigrants contribute more than seven billion dollars per year to the U.S. Social Security system. Not a single undocumented immigrant will ever be eligible to collect the benefits they currently pay into the system.

In the House of Representatives, Tom Tancredo (R-CO) proposed his own legislation in July 2005. His bill would make it a felony to enter the United States without documentation and would put the burden of enforcement on the Department of Homeland Security. Representative James Sensenbrenner (R-WI) pushed his own agenda—the Border Protection, Antiterrorism, and Illegal Immigration Control Act of 2005—through the House Judiciary Committee (on which he serves as chairman) and on to the House floor for debate in December. On 16 December 2005, this so-called Sensenbrenner Bill (H.R. 4437) passed the House of Representatives by a vote of 239–182. The tone of this bill frightened many people in the United States. The Sensenbrenner bill (if turned into law) would criminalize all undocumented persons as "aggravated felons" and would charge anyone who offered any type of aid or help to an undocumented person with an aggravated felony. In other words, people handing out sandwiches at a soup kitchen that serves the poor and/or undocumented could, in theory, be arrested! This bill focuses exclusively on enforcement, punishment, and deportation. It neither offers a guest worker program nor any sort of "pathway to citizenship," as called for by more thoughtful legislators.

Sensenbrenner's bill provoked a storm of controversy. First, Cardinal Roger Mahoney of the Roman Catholic Archdiocese of Lost Angeles urged parishioners in an Ash Wednesday homily (on 1 March 2006) to defy any law that criminalizes the Good Samaritan. Mahoney's criticism of the House legislation made national news and sparked popular organization on a massive scale. In fact, on 25 March in Los Angeles, more than half a million people peacefully protested against the excesses of the Sensenbrenner legislation, and other protests were organized in cities with a significant Hispanic presence. For example, about 50,000 people protested in Denver on the same day, and police estimated that 20,000 demonstrated in Phoenix the previous day. The U.S. Senate took note of these protests, remembering how Governor Pete Wilson's political career ended after he supported the extreme Proposition 187 in 1994 which (though never implemented) sought to deny essential state services to undocumented persons living in California.

On Monday, 27 March 2006, the U.S. Senate Judiciary Committee voted 12–6 in favor of a more moderate immigration restructuring plan. The chairman of that committee, Arlen Specter (R-PA) has pushed for a "pathway to earned citizenship" for undocumented persons based on good behavior, a steady work record, and payment of a $2,000 fine. The right wing of the Republican party views this sensible approach as providing "amnesty" for lawbreakers, but Specter and other moderate lawmakers refute such rhetoric. Senator Bill Frist (R-TN) broke with the recommendations of the Judiciary Committee; Frist supports a "guest worker" program but strongly opposes a pathway to earned citizenship. President Bush hopes to sign a comprehensive immigration bill that includes tightening security along the U.S.-Mexican border and a pathway to earned citizenship for undocumented workers in addition to the creation of a guest worker program. The intensity of debate and the deep divisions over immigration among Republican legislators (as of late March 2006) suggest that a comprehensive immigration reform bill might have to wait until after the November mid-term elections.

The United States is a country of immigrants. Immigrants from Latin America live among us, and their presence is not confined solely to California, Texas, and Florida. Latin American immigrants have provided a dynamic boost to our economy, and to U.S. culture. They come here looking for work and find it in abundance in the strawberry fields of California, the carpet mills of Georgia, the meat packing plants in Nebraska, and the poultry processing plants of Arkansas. Now is the time for rational and reasonable immigration reform to emerge from the U.S. Congress. The strength of the United States lies in its diversity, openness, and willingness to provide opportunities to those who want to work and live here. Blaming the poorest and most vulnerable among us—undocumented immigrant workers—for the economic, social, and political problems that face our nation is misguided, counter-productive, and contrary to our country's core values.

24

The Forgotten Relationship

Jorge G. Castañeda

Jorge Castañeda sees the aftermath of 9/11 as the death knell of what could have become, for the Bush administration, a more forward-looking, engaged, and enlightened policy toward Latin America. The absence of an extra-hemispheric threat brought on by the collapse of the Soviet Union and the end of the Cold War, and the George W. Bush administration's commitment to make Latin America the cornerstone of U.S. foreign policy seemed to usher in a period reminiscent of the Good Neighbor policy. Immediately after 9/11, U.S. policy focused on security matters resulting in a constricted, rather than expansive, relationship with Latin America. Castañeda aptly argues that the United States could have maintained a robust antiterrorism policy while expanding a common agenda for the hemisphere. Now, Latin Americans worry about the reemergence of U.S. hegemony in the aftermath of 9/11. In the meantime, political, social, and economic challenges in Latin America grow, threatening democratic rule and economic development. Castañeda warns that ignoring critical challenges and opportunities in Latin America will prove costly for the United States in the near future.

RETHINKING U.S.–LATIN AMERICAN TIES

Free from the strategic and ideological rigidities of the Cold War, Latin America in the mid-1990s looked forward to a more realistic and constructive relationship with the United States. The first Summit of the Americas in 1994, which launched negotiations on the Free Trade Area of the Americas (FTAA), symbolized the renewal of goodwill and cooperation in the region. The summit led to a series of hemisphere-wide meetings at various levels throughout the 1990s that offered a new model for political relations between the United States and Latin America (most notably the Williamsburg and Bariloche defense ministerial meetings). This new diplomacy for the first time presumed to treat all the re-gion's nations (with the exception of Cuba) as equals. The summitry also sent a powerful message throughout the hemisphere by implicitly stating that the suc-cess of the entire endeavor depended on the coordinated progress of all nations in the Americas.

A sign of the times was the lessened rhetorical confrontation between most Latin American nations and their powerful northern neighbor. Some unilateral U.S. policies—such as the process of "certifying" countries' cooperation with the U.S. drug war or the Helms-Burton legislation, which placed sanctions on any country that traded with Cuba—faced firm regional opposition. But Latin American countries felt increasingly more at ease when discussing certain issues with Washington that in the past had been highly controversial, such as democ-racy and human rights promotion or combating corruption. A consensus devel-oped, stronger than at any time in the past half-century, on what constituted a common agenda for hemispheric relations and how to address it.

By the end of the last decade, however, the progress seemed to wind down. And the terrorist attacks in New York and Washington sounded the death knell of what could have become the new Bush administration's more forward-looking, engaged, and enlightened policy toward the rest of the hemisphere. The resulting post–September 11 picture is not pretty from a Latin American point of view, al-though there is certainly no lack of understanding or even support throughout the Americas for the U.S. fight against terrorism. But the United States has replaced its previous, more visionary approach to relations in the western hemisphere with a total focus on security matters. This disengagement is dangerous because it un-dermines the progress made in recent years on economic reform and democrati-zation. Rarely in the history of U.S.–Latin American relations have both the chal-lenges and the opportunities for the United States been so great. It is certainly not a time for indifference.

ROLLBACK

The events of September 11 preempted the Bush administration's initial plans to employ a more open approach within the western hemisphere. Indeed, security and counterterrorism concerns quickly, and perhaps understandably at first, overshadowed any other issue. For example, one immediate casualty of the em-phasis on homeland security was the initiative to create a comprehensive and long-term solution to the problem of migration flows from Mexico to the United States. Other setbacks swiftly followed. By early 2002, the Bush administration had broadened the Plan Colombia antidrug initiative to include direct anti-insurgency efforts. This decision was motivated both by a sense that any area plagued by armed instability was a potential host for terrorism and by the collapse of the Colombian peace process. The international antiterrorist campaign further led to a disengagement from the economic troubles brewing in Argentina, Uruguay, and Brazil. In particular, the U.S. Treasury Department's inaction turned the tragedy of Argentina's financial collapse into a painful lesson in international laissez-faire. In Venezuela, moreover, social polarization, political instability, and growing anti-American sentiment were largely ignored at the policymaking level, even if intellectual concern in Washington among officials and think tanks was acute and increasing.

But perhaps more than these country-specific crises, the main reason to worry about the redirection of U.S. attention lay in the broader patterns emerging in Latin America. First and foremost was the lack of tangible results from years of economic reform. By the turn of the new century, it had become quite clear that the structural changes implemented in virtually every Latin American economy over the past two decades had not brought about the desired results. Growth rates remained far below expectations or even previous achievements. Even Chile, for many years the only showcase of successful economic reform, had run out of steam, averaging barely 3 percent growth between 1999 and 2002. This situation not only discredited the reforms themselves but invited the advent of alternatives, some of which inevitably are "anti-neoliberal."

The disappointing results, moreover, brought into question the other great regional achievement of recent times: the broad and deep consolidation of democratic rule throughout the hemisphere. Those who became familiar at the same time with open economies and open societies channeled, perhaps unavoidably, their frustrations about weak economic performance into anger at the political process. People increasingly blamed democracy for economic stagnation, or at least for failing to deliver economic growth. Consequently, governance began to falter: democratic regimes with nothing to show for their efforts found themselves increasingly impotent and isolated, blamed for everything from the impact of unpredictable weather to international economic trends to crime and corruption. The dwindling enthusiasm for economic reform and representative democracy was revealed in poll after poll and in one election after another. And, as a result, the region today faces an increasingly unpredictable future.

U.S.–Latin American relations are also mired in uncertainty. In the post–September 11 world, Latin America finds itself consigned to the periphery: it is not a global power center, but nor are its difficulties so immense as to warrant immediate U.S. concern. In many ways, the region, at least in terms of U.S. attention, has become once again an Atlantis, a lost continent. Perplexing bureaucratic conundrums—for instance, the lengthy absence of a permanent U.S. assistant secretary of state for western hemisphere affairs—and new agency priorities have left many Latin American capitals in a diplomatic vacuum. This situation has developed despite Secretary of State Colin Powell's and National Security Adviser Condoleezza Rice's excellent and perhaps unprecedented personal relationships with many of their colleagues in the region. On top of it all, Latin American leaders and diplomats have a nagging feeling that whenever they point out the obvious lack of U.S. attention to regional problems or bilateral agendas, their views are received in Washington with impatience and even irritation.

Indeed, as the post–September 11 world grows increasingly complex, the western hemisphere still reveals a relatively simple pattern: the reassertion of U.S. hegemony. The central question thus becomes whether the United States is willing to work with Latin America to achieve a durable framework for regional relations and how it would accomplish this. The United States can be a positive influence in the hemisphere and it can, more than ever, contribute to the successful resolution of the region's challenges.

UNQUIET QUARTET

To better understand the challenges—and the opportunities—of Latin America today, one ought to focus on four countries: Mexico, Colombia, Argentina, and Venezuela. Their problems have diverse sources but all would benefit from vigorous U.S. engagement.

Dealing with Mexico is in many ways the most important regional task facing the Bush administration. The matter can be summed up simply: President Vicente Fox's consolidation of Mexico's first democratic transfer of power must be—and be seen to be—a success. There is nothing more important to the United States than a stable Mexico, and today a stable Mexico means a democratic one. And the United States has a huge role in making Mexico's transition to democracy a success, or in contributing to its failure. The success or failure of this experiment will be judged in Mexico ultimately in the light of the country's economic performance—which has not been impressive these past two years. But Mexicans will also judge the state of their country's relations with the United States. They will look to see whether Presidents Fox and Bush deliver on the ambitious bilateral agenda they sketched out at their historic February 2001 meeting at Fox's ranch in Guanajuato, Mexico. On issues of trade, drug enforcement, the border, building a North American Economic Community, energy, and, most significantly, immigration, the two countries set out a bold series of goals to meet by the end of Bush's first term, if not sooner.

Indeed, in the first eight months of their respective presidencies, Bush and Fox achieved a fundamental breakthrough on immigration. By the time of the Guanajuato meeting, both sides had identified the core policies needed to tackle undocumented migration flows from Mexico to the United States: an expanded temporary-worker program; increased transition of undocumented Mexicans already in the United States to legal status; a higher U.S. visa quota for Mexicans;

enhanced border security and stronger action against migrant traffickers; and more investment in those regions of Mexico that supplied the most migrants. The speed with which both governments carried out these negotiations certainly captured the political imagination of both societies. Fox's resounding state visit to Washington on the eve of the September 11 terrorist attacks further lifted the new initiatives and underscored both leaders' commitment to them.

But the symmetry ends there: Fox staked much more on this partnership than Bush did. And since the Mexican president has little to show for his gamble, he has paid a high domestic political price for his willingness to bring about a sea change in Mexico's relations with the United States and the rest of the world. Indeed, this change has been on the order of what President Carlos Salinas did with Mexico's economy or what President Ernesto Zedillo did with the nation's political system. Hence the centrality of immigration in the bilateral relationship today: both Bush and Fox stated dramatic goals and raised expectations enormously. The United States understandably was forced to put the issue on hold for a time. But what was initially portrayed as a brief interlude will now probably stretch through Bush's entire first term.

It will be almost impossible to point to success in the bilateral relationship without a deal on immigration. And unless there is such a breakthrough, Fox's six-year term in office, nearly half over, may well be seen in Mexico as an exercise in high expectations but disappointing results. To avoid a breakdown in relations, Bush must make a state visit to Mexico City this year. He should take with him sufficient progress on key issues—immigration; trade concerns relating to sugar, tuna, trucking, and the North American Free Trade Agreement's agricultural chapter; and funding for heightened security and the expedited passage of people and cargo at the border—to show that Mexico remains a top priority for his administration. Bush must also show that he is willing to spend political capital to ensure the success of Fox's push for true Mexican democracy. Washington may have so far missed an opportunity to present its relationship with Mexico City as a model for the rest of the hemisphere and, indeed, for the rest of the developing world—an example of how a rich and powerful neighbor and a still relatively poor and weak one can get along and contribute to each other's success. But the window of opportunity has not been shut. In the aftermath of the current conflict with Iraq, the United States would benefit hugely by demonstrating that it can construct alliances beyond its traditional circle of friends.

Colombia is almost as important as Mexico to the United States because of the U.S. stake in that country's fight against drug traffickers and insurgents. The problems inherent in such a conflict are manifest. The downing of a U.S.-manned intelligence flight in mid-February close to territory controlled by the Revolutionary Armed Forces of Colombia (known by its Spanish acronym, FARC) was a tragedy waiting to happen. Indeed, rather than being an isolated event, it seems to be a deliberate escalation of FARC's war against the administration of President Alvaro

Uribe and the United States. The apparent kidnapping of three U.S. intelligence officials, in the context of deadly bombings in several Colombian cities, underscores the nature of the U.S. and Colombian dilemma. On the one hand, the peace process and the "all-talk, no-fight" policy pursued by former President Andrés Pastrana ended in utter failure because of the guerrillas' total unwillingness to negotiate. But the "all-fight, no-talk" strategy employed by Uribe has led to a predictable outcome: the FARC has unleashed a wave of terror and violence identical to those loosed previously by the insurgents and the drug traffickers. The country, moreover, seems hardly willing to pay the price required for a military victory over the guerrillas or even for an offensive long and intense enough to force them to negotiate in good faith. Uribe's choice is as illusory and one-sided as Pastrana's, and U.S. support for it is equally misplaced.

Is there a solution? Perhaps, but it is not cheap, complete, or quick. The broad outline of a long-haul strategy should be built around three components. First, Uribe should fight and talk simultaneously, as guerrillas themselves have always done. He should up the ante militarily and continue to receive U.S. support in that effort, but he should also restart negotiations with the FARC and again move forward in talks with the rival National Liberation Army (ELN). Uribe should be able to count on firm and vocal backing from the Bush administration on that score as well. This cooperation should include, if necessary, direct talks between the United States and the FARC and also the ELN—something that Washington has been unwilling to do since three American anthropologists were murdered four years ago near the Darien Gap. Second, the United States should at all costs avoid direct involvement on the ground, regardless of legalistic distinctions between contractual and official personnel, or between trainers, advisers, and combatants, be they overt or covert. Doing otherwise, no matter how great the temptation, will only mire the United States in this conflict.

Finally, Washington and Bogotá should involve the rest of the hemisphere, especially Brazil and Mexico, in the Colombian peace process. These countries should act mainly, but perhaps not only, as mediators. Brazil has proved notably reluctant to participate in the Colombian crisis other than by tightening controls on its border. Brazil's new president, Luis Inácio Lula da Silva, however, may be more forthcoming than former president Fernando Cardoso, especially if cajoled by Mexico in that direction. Other countries, not just in the region but also in Europe, could also help Colombia by isolating the FARC internationally, as Mexico did by closing down the FARC's office in Mexico City. Governments should also investigate potential ties between the FARC and other regional players, such as Cuba. Not only would such outside involvement improve the prospects for negotiating success, but it would also provide political cover for Uribe in what can only be a bitter and bloody struggle.

The third trouble spot is Argentina. Its economic crisis, although contained, is certainly not over. And the longer-lasting consequences of the collapse of the

Southern Cone economy are as yet unclear, both for Argentina and for the rest of South America. Partly for reasons of timing (when the crisis exploded the Bush administration still thought it could easily break with the precedents set by previous bailouts from the International Monetary Fund) and partly for circumstantial reasons (Republican dislike for the IMF and former treasury secretary Paul O'Neill's perceived dislike for Argentina), Washington seemed willing to let Argentina "sink until it hit bottom," as one Western leader put it. But neither has it sunk completely nor recovered fully from the collapse of its currency and the deep depression of its economy. As a result, U.S. support for an agreement with the IMF had to be channeled through the government of President Eduardo Duhalde. This approach ultimately translated into backing for a deal that possesses serious flaws and may not even be implemented fully by the next Argentine president, who is to be elected in late May or early June.

Thus it would seem to make more sense for the United States to fully engage Argentina and provide solid support for the new government. At the same time, Washington should urge Buenos Aires to carry out the political and institutional reforms that that nation (and for that matter, all of Latin America) desperately needs. The new president, whatever his or her political persuasion, will require a lot of help, primarily in the form of economic assistance, and the United States should make that assistance available. This support would not be a case of throwing good money after bad. Intervention costs less earlier than later, and benign neglect is not an option, as the economic spillover from Argentina to Uruguay and Paraguay and the political shock waves hitting Brazil and Bolivia have already shown.

Finally, there is Venezuela. After excessive irritation with President Hugo Chávez during the first year of the Bush administration, Washington's attitudes toward the Venezuelan regime had shifted rather remarkably by the time of the attempted coup in April 2002. The unlikely, worst-case explanation of what happened is that the U.S. government bestowed a smile and a wink on the bungling conspirators during the crisis leading up to the coup attempt; the best and most likely rendition is that Washington displayed an almost unheard-of degree of indifference toward those events. Concern did set in after the coup started, but it was once again overtaken by distance and by growing concern with other issues (increasingly, Iraq). Only as 2002 ended did Washington concentrate again on Venezuela, as the oil workers' strike and Chávez's decision to hold onto power at all costs plunged the country into chaos. Secretary Powell then began to consider diplomatic options to work with the Organization of American States and its secretary-general, César Gaviria, as well as with former U.S. president Jimmy Carter. The United States agreed to join the "Group of Friends" of Venezuela created in January, which also included Mexico, Brazil, and Chile, as well as, perplexingly, Spain and Portugal. But that diplomatic effort never got off the ground, Chávez eventually broke the oil strike, and the opposition, the United

States, and the rest of Latin America ended up right back where they started more than a year ago.

On the one hand, Venezuela has a democratically elected president. He may have polarized public opinion and driven the country into the ground in response to an irresponsible opposition, but he can hardly be characterized as a communist or a traditional Latin American dictator. On the other hand, the level of animosity in Venezuelan society and the magnitude of the economic collapse guarantee that the crisis will continue. Chávez will retaliate against his opponents, they will continue to plot and demonstrate against the government, and all of this will put the country's fragile institutions to a terrible test and frighten its neighbors and friends who know that such situations never end well.

This is perhaps why, now that tensions have slightly receded, it might be time for Washington to participate in a less formal, more realistic initiative together with Chile, Brazil, and Mexico. Such an effort should seek to place a series of compromise proposals on the table, and then use different methods to transform them into offers that neither party could refuse. The United States can, as it did in the Central American peace talks nearly fifteen years ago, deliver the opposition. And the major Latin American countries might be able to convince Chávez that it is in his interest to cut a deal that is less than perfect, but that will allow him either to depart in a dignified manner or to continue to govern in a reasonably effective way. Just as some insisted that no Group of Friends would be viable without the United States, there is no way out of the Venezuelan imbroglio without American engagement. The cost of letting these wounds fester is steep: for the Venezuelan people; for neighboring countries such as Brazil and Colombia; for Mexico, now one of the largest investors in Venezuela; and for the United States, which still relies on the country for more than 15 percent of its crude oil imports.

LOOK ON THE BRIGHT SIDE

If the preceding cases resemble a long list of brewing regional troubles, there are also a couple of bright spots in the region, where the United States has proceeded judiciously and can continue to do so with ease. Moreover, Washington with a few relatively simple steps can do much to bridge the gap with the rest of the region.

The Bush administration, and its insightful and skillful trade negotiator, Robert Zoellick, concluded a sophisticated free trade agreement with Chile in December 2002. Chile's economic and social situation, although lacking the spectacular results of the period from 1985 to 1999, is also solid and secure. Thus, just staying the course with Santiago would be fine policy for Washington. In addition, Chile has adroitly managed its relations with the United States, engaging intelligently and effectively with it both at the UN Human Rights Commission and at the Security Council. President Ricardo Lagos is rightly considered Latin America's elder statesman today; when he speaks on international matters, everyone in the region listens.

Brazil is the region's other bright spot, perhaps of greater import because, in the end, size does matter. Washington dismissed ideological prejudices and played its cards right during the presidential campaign that took Lula (as the new Brazilian president is universally known) to power. The Bush administration has refrained from estranging the new government and has constructively engaged Lula's team on a potentially divisive issue, the involvement of the Group of Friends in Venezuela. Brazil's new leader, for his part, has chosen a wise course of avoiding confrontation with the United States and pursuing domestic policies that are acceptable to the markets and would not ultimately scare the Bush administration into being more assertive. Yet Lula has not betrayed his platform or his followers. He is implementing many of his campaign promises, his social programs are ambitious yet feasible, his team is diverse and representative, and he could well be the harbinger of the great transformation, or aggiornamento, of the Latin American left that has been so long in coming.

Washington should do everything it can to help Lula succeed. It can go beyond benevolent neutrality to actively endorsing his regime with the markets, the IMF, and the World Bank; the United States can become a cheerleader for Lula, obviously not on ideological grounds, but because he is a democratically elected leader with sound social and economic policies. The value of such an effort is the same as it would be in Mexico: contributing to a Lula success story would generate enormous benefits for Washington. The reward would be not only the stability of Brazil, something of paramount value to the region and the United States. Most important, such a policy would show that the Bush administration can work constructively with regimes that are not its ideological soul mates, but that are nonetheless willing to reach out to the United States and find common ground. Again, as in relations with Mexico, this is no small matter in the aftermath of conflict with Iraq and U.S. estrangement from the rest of the world.

That common ground is not as difficult to reach as some may think, particularly when looking at the broad problems that Latin America faces and how the United States can address them. Economic stagnation is of course the most salient one, as well as the single issue felt most directly by the region's inhabitants. The core concern here is restarting economic expansion, at a time when regional growth rates have once again dropped to very low levels. In addition to the debacles in Argentina and Venezuela last year, Mexico and Brazil both suffered practically flat economic performances in 2002, and the prospects for 2003 are dropping daily. The United States can play a role here, both through its own economic recovery and by pushing for a more open trade agenda in the new World

Trade Organization (WTO) talks leading up to the ministerial meeting in Cancún, Mexico, next September. The U.S. stance in the WTO's "Development Round" has in fact been more constructive than the European Union's. But other U.S. steps—such as implementing huge agricultural subsidies and steel import tariffs—have deeply disturbed many in Latin America, particularly those in countries such as Argentina and Brazil, for whom agricultural or steel exports are crucial. The United States can do much more to open up its markets in these areas.

Washington can also add a new dimension to the FTAA agenda, which is partly dormant as a result of Argentine, Brazilian, and Mexican wariness. Since the third Summit of the Americas in 2001, many countries have pointed out that free trade on its own will not easily or automatically pull up the least developed countries in the region. Accordingly, they have called for the inclusion of some type of resource-transfer mechanism for the poorest parts of the hemisphere. Again, such a step may not be ideologically palatable to the Bush administration, but it would be in the U.S. national interest. Like the equally counterintuitive announcement of gradual increases in the U.S. foreign aid budget at the Monterrey development summit in March 2002, a resource-transfer proposal would be extremely well received in Latin America and would provide a stimulus to the faltering free trade negotiations.

With respect to issues of good governance, the United States can also help solve some of Latin America's most intractable problems. Many in the region today believe that the main obstacles to growth are neither the weakness of economic reforms (essentially the conservative view) nor the nature of the reforms themselves (the left's perspective) but rather the poor quality of governmental institutions and corporate practices. Reforming both is perhaps the region's greatest challenge—and last opportunity—to return to growth. These reforms require political will, resources, and a friendly international environment. They could include jettisoning Latin America's two-centuries-old system of presidential regimes, which have never worked under truly democratic rule or with open societies. And they could also foster a crusade to establish the rule of law throughout the region. In too many nations, human rights, property rights, due process, an efficient and accessible judicial system, and brief, nonprogrammatic constitutions are either insufficiently represented or inadequately respected. Through the World Bank, the U.S. Agency for International Development, bilateral agreements, and other regional mechanisms, Washington could contribute actively to the modernization of Latin American institutions and thus help remove the remaining obstacles to renewed economic expansion.

By doing so, the United States would also send a strong signal that it is committed to democracy in Latin America. The U.S. response to the recent Venezuelan coup attempt was not a shining moment in this regard. The potential lack of compliance with human rights considerations in current and future anti-insurgency campaigns in Colombia could be another setback. Thus the Bush administration must emphasize that its support for democracy and human rights in Latin America holds regardless of the specific regimes this policy may help or the specific obstacles this may generate with respect to other goals. This commitment is essential to U.S. credibility in the region. Moreover, the United States would firmly establish itself as an ally in building democracy, rather than a hindrance or a fickle companion that engages or disengages depending on its interests.

A final area in which the United States and Latin America could cooperate fruitfully is in the conduct of international diplomacy. For instance, Chile's and Mexico's role on the UN Security Council can have an important effect on U.S.–Latin American relations. Although neither voted against the United States, they clearly felt reluctant to go along with the use-of-force resolution sponsored by the American, British, and Spanish delegations. This may have generated some irritation in Washington, but the Bush administration should use this opportunity to show that friendly relations do not require unconditional support and that there are no hard feelings. Nevertheless, both Santiago and Mexico City remain committed to working with Washington to provide diplomatic leadership on important regional issues such as the Special Conference on Hemispheric Security, which will take place in Mexico City during the summer.

BRAVE NEW CONTINENT

The challenges that Latin America faces today, even for a part of the world accustomed to adversity, are awesome. If those challenges are compounded by the lack of a bold, ambitious, and enlightened U.S. approach to the region, then undoubtedly they will be still more daunting. And yet the opportunities are also greater today than ever before. The Cold War is long gone. Democracy has taken hold nearly everywhere in the region, as has at least the principle of respect for human rights. Many Latin American governments, perhaps starting with Mexico, are accepting that there is no better ally for domestic change than scrutiny, commitment, and support from abroad—preferably multilateral in nature, although bilateral ties can certainly play a part.

Across the region, people now realize that market economies of one sort or another—not necessarily the "one-size-fits-all" model purveyed by the Washington Consensus—are here to stay, and that their advent is not such a bad thing. And increasingly broader swaths of Latin American societies now accept that globalization and closer ties with the United States are facts of life, and not necessarily undesirable ones. The United States, despite its sporadic bouts of parochialism and unilateralism, and its reduced attention span, has shown open-mindedness in recent times. For instance, the early Bush administration, the AFL-CIO, and Federal Reserve Board Chair Alan Greenspan all accepted in principle a new pro-migration stance toward the region. The U.S. Congress has also virtually suspended the much-loathed counterdrug certification process. So there is progress to cheer about, but clearly much more to hope for. To turn hope into reality, the entire region needs leadership, vision, and the will to achieve. Both Latin America and the United States have ample reserves of all three.

25

The United States and Latin America through the Lens of Empire

Michael Shifter

Michael Shifter, senior fellow at the Inter-American Dialogue in Washington, D.C., documents the growing resentment in Latin America toward U.S. policy in the region, specifically after 9/11 when many key opportunities to deepening a common hemispheric agenda were squandered as President George W. Bush emphasized security and unilateralism in his administration's foreign policy. The Bush administration's unilateral approach has reminded Latin Americans of the not-so-distant past when hegemonic presumption dominated hemispheric relations. According to Shifter, there is a growing sense in Latin America that since 9/11 the United States is largely "unresponsive and disengaged" from the region's deepening social and economic problems—"while expecting unquestioning support and loyalty for its own specific agenda." Shifter is not optimistic that the United States will reengage Latin America, despite increasing social dislocations and rising tensions that threaten stability and ultimately U.S. strategic interests in the region.

For many Latin Americans, President George W. Bush's November 6, 2003, speech before the National Endowment for Democracy touched on an all-too-familiar theme. Bush boldly called for a democratic revolution, led by the United States, in Iraq and the Middle East. Two decades earlier, President Ronald Reagan had delivered a similarly audacious address to the British Parliament, one that laid the groundwork for the creation of the endowment itself. Just as Bush has now targeted the "axis of evil," Reagan had assailed the Soviet Union's "evil empire." Then, however, the principal theater the U.S. president had in mind for his democracy mission was not thousands of miles away, in the Middle East, but much closer to home, in Central America.

Not surprisingly, Latin Americans are perhaps peculiarly sensitive to the stunning projection of U.S. power in Iraq in 2003. The terms that are increasingly

275

fashionable in describing international affairs—"unilateralism," "hegemony," "empire"—have long been used in analyses of inter-American relations. The vast asymmetry of power between the United States and the countries to its south has been a fundamental feature of the region's historical landscape. The Manichaean "you're either with us or against us" formulation has been implicit, and long assimilated.

With the collapse of the Berlin Wall, the use of terms such as empire and hegemony, tailored over decades to Cold War realities, was substantially attenuated. Starting with the administration of George H. W. Bush (1988–1992), a window of opportunity opened for referring, without irony, to the prospect of constructing political partnerships and striving to become "enterprises of the Americas." Fresh and original ideas for defending democracy and extending commerce in the Americas offered considerable promise for more productive hemispheric cooperation.

Today that promise has largely faded. Relations between the United States and Latin America have acquired a rawness and a level of indecorum that recall previous eras of inter-American strain and discord. In the past, the rough edges had occasionally been blunted and softened, not only during the post–Cold War interlude of the 1990s, but also at various other moments, such as the 1930s and early 1960s. Although Latin Americans have always resisted and opposed U.S. power, from time to time their demands have been at least partially addressed.

Yet, at the beginning of the twenty-first century, the quality of American "exceptionalism" that sociologist Seymour Martin Lipset called a "double-edged sword"—characterized, on the one hand, by generosity and democratic openness and, on the other, by unbridled moralism, bordering on intolerance—has tilted decidedly toward the latter. An unvarnished sense of superiority, displayed proudly on the regional and global stage, has revived the resentment and distrust of Latin Americans toward the United States that had recently shown signs of receding. It is an attitude captured in a November 2003 survey by Zogby International among key opinion makers in six Latin American countries, which showed that a startling 87 percent of respondents had a negative opinion of President Bush.

HISTORICAL BAGGAGE, AND LESSONS LEARNED

The United States has rarely exhibited the characteristics of an empire or imperial power in a classical sense. Unlike Britain, France, or Spain in previous eras, the United States has shown little propensity to completely take over another territory and control its institutions. Instead, since the elaboration of the Monroe Doctrine in 1823, there has been a tendency to keep other great powers out of the

Western Hemisphere and permit national, independent development—provided that it posed little threat to the region's stability and assured the primacy of U.S. interests.

In the early part of the twentieth century especially, the U.S. role in Central America and the Caribbean was marked by various occupations carried out by the U.S. armed forces when it was deemed necessary to protect American economic and strategic interests and to spread American values. Nicaragua, Haiti, the Dominican Republic—all at one time were occupied, often for considerable stretches. The occupations, which generally came to an end by the 1930s, proved difficult, and had mixed results at best. These experiences account, in part, for the enormous skepticism in much of Latin America about the current U.S. occupation of Afghanistan and Iraq.

The Cold War saw the United States return to Latin America in an attempt to assert its ideological hegemony and maintain the hemisphere as its sphere of influence, if not control. Whatever Washington perceived as an extension of Soviet influence in the hemisphere was typically met with a swift and severe response. This was the case even before the 1959 Cuban revolution (for example, in Guatemala in 1954), but became especially pronounced after the installation of a Communist government just off the U.S. mainland. It would be hard to overstate the effect of Fidel Castro's regime in shaping U.S.–Latin American policy through the Cold War—and even since the Cold War's end. The U.S. intervention in the Dominican Republic in 1965, and the U.S. pressure that helped result in the 1973 military coup against Chile's elected president, Salvador Allende, can best be understood against this Cold War backdrop.

In the 1980s, the Cold War's intense ideological battle became concentrated in Central America, where the Reagan administration backed an authoritarian government in El Salvador to prevent a powerful leftist insurgency from taking over. The United States also waged a proxy war through the "contras" in Nicaragua, then controlled by a Sandinista government with close ties to Cuba and the Soviet Union.

The U.S. obsession with security questions in the 1980s rendered a productive relationship with Latin America virtually impossible. Sharp differences in priorities had always existed, but occasional U.S. initiatives in response to Latin American concerns attempted to bridge them. Franklin Roosevelt's Good Neighbor Policy of the 1930s, a serious effort to engage constructively with the region, was one example. Another was John Kennedy's lofty Alliance for Progress. No doubt calculated to counter the appeal ol Castro's regime, it nonetheless projected a commitment to Latin America's social reform agenda. Although these initiatives did not transform the hemisphere's power relations, they did display a concern for Latin America's acute social conditions and reflect an effort to identify common interests, thereby cushioning the negative effects of U.S. hegemony.

THE GEORGE H. W. BUSH AND CLINTON ERAS

In fundamental respects, the first Bush administration reflected continuity with the U.S. policies toward Latin America whose antecedents were Roosevelt's Good Neighbor Policy and Kennedy's Alliance for Progress. Transformations on the world stage—most notably the fall of the Berlin Wall—coupled with important changes in Latin America's political landscape toward more democratic rule, created fertile and favorable conditions for a more serious engagement with the region.

This period saw new precedents set in the critical areas of democracy and trade. Roughly coinciding with the end of Chilean dictator Augusto Pinochet's extended military rule, member governments of the Organization of American States, meeting in Santiago, Chile, in June 1991, approved a resolution that marked a sharp departure in inter-American norms. For the first time, any interruption in democratic, constitutional rule would become a matter of regional concern and would trigger a hemispheric response. That resolution, which has been invoked four times since its adoption, formed the cornerstone of the widely touted Inter-American Democratic Charter that was approved a decade later at an OAS General Assembly in Lima, Peru. The charter codified or systematized all the democracy-related declarations and resolutions that had been adopted over the previous decade, essentially giving these declarations and resolutions greater force.

The notion of creating a hemisphere-wide free trade area can also be traced to the first Bush administration. The Enterprise of the Americas initiative, launched in 1990, recognized the concerns of Latin American leaders who had expressed keen interest in securing greater access to U.S. markets for their countries' products. Such responsiveness and engagement were welcomed south of the Rio Grande, and especially in Mexico. It was during the first Bush administration that the final terms of the North American Free Trade Agreement (NAFTA), involving the United States, Canada, and Mexico, were negotiated and signed. The U.S. Congress approved the treaty in 1993, under the Clinton administration. The first Bush administration was responsive to Latin American concerns about foreign debt as well, devising the Brady Plan—after Treasury secretary Nicholas Brady—to reduce the region's $450 billion in foreign debt.

Other nods to Latin America did not go unnoticed in the region. With the end of the Cold War, Washington became more committed to achieving a peaceful resolution to longstanding conflicts in Central America—in Nicaragua in 1990 and El Salvador in early 1992 under the first Bush administration, and then in Guatemala under Clinton in 1996. The U.S. role helped overcome doubts about whether the United States was prepared to apply its power constructively in former Cold War battlegrounds. The first Bush administration also participated in two antidrug summits—in Cartagena, Colombia, and San Antonio, Texas—

during which the U.S. president met with his Andean counterparts in a multi-lateral framework.

The momentum toward greater cooperation continued into the two terms that Bill Clinton served between 1992 and 2000. This era saw not only the passage of NAFTA, but also the convening of the Summit of the Americas, featuring all the hemisphere's elected leaders, in December 1994 in Miami. The summit was the first meeting of its kind in a quarter of a century. It set the goal of negotiating a Free Trade Area of the Americas (FTAA) by January 2005.

Two months before the summit, the Clinton administration used the threat of force to return to office the democratically elected leader of Haiti, Jean-Bertrand Aristide. This was in striking contrast to historical images of the United States propping up authoritarian regimes. It offered further evidence that the U.S. government could use its power to advance legitimate democratic rule in the hemisphere.

The momentum stalled, however, in the latter part of the 1990s. Economic and political conditions in many Latin American countries deteriorated. In Venezuela, which endured two successive lost decades, strongman Hugo Chávez was elected president in December 1998, while in Peru, President Alberto Fujimori further entrenched his authoritarian rule. In short, a malaise gripped much of the region, making it less attractive to Washington. In addition, the U.S. Congress continually denied Clinton the "fast track" authority he sought to negotiate trade agreements without congressional amendment, reflecting a more inward-looking society and the growing salience of domestic politics—in this case, pressure from labor unions identified with the Democratic party—in shaping U.S. hemispheric policy.

Latin Americans were deeply suspicious of what they regarded as unilateral moves in Colombia that culminated in the July 2000 approval of some $1.3 billion in U.S. security aid to fight the drug war in that country. To be sure, Washington was responding to a deeply troubling situation: a democracy under siege. But the elements of the final assistance package nonetheless centered chiefly on combating drugs, a narrow piece of the wider problem, and mostly through law enforcement efforts. A more comprehensive strategy, embracing key dimensions of social development and institutional reform, was lacking.

GEORGE W. BUSH AND 9/11

The election in November 2000 of George W. Bush generated varied expectations about how the United States would approach hemispheric relations. Two separate tendencies within the executive branch could be discerned. That Bush appeared comfortable with Latin America—he had served as governor of Texas—and had initially evinced great enthusiasm for a tightly knit inter-American community, seemed to bode well for hemispheric relations. At the same time, senior officials such as national security adviser Condoleezza Rice showed little sympathy for the kind of "nation-building" mission the Clinton administration had carried out in Haiti and instead signaled that the new administration would pursue hard-headed policies, emphasizing the defense of vital national interests.

The first nine months of the Bush administration provided evidence of both of these tendencies. Bush met with many of the region's leaders, attended the third Summit of the Americas in Quebec, and cultivated a particularly close relationship with Mexican President Vicente Fox. At the White House on September 5, 2001, Bush famously referred to Mexico as "our most important relationship." Unlike its predecessor, however, Bush's team at the Treasury Department eschewed anything resembling a bailout in dire financial situations like the rescue the Clinton administration had provided to Mexico during the 1995 peso crisis. Thus, the deepening Argentine predicament in 2001—marked by unsustainable deficits, which resulted in widespread social unrest and the forced resignation of the country's president—was treated as merely a fiscal problem and initially elicited indifference from Washington. Eventually, however, the United States voted in favor of an IMF loan of nearly $3 billion to Argentina in January 2003, and also participated in an IMF aid package to Brazil.

The attacks on the World Trade Center and Pentagon on September 11, 2001, dramatically eclipsed the incipient Bush administration approach to Latin America. The traumatic events engendered a sense of vulnerability and fear in American society, and transformed Bush into a wartime president. The moralist side of American exceptionalism described by Lipsct was activated with unprecedented force. Crystallizing the emerging foreign policy concept was a new doctrine of "preemption," developed in the Bush administration's September 2002 *National Security Strategy*. The strategy made it clear that America would not hesitate to use power preemptively to protect itself. For the United States, this marked a departure. As historian Arthur Schlesinger noted in the October 23, 2003, *New York Review of Books*, "Mr. Bush has replaced a policy aimed at peace through the prevention of war by a policy aimed at peace through preventive war."

Much of the rest of the world overwhelmingly rejected this formulation. The response in Latin America was similar, but it had a distinctive twist. For Latin Americans, the practice of preventive military action by the United States had a long history, especially in Central American and Caribbean countries. It can be plausibly argued that the use of us force in 1983 in Grenada, or in 1989 in Panama, were early examples of preventive military action. But making the practice a matter of doctrine touched a raw nerve in Latin America, since it showed a blatant disregard for the precepts of international law. It also raised the specter of future U.S. military adventures in the region, employing the war on terror as a justification.

The region has been sensitive as well to the treatment of prisoners of America's "war on terror" who are being held at the detention center in Guantanamo, Cuba. In this U.S.-controlled territory, secured as a result of what many Latin Americans see as an imperialist war, basic standards of due process have not been respected and followed. Although at the end of 2003, U.S. courts had begun to raise serious objections to such treatment, the reports from Guantanamo have not helped enhance U.S. credibility as a guardian of human rights and constitutional protections. Some comments in the Latin American press have been unsparing (one Colombian columnist referred to Guantanamo as the U.S. "gulag"). Guantanamo, and the specter of military tribunals for suspected terrorists, raised the perennial question of double standards, and supplied ammunition for Latin Americans subjected to U.S. sermons on the importance of adhering to the rule of law.

As the war on terror became the overriding priority of U.S. foreign policy, claims of interest in and concern for Latin America within the Bush administration rang increasingly hollow. Senior officials became more and more distracted from a region that was supposed to be high on Washington's agenda. It is true that in September 2003 the U.S. Congress, for the first time in five years, confirmed an assistant secretary of state for Western Hemisphere affairs, Roger Noriega. But, given that U.S. prestige and credibility were on the line in Iraq and the war on terror, it would take a superman to successfully engage interest in Latin America among the most senior-level decision makers in Congress and the administration. Latin Americans hoped not so much for increased attention—the demand, after all, has a paternalistic ring to it—but rather a strategy that sought to take better advantage of the many mutual interests shared by the United States and Latin America.

Washington's distraction, indifference, and failure to seriously consider Latin America's own concerns have exacted considerable costs. The Bush administration's initially mishandled response to the April 2002 military coup against Venezuelan President Hugo Chávez—failing to show any concern and instead expressing undisguised glee—eroded the administration's credibility on the democracy question. That blunder effectively sidelined any potential U.S. leadership role in trying to assure a peaceful, constitutional resolution to Venezuela's political crisis.

From Latin America's perspective, Washington also bore some responsibility for the democratic setback that Bolivia suffered in October 2003. The government of President Gonzalo Sánchez de Lozada, which had faithfully implemented the various economic and drug policy recipes advocated by Washington, could not withstand the enormous social pressure brought by a variety of angry and frustrated sectors, particularly the well-organized indigenous groups and coca growers. As was widely reported after the collapse of his government, President Sanchez de Lozada had in 2002 requested some $150 million in development assistance from Washington to deal with growing strain and unrest. He was rebuffed by the Bush administration, which offered merely $10 million. The Bolivian president was prescient in anticipating that, without the requested aid, he would have trouble surviving in office.

The Bolivian case underscores the myopia of a longstanding U.S. drug policy excessively focused on law enforcement objectives—a policy that gives scant attention to social development issues and fails to take into adequate account its effects on democratic governance. More important, what happened in Bolivia illustrates a deeper malaise throughout the troubled Andean region that also extends to other pockets of concern in Latin America. Bolivia conveys a sense of an already fragile region breaking further apart, devoid of a coherent framework for political and economic development.

In this regard, the Latinobarometro's comparative surveys offer little to cheer about. As the October 30, 2003, *Economist* summed it up, "A bare majority of Latin Americans are convinced democrats, but they are deeply frustrated by the way their democratic institutions work in practice." In 10 of the 17 Latin American countries polled, support for democracy has dropped significantly, and steadily, since 1996. Notably, 52 percent of the sample agreed with the statement: "I wouldn't mind if a non-democratic government came to power if it could solve economic problems." Levels of confidence and trust in the region's political leaders and institutions—political parties are particularly discredited—remain alarmingly low.

Such worrying results are impossible to separate from Latin America's stubbornly stagnant economies. Many of the region's citizens are profoundly disenchanted with market-oriented prescriptions that they see as having yielded only greater corruption, few tangible benefits, and deepening social inequalities. Whether one refers to the precepts of "neoliberalism" or, as shorthand, the "Washington consensus," there is clearly a major backlash in much of Latin America. Bolivia highlights the spreading angst about lack of national control in the context of globalization as indictments of privatization gain growing support.

Increasing social dislocations and rising tensions are understandably of primary concern for most Latin Americans. Yet, in Washington, the war on terror, perhaps also understandably, is of overriding concern. The result is a disturbing disconnect that, as Latin America's social disintegration and the U.S.-led war continue, could become even wider. The common language of open democracies and free markets used in the past decade by reform-minded opinion leaders throughout the hemisphere has less and less resonance. And, as the Latinobarometro poll reports, at least among Mexicans and South Americans, regard for the United States in the past two years has fallen sharply. True, the unilateral U.S. military adventure in Iraq in large measure accounts for the drop. But the sense that the United States has mainly been unresponsive to and disengaged from Latin America's deepening concerns—while expecting unquestioning support and loyalty for its own specific agenda—also helps to explain the growing anti-American sentiment in the region.

THE TEST OF HEGEMONY: TRADE AND BRAZIL

Although the Bush administration has not strayed from Washington's traditional indifference to Latin America's social distress and political turmoil, it has been far more engaged and energetic in seeking to advance the trade agenda. President Bush managed to secure the "fast track" trade authority that President Clinton failed to obtain, and achieved a long-awaited bilateral trade agreement with Chile. In late 2003, the United States announced a free trade agreement with four Central American countries, and prospects for reaching deals with Colombia and Peru looked promising. U.S. trade representative Robert Zoellick has, more than any other senior Bush administration official, engaged Latin America—responding to the region's interest in obtaining access for its products to U.S. markets.

Although there has been undeniable progress in this area, trade issues also pose significant challenges to inter-American relations and represent a fundamental test of the relationship between the United States and Brazil. Agreement between these two large countries is essential if there is to be any possibility of moving toward the goal of a Free Trade Area of the Americas, which has been generally supported by the hemisphere's elected governments since 1994. And on a wide array of other critical issues affecting the hemisphere, it is difficult to imagine important advances without close cooperation between the United States and Brazil.

The election of Luiz Inácio Lula da Silva as Brazil's president in October 2002 left Washington palpably nervous; it did not know what to expect from the leftist leader of the Workers Party. Yet 2003 proved to be the year of Lula (as he is commonly known) in Latin America. Impressively, he has so far sustained what might ultimately prove an impossible balancing act: straddling the worlds of the financial establishment and its critics. No other leader, for example, participated in both the World Economic Forum in Davos, Switzerland, and its counterpoint, the Social Forum in Porto Alegre, Brazil. Lula appears to be the quintessential pragmatist, displaying a penchant for fiscal discipline and other economic policies associated with the Washington consensus. At the same time, unless he can make progress in tackling Brazil's immense social agenda and particularly its glaring inequalities, Lula risks disappointing many of his supporters, in Brazil and throughout Latin America, who have high hopes and expectations for another "way" in a frustrated region searching for alternatives.

Lula has surprised many observers not only with his pragmatism in national policies, but also because of his assertive role in regional affairs. Building on Brazil's self-image as a regional power, with disproportionate significance in South America, Lula has taken the initiative in dealing with difficult situations in Venezuela, where he launched a Group of Friends mechanism to deal with the clash between President Chávez and his opponents, and in Colombia, where he offered support to President Alvaro Uribe in his pursuit of democratic security. Lula has also sought to strengthen his relationship with Argentina, particularly the government of Nestor Kirchner, to further consolidate MERCOSUR, the Southern Cone trade group. Indeed, Lula has staked out a position on reaching an FTAA pact, consistent with his predecessors, that emphasizes the importance of U.S. concessions in lifting agricultural subsidies as a precondition for corresponding concessions on the Brazilian side.

Questions related to a trade agreement aside, what is crucial in the coming period will be the capacity of both the United States and Brazil to reach an accommodation and tolerate what are bound to be inevitable differences on policy issues. From all indications, the U.S. government is split on how to deal with Brazil's attempt to establish itself as a regional power. (The Brazilian government appears similarly divided regarding the United States.) Growing strains between the two countries were apparent during the World Trade Organization meeting in Cancun, Mexico, in September 2003, and the gathering of trade ministers in Miami in November 2003. But the question is: will the United States exercise its hegemonic presumption in this context and show little tolerance for Brazil's heightened activism, or will it pursue an understanding with another regional power in this hemisphere? Will accommodation or an adversarial posture prevail? Can the United States accept real policy differences for the sake of building a broader relationship? There is no better opportunity for Washington to forge a strategic partnership and restore the declining goodwill among many Latin Americans toward the United States.

BACK TO THE BACKYARD?

How the United States deals with Brazil's evolving role in the hemisphere in the coming years will largely determine America's ability to adjust its thinking to the region's new realities. Analysts have long used the image of the "backyard" to depict U.S. conceptions of Latin America, especially Central America. But in the context of globalization—where national problems have worldwide ramifications—such conceptions are woefully inadequate.

The regional test for the United States also includes its relationship with Mexico, which is fundamental to constructing a vital hemispheric community. After the September 11 attacks, no country has experienced more friction with the

United States at the highest political levels than Mexico. Perhaps expectations were unrealistically high, but President Bush, based on his previous foreign policy experience and friendship, initially looked south, toward President Fox. The strain that developed after the attacks—Washington felt that Mexico did not show sufficient solidarity—was exacerbated once the Iraq enterprise started, and Mexico, as a member of the United Nations security Council, had to take a public stand on the U.S. decision to go to war. Mexico's opposition to the U.S. position did not sit well with Congress and, especially, the Bush administration.

Not surprisingly, toward the end of 2003 signs appeared that the bilateral relationship was on the road to repair. Summits held in Mexico in October 2003 and January 2004 should help reengage Washington with the bilateral agenda. Electoral politics in advance of the U.S. presidential election of 2004—Mexicans make up a growing share of the voting population in key states—have also prompted another glance south.

President Fox, for his part, dismissed Mexico's ambassador to the United Nations, Adolfo Aguilar Zinser, in November 2003 for suggesting in a speech that the United States treats Mexico like its "backyard." While one can question Aguilar Zinser's discretion and diplomacy for such a remark, a shrinking number of Mexicans—and Latin Americans generally—would probably take issue with his characterization. It is a measure of how sour feelings have become since NAFTA was signed a decade ago.

Relations between the United States and Latin America—like those between the United States and Mexico—have often suffered from unrealistic expectations. Unless vital national security interests have been perceived to be at stake, as was the case in Central America in the 1980s, Latin America has not been a top priority for Washington, and that is unlikely to change in the foreseeable future. Still, the unmitigated projection of U.S. power in the world, combined with the assumption that Latin America will automatically go along with any policy put forward by Washington, creates an unnecessary rift and strain in the Western Hemisphere.

The United States has instruments and resources at its disposal—and there are ample historical precedents—to mollify the virulent anti-Americanism that has returned to Latin America. Higher levels of engagement and greater responsiveness from Washington to the region's agenda—to create jobs, stimulate growth, and reduce crime—could once again put the first Bush administration's vision of a productive partnership in the Americas within reach.

26

U.S. Influences in Latin America: The Environmental Impact of Trade and the Sustainability Agenda

Wesley Ingwersen and Laura Ávila

This chapter focuses on important environmental concerns that, since the Rio Declaration on Environment and Development (1992), have framed academic debate as the American economies gravitate toward trade liberalization, open markets, and trading blocs. Authored specifically for this second edition, the chapter helps readers understand the impact of free trade on the environment; this chapter offers case studies and examples from recent Mexican, Chilean, and Cuban history and provides a thoughtful, balanced perspective on the often neglected environmental impact of trade. A serious, integrative study of political, diplomatic, economic, and social trends in the Americas cannot eschew consideration of the physical environment. Ingwersen and Ávila's chapter demonstrates the importance of interdisciplinary approaches and challenges researchers to consider the environment as "actor" in future studies of U.S.–Latin American relations.

At the end of the temperate growing season, individuals of hundreds of different bird species depart their U.S. homes for wintering grounds all over Latin America. Crossing political boundaries means nothing to these birds beyond the physical challenge posed when boundaries are formed by geographic features like the Gulf of Mexico. Some birds, like the Swainson's hawk, traverse nearly the length of the north-south corridor of the Americas from the prairies of western Canada and the United States to the *pampas* of Argentina in search of food (Weidensaul 1999).

People of the Americas and their institutions, like birds, are continually scavenging resources within and across sometimes arbitrary political boundaries without regard for the manifold effects on the environment. Competition over and claims for limited natural resources, both "transboundary" (species ranges, ecosystems, air, and water) and those that exist entirely within the political boundaries of nations, have been and continue to be disputed throughout the Americas. For example, U.S. corporations purchase land in Latin America to produce tropical fruit to export to the United States. Others establish factories in Latin America to manufacture goods with less expensive labor. Farmers from Latin America seek to expand sales of their products to the larger customer base in the United States. These are a few common scenarios in a busy culture of material exchange between the United States and Latin America. Political leaders in the United States and Latin America who support the neoliberal economic model are increasingly eager to develop policies that facilitate the flow of capital and goods between the United States and Latin America. The most significant of these agreements in place, the North American Free Trade Agreement (NAFTA), stimulated significant economic growth between the U.S., Canadian, and Mexican economies. In July 2005, the United States ratified the Central American Free Trade Agreement-Dominican Republic (CAFTA-DR), which will lift barriers between the United States and Central American countries as well as the Dominican Republic. These and other bilateral trade agreements and treaties are potential predecessors of a larger Free Trade Area of the Americas (FTAA), which, in theory, would create a zone where capital and goods could flow without tariffs through most of the hemisphere. Concurrent with the expansion of free trade, international concern for the planet's future under increasing strain from human demand prompted the first "Earth Summit" in 1992 and the Rio Declaration on the Environment, a resolution for sustainable development. Serious discussion of sustainability has since trickled down to influence regional and domestic policy in the Americas.

From an ecological point of view, the unrestricted flow of goods across the hemisphere encouraged by these agreements speeds up the metabolism of the economy, which accelerates both the consumption of resources and the creation of waste. Free trade agreements open new international markets, generating demands for goods and services, while increasing demands on environmental resources. Because of the size of the U.S. market and its investment power, the U.S. push for free trade in the Americas has and will continue to create patterns of production and consumption that the environment potentially cannot support.

The breadth of consideration of the environment is greatly enhanced when the environment is understood as the source of all wealth in human society and the ultimate destination of all of our wastes (figure 26.1).

Natural resources like mineral deposits, soils, forests, freshwater, and fisheries are the backbone of subsistence economies and modern economies alike, and are required for any product, from bananas to high-end manufactured goods like automobiles or computer chips. The limited quantity of these resources ultimately limits the amount of production. Yet since goods and services are nec-

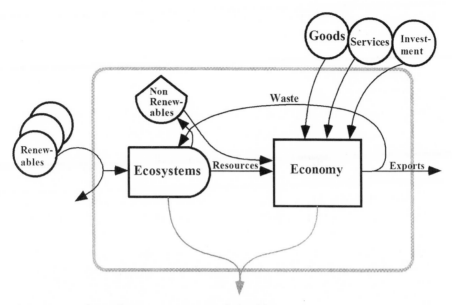

Figure 26.1. The Environment-Economy Relationship

essary for the maintenance of populations, some degree of burden will inevitably be placed on the environment. This means that every production process ultimately involves an environmental cost-benefit trade-off.

A MARKET-DRIVEN APPROACH: THE ENVIRONMENTAL KUZNETS CURVE

A general increase in environmental quality concurrent with an increase in income is the premise of the environmental Kuznets curve, an elaboration of the income equality theory of Simon Kuznets. Used as a key paradigm of the environment–economic development link in the World Bank's 1992 World Development report, the Kuznets curve is an upside down U-shape that suggests pollution at first increases with economic development but levels off when per capita income approaches a moderate level, and subsequently declines (Grossman and Krueger 1991). Together with capable institutions and enforced environmental regulations, this theory is used to show that market forces are the key drivers of environmental improvement, functioning via the spread of technology that improves efficiency and reduces emissions. Though evidence suggests the curve is only relevant for certain pollutants in nations that have followed expected development trajectories, this theory still serves as a strong underlying justification by U.S. administrations that free trade must be the underlying strategy of environmental sustainability.

What a Market-Based Approach Leaves out:
The Economy Price Gap and the Unrealized Costs of Trade

When resources are extracted by humans or manipulated to produce goods and the raw resources or products are transformed into commodities, the price attached to the resource does not embody the sum of environmental energies required to make them (Odum 1996). When prices are determined from the supply side, which is through the cost of extraction/production, they only embody the energy from the inputs controlled by man. And since the environment does not get paid for them, they are "free." Any product that requires the environment as a direct or indirect input has an energy value that is much greater than the assigned dollar value. Thus when a primary product is exported out of the country, the foreign buyer reaps the marginal environmental benefit of the product. For example, the formation in Mexico of offshore petroleum required millennia of environmental energy to develop the ecosystems from which arose abundant organic matter, then additional millennia for geologic forces to transform and concentrate that dead organic material into oil. When PEMEX, the nationalized petroleum company of Mexico, extracts this oil from underneath the Gulf of Mexico and refines it into gasoline, the price of the gasoline only incorporates the cost of the company's activities. When the oil is sold to the United States, the millions of years of environmental energy used to make an excellent energy source are consumed in the United States. A portion of a limited resource is depleted, and the environmental benefit leaves Mexico. The money that Mexico receives from U.S. consumers does not have, hidden in it, an equal amount of "free energy," because the U.S. economy is more service-oriented. Because Latin American exports are dominated by primary products and raw materials, the region bears a significant natural resource cost with trade. Nevertheless, most proponents of free trade see this environmentally costly export pattern as a mere "temporary stage" of development for resource-rich regions like Latin America.

TRADE IN THE AMERICAS

The natural bounty of Latin America has functioned and continues to do so as a source of wealth. Since the early colonial period, the region has been structured and driven by the export of raw materials (i.e., minerals, metals) and primary products (i.e., timber, agriculture). Economic reforms during the last two decades have encouraged less restrictive trade. The sum of goods and services now traded between the United States and Latin America comprises a significant part of the goods and services cycling through the U.S. economy, and often a dominant portion of those in Latin American economies. Trade in goods has more than doubled in the last decade: Between 1994 and 2004 exports to Latin America (from the United States) increased 171 percent while imports increased over 250 percent. Trade in services is smaller but still significant—the U.S. exports more transportation, business, and technical services than it imports from Latin America. Money is also flowing via investment, though predominately in one direction (i.e., from the United States to Latin America). U.S. foreign direct investment in Latin America increased threefold during the 1990s, from an average of US $16.5 billion/year in the early part of the decade to an average of US $58.2 billion/year near decade's end. Whether through goods, services, or investments, each dollar traded is intrinsically tied to some aspect of the environment. The sheer increase in volume of trade and its continuing expansion warrant an investigation into the environmental effects and impacts associated with this process.

THEORIES OF TRADE AND THE ENVIRONMENT

International trade agreements influence the formation of patterns of production and often accelerate the rate of development, both of which have a broad range of implications for the environment. The Organization of Economic Development (OECD) has classified the environmental effects of trade into three categories (UNEP and IISD 2000):

(1) *Product* effects: Effects of the traded good itself or the technology used in production.
(2) *Scale* effects: Effects on the level of economic activity, typically involving increases in efficiency but also increasing environmental damage. Subsequent accumulation of wealth in society may increase consumption patterns, further burdening resource use.
(3) *Structural* effects: Changes in the structure of economies. The relative share that sectors contribute to the GNP change, causing a change in the nature and extent of resource use and environmental pollution.

THE ENVIRONMENTAL IMPACT OF RECENT TRADE AGREEMENTS IN THE AMERICAS

By the early 1990s, environmental considerations could no longer be ignored on the international trade agenda. During that decade, the United States and Europe began using environmental safeguards in international trade. New regulations imposed upon producers in developed countries increased costs and reduced the competitiveness of exports from the developed countries; thus a strange conglomeration of advocacy groups (agribusiness, environmental advocates, etc.) supported trade barriers for products coming from Latin America and the developing world that did not meet the same environmental standards (Vogel 2003). The first major dispute arose from a U.S. ban on Mexican tuna because of fishing methods that resulted in high dolphin mortality. The dispute was settled by the GATT (General Agreement on Tariffs and Trade) in favor of Mexico in 1991, which argued that nations have the right to self-determine their own environmental standards. The case was one of the most controversial in the history of the GATT tribunal, and environmentalist outcry at the decision carried over into the lobbying effort for inclusion of environmental protections in the North American Free Trade Agreement (NAFTA). Despite an initial resistance to including environmental provisions, the Mexican government finally conceded, and NAFTA included the first significant environmental protection policies in an international trade agreement.

NAFTA

The North American Free Trade Agreement lifted tariffs on goods exchanged between the United States, Mexico, and Canada. Signed concurrently with NAFTA, an environmental side agreement, The North American Agreement on Environmental Cooperation (NAAEC), created the North American Commission for Environmental Cooperation (CEC), a tri-national body designed to address regional environmental concerns, promote research and capacity building, and serve as a dispute-resolution entity.

The NAAEC did not create an independent or consistent set of environmental regulations for the region, but rather guarantees the right of each nation to write its own environmental and development regulations (Article 3, NAAEC); this prevents the enforcement of one country's environmental standards in the territory of another (Article 37, ibid). In addition to the CEC, two other entities were formed to contend with the environmental repercussions of NAFTA, the Border Economic Cooperation Commission and the North American Development Bank. These organizations foster and fund environmental infrastructure projects in the border region. Beyond the institutions created by the NAAEC, U.S. and Mexican environmental agencies continue to engage in joint cooperation to help identify and resolve environmental problems along the border.

THE BORDER REGION

Environmental problems continue (even in the post-NAFTA period) to strain and damage resources in the U.S.-Mexico border region. Poor air quality, insufficient water supplies, hazardous waste spills, and other threats have presented risks to ecosystems and human health. The manufacturing sector is especially prominent along the border. Due to the heavy contribution of manufactured goods in the makeup of Mexican exports to the United States, common concern for the Mexican environment inspired by free trade focuses on manufacturing rather than the natural resource or agriculture sectors. Perhaps the most publicized environmental concerns surround the assembly plants, or *maquiladoras*. NAFTA did not initiate the concentration of industry along the U.S.-Mexican border—the bilateral "maquiladora" program in 1965 first created incentives for U.S. companies to set up assembly plants across the border. Yet the number of *maquiladoras* doubled during the 1990s after NAFTA's passage (Roberts and Thanos 2003).

HAZARDOUS WASTE

The *maquiladoras* (including television, electronics, textile, and furniture plants) generate by-products classified as hazardous waste. Disposal of hazardous waste is now regulated on both sides of the border by U.S. and Mexican environmental agencies, but the infrastructure does not always exist to manage these wastes, and until 1996 Mexico had no hazardous waste management facilities in place and no clear regulations for the siting of proposed facilities. Growing citizen activism and joint ventures between U.S. and Mexican entities to improve waste tracking and establish waste recycling facilities in Mexico (Jacott et al. 2000), appear to be diminishing the hazardous waste problem. Nevertheless, capacity for enforcement of handling and cleanup of hazardous waste in Mexico is weaker than in the United States, which puts public and environmental health at greater risk on the Mexican side of the border.

AIR POLLUTION

Industry in Mexico is responsible for 90 percent of some primary air pollutants like sulfur and nitrogen oxides. Since the enactment of NAFTA, output of four primary pollutants has nearly doubled, but air pollution intensity, a measure of pollutant per dollar of product, has hovered around the same level (Gallagher 2002). On average facilities were just as dirty after five years under NAFTA. Industrial production is increasing in Mexico with greater air quality cost than equivalent increases in production in the United States.

WATER ISSUES

For 1,300 miles the Rio Grande flows the length of the Texas-Mexico border from west to east. The United States and Mexico still divide the water according to a 1906 treaty, with 79 percent of the water permitted for withdrawal by the

United States, 14 percent by Mexico, and the remaining 6 percent left for the river. Water from the Rio Grande has provided for cotton and citrus production in New Mexico, but the heavy withdrawals of water and runoff of fertilizers and pesticides into the river pollutes it before it even reaches the Mexican border. Following the build-up of industry and concurrent population increases after the 1960s, industrial waste and urban wastewater added further to the pollutant load in the river. By the time NAFTA was instituted, water monitoring revealed at least one toxic substance in each of nineteen river monitoring stations along the border. Two native species of fish had become extinct. In the mid-1990s the six largest Mexican border cities were dumping an average of 151 million gallons of untreated wastewater into the river daily (TCP 2000). But in the last ten years, NAFTA-born agencies helped fund the creation of wastewater treatment plants in all of these cities. Water quality has since improved, but still many segments of the river present dangers to aquatic life and recreational use. Moreover, increasing population and industrial growth threatens to dry the river before it reaches the Gulf of Mexico; this actually occurred during a period of drought in 2001.

BEYOND THE BORDER

Issues of environmental degradation extend beyond the U.S.-Mexico border region and involve other sectors of the economy. Pressure from Mexican *maquiladoras* is felt in industrial centers in the Mexican interior, in the states of Puebla and Mexico. Nonindustrial sectors like agriculture and forestry tend to be more widely dispersed across the landscape. Of the vast agricultural area of Mexico, nothing occupies more area and diverse terrain than corn. Corn, used in the making of tortillas, has long been the main staple of the Mexican diet and an integral part of the economic and cultural fabric of society. But in the years following NAFTA, cheap corn from the United States, grown on input-intensive, well-subsidized, large-scale farms, began to flow into Mexico. The Mexican government had expected NAFTA to create structural changes in the agriculture sector with much of the land under corn cultivation shifting to more labor-intensive crops like fruits and vegetables, where Mexico had a competitive advantage. Two plans were set in place to mitigate the hardships faced by corn farmers. First, NAFTA established a quota system that gradually reduced tariffs on corn imports into Mexico over fifteen years. Second, the government planned to fund programs to support the transition from corn to the cultivation of other crops. But economic crisis in Mexico during the first two years of NAFTA (1994–1996) resulted in the government's failure to implement either program. As a result, corn imports were much higher than anticipated, and the price of corn on the market dropped, hurting Mexican farmers. Without the support for and knowledge of diversification, corn farmers have actually increased their corn output by spreading cultivation to increasingly sensitive and protected lands (Nadal 2002). Further, to reduce inflation and spending, the government cut subsidies to (corn) tortilla mills and ended price controls on tortillas, resulting in an increase in the price of tortillas for the Mexican consumer. Thus poor anticipation and planning by the Mexican government to manage NAFTA-induced changes to the corn industry has caused hardships for both the corn producer and consumer, and has placed increasing pressure on the environment.

THE U.S.-CHILE FTA

In terms of economic growth and distribution of wealth, neoliberal economic reform in Chile has had more success than in any other Latin American nation. A series of economic and structural reforms that began in the 1970s has resulted in aggressive annual GDP growth. A shift in export composition from natural resource exports, dominated by copper, to primary product exports, including grapes, fish, and apples, has been one of the most successful elements of the economic restructuring. Chile exploits a niche in the market for seasonal fruits in the Northern Hemisphere. The topography, latitude, and ample rainfall in Chile are conducive to growing the temperate fruits that are a staple of U.S. diets—at the opposite time of the year as they are grown in northern climates. Large- and mid-scale Chilean farmers tending land in the central valleys have prospered by switching to these nontraditional fruit products. The predominant style of agriculture that has arisen is similar to that of commercial agricultural operations in the United States—a monoculture that requires large quantities of pesticides and fertilizers, and that places increased pressures on the surrounding environment. The growth of the fruit industry has affected landholding patterns, increasing the disparity between the rich and poor in areas not suitable for farming nontraditional fruits.

The economic boom, among other factors, inspired the U.S. initiation of a free trade agreement with Chile in 2002. The FTA, signed into law in 2003, opens up the Chilean market to agricultural imports from the United States and bans the use of subsidies for exports to the United States. The FTA requires, among basic environmental provisions and bilateral programs, that each country enforce and improve national environmental regulations. But in Chile the FTA will likely promote rather than subdue the prevailing pressures that nontraditional export agriculture is placing on the environment. If scale effects ensue and production increases, land conversion to intensive agriculture is likely to continue at an unrealized cost to the natural ecosystems; this tradeoff has serious implications for sustainability of production and has not yet been addressed in the text of the FTA.

CUBA AND ENVIRONMENTAL
IMPLICATIONS OF ECONOMIC ISOLATION

The island nation of Cuba, embargoed by the United States since 1962, and for the last fifteen years importing drastically less than it did in the 1980s, represents the extreme of economic isolation in the Hemisphere and the opposite of a liberalized trade-driven economy. Cuba was heavily dependent on the patronage of the Soviet Union until it collapsed in 1989, which caused an immediate economic decline on the island. The GDP fell 85 percent in two years and the average daily caloric intake decreased from 3,000 to 1,800 (McKibben 2005). The subsequent response of the Castro government was a vast economic reorganization that allowed society to function with a significantly limited resource base. A regression from an industrial to a low-input agrarian economy marked this so-called Special Period in the 1990s, during which the economy grew steadily, albeit slowly. The radical innovations in organic agriculture that accompanied the economic restructuring have captured the attention of progressive environmentalists, many of whom see new practices in urban gardening, small farmer entrepreneurship, and clever adaptation of old technologies as models for an environmentally sound agriculture. About 200 *organopónicos* (urban gardens) were formed in Havana and supply nearly all of the vegetables consumed in the city, typically substituting antagonistic fungi and compost for artificial pesticides and fertilizers, and humans for mechanized labor. The *organopónicos* grow food with less energy input, create jobs, and pose less of a threat to environmental health than traditional farming. Though there is high employment and sufficient food under the new model, living a lower-energy lifestyle is not preferred by all Cubans, and would not be an acceptable standard of living to the majorities in developed nations. Significant long-term environmental threats exist in Cuba as elsewhere—soil erosion, decaying water systems, biodiversity losses, and improper hazardous waste disposal are a few of the documented environmental problems that Cuba is facing. Though some of these environmental problems may be residuals from the previous economic regime, Cuba lacks the fiscal capacity to solve them. Even in terms of resource use, Cuba may not, based on its current status, meet a strict definition of environment sustainability: for instance, in addition to the aforementioned environmental problems, Cuba still depends on oil for electricity production. But the nation has low electricity use per capita and low carbon dioxide emissions per capita, and treats a high portion of domestic wastewater. Cuba uses less energy and material input and is more resource-efficient than the United States and other Latin American countries.

FURTHER ENVIRONMENTAL CONSEQUENCES OF TRADE

Hemispheric trade is inevitably shaped by social, economic, and geographic realities, none more powerful than the pronounced economic asymmetry between the United States and the Latin American nations. The United States has the most highly developed service economy, and as a result, a far greater number of transnational corporations (TNCs), capable of developing business overseas, are headquartered in the United States. As dominant actors in trade, TNCs can accelerate economic growth in developing nations, but they may cause irreparable changes in the environment in the process. Large scale TNC agriculture and mining operations present vivid examples of the environmental costs of resource export. U.S.-based Newmont Mining Corporation operates a gold mine at Yanacocha in the Andean highlands of Peru, which is the largest foreign investment in the country. Gold from the mine has generated $7 billion in profit at the expense of thirty tons of soil removed for each ounce of gold, large quantities of freshwater used, and a persistent threat of soil and water contamination (Perlez and Bergman 2005). Most of Newmont's revenue leaves Peru as does the resource, resulting in a large environmental loss and limited economic gain for Peruvians. Free trade agreements, including NAFTA and the Chile-FTA, tend to offer investment incentives that prevent host government interference with TNC business affairs. TNCs are required to comply with domestic environmental regulations, and they are conceivably more efficient producers than domestic industries, and thus may reduce product effects of trade. Some TNCs choose to institute environmental management programs, but under FTAs, developing nations are at risk of TNCs that act only in their own interest.

One the most obvious obstacles of trade in the Americas is the distance that separates the United States and Latin America. The greater the distance between origin and destination of a product, the greater the cost of transportation. The bulk of trade goods travels overseas on container ships. Large quantities of fossil fuels are required to power these ships between ports. Combustion of these fuels result in emissions of pollutants to the air along the traveling route and in the periphery of the ports. Additional environmental burden is created by overland transportation infrastructure, as goods arriving must be distributed to population centers scattered throughout the country. In comparison with local and domestic goods, international goods inherently have a greater energetic and emissions burden associated with transport.

The geographic distance, coupled with cultural and political divides, also obscures the supply chain that connects consumers with producers. Consumers may be agents of unnecessary social and environmental costs by supporting bottom-line production practices. Certification agencies grant labels to identify goods produced in a socially and environmentally responsible manner. Examples of labels for Latin American coffee imported to the United States include a "Fair Trade Certified" certification offered by TransFair U.S.A, and the "Bird Friendly®" certification offered by the Smithsonian Migratory Bird Center. Such green labeling efforts improve the transparency of product life cycles and the accountability of producers. Currently, though, free trade agreements do not provide incentives for labeled products, and price-driven consumption may limit the market of labeled goods to conscientious consumers willing to pay a premium for them.

SUSTAINABLE DEVELOPMENT

The 1987 Brundtland Commission coinage of the term "sustainable development" followed from an international recognition of the impact of human development upon the integrity of natural systems and the limited future capacity of those systems to continue sustaining human communities. The theory of sustainable development posits that in balancing social, economic, and environmental interests we may "meet the needs of the present generation while not compromising the ability of future generations to meet their own needs" (UN 1992). The loosely defined objective of sustainable development was incorporated into the Agenda 21 global action plan, which was adopted in 1992 by 178 countries at the first "Earth Summit" in Rio de Janeiro. Since then the Organization of American States (OAS) has created a commission, the Office for Sustainable Development and Environment, to oversee the enactment of Agenda 21 and successive international mandates on sustainable development within the Americas.

Though sustainable development has been the dominant international environmental initiative of the last two decades, the strength of the paradigm as a vehicle for environmental protection has been crippled by the lack of a salient picture of future capacity to sustain human life and a lack of international consensus on standards for development. As it stands, U.S. policy that incorporates the rhetoric of sustainable development has been stretched to support a continuation of current economic models. Today the Bush administration affirms an agenda agreed to by the World Trade Organization (WTO), that trade liberalization is the best mechanism for promoting sustainable economic growth in the developing world (CEQ 2005). Bilateral and regional trade agreements brokered with Latin American nations have, since the 1992 Rio Summit, represented the U.S. policy on sustainable development via trade liberalization in the region, and have largely proceeded without thorough assessments of potential environmental impacts.

An examination of current resource flows makes it immediately apparent that our use of resources exceeds the renewable resource flows of ecosystems: world economies, especially in the larger, developed countries, are powered by finite sources of energy, mainly fossil fuels. And while average consumption across the region may exceed natural capacity, many people still live without adequate resources. Societies in Latin America, on the whole, are characterized by greater economic inequality than any other major region of the world. Poor social conditions result from the failure to sustain economies and preserve the environment. The National Population Council of Mexico attributes rural poverty and exodus in Mexico partially to deforestation and the subsequent depletion of water resources that threaten agriculture and habitation (EcoAméricas, 2004). It is becoming increasingly apparent that environmental ills reverberate through economy and society. While there are many interrelated objectives of sustainable development, the challenge for future policymakers involves satisfying interrelated, but sometimes contradictory, sustainable development objectives.

FREE TRADE AND SUSTAINABILITY: HARMONIOUS OR ANTITHETICAL PRINCIPLES?

At the ten-year anniversary of the Rio Summit in 2002, the nations of the world gathered again to discuss implementation of the new guiding principle of sustainable development at the World Summit on Sustainable Development in Johannesburg. The key document that emerged was a Plan of Implementation (JPOI), which fleshed out recommendations for policy measures to meet sustainable development goals based on the ideals incorporated in the 1992 Rio Declaration. There are many trade-related resolutions therein supporting the continued liberalization of international trade for the benefit of sustainable development. The plan encourages continued facilitation of the opening and capacity building of developing country markets. But it also places the weight of the responsibility on the shoulders of the wealthier nations for assuring that developing countries open their markets and stimulate production in an environmentally sound fashion. Means still need to be clarified for developed nations to facilitate the flow of direct foreign investment, transfer of technology, scientific capacity building, and the creation of institutional support structures in developing countries. In the JPOI, the free market mechanisms are coupled with a challenge to wealthier nations to prevent growth from occurring in ways that are unsustainable.

The assumption that underlies the JPOI—that free trade policy and sustainability are commensurate—has preempted the conclusions of the scientific community. The scientists' skepticisms are justified, and the UN stance defies the intuition of those who have witnessed the changes that follow unbridled economic activity (i.e., those who state that sustainability is not resulting from free trade). But few convincing arguments can be levied for surmounting the north-south asymmetries without the instrument of trade. The Mexican Action Network on Free Trade has summed up this dilemma concisely: "The market and world economy have a role to play in the national project of long-term sustainable development but the definition of that project cannot be left to the market" (Carlsen and Salazar 2002).

CONCLUSION

Trade agreements have been the centerpiece of U.S.–Latin American relations over the last 15 years, and the prospects for expanding free trade between the United States and Latin America are strong. On the table for the United States is an FTA with the Andean nations. Negotiations with Bolivia, Colombia, Ecuador, and Peru began in 2004, though over 6,000 goods already enter the U.S. market duty free from the Andean nations as a result of the earlier Andean Trade Promotion and Drug Eradication Act (ATPDEA), which was renewed and expanded in 2002. FTAs were signed with Peru in December 2005, and with Colombia in February 2006. But the importance of these bilateral agreements is dwarfed by the larger regional agreements on the horizon. At the time of this writing nearly every participatory nation, including the United States, has ratified CAFTA-DR, a regional free trade agreement between the United States and the Central American nations. And though the hemispheric integration plan, the FTAA, seems to be stalled because of dissent from Venezuela and the Mercosur nations, there is a strong tide in the rest of Latin America to join in FTAs proposed and pushed for by the Bush administration. The fears among Latin American leaders who believe that environmental provisions could forestall economic benefits from trade are again pushing environmental consideration to the periphery in FTA discussions.

The trade agreements brokered by the United States in the last decade with Latin American partners are not, on the whole, inconsistent with the Johannesburg Plan of Implementation (2002), which reaffirmed free trade as the primary driver of environmental sustainability. However, in the case of NAFTA, organizations and regulatory bodies designed to protect the environment have not been strong enough to counter the trend toward environmental degradation correlated with extraordinary growth in trade. It appears that the U.S.-Chile FTA is facing similar structural shortcomings. CAFTA-DR contains an environmental chapter and an environmental side agreement, like NAFTA, but these provisions lack a clear enforcement mechanism to prevent environmental abuse. Sustainable development initiatives and policies are being sidelined in favor of market forces. When considering free trade agreements, it is in the best interest of all citizens of the Americas to focus on environmental factors that protect finite natural resources, while ensuring that water and air remain safe and clean. Our commitment and dedication to these important initiatives will impact the future social, political, and economic health of all of us who inhabit the Americas.

SOURCES CITED

Carlsen, Laura, and Hilde Salazar. 2002. Limits to Cooperation: A Mexican Perspective on the NAFTA's Environmental Side Agreement and Institutions. In *Greening the*

Americas: NAFTA's Lessons for Hemispheric Trade. Edited by Carolyn Deere and Daniel Esty. Cambridge, MA: MIT Press.

CEQ. 2005. *A Successful World Summit on Sustainable Development*. White House Council of Environmental Quality. www.whitehouse.gov/ceq/worldsummit.html (accessed June 19, 2005).

EcoAméricas. October 2004. *Around the Region*. www.ecoamericas.com (accessed September 10, 2005).

Gallagher, Kevin. 2002. Industrial Pollution in Mexico. In *Greening the Americas: NAFTA's Lessons for Hemispheric Trade*. Edited by Carolyn Deere and Daniel Esty. Cambridge, MA: MIT Press.

Grossman, Gene, and Alan Krueger. 1991. *Environmental Impacts of a North American Free Trade Agreement*. Princeton, NJ: Princeton University Press.

Jacott, Marisa, Cyrus Reed, and Mark Winfield. 2000. The Generation and Management of Hazardous Wastes and Transboundary Hazardous Waste Shipments Between Mexico, Canada, and the United States, 1990–2000. In *The Environmental Effects of Free Trade: North American Symposium for Understanding the Linkages Between Trade and the Environment*. Edited by CEC. Washington, DC: CEC.

McKibben, Bill. 2005. The Cuba Diet. *Harper's*, April, 61–69.

Murray, Warwick E., and Eduardo Silva. 2004. The Political Economy of Sustainable Development. In *Latin America Transformed: Globalization and Modernity*. Edited by Robert N. Gwynne and Cristobal Kay. London: Oxford University Press.

Nadal, Alejandro. 2002. Zea Mays: Effects of Trade Liberalization of Mexico's Corn Sector. In *Greening the Americas: NAFTA's Lessons for Hemispheric Trade*. Edited by Carolyn Deere and Daniel Esty. Cambridge, MA: MIT Press.

Odum, H. T. 1996. *Environmental Accounting*. New York: John Wiley & Sons.

Office of the United States Trade Representative. 2002. *Free Trade with Chile: Summary of the U.S.-Chile Free Trade Agreement*. www.ustr.gov (accessed October 12, 2005).

Perlez, Jane, and Lowell Bergman. 2005. Treasure at Yanacocha: Tangled Strands in Fight Over Peru Mine. *New York Times*, October 25.

———. 2005. *U.S. Trade 2004*. Washington, DC.

Roberts, J. T., and N. D. Thanos. 2003. *Trouble in Paradise: Globalization and Environmental Crisis in Latin America*. New York: Routledge.

TCPS. 2000. *Texas Environmental Profiles: Border Water Quality Issues*. Texas Center for Policy Studies and Environmental Defense. www.texasep.org/html/wql/wql_1sfq_brdr.html (accessed August 6, 2005).

UN. 1992. *Rio Declaration on Environment and Development*. Rio de Janeiro: United Nations.

UNEP and IISD. 2000. *Environment and Trade: A Handbook*. Winnipeg: International Institute for Sustainable Development.

Vogel, David. 2003. International Trade and Environmental Regulation. In *Environmental Policy: New Directions for the Twenty-First Century*. Edited by N. J. Vig and M. E. Kraft. Washington, DC: CQ Press.

Weidensaul, Scott. 1999. *Living on the Wind: Across the Hemisphere with Migratory Birds*. New York: North Point Press.

Wheeler, D. 2000. *Racing to the Bottom? Foreign Investment and Air Quality in Developing Countries*. Washington, DC: World Bank.

27

Resistance and Alternatives to Globalization in Latin America and the Caribbean

Richard L. Harris

Professor Richard L. Harris of California State University–Monterey Bay suggests that despite the failings and popular resistance to neoliberal policies and globalization, which have only exacerbated the difficult socioeconomic conditions of many Latin Americans, left and center-left movements and political parties have failed to develop a coherent social democratic alternative to neoliberalism and structural adjustment. Organizations have developed some interesting proposals but none have been adopted by the "pragmatic reformists" who seem content with offering adjustments to neoliberalism rather than mobilizing the disenfranchised social groups to implement a radically different social or democratic project. In this chapter, Harris describes the efforts by some groups such as the Landless Rural Workers' Movement (MST) in Brazil, the Zapatistas in Mexico, and the World Social Forum to organize and mobilize Latin American society in favor of a new development model.

What is often referred to as the "globalization," or the increasing integration, of the Latin American and Caribbean region (as well as other regions) into the contemporary global capitalist system has not propelled the people living in this important part of the world into a new era of postmodernity (Harris and Seid 2000, 2). Many of the "old" problems and issues confronted by the societies in this region during the twentieth century persist. In fact, the effects of contemporary globalization—perhaps best defined as the global expansion of late-twentieth-century capitalism or what has been called "turbo-capitalism" (Luttwak 1999)—have aggravated most of the chronic problems of the Latin American and Caribbean societies while adding new ones. Most of these problems are still best characterized in terms of such "classical" or "modernist" concepts as corporate capitalism, imperialism, neocolonialism, economic exploitation, political repression, social inequality, and social injustice.

Since the early 1980s, neoliberalism has provided the ideological justification for a series of so-called structural reforms carried out by most of the governments in the region. These policies are based on the "Washington consensus" of the international financial institutions (Bulmer-Thomas 1996; Green 1995, 2–4) that have propagated this "free-market" and "free-trade" ideology to justify the so-called financial stabilization and structural adjustment programs that they have insisted governments in Latin America and the Caribbean (as well as other parts of the world) impose on their popular classes. These measures have been aimed at making sure these governments pay off the large external debts that they assumed during the 1970s and 1980s, opening up their economies to transnational capital and increasing the "integration" of these economies into the global market (Harris 2000, 142–43).

The continued electoral support for neoliberal regimes in Latin America and the Caribbean "has led conservative commentators to argue that neoliberalism has become the hegemonic ideology, or in less elegant terms, that it has become the accepted political discourse of the masses" (Veltmeyer, Petras, and Vieux 1997, 213). It has even influenced leftist political parties and intellectuals throughout Latin America and the Caribbean to accept as a fait accompli many of the neoliberal structural reforms that have been implemented in their countries the past decade or so. However, while the centrist political regimes and the "leftist pragmatists" in the opposition parties have accepted these neoliberal reforms as part of the current reality, there has been increasing popular resistance to these policies throughout the region.

The hemispheric Free Trade Area of the Americas (FTAA), first proposed by the Clinton administration and now being promoted by the Bush administration, is intended to bring all the North American, Latin American, and Caribbean countries into a single hemispheric trade association that removes trade barriers and promotes the development of inter-hemispheric trade and the development of the economies of the countries involved. Strong opposition within the United States to expansion of the North American Free Trade Association (NAFTA), led by the U.S. labor and environmental movements but also involving nationalist elements in the Republican-controlled U.S. Congress, forced the Clinton administration and the North American–based transnational corporations to postpone their plans to expand NAFTA in the late 1990s. However, the current administration of George W. Bush has succeeded in advancing this project under the guise of a rejuvenated FTAA (Katz 2002). Despite the unprecedented popular protests that confronted the FTAA summit in Quebec City in April 2001, the heads of thirty-four countries in the Americas who attended this meeting produced a draft agreement, and negotiations are now taking place to produce a second version of this agreement. The negotiations for the FTAA are supposed to be concluded by January 2005 so that the treaty can be put into force by December 2005, thereby creating a "free-trade area" for the entire Western Hemisphere (FTAA, 2002).

POPULAR RESISTANCE TO GLOBALIZATION AND NEOLIBERALISM

The role of the state throughout Latin America and the Caribbean in regulating the economies of the countries in the region has declined significantly as a result of neoliberal "reforms" that have led to the privatization of state assets, the deregulation of many economic activities, and the drastic reduction of government expenditures on public subsidies, public services, and public employment. Nevertheless, authoritarian governmental bureaucracies and a considerable degree of centralized state power still remain in most of the Latin American and Caribbean countries. In fact, the neoliberals' rhetoric about limiting the role of the state in the economy is in fact a cover for redirecting the state's role in the economy away from serving the needs of the popular classes toward serving the special interests of the upper classes and the transnational corporations. As Clive Thomas (1989, 344) noted in the 1980s:

> We are witnessing efforts to alter the direction of state activity, and not in fact a movement to liquidate the centrality of its "economic function" [and] . . . this shift in direction may well be paralleled with more openly activist roles for the state in the process of economic concentration and the further hierarchicalization of economic and social relations. Already measures have been taken to reduce the role of the state in providing welfare, basic needs, unemployment relief, and so on. This legitimizes the social and economic inequality of capitalism under the guise of disinvolvement.

More than one critical observer has noted the hypocrisy inherent in this anti-statist rhetoric. For example, the noted Latin American scholar Atilio Boron has criticized the neoliberal ideology as being merely ideological camouflage for what are in fact inherently antidemocratic objectives and practices. According to Boron (1995, 64):

> The alleged anti-statism of the modern crusaders of neoliberalism is actually a frontal attack against the democratization that the popular classes and strata were able to construct despite the opposition and sabotage of capitalist interests. What Friedmanities and others alike are in fact preoccupied with regarding the modern state is not its excessive size nor its deficit spending but the intolerable presence of the masses saturating all of its interstices. Governments of neoliberal inspiration have fully shown that when they carry out the recommendations of their mentors, they confirm the bourgeoisie's addiction to deficit spending and to the

hypertrophied state (while cutting social expenditures, thereby suffocating the vitality of democratic institutions).

The neoliberal politicians in the Latin American countries reflect this duplicity in both their pronouncements and their policies. Most of the Latin American and Caribbean governments have selectively applied the neoliberal injunctions to downsize the state, and, of course, a few have actively resisted these neoliberal reforms (e.g., the Cuban government and the administration of President Hugo Chávez in Venezuela).

One of the most disturbing features of the contemporary political scene in Latin America and the Caribbean is the lack of governmental responsiveness to the needs of the majority of the population even though the formal mechanisms of democratic politics have been established in most of the countries of the region. This lack of responsiveness—perhaps the most deleterious effect of the contemporary process of capitalist globalization and the neoliberal reforms associated with it—has undermined the embryonic democratization of the region's political systems.

Boron (1995, 211) has effectively characterized the effects of neoliberal reforms on the democratization of the region:

Neoliberal policies have augmented the share of the very rich in the national income . . . aimed at deregulating markets, at privatization and liberalization, [these policies] have had as one of their consequences the extraordinary reinforcement of the bargaining power of a handful of privileged collective actors, whose demands gain direct access to the upper echelons of the government and the central bureaucracy. Therefore, the quality of democratic governance is not only impaired by the deterioration of the material foundations of citizenship: these fragile democratic experiments are also endangered by the fact that, deaf to the reasonable and legitimate expectations of the underlying population, they tend to magnify the strength of the dominant classes and, as a result, to further reinforce the role of naked, noninstitutionalized power relations.

In most of these countries, the urban working class, the peasantry, rural workers, the lower sectors of the salaried middle class, the members of the large informal sector, and the indigenous communities have been largely excluded or marginalized from the political arena. Taken together, these various classes and sectors represent anywhere from two-thirds to three-quarters of the population, depending on the demographic profile of each country.

Past efforts to organize and unite these classes and sectors for the purposes of representing their interests in the centers of state power have proved politically difficult and at times quite dangerous. In the past, the political mobilization of these sectors of the population has provoked the violent reaction of the military, police, and right-wing paramilitary groups, and it has also been obstructed by traditional forms of political co-optation such as clientelism, patronage, and corporatism, which the political elites have used quite effectively in most cases to subordinate and divide these classes and sectors of the population (Nef 1995, 84–89).

During the 1980s and 1990s, many of the more politically active members of the intelligentsia in the region assumed moderate political positions (in contrast to the more radical politics of the intelligentsia in the 1960s and 1970s). They distanced themselves from the popular classes and social sectors just mentioned and often accommodated their views to the prevailing neoliberal orthodoxy (Petras and Morley 1992). Many formerly leftist political parties and organizations (such as the trade unions) moved toward the political center or assumed a relatively low political profile, and some political organizations and movements opposed to the status quo fell into organizational and/or ideological disarray.

The progressive forces with the most potential to oppose the expansion of global capitalism and neoliberalism have been weakened and disoriented by major political and ideological transformations at the global level, such as the end of the Cold War, the collapse of the Soviet Bloc, and the perceived triumph of the forces of global capitalism over the previously opposing forces of revolutionary nationalism and socialism. Moreover, these forces and other opponents of contemporary turbo-capitalism have also been handicapped by their failure to develop an effective strategy for mobilizing the majority of the population against the forces of capitalist globalization and their countries' neoliberal regimes.

Revolutionary movements and insurgent groups such as those that existed in Central America during the 1970s and 1980s have been forced to give up their armed struggles for revolutionary nationalism, popular democracy, and socialism. In many cases, they have been absorbed into the conventional political process under neoliberal regimes. The revolutionary regime in Cuba has miraculously survived the collapse of the Soviet bloc and the continued economic and political embargo of the United States. However, it has been forced by the end of the Cold War and the "triumph" of global capitalism to seek increasing accommodation with the global capitalist system in order to survive (Blanco 1995; Dilla Alfonso 2000). Nevertheless, it is a vocal critic of neoliberalism and the effects of capitalist globalization and is actively opposing the establishment of the FTAA (Castro 2000).

As mentioned above, the neoliberal stabilization and structural reforms undertaken by most of the governments in the region have met with a wide range of popular resistance (see Harris 1999). At times, this resistance has taken relatively peaceful and legal forms of expression such as electoral opposition, lawsuits and court action, peaceful demonstrations, rallies, picketing, work stoppages, and strikes. But there has also been an increasing incidence of extralegal and at times violent manifestations of popular resistance, ranging from the blockage of roads and highways to land occupations, urban riots, bombings, guerrilla warfare, and even popular insurrections. The recent crisis in Argentina has provoked opposition to the country's neoliberal regime that has resorted to nearly all of these forms of popular resistance.

The continuing popular resistance to neoliberalism and globalization in the region, however, has not succeeded in stopping the globalization of most of the region's economies or the continued implementation of the neoliberal project. As Duncan Green (1995,165) of the Latin American Bureau in London has noted in his insightful study of the effects of neoliberal policies on Latin America, popular resistance to neoliberal policies in Latin America and the Caribbean has so far failed to produce a viable alternative to these policies:

> Social and political unrest have become the norm, as continued opposition to the impact of structural adjustment has sputtered and occasionally ignited in sporadic riots, strikes, rural uprisings, land takeovers and increasingly, electoral victory for presidential candidates promising to soften the impact of adjustment. In general, however, the opposition is scattered and incoherent, dogged by its lack of a coherent alternative. Grassroots political leaders and intellectuals alike bemoan the opposition's inability to move from *protesta* (protest) to *propuesta* (proposal).

Green's assessment is based on what he characterizes as the "austerity protests" in Latin America that have taken place during the past two decades or so. These austerity protests, sometimes called "IMF riots" because they have tended to be associated with the economic austerity measures recommended to the Latin American governments by the International Monetary Fund, have generally occurred in response to neoliberal stabilization and structural adjustment policies.

Since the mid-1990s, there has been a notable upsurge in popular resistance to the neoliberal policies of the Latin American and Caribbean governments. The privatization of public enterprises, worker layoffs, the dismantling of agrarian reform laws, the reform of the labor laws to permit a more "flexible" deployment of the workforce, rising prices on basic commodities, falling real wages, and widespread unemployment and underemployment have provoked wave after wave of protest. One of the most notable examples of this resistance is the popular uprising that took place in southern Mexico at the beginning of 1994. Led by armed elements of the Ejército Zapatista de Liberación Nacional (Zapatista Army of National Liberation—EZLN), a large proportion of the indigenous population of the state of Chiapas rose up in protest against the Mexican government's neoliberal economic reforms and the terms of Mexico's entry into NAFTA. As the following quote from Neil Harvey's (1996, 188) insightful analysis of the Zapatista rebellion indicates, this uprising was in large part a response to the effects of the government's neoliberal economic reforms on the Mexican peasantry:

> Since the 1970s, politically independent movements had fought first for land and then for the appropriation of the productive process. Both of these fronts of strug-

gle had evolved within an institutional framework of extensive state intervention in rural development. This framework began to be transformed with the liberalization of trade in 1986 and the subsequent withdrawal of agricultural subsidies, the privatization of state enterprises, and the reforms to Article 27 [the agrarian reform provisions of the Mexican Constitution]. In the early 1990s, the new challenge for *campesino* organizations became the defense of small producers in an increasingly liberalized market. The Chiapas rebellion revealed that the earlier struggles for land and autonomy were still alive, but it also revealed resistance to reforms that would force *campesinos* out of the market and off the land.

For similar reasons, there has been a wave of mass land invasions in Brazil organized by the Movimento dos Sem Terra (Landless Movement—MST) since the mid-1990s (Veltmeyer, Petras, and Vieux 1997, 192–94). Among the critical issues addressed by the MST are the Brazilian government's neoliberal policies that support the narrow agro-export interests of the large agricultural producers at the expense of Brazil's poor small producers, landless peasants, and agricultural workers.

The increasing globalization of the region's economies has provoked the active resistance of many local communities and social groups in Latin America that see their survival as increasingly threatened by the adverse economic, political, and cultural effects associated with the accelerated integration of their societies into the global capitalist economy. It is important to note that, as evidenced in the case of the Zapatistas in Mexico and the Confederación de Nacionalidades Indígenas del Ecuador (Confederation of Indigenous Nationalities of Ecuador—CONAIE), indigenous peoples have been among the most active opponents of these reforms and their consequences (Korten 1995, 295). They constitute a sizable proportion of the population in many Latin American countries, and their political resistance is increasingly connected with the struggles of peasant unions and rural workers (Robinson 1998–1999, 123). Moreover, in many cases they are involved in international alliances and collaborate with similar groups and communities in other countries. As Joshua Karliner (1997, 199) has observed, these "communities and organizations are increasingly working together across national boundaries," and this "kinetic activity" provides evidence of "a somewhat dispersed but burgeoning process of grassroots globalization."

The global media, particularly the Internet, have contributed to this phenomenon of "grassroots globalization" through the international diffusion of information about the political strategies and mobilization of local communities and social groups in different parts of the world that oppose the current neoliberal agenda and the processes and effects of globalization. This global diffusion process has created a global demonstration effect in the sense that the activation of an increasing number of groups and communities has been inspired by what they learn from the global media about the resistance of other groups like themselves (Robertson 1992, 166–72). Taking their cue from the example set by movements such as the Zapatistas in Mexico, these groups have learned to use the global media networks to obtain international solidarity and support for their causes. The Zapatista movement's use of the Internet and other global means of communication has garnered support for their movement throughout Mexican society as well as the rest of the world and "sparked a worldwide discussion of the meaning and implications of the Zapatista rebellion for many other confrontations with contemporary capitalist economic and political policies" (Cleaver 2002).

In many cases, these indigenous movements and communities have formed and/or joined broader social movements and political organizations that are distinguished from the older social movements and political parties in their countries by their grassroots leadership and organizing tactics and by their efforts to obtain the support of international public opinion for their struggles. As a result, the struggles of these movements at the grassroots level against globalization and neoliberalism and in favor of basic human rights, protection of the natural environment, and social justice have "become a transnational concern in which domestic and foreign activists work together to influence international public opinion" through networks of "international communications that have only become feasible in the computer age" (Karliner 1997, 174). As a result, many of these new social movements now maintain international linkages with progressive political parties and progressive international nongovernmental organizations that have chosen to support them in order to promote their own specific goals (Karliner 1997, 197–223).

The most recent and perhaps most significant expression of international popular resistance to neoliberalism and capitalist globalization has been the formation of the World Social Forum (WSF), which has now held two annual meetings (in 2001 and 2002) in Porto Alegre, Brazil. These two meetings were attended by a remarkable diversity of activists and representatives of hundreds of organizations from all over the world. Generally speaking, the groups and organizations represented at these two meetings have in common their opposition to the neoliberal regimes in their countries and the "globalization from above" imposed on their societies by the major actors and forces in the contemporary global capitalist system. The representatives of grassroots social movements and progressive organizations from Latin America and the Caribbean have been a major force at both of these meetings. In fact, Latin American and Caribbean activists and progressive organizations are now providing the organizing leadership, along with their European counterparts, for what the mainstream media have come to call the "antiglobalization movement."

The WSF has not yet produced a comprehensive alternative project that can serve as a viable alternative to the neoliberal project and capitalist globalization, but the participants at the 2002 meeting—titled "Another World Is Possible"—did agree on the following (Cooper 2002, 13): (1) They need to reposition their growing global movement from its perceived stance of opposition to neoliberalism and globalization to a more affirmative stance based on the promotion of a viable alternative or alternatives to the existing global order and the neoliberal project. (2) Under the banner of "Shrink It or Sink It," they also need to escalate the existing international struggle against the WTO to reduce its powers or shut it down completely. (3) In the Western Hemisphere, they need to wage an all-out campaign against the FTAA through organizing "national plebiscites" throughout the region to expose the little-known fact that it will give transnational corporations the power to override the laws and regulations of all the national governments that become members. (4) They need to work for the creation of new international organizations to replace the IMF and the World Bank and "devolve production and trade decisions to national economies" so that they can "pursue diverse development strategies and not be bound to one centralized model" (Cooper 2002, 13). Although there was widespread agreement on these general goals, there was disagreement on many others, and a clear division emerged between the "reformers" and the "radicals" over both the ends and means that should be pursued by those who are opposed to the current global order.

The organizers of the 2002 WSF were largely reformists. The more radical movements in the region such as the Zapatistas and the Fuerzas Armadas Revolucionarias de Colombia (Revolutionary Armed Forces of Colombia—FARC), were not invited to participate in the forum on the grounds that they were "political movements" (Petras, 2002). Not even the Asociación Madres de Plaza de Mayo (Association of the Mothers of the Plaza de Mayo), one of the most prominent human rights organizations in Argentina, was invited, but the leaders of the Brazilian MST protested its exclusion and paid the air fare for one of its leaders to attend the meeting. Put simply, the differences between the reformist and radical elements within the WSF reflect the differences that exist throughout Latin America and the Caribbean between those who believe it is possible to *reform* the existing neoliberal regimes in their countries and the global capitalist system and those who believe that both must be replaced by a new social order. The observations of James Petras (2002) on these differences at the 2002 WSF meeting reveal this distinction quite clearly:

> The division between reformists and radicals was most evident in their definitions of what they considered to be the central most important aspect of the struggle and in their proposals. The reformists still talked about opposing globalization and added to this opposition to Yankee militarism. The radicals linked the expansion of the multinational corporations to the imperialist states and used the language of anti-imperialism. This was not just a rhetorical difference. It is a difference rooted deeply in the orientations and the strategic perspectives of their opposing positions.

As Petras also observes, in their discussions about "alternatives" the reformists tended to discuss the possibility of creating more humanitarian forms of "globalization" while the radicals preferred to speak about fighting "imperialism" and tried to broaden the discussion of alternatives to put "socialism on the table." According to Petras, the final declaration of the forum represented a compromise between the reformists and the radicals. On one hand, they agreed on a radical diagnosis of the problems confronting humanity and agreed to organize a series of popular mobilizations in various parts of the world throughout 2002. On the other hand, their new goals reflect the moderate, nonviolent orientation of the reformists rather than the demands of the radicals for a strategy aimed at defeating imperialism and creating participatory forms of socialism at the grassroots level.

THE NEED FOR A VIABLE ALTERNATIVE

In view of the foregoing analysis, it is clear that viable alternative courses of development are needed that genuinely serve the needs of the majority of the population in Latin America and the Caribbean. The strength of the neoliberal regimes in the region is that they have presented a coherent strategy that appears to be in step with the times. However, the "unending series of adjustments, each implemented with the promise that it would be the final one," has begun to erode the credibility of these regimes and led to "downward social mobility for key supporters of the neoliberal model—not only the poor and public employees, but sectors of the professional and business class who [have been] badly hit" by these adjustments, so much so that even "sectors of the military and church hierarchy" have begun to question the viability of the neoliberal agenda (Veltmeyer, Petras, and Vieux 1997, 221).

The center-left opposition parties and movements in most of the Latin American countries have failed to take full advantage of this situation. They have failed to win major electoral victories over the neoliberals because they have been unable to offer the electorate a viable alternative to the neoliberal agenda. Moreover, the neoliberal political forces in power have successfully exploited the authoritarian legacy of fear and insecurity in the political culture of most of these countries. This political legacy stems from the recent past experience with military rule and the ruthless political repression of the left and other popular-based political movements by the military, the police, and right-wing paramilitary groups. The neoliberal political forces in the region also have used their privileged access to the elite-controlled mass media and extensive campaign funds provided by the upper classes to maintain their hold on political power (Veltmeyer, Petras, and Vieux 1997, 214–15).

The center-left parties have largely abandoned their previous social democratic and social reformist agendas for a more pragmatic "social liberal" agenda that is hardly distinguishable from that of the neoliberals except that they advocate more state expenditures on social programs (Otero 1996, 240–43). They have also tended to shy away from mobilizing the popular classes through general strikes and mass demonstrations. Instead, they have focused on parliamentary and electoral politics, even though popular resistance to these regimes has continued to erupt in the streets, factories, universities, and countryside while they sit in their offices and parliamentary chambers.

To displace the neoliberals from power, the parties of the left and center-left and other organized progressive political forces in Latin America will need to overcome their differences, join together in a broad political front, and mobilize broad-based popular support for a viable alternative project of inward-oriented and ecologically sustainable social, economic, and political development. This alternative project will have to respond to the needs and interests of the diverse, multi-class spectrum of social movements and grassroots organizations that have arisen in opposition to the neoliberal project and the imposed integration of these societies into the global capitalist economy (Green 1995, 195). In the past, center-left and leftist political movements have won electoral victories in Latin America "when the elections were the *culmination* [emphasis added] of mass mobilizations and struggles, land occupations, and urban movements" that polarized the population in a manner favorable to an electoral victory by these forces (Veltmeyer, Petras, and Vieux 1997, 218). To reverse the tide of neoliberalism and globalizing turbo-capitalism, the opposing forces need to adopt this kind of mobilizing strategy for the purposes of gaining political power so that they can promote an alternative project of social, economic, and political development that is both inward-oriented and ecologically sustainable.

To date, leftist and progressive forces in Latin America have not been able to put forward either a viable social democratic or a credible democratic socialist project as an effective alternative to the neoliberal agenda. However, the basic elements of these two alternatives to the turbo-capitalism of the neoliberals would appear to be needed in any alternative project that provides a viable course of sustainable economic development based on social equity, popular democracy, and the protection of the natural environment. An "alternative state" is also needed to implement a viable alternative project of this nature. As Leon Panitch (1996, 88) has argued:

> A "possible alternative state" to those sponsoring globalization amid competitive austerity today would have to be based on a shift toward a more inwardly oriented economy rather than one driven by external trade considerations. This in turn would mean placing greater emphasis on a radical redistribution of productive resources, income and working time. This could only be democratically grounded . . . insofar as production and services were more centered on local and national needs where the most legitimate democratic collectivities reside.

At the 2002 WSF meeting in Porto Alegre, Alberto Arroyo of the Red Mexicana de Acción frente al Libre Comercio (Mexican Action Network Against Free Trade—RMALC) also spoke of this need for a new *kind* of state: "When we are talking about a new and strengthened role for the state, we have to be talking about a new kind of state—one subject to real democratic controls by civil society" (quoted in Cooper 2002, 13). Arroyo was one of the main contributors to an important document titled "Alternatives for the Americas: Building a People's Hemispheric Agreement" that was produced for the People's Summit of the Americas held in Santiago, Chile, in April 1998, at the same time as the FTAA Summit of the Americas, headed by U.S. President Bill Clinton. This document— produced by a coalition of Canadian, U.S., and Mexican activists—focuses on "building a hemispheric social alliance around concrete, viable alternatives" for the future development of the hemisphere. It is based on a vision of the future that is radically different from that of the neoliberal governments of the region and the proponents of the FTAA.

In this document—remarkable in its vision, comprehensiveness, and specificity—the authors proclaim that "at this stage of the struggle, it is not enough to oppose, to resist and to criticize," it is also necessary "to build a proposal of our own and fight for it" (Alternatives 2002). The document lays out a framework for the development of such a proposal. The authors argue that as far as the state is concerned, "The key is for nations to open themselves to the world based on their own plans for fair and sustainable development led by democratic governments, rather than leaving the future of such development to market forces. Economies that are open are all the more reliant on regulations at the national and international levels, and require a state that is strong enough to promote and enforce them." They emphasize that what they propose is a democratic state that "radically challenges corruption at every level" and that is both "economically and socially accountable to its citizens."

According to the authors of this document, what is needed is a new kind of state that performs "a qualitatively new role within the economy"—one that involves the development and implementation of a "democratically established national development plan." However, they continue:

> We are not proposing an oversized state burdened by huge, inefficient enterprises. The number and size of public corporations is less important than the role they fulfill. Society, not only governments, should make decisions relating to industries in the public realm. The goal should not be traditional protectionism, but building a state accountable to society that can implement a democratically established national development plan. This may involve the protection of certain sectors considered strategic within a country's plan, but more importantly, it means promoting forward-looking development. Regulation does not imply inhibiting private initiative. On the contrary, it means establishing clear rules, balancing rights and obligations, and ensuring that both national and international capital promote a country's fair and sustainable development. This renewed role for the state implies international regulations that must be determined democratically and through consultation with citizens. Sovereignty belongs to the people, who may decide to submit to international regulations *if* [emphasis added] it is in their collective interest.

Thus, the authors of the document make it clear that the kind of state that is needed in Latin America and the Caribbean is one quite different from those that now exist. They do not offer any proposals for bringing this new kind of state into being; and it is difficult to imagine how the kind of democratic, strong state they propose could be established under present conditions in most of Latin America and the Caribbean.

Nevertheless, if popular resistance to the many adverse effects of neoliberalism and turbo-capitalism continues to grow in Latin America and the Caribbean as it has over the past decade or so, then the conditions for the mobilization of broad-based popular movements capable of changing the existing social order will almost surely emerge. To facilitate this course of development, progressive parties, movements, and organizations throughout the region and their allies outside it need to formulate and propagate alternative projects that are clearly preferable to the neoliberal one. It now seems clear that such projects must provide feasible and attractive strategies for moving from the prevailing export-oriented neoliberal model of capitalist development to a new inward-oriented model of sustainable development, probably based on some combination of social democracy and democratic socialism but tailored to the diverse conditions, political history, and cultural values of the societies involved. These projects must also provide feasible frameworks and strategies for new forms of international cooperation and regulation that will support the democratic forms of inward-oriented and sustainable development that are needed at the societal level. At the same time, they must contribute to the establishment of a new global trading system based on "fair trade" to replace the present global capitalist system based on "free trade."

Finally, the implementation of a successful alternative project will require the creation of an alternative state that provides for bottom-up democratic control over the economy at the national level and the effective regulation of the linkages between the national economy and the larger global economy at the international level. Until this happens, it is at least safe to predict that there will be continuing popular resistance to neoliberalism and to the globalization of the Latin American and Caribbean economies—primarily because of the widespread suffering they will continue to impose upon the majority of the population. To quote from a recent commentary by Eduardo Galeano (2002) on the massive popular mobilization generated by the recent collapse of the Argentine economy, "The people, tired of being spectators of their own humiliation, have made it on to the playing field. It won't be easy to get them off."

REFERENCES

Alternatives. 2002. "Alternatives for the Americas: Building a People's Hemispheric Agreement." www.web.ca/-comfront/alts4americas/eng/cover.html (accessed March 22, 2002).

Blanco, Juan Antonio. 1995. Cuba: Crisis, ethics, and viability. In *Latin America Faces the Twenty-First Century: Reconstructing a Social Justice Agenda*. Edited by Susanne Jonas and Edward McCaughan. Boulder, CO: Westview.

Boron, Atilio. 1995. *State, Capitalism, and Democracy in Latin America*. Boulder, CO: Lynne Rienner.

Bulmer-Thomas, Victor. 1996. Introduction. In *The New Economic Model in Latin America and Its Impact on Income Distribution and Poverty*. Edited by Victor Bulmer-Thomas. New York: St. Martin's Press.

Castro, Fidel. 2000. On globalisation. Speech presented at the opening session of the South Summit in Havana on April 12, 2000. archive.8m.net/castro.htm (accessed June 7, 2002).

Cleaver, Harry. 2002. Zapatistas in cyberspace: A guide to analysis and resources. www.eco.utexas.edu/faculty/Cleaver/zapsincyber.html (accessed March 21, 2002).

Cooper, Mark. 2002. From protest to politics: A report from Porto Alegre. *The Nation*, March 11, 11–14.

Dilla Alfonso, Haroldo. 2000. Cuba: El curso de una transition incierta. *Memoria* 132. www.memoria.com.mx/132/Dilla.htm (accessed March 21, 2002).

FTAA (Free Trade Area of the Americas). 2002. Overview of the FTAA process. www.ftaa-alca.org/View_e.asp (accessed March 21, 2003).

Galeano, Eduardo. 2002. Argentina pays debt—to democracy. *The Progressive*. www.progressive.org/0901/gal0202.html (accessed March 20, 2002).

Green, Duncan. 1995. *Silent Revolution: The Rise of Market Economics in Latin America*. London: Cassell.

Harris, Richard. 1999. Popular resistance to neoliberalism in Latin America. In *Globalization and the Dilemmas of the State in the South*. Edited by Francis Adams. New York: St. Martin's Press.

———. 2000. The effects of globalization and neoliberalism in Latin America at the beginning of the millennium. In *Critical Perspectives on Globalization and Neoliberalism in the Developing Countries*. Edited by Richard Harris and Melinda Seid. Leiden: Brill.

Harris, Richard, and Melinda Seid. 2000. Critical perspectives on globalization and neoliberalism in the developing countries. In *Critical Perspectives on Globalization and Neoliberalism in the Developing Countries*. Edited by Richard Harris and Melinda Seid. Leiden: Brill.

Harvey, Neil. 1996. Rural reforms and the Zapatista rebellion: Chiapas 1988–1995. In *NeoLiberalism Revisited: Economic Restructuring and Mexico's Political Future*. Edited by Gerardo Otero. Boulder, CO: Westview.

Karliner, Joshua. 1997. *The Corporate Planet: Ecology and Politics in the Age of Globalization*. San Francisco: Sierra Club Books.

Katz, Claudio. 2002. Free trade area of the Americas: NAFTA marches south. *NACLA Report on the Americas* 35 (January/February): 27–31.

Korten, David. 1995. *When Corporations Rule the World*. San Francisco: Berrett-Koehler.

Luttwak, Edward. 1999. *Turbo-Capitalism: Winners and Losers in the Global Economy*. New York: HarperCollins.

Nef, Jorge. 1995. Demilitarization and democratic transition in Latin America. In *Capital, Power, and Inequality in Latin America*. Edited by Sandor Halebsky and Richard Harris. Boulder, CO: Westview.

Otero, Gerardo. 1996. Mexico's economic and political futures. In *NeoLiberalism Revisited: Economic Restructuring and Mexico's Political Future*. Edited by Gerardo Otero. Boulder, CO: Westview.

Panitch, Leon. 1996. Globalization, states, and left strategies. *Social Justice* 23: 79–89.

Petras, James. 2002. Una historia de los foros. www.forumsocialmundial.org.br/esp/ balanco_JamesPetras_esp.asp (accessed March 21, 2002).

Petras, James, and Morris Morley. 1992. *Latin America in the Time of Cholera*. New York: Routledge.

Robertson, Roland. 1992. *Globalization: Social Theory and Global Culture*. Newbury Park, CA: Sage.

Robinson, William. 1998–1999. Latin America and global capitalism. *Race and Class* 40: 120–29.

Thomas, Clive. 1989. Restructuring the world economy and its political implications for the Third World. In *Instability and Change in the World Economy*. Edited by Arthur MacEwan and William Tabb. New York: Monthly Review Press.

Veltmeyer, Henry, James Petras, and Samuel Vieux. 1997. *Neoliberalism and Class Conflict in Latin America*. New York: St. Martin's Press.

28

Beyond Benign Neglect:
Washington and Latin America

Arturo Valenzuela

According to Arturo Valenzuela, director of the Center for Latin American Studies at Georgetown University and senior director for Western Hemisphere at the National Security Council in the Clinton administration, President George W. Bush lost critical momentum and key opportunities to focus U.S. attention on the pressing issues facing Latin America. Much of the goodwill offered by political elites throughout Latin America dissipated with the Bush administration's decision to declare war on Iraq without support of the United Nations. What added insult to injury was the hostile way in which Mexico and Chile, members of the UN Security Council, were treated by the administration for not supporting U.S. policy. Along with heavy-handedness and neglect, Valenzuela attributes Latin Americans' extraordinarily negative view of the Bush administration to its poor handling of crises in the region, such as those in Argentina and Venezuela, and its inability or unwillingness to look beyond trade as a solution to Latin America's social and economic ills. The author recommends that the U.S. focus its resources and attention on strengthening democratic political institutions and multilateral regional institutions as a strategy to reengage Latin Americans as they confront a myriad of complex social, economic, and political challenges.

In the years after the end of the Cold War, the administrations of Presidents George H. W. Bush and Bill Clinton moved to implement a new agenda for the Western Hemisphere. This included helping to end the civil conflicts in Central America that had raged during the 1980s and embarking on a concerted initiative aimed at liberalizing trade, implementing economic reforms, protecting and strengthening democratic institutions, resolving border disputes, ensuring security, and addressing transnational challenges such as drugs and migration flows.

The United States shifted the definition of its interests in the region from containing the spread of communism to working to promote political stability, security, prosperity, and trade. It did so by seeking to strengthen multilateral frameworks for cooperation while minimizing unilateral actions. Washington attempted to set a tone of mutual engagement and respect largely absent in the long, often testy relations between the hemispheric superpower and its southern neighbors.

Out of this engagement came the negotiations for a North American Free Trade Agreement (NAFTA) and the subsequent Summit of the Americas process. That process, which brought together all the hemisphere's heads of state, led to negotiations for a Free Trade Agreement of the Americas (FTAA), the forging of a Convention against Corruption, the strengthening of the Organization of American States' ability to come to the collective defense of democracy, and the establishment of a multilateral system for gauging progress on drug eradication.

CRISIS MANAGEMENT

The new framework for hemispheric cooperation also contributed to the development of collaborative mechanisms to address specific regional crises. After the signing of NAFTA, U.S. interests and the well-being of countless Mexicans would have been severely affected had the Mexican peso crisis of late December 1994 been permitted to spin out of control. In one of the most important actions of his presidency, Clinton made use of broad executive powers to configure a massive support package for Mexico, combining funds from the United States and international financial institutions, to bolster the value of the peso. In an era of globalization of international financial markets, the United States also helped structure a financial assistance package for Brazil in 1998, thereby averting a serious downturn in Latin America's largest economy, which had weathered with difficulty the shock of the Asian financial crisis the previous year.

Similarly, U.S. leaders worked closely with their counterparts in the region and through the O.A.S. to address political crises. After the military coup that overthrew Haitian President Jean-Bertrand Aristide in 1991 and the "self-coup" by Peruvian President Alberto Fujimori (who closed Peru's Congress with support of the armed forces), the elder Bush's administration sought ways to reestablish constitutional rule together with other governments and the Organization of American States. When an embargo endorsed by the OAS failed to restore democracy in Haiti, the newly elected Clinton administration, backed by a United Nations mandate, moved to restore Aristide to office. Facing challenges to democracy in the Dominican Republic, Guatemala, Ecuador, Paraguay, and Peru, hemispheric leaders, working in coordination with the OAS, succeeded in preventing overt military involvement in politics and maintaining constitutional order.

Finally, despite a significant decline in resources for bilateral assistance to the region, the Clinton administration struck a deal with the Republican-controlled Congress to provide increased support for Colombia in its efforts to fight insurgents financed by the profits of illegal drugs sold in the United States and Western markets. Washington also sought to "internationalize" support for Colombia and the Andean region in Europe and the hemisphere.

DISAPPOINTMENTS, DIVERSIONS

Irritants did remain in inter-American relations despite the new tenor of engagement. Latin American leaders, who had pressed strongly for the free trade agenda in the summit process, were disappointed when President Clinton was not able to obtain fast-track negotiating authority from Congress, which would have permitted the conclusion of a free trade agreement with Chile and given impetus to the FTAA process. At the same time, officials and the public viewed as arbitrary and patronizing congressional requirements that the president annually certify the degree of individual country cooperation with the United States on drug eradication efforts in order to receive U.S. assistance.

U.S. attention to the former Soviet Union and crises in the Balkans, the Middle East, and Haiti also diverted resources that were needed to support the ongoing peace process in Central America and help address the challenges faced in the Caribbean and the Andes. Meanwhile, Congress, taking its cues from Republican Senator Richard Helms, the chairman of the Senate Foreign Relations Committee, showed reluctance to engage the world by committing funds for foreign assistance and the operation of multilateral institutions.

On assuming office in 2001, President George W. Bush promised to further increase U.S. engagement by making the Western Hemisphere the highest priority of the new administration's foreign policy, underscoring his skepticism with the foreign policy activism of the Clinton administration in the Balkans and the Middle East. Placing a particular focus on Mexico, the first foreign country he visited after the election, the new president signaled a willingness to forge new ground on immigration policy, while picking up on the stalled FTAA process and continuing antidrug efforts in the Andes.

Leaders throughout the Americas welcomed the Bush administration's declared commitment to the hemisphere at a time when much of the initial enthusiasm with economic and political reform had lost its luster. With some notable exceptions, economic reversals and weak and inefficient governments had seemed to leave many states incapable of addressing the persistence of massive poverty and increased inequality. With Washington's renewed focus on the region many leaders hoped that the negative trends could be reversed.

THE SOURCES OF ILL WILL

As the Bush administration prepares to embark on its second term in office, what is the verdict in the region on the president's first four years?

Judging from public opinion surveys, editorial opinion, and the private views of high-ranking officials throughout Latin America, the reelection of President Bush was not welcome news. This fact places considerable pressure on the administration as it moves to redefine its policies toward the region in the months ahead. A Zogby poll of elite opinion conducted for the University of Miami in 2002 showed that 87 percent of the leaders polled had an unfavorable opinion of President Bush's performance and only 12 percent felt that he was making a good or excellent effort in dealing with the hemisphere. A September 2004 poll of mass public opinion by the Program on International Policy Attitudes at the University of Maryland confirmed that displeasure with Bush's international policies had contributed to a sharp drop in positive perceptions of the United States.

Indeed, 78 percent of Mexicans claimed that U.S. foreign policy had led them to view the United States unfavorably, while only 18 percent said that they had improved their estimation of their neighbor to the north. This pattern was repeated in Brazil (66 percent to 17 percent), Argentina (65 percent to 5 percent), and Uruguay (51 percent to 5 percent). By smaller margins, sentiments toward the United States had deteriorated in the Dominican Republic (49 percent to 37 percent), Colombia (44 percent to 29 percent), Bolivia (38 percent to 14 percent), and Peru (27 percent to 20 percent). The only country where views of the United States resulting from Washington's foreign policy were virtually tied was Venezuela (34 percent to 33 percent)—reflecting the polarization in that country and the perception that the Bush administration was more partial to the opposition than the Hugo Chávez government. It is not a coincidence that in all the countries surveyed, respondents favored the election of John Kerry over George W. Bush in 2004 by large margins.

How should we account for such sentiments? They are clearly not related to the fact that the United States had to focus its attention on the terrorist threat after the attacks on the World Trade Center and the Pentagon on 9/11. The attacks elicited an unprecedented outpouring of sympathy and solidarity with the United States, and few questioned the wisdom of the retaliatory war on Al Qaeda and the Taliban.

Much of that goodwill was dissipated when the United States decided to go to war against Iraq without obtaining the sanction of the UN Security Council. The administration's invocation of a doctrine of preemptive war provided unsettling reminders of the days of unilateral U.S. intervention in the internal affairs of countries in the Western Hemisphere. It was viewed as a repudiation by the United States of efforts strongly supported by Latin Americans over several decades to establish and consolidate international institutions and international law as a way to encourage the peaceful resolution of conflicts in the conduct of international affairs.

Both leaders and mass publics strongly approved of the position taken by Mexico and Chile, the two nonpermanent members from the Americas on the UN Security Council, whose representatives joined the council majority in opposing a vote authorizing war in Iraq. Despite enormous pressure from the United States to support a second resolution sanctioning a U.S.-led war against Saddam Hussein, both countries argued that there was inconclusive evidence of the existence of Iraq's reconstituted weapons of mass destruction and that UN inspectors should be allowed to continue their work before force was authorized. Chile and Mexico believed with the council majority that the work of the United Nations had "contained" the military threat posed by Iraq. Chile did propose a compromise resolution providing for specific benchmarks and timelines for Iraqi compliance before war could be authorized, only to be publicly rebuffed by a White House intent on going to war.

PRESSURES AND PUNISHMENTS

Adding insult to injury was the U.S. administration's reaction in the aftermath of the Security Council's failure to give a green light to Washington's military intentions. Viewing the stand taken at the UN by the two Latin American countries as a betrayal of friendship, President Bush refused to take Mexican President Vicente Fox's phone calls and pointedly declined to reopen the promising discussions initiated with Mexico on immigration reform. The signing of a free trade agreement between Chile and the United States on June 6, 2003—originally one of the high points of administration policy in the region—was consigned to a ministerial level event in Miami while Singapore, which openly supported the United States in Iraq, celebrated its trade-pact-signing a month earlier in a White House ceremony.

At the same time, the administration placed strong pressure on Colombia, the largest recipient of U.S. aid in the hemisphere, and several Central American countries to endorse and support U.S. actions as part of the "coalition of the willing" in the Iraq War. Colombia and Costa Rica joined the coalition, and Nicaragua, Honduras, El Salvador, and the Dominican Republic made small troop commitments, although only El Salvador continued to maintain troops in Iraq at the beginning of President Bush's second term in office.

Pressure to support the war coincided with additional entreaties to sign bilateral immunity agreements with the United States. Through these agreements countries that are signatories to the International Criminal Court (ICC) would pledge not to surrender U.S. citizens within their jurisdiction to the court, lest they lose U.S. military and nonmilitary assistance, much to the annoyance of leaders throughout the region who chafed at these tactics and for the most part refused to abide by them. Small countries in the Caribbean that had strongly supported the ICC were particularly incensed at this pressure and chose to rebuff the United States, thereby jeopardizing significant bilateral assistance.

Revelations of widespread abuse of prisoners in Iraq and at the U.S. facility at Guantanamo Bay, at the hands of U.S. personnel and in contravention of the Geneva accords, further tarnished the image of the United States. It also undermined the administration's argument that American citizens should be immune from prosecution before the ICC because the United States adheres to the highest standards of justice and simply fears the political prosecutions of its citizens. In an era when heads of state and top officials meet frequently and are scrutinized by ubiquitous mass media, the elements of a foreign policy based on retribution and arm-twisting became widely known, contributing further to the image of the United States as a bully on the world stage.

WASHINGTON'S HEAVY HAND

Problems with Washington during President Bush's first term did not stem exclusively from dissent over the war in Iraq and pressure to fall in line with U.S. global objectives. Although professing goals in the hemisphere similar to those espoused by his father and President Clinton—continuing the Summit of the Americas process, making headway on regional free trade agreements, and supporting Andean counter-drug activities—Bush took a decidedly different approach to managing regional crises, notably in the cases of Argentina, Venezuela, Bolivia, and Haiti, all of which tarnished Washington's image in the region. The handling of these crises tended to overshadow administration accomplishments, including renewed anticorruption initiatives, improved cooperation on security matters, and progress on trade as evidenced by the pact with Chile and the successful negotiation of a Central American Free Trade Agreement, still subject to ratification.

From the outset, the U.S. Treasury Department made it clear that it viewed support for countries in financial difficulties as a "moral hazard" problem—that is, the U.S. taxpayer should not be called on to bail out investors who made poor choices, even if it means that a country's financial system might collapse. Argentina was caught in a particularly vicious circle. Having pegged its currency to the dollar, the country became increasingly uncompetitive in world markets, particularly after Brazil devalued. As the cost of servicing its debt skyrocketed and the government found it politically untenable to implement further austerity measures, it was only a matter of time before pressure on the currency would lead to devaluation and render payment on dollar-denominated debt virtually impossible. Although Washington reversed its stand and sought at the last minute to prevent the collapse of the Argentine economy by structuring a financial support package in 2001, that support was too little and too late. It also came without a concerted and well-crafted effort to engage Argentine authorities in a joint strategy to help cushion the economic crisis.

Contrary to the assumptions of U.S. policy makers, the Argentine financial crisis that forced the resignation of President Fernando de la Rua in 2001 not only affected Argentina but also sent a pall over vulnerable economies in the region already suffering from a downturn in the international economy. Throughout the hemisphere serious doubts were raised about the wisdom of economic stabilization and structural reform policies promoted by the United States and the advertised benefits of growth based on increased trade alone. It is no accident that the sharpest drop in favorable attitudes toward the United States came in Argentina.

In Venezuela, the administration's initial support for the formation of an unconstitutional ad hoc government established by the military after the forced (though short-lived) resignation of President Hugo Chávez in April 2002 constituted a significant blow to hemispheric efforts to support adherence to the institutional order and the rule of law in the region. Deviating sharply from the policies pursued by its two predecessors, the Bush administration refused to call on the established mechanisms of the OAS to prevent the interruption of the democratic process.

The United States did belatedly turn to the OAS, but only after it became clear that President Chávez's supporters in the military and on the street had reversed the outcome and reinstated the elected president. By equivocating in the face of the unconstitutional removal from office of an elected leader whom Washington did not like, the administration contributed to undermining the United States' political and moral authority as a country committed to supporting the democratic process. It also damaged the effectiveness of the OAS and its newly approved "democratic charter" as instruments for safeguarding democracy. Ironically, Washington's posture damaged its ability to deal with the mercurial Venezuelan president and his government, which wrongly assumed that the United States was actually behind the coup attempt.

SHOT IN THE FOOT

In Bolivia, the Bush administration undermined its own preferred presidential candidate in the electoral campaign of 2002 when the U.S. ambassador openly declared his opposition to the candidacy of the leader of the coca producers union, thereby boosting his popularity and bringing him within a fraction of gaining the highest plurality of votes in the race. Gonzalo Sánchez de Lozada, who had served as president of Bolivia in the 1990s, was elected to office but soon faced a mutiny by poorly paid police officers. In a climate of growing civil unrest he desperately sought $100 million in U.S. support to cover severe budget shortfalls. On a trip to Washington, including a visit with President Bush, he was rebuffed and provided with a minute portion of his request.

Only after Sánchez de Lozada was forced to resign the presidency in 2003, after dozens of protesters were killed by the armed forces, did Washington and the international financial institutions significantly increase their financial support for Bolivia. By then policies that could have helped resolve Bolivia's chronic problems, including the construction of a pipeline to export natural gas, had become politically untenable.

Finally, in Haiti, the administration's unwillingness to engage the island's daunting problems and its personal distaste for Haiti's elected leader contributed to a severe deterioration of public order. This in turn helped force the ouster of another elected president, setting back the unfinished if limited progress that country had made in struggling to establish institutional order. When Haiti was overrun by rebels associated with remnants of the disbanded Haitian military, Secretary of State Colin Powell correctly argued that the solution to the crisis required respect for the constitutional order and the legitimacy of the elected president, Aristide.

The State Department's efforts to mediate the crisis were half-hearted at best. When the opposition refused to accept its terms the administration made it clear that there would be no support for the beleaguered president from the international community, thereby encouraging his ouster in 2004. "I am happy he is gone. He'd worn out his welcome with the Haitian people," proclaimed Vice President Dick Cheney.

By turning its back on Haiti, the administration also turned its back on the OAS and the efforts by other Caribbean states to mediate the political conflict on the island. The departure of President Aristide and his replacement with an ad hoc government did not resolve the country's problems; it only made them worse. By encouraging the removal of a figure, however flawed and controversial, who was the legitimate head of state and who continues to command strong allegiance, Washington aggravated the polarization of the country and made more difficult the restructuring of a semblance of institutional order.

A NEW AGENDA

Now that he has been reelected, how can President Bush reverse the growing dissatisfaction with U.S. policy in the hemisphere? His administration will continue to be judged as much for its global policy as for its policy toward the region. If the president in his second term succeeds in reengaging with America's traditional allies in Europe and moves toward projecting a constructive approach to multilateral cooperation, some of the standing that the United States has lost in the eyes of the world's leaders and mass publics will be regained. With respect to Latin America, the president and his administration need to signal that they really do care.

On substance, administration officials should continue to press for the Free Trade Agreement of the Americas. It is not clear, however, whether the administration's strategy of negotiating subregional agreements with Central America and the Andean region will provide the necessary building blocks to conclude a broader hemispheric agreement that includes Brazil. Indeed, partial agreements may increase the difficulty of negotiating a more comprehensive trade pact by introducing standards that might make compromises with Brazil harder to make. In any case, the White House must first ensure Senate confirmation of the Central American Free Trade Agreement, something that is not assured despite the strengthening of the president's majorities in Congress.

The administration will have to move beyond the talking points of the 1990s—that the hemisphere's problems can be solved with "trade not aid"—and recognize that economic reforms are simply not enough to address the continued ills of a region characterized by slow growth and increased inequalities. With as many as 150 million people living on $2 per day, Latin America's problems require attention to investment in infrastructure and people, particularly through educational opportunities for marginalized populations. This requires a further strengthening of state institutions and the ability of governments to generate additional revenues for public investments.

It is also clear that the establishment of electoral democracies is not the same as the consolidation of viable democratic regimes, and this consolidation is a complex and lengthy process. U.S. budget deficits and commitments in Iraq make it unlikely that the United States will be in a position to provide additional resources for development efforts in the region. Despite an increase in the foreign aid budget, Latin America continues to lag. Only three countries in the region now qualify for funding under the Millennium Challenge Account, an innovative program that increases foreign aid to the poorest countries, but only if they exhibit good governmental practices and low levels of corruption.

With regard to Mexico and Central America, President Bush faces a significant challenge if he intends to honor the pledge he made in 2000 to implement migration reforms. It is not true that immigration reform fell victim to 9/11. Promising steps to create expanded temporary worker programs and a path to normalize the status of undocumented immigrants in the United States were set aside before the terrorist attacks because of strong objections from conservatives in the Republican party fearful that the issue would cost the president his reelection.

To enact immigration reform the president will have to reach out to Democrats to cobble together a pro-reform agenda. He will not succeed in getting that support if he shelves proposals to create a path for citizenship for the millions of undocumented workers already in the United States. Bush will have to be willing to stand on principle to obtain immigration reform despite significant dissent from his hard-line base, something he has not been prepared to do so far.

The second Bush administration may also have to manage a response to political change in Cuba. Now that the president has been reelected he should pay serious attention to growing sentiments within his own party and within the Cuban-American community in support of a substantial shift in policy, one aimed at ensuring a "soft landing" in Cuba—a transition not premised on the violent overthrow of the regime but on Cuba's evolution toward a more open and democratic society.

Finally, the administration should renew its commitment to effective regional institutions, including the OAS. Multilateralism does not mean turning over vexing problems such as the crises in Venezuela and Haiti to the OAS secretariat. It means genuine engagement with leading countries to strengthen collective solutions to the region's problems that can be implemented with the organization's administrative help. Washington needs to view the leadership of the OAS as a tool to promote effective dialogue, not as a reward for loyalty to U.S. foreign policy objectives elsewhere in the world.

President Bush can make great strides in remedying hostility to his policies by renewing the multilateral dialogue begun with the countries of the hemisphere by his immediate predecessors. Without clear and concerted engagement and a recognition that the consolidation of democracy in Latin America is far from a foregone conclusion, Washington will be unable to regain the momentum for progress lost over the past four years.

Notes

INTRODUCTION

1. See Charles Gibson, *Spain in America* (New York: Harper and Row, 1966); Stanley Stein and Barbara Stein, *Colonial Heritage of Latin America* (New York: Oxford University Press, 1970).

2. See Lewis Hanke, ed., *Do the Americas Have a Common History?* (New York: Knopf, 1964).

3. John Lynch, *Spanish-American Revolutions, 1808–1826*, 2nd ed. (New York: Norton, 1986), 5.

4. See Lester Langley, *America and the Americas: The United States in the Western Hemisphere* (Athens: University of Georgia Press, 1989).

5. Francisco Garcia, *Latin America: Its Rise and Progress* (London: Cassell, 1913).

6. Quoted in James D. Cockroft, *Latin America: History, Politics, and U.S. Policy*, 2nd ed. (Chicago: Nelson-Hall, 1996). See also Arthur Whitaker, *The United States and the Independence of Latin America, 1800–1830* (Baltimore: Johns Hopkins University Press, 1930); John Johnson, *A Hemisphere Apart: The Foundations of United States Policy toward Latin America* (Baltimore: Johns Hopkins University Press, 1990); Piero Gleijeses, "The Limits of Sympathy: The United States and the Independence of Spanish America," *Journal of Latin American Studies* 24 (1991): 481–505.

7. Lars Shoultz, "U.S. Values Approaches to Hemispheric Security Issues," in *Security, Democracy, and Development in U.S.–Latin American Relations*, ed. Lars Schoultz, William C. Smith, and Augusto Varsas, 33–34 (New Brunswick, N.J.: Transaction, 1994).

8. See Frederick Merk, *Manifest Destiny and Mission in America History: A Reinterpretation* (New York: Knopf, 1963).

9. Albert Weinberg, *Manifest Destiny: A Study of Nationalist Expansionism in American History* (Baltimore: Johns Hopkins University Press, 1935).

10. Dana Munro, *Intervention and Dollar Diplomacy in the Caribbean, 1900–1921* (Princeton, N.J.: Princeton University Press, 1964).

11. Bryce Wood, *The Making of the Good Neighbor Policy* (New York: Columbia University Press, 1961); David Green, *The Containment of Latin America: A History of the Myths and Realities of the Good Neighbor Policy* (Chicago: Quadrangle, 1971); Irwin Gellman, *Good Neighbor Policy: United States Policies in Latin America* (Baltimore: Johns Hopkins Press, 1979).

12. Fredrick Pike, *FDR's Good Neighbor Policy: Sixty Years of Generally Gentle Chaos* (Austin: University of Texas Press, 1995).

13. See Helen Delpar, *The Enormous Vogue of Things Mexican: Cultural Relations between the United States and Mexico, 1920–1935* (Tuscaloosa: University of Alabama Press, 1992).

14. Martin Needler, *The United States and Latin American Revolution* (Boston: Allyn and Bacon, 1972).

15. See Jan Knippers Black, *United States Penetration of Brazil* (Philadelphia: University of Pennsylvania Press, 1977).

16. Louis Halle, another important American diplomat of the time, had an opposite view of U.S. policy toward Latin America. In an article in *Foreign Affairs* that he signed "Y," Halle recommended a policy that would promote democracy and "encourage the Latin American states to participate responsibly in the councils of the world." See Y, "On a Certain Impatience with Latin America," *Foreign Affairs* 28, no. 4 (July 1950): 565–79

17. Gaddis Smith, *The Last Years of the Monroe Doctrine* (New York: Hill and Wang, 1994), 67.

18. Jan Knippers Black, *Sentinels of Empire: The United States and Latin American Militarism* (New York: Greenwood, 1986).

19. John Dreier, *The Alliance for Progress* (Baltimore: Johns Hopkins University Press, 1962).

20. Ronald Scheman, ed., *The Alliance for Progress: A Retrospective* (New York: Praeger, 1988).

21. See James Petras and Morris Morley, *The United States and Chile: Imperialism and the Overthrow of the Allende Government* (New York: *Monthly Review*, 1975).

22. Peter Smith, *Talons of the Eagle: Dynamics of U.S.–Latin American Relations* (New York: Oxford University Press, 1996), 188.

23. See Robert Pastor, "The Carter Administration and Latin America: A Test of Principle," in *United States Policy in Latin America: A Quarter Century of Crisis and Challenge, 1961–1986*, ed. John D. Martz (Lincoln: University of Nebraska Press, 1988), 61–97.

24. Jeane J. Kirkpatrick, "Dictatorship and Double Standards," *Commentary* 68 (November 1979): 34–45.

25. See Howard Wiarda, *American Foreign Policy toward Latin America in the 80s and 90s: Issues and Controversies from Reagan to Bush* (New York: New York University Press, 1992), 12–34.

26. See Richard Newfarmer, ed., *From Gunboats to Diplomacy: New U.S. Policies for Latin America* (Baltimore: Johns Hopkins University Press, 1984); Morris Blachman, William Leogrande, and Kenneth Sharpe, eds., *Confronting Revolution: Securing through Diplomacy in Central America* (New York: Pantheon, 1986).

27. Dov S. Zakheim, "The Grenada Operation and Superpower Relations: A Perspective from the Pentagon," in *Grenada and Soviet/Cuba Policy: Internal Crisis and*

US/OECS Intervention, ed. Jiri Valenta and Herbert Ellison (Boulder, Colo.: Westview, 1986), 176.

28. For a historical and sociological study of the roots of revolution in Central America, see Jan Flora and Edelberto Torres-Rivas, eds., *Sociology of Developing Societies: Central America* (New York: *Monthly Review*, 1989).

29. See *Report of the National Bipartisan Commission on Central America* (Washington, D.C.: Government Printing Office, 1984).

30. For a review of the Contadora process, see Bruce Bagley, ed., *Contadora and the Diplomacy of Peace in Central America: The United States, Central America, and Contadora* (Boulder, Colo.: Westview, 1987).

31. Robert Pastor, ed., *Latin America's Debt Crisis: Adjusting to the Past or Planning for the Future?* (Boulder, Colo.: Westview, 1987).

PART I

1. David Bushnell and Neill Macaulay, *The Emergence of Latin America in the Nineteenth Century* (New York: Oxford University Press, 1988), 25.

CHAPTER 2

1. Quoted in R. W. Van Alstyne, *The Rising American Empire* (New York: Oxford University Press, 1960), 184.

CHAPTER 9

1. Graham Cosmas, *An Army for an Empire: The United States Army in the Spanish-American War* (Columbia: University of Missouri Press, 1971), 308–9; Edmund Moris, *The Rise of Theodore Roosevelt* (New York: Coward, McCann, & Geoghegan, 1979), 626.

2. Grover Flint, *Marching with Gómez* (Boston: Lanson and Wolfe, 1898).

3. Gerald Linderman, *The Mirror of War: American Society and the Spanish American War* (Ann Arbor: University of Michigan Press, 1974), 137–45.

4. Charles Post, *The Little War of Private Post* (Boston: Little, Brown, 1970), 260–61.

5. Russell Alger, *The Spanish-American War* (New York: Harper and Bros., 1901), 426.

6. Hugh Thomas, *Cuba: The Pursuit of Freedom* (New York: Harper and Row, 1971), 417–35.

7. Quoted in J. H. Hitchman, *Leonard Wood and Cuban Independence, 1898–1902* (The Hague: Martinus Nijhoff, 1971), 6.

8. Military Government of Cuba, *Civil Report of Major-General John R. Brooke, 1899* (Washington, D.C., 1900), 6–7; idem, *Report of Brigadier-General William Ludlow, July 1, 1899, to May 1, 1900* (Washington, D.C., 1900), 6–9.

9. Hitchman, *Leonard Wood and Cuban Independence, 1898–1902*, 17–18; Brooke to Adj. Gen., Feb. 15, 1900, Wood Papers, LC MS Div.

10. Herman Hagedorn, *Leonard Wood* (New York: Harper & Bros., 1931), 1:260–61.

11. Quoted in ibid., p. 285. See also Military Government of Cuba, *Civil Report of Brigadier-General Leonard Wood, 1902* (Washington, D.C., 1902), 4.

12. Hitchman, *Leonard Wood and Cuban Independence, 1898–1902*, 31; Robert Bullard, "Education in Cuba," *Educational Review* 39 (April 1910): 31; Military Government of Cuba, *Civil Report of Brigadier General Leonard Wood, 1901*, 15 vols. (Washington, D.C., 1901), 1:21, 48–49; David Healy, *The United States in Cuba, 1898–1902: Generals, Politicians, and the Search for Policy* (Madison: University of Wisconsin Press, 1963), 179–88.

13. Root to Wood, Feb. 9, 1901, Elihu Root Papers, box 168, LC MS Div.

14. Wood to Root, Mar. 23, 1901, Root Papers, box 168, LC MS Div. For a more critical interpretation of American involvement in the war and the character of the occupation that followed, see Philip S. Foner, *The Spanish-Cuban-American War and the Birth of American Imperialism, 1895–1902*, 2 vols. (New York: Monthly Review Press, 1972), vol. 2, esp. 339–465.

CHAPTER 10

1. Joseph Bucklin Bishop, *Theodore Roosevelt and His Time Shown in His Own Letters*, vol. 1 (New York: C. Scribner's Sons, 1920), 278 [author's note].

2. Theodore Roosevelt, *An Autobiography* (New York: Macmillan, 1913). At the University of California, March 11, 1911, he declared: "I took the Canal Zone" [author's note].

CHAPTER 13

1. John Lewis Gaddis, *The United States and the Origins of the Cold War, 1941–1947* (New York : Columbia University Press, 1972), 23–31, discusses pre-1945 planning for an international organization. Robert A. Divine, *Roosevelt and World War II* (Baltimore: Johns Hopkins Pess, 1969), 49–71, analyzes President Roosevelt's position on the subject. Thomas M. Campbell, *Masquerade Peace: America's UN Policy, 1944–1945* (Tallahassee: Florida State University Press, 1973), is a useful study. See also Ruth B. Russell, *A History of the United Nations Charter* (Washington, D.C.: Brookings Institution, 1958), 1–548, for a detailed account of the period prior to the San Francisco Conference.

2. For analyses of the Good Neighbor policy see Bryce Wood, *The Making of the Good Neighbor Policy* (New York: Columbia University Press, 1961); Samuel Flagg Bemis, *The Latin American Policy of the United States: An Historical Interpretation* (New York: Harcourt, Brace, 1943), 256–393; David Green, *The Containment of Latin America: A History of the Myths and Realities of the Good Neighbor Policy* (Chicago: Quadrangle, 1971); Dick Steward, *Trade and Hemisphere: The Good Neighbor Policy and*

Reciprocal Trade (Columbia: University of Missouri Press, 1975). Two works that center on the post-1945 Latin American policy of the United States are R. Harrison Wagner, *United States Policy Toward Latin America: A Study in Domestic and International Politics* (Stanford, Calif.: Stanford University Press, 1970), and David Green, "The Cold War Comes to Latin America," in *Politics and Policies of the Truman Administration*, ed. Barton J. Bernstein (Chicago: Quadrangle, 1970).

3. For a summary of the Chapultepec Conference, see J. Lloyd Mecham, *The United States and Inter-American Security, 1889–1960* (Austin: University of Texas Press, 1961), 246–59. For a firsthand account see Thomas M. Campbell and George C. Herring, eds., *The Diaries of Edward R. Stettinius, Jr., 1943–1946* (New York: New Viewpoints, 1975), 260–93 (hereafter cited as Stettinius, *Diaries*). For documents on conference preparations and proceedings, see Department of State, *Foreign Relations of the United States: Diplomatic Papers*, 1945, Volume IX, The American Republics (Washington, 1969), 1–153 (hereafter cited as FR 1945 IX). [Harley A. Notter], Postwar Foreign Policy Preparation, 1939–1945 (Washington, D.C. 1949), 398–407, discusses the Chapultepec Conference, with some attention to Latin American concern about the Dumbarton Oaks proposals. The Stettinius quotation is from *Diaries*, 284. The text of the Act of Chapultepec is in Arthur M. Schlesinger, Jr., ed., *The Dynamics of World Power: A Documentary History of United States Foreign Policy, 1945–1973*, 5 vols. (New York: Chelsea House, 1973), vol. 3, Robert Burr, ed., *Latin America*, 3–5 (hereafter cited as Burr, *Latin America*). See also Campbell, *Masquerade Peace*, 111–29, and Russell, *United Nations Charter*, 551–69.

4. Memo of conversation by Merwin L. Bohan, Technical Officer of the U.S. Delegation, Mexico City, 29 January 1945, FR 1945 IX: 72–73 (source of the Padilla quotation); Stettinius, *Diaries*, 277–78.

5. Stettinius, *Diaries*, 353–66; Campbell, *Masquerade Peace*, 159–75. For a major collection of documents on the San Francisco Conference, see Department of State, *Foreign Relations of the United States: Diplomatic Papers*, 1945, Vol. I, General; The United Nations (Washington, D.C. 1967), 1–1432; scattered throughout these pages are many documents related to Latin America. Russell, *United Nations Charter*, 625–932, discusses the San Francisco Conference in great detail.

6. Stettinius, *Diaries*, 354.

7. Ibid., 349–56; Campbell, *Masquerade Peace*, 165–75.

8. Sumner Welles, *Where Are We Heading?* (New York: Harper and Brothers, 1946), 190–204; "Final Act of the Third Meeting of Ministers of Foreign Affairs of the American Republics, Rio de Janeiro, January 28, 1942," in Department of State Bulletin, VI (7 February 1942): 118–34; Ernest R. May, "The 'Bureaucratic Politics' Approach: U.S.-Argentine Relations, 1942–47," in *Latin America and the United States: The Changing Political Realities*, ed. Julio Cotler and Richard R. Fagen, 129–63 (Stanford, Calif.: Stanford University Press, 1974); Department of State, *Foreign Relations of the United States: Diplomatic Papers*, 1944, vol. 7, *The American Republics* (Washington, D.C. 1967), 252–88 (documents on U.S. refusal to recognize the Farrell government).

9. Stettinius, *Diaries*, 261, 286–88, 309–10, 324–25, 341–48; "Memorandum on the Argentine Problem," FR 1945 IX: 448–51; Chargé Edward L. Reed to Secretary of State, 27 March 1945, ibid., 371; Stettinius to the President, 8 April 1945, ibid., 376; George S. Messersmith to Secretary of State, 4 April 1945, ibid., 151–53; Harry S. Truman,

Memoirs, Vol. I, *Year of Decisions* (Garden City, N.Y.: Doubleday, 1955), 281–82; Stephen Clissold, ed., *Soviet Relations with Latin America, 1918–1968: A Documentary Survey* (London, New York: Oxford University Press, 1970), 173–74; Campbell, *Masquerade Peace*, 162–63.

10. Stettinius to Truman, 16 April 1945, Office File (OF) #247, the Papers of Harry S. Truman, Truman Library, Independence, Missouri (hereafter cited as Truman Papers); Spruille Braden, *Diplomats and Demagogues: The Memoirs of Spruille Braden* (New Rochelle, N.Y.: Arlington House, 1971), 319–43; Braden, "Latin-American Industrialization and Foreign Trade," in *Industrialization of Latin America*, ed. Lloyd J. Hughlett, (Westport, Conn.: Greenwood Press 1970), 486–93; Dean Acheson, *Present at the Creation: My Years in the State Department* (New York: Norton, 1969), 157–60, 187–88; Welles, *Where Are We Heading?* 214–18; FR 192S IX: 380–412 (documents for period of Braden's ambassadorship); Green, *The Containment of Latin America*, 250–54.

11. Documents on the origins, announcement, and response to the Rodriguez Larreta proposal are in FR 1945 IX: 185–21; see especially Rodriguez Larreta to Secretary of State James F. Byrnes, 21 November 1945, ibid., 190–96 (text of the proposal). Rodriguez Larreta explained his purposes and principles in "El derecho a la intervención colectiva," Combate 2 (July 1959), 23–26. See also Welles, *Where Are We Heading?*, 225–27; Acheson, *Present at the Creation*, 188; and Gordon Connell-Smith, *The Inter-American System* (London: Oxford University Press, 1966), 142–44.

12. For information on the development and publication of the Blue Book, see Braden, *Diplomats and Demagogues*, 356–57; Byrnes, "Memorandum for the President, Subject: Argentine Complicity with the Enemy," 8 February 1946, in Truman Papers, President's Secretary's File (PSF), Subject File (SF) #170, Argentina Folder #1. An original typed and edited copy of the Blue Book, entitled *Consultation among the American Republics with Respect to the Argentine Situation*, is in Truman Papers, PSF-SF #170, Argentina Folder #2; excerpts from the Blue Book are in Burr, ed., *Latin America*, 20–26; Secretary of State to Chargé John M. Cabot, 8 February 1946, in Department of State, Foreign Relations of the United States, 1946, vol. 11, *The American Republics* (Washington, D.C. 1969), 201 (hereafter cited as FR 1946, XI); Secretary of State to Diplomatic Representatives in the American Republics Except Argentina and Haiti, 9 February 1946, ibid., 204–5. Argentine reaction to the Blue Book can be traced in: Cabot to Secretary of State, 14 February 1946, ibid., 212; Cabot to Secretary of State, 15 February 1946, ibid., 213–14; Cabot to Secretary of State, 29 March 1946, ibid., 240; J. Edgar Hoover to Brigadier General Harry H. Vaughn, 20 February 1946, in Truman Papers, PSF-SF #167, Folder FBI-Argentina; Hoover to Vaughn, 21 February 1946, ibid.; Brigadier General A. R. Harris, Military Attache, Report No. R-1 13–46, 26 February 1946, in Record Group 226, Records of the Office of Strategic Services, XL44751, Box 353 (hereafter cited as RG 226, OSS). Reaction in other Latin American countries is indicated in Ambassador John F. Simmons to Secretary of State, 11 February 1946, FR 1946 XI: 205–6; Ambassador Claude G. Bowers to Secretary of State, 23 February 1946, ibid., 219–20; Ambassador William D. Pawley to Secretary of State, 25 February 1946, ibid., 222; Robert Newbegin, memo of conversation with Ambassador Gufflermo Sevilla Sacasa, 1 March 1946, ibid., 227–28. Comments on the Argentine election are in Cabot to Sec-

retary of State, 25 February 1946, ibid., 221; Brigadier General Harris, Report No. R-1 18–46, 27 February 1946, RG 226, OSS, XL44895, Box 353; Representative Joseph C. Baldwin, 17th Cong. District, N.Y., to Truman, 13 April 1946, in Truman Papers, PSF-SF #170, Argentina Folder #2.

13. On Messersmith's appointment, see Byrnes to Truman, 9 April 1946, Truman Papers, OF #1370, Folder #496; Braden, *Diplomats and Demagogues*, 358–63. In the Truman Papers, PSF-SF #170, Argentina Folders #2 and 3, are originals and/or copies of many letters Messersmith wrote to Truman, Byrnes, and Acheson, their internal correspondence, and their replies to Messersmith; for example see Messersmith to Truman, 15 June 1946, including copy of Messersmith to Byrnes, 15 June 1946 (27 pages); Acheson to Truman, 12 July 1946; Truman to Acheson, 22 July 1946; Messersmith to Acheson, 16 August 1946; Messersmith to Byrnes, 16 August 1946; Acheson to Messersmith, 29 August 1946; Acheson to Truman, 29 August 1946; Truman to Messersmith, 6 September 1946; Messersmith to Byrnes, 12 October 1946; Messersmith to Acheson, 16 October 1946. Dispatches illustrating Messersmith's contention that Argentina was eliminating Axis influences are Messersmith to Secretary of State, 24 June 1946, FR 1946 XI: 263–65; Messersmith to Secretary of State, 25 June 1946, ibid., 265–66; Messersmith to Secretary of State, 24 July 1946, ibid., 282–83. Messersmith's references to the Soviet threat are Messersmith to Acheson, 2 October 1946, ibid., 321–22; Messersmith to Byrnes, 9 October 1946, attached to Messersmith to Truman, 9 October 1946, in PSF-SF #170, Argentina Folder #3.

14. Byrnes to Truman, 9 January 1947, Truman Papers, OF #1370, Folder #496; Acheson, *Present at the Creation*, 189–90; Braden, *Diplomats and Demagogues*, 363–70; Messersmith to Secretary of State George C. Marshall, Department of State, Foreign Relations of the United States, 1947, vol. 8, *The American Republics* (Washington, D.C., 1972), 201–2 (hereafter cited as FR 1947, VIII); Truman to Braden, 4 June 1947, Truman Papers, President's Personal File (PPF) #3295; *New York Times*, 6 June 1947, clipping in Truman Papers, OF #1052, Folder #366.

15. Chargé Guy W. Ray to Secretary of State, 14 August 1947, FR 1947 VIII: 205–9; Ambassador James Bruce to Truman, 4 February 1948, in Truman Papers, PSF-SF #170, Argentina Folder #3; Ray to Ambassador Ellis Briggs, 20 February 1948, in Department of State, Foreign Relations of the United States, 1948, Vol. IX, T*he Western Hemisphere* (Washington, D.C., 1972), 281–82 (hereafter cited as FR 1948 IX); Bruce to Secretary of State, 28 April 1948, ibid., 288.

16. See Department of State, Inter-American Conference for the Maintenance of Continental Peace and Security, Quitandinha, Brazil, August 15–September 12, 1947: Report of the Delegation of the United States of America (Washington, 1948). See also "Memorandum for the President, Subject: Inter-American Mutual Assistance Pact," 30 November 1945, in Truman Papers, White House Central Files, Confidential File (WHCF-CF), Box #33, Folder #3; "Proposals by the United States for the Provisions of an Inter-American Treaty of Mutual Assistance," enclosed in a circular from Secretary of State to Diplomatic Representatives in the American Republics Except Argentina, 13 December 1945, FR 1945 IX: 168–71; Acheson to Diplomatic Representatives in the American Republics Except Haiti and Argentina, 1 April 1946, FR 1946 XI: 9–12.

17. Ray to Secretary of State, 1 August 1947, FR 1947VIII: 31; Braden to Acheson, 29 May 1947, ibid., 2.

18. Marshall to Acting Secretary of State, 16 August 1947, ibid., 35; Marshall to Acting Secretary of State, 18 August 1947, ibid., 36; Marshall to Acting Secretary of State 19 August 1947, in Truman Papers, PSF-SF #162, Folder Rio de Janeiro Conference; Robert M. Lovett, Acting Secretary of State, to U.S. Delegation, Petropolis.

19. Memo by Edgar L. McGinnis of the State Department Division of North and West Coast Affairs, 3 September 1947, ibid., 78–79 (a summary of Truman's address). The text of Truman's address is in Burr, ed., *Latin America*, 36–40; the quotation is on 38–39. See also Gordon Connell-Smith, *The United States and Latin America: An Historical Analysis of Inter-American Relations* (London: Heinemann Educational, 1974), 199.

20. Connell-Smith, *The US and Latin America*, 196. The text of the Rio Pact is in Burr, ed., *Latin America*, 30–35. There is an analysis of the treaty in Acting Secretary of State Lovett to Truman, 1 December 1947, FR 1947 VIII: 90–93. See also Jerome Slater, *The OAS and United States Foreign Policy* (Columbus: Ohio State University Press, 1967), 19–38.

21. The text of Vandenberg's radio address of 4 September 1947 is in "The Inter-American Conference for the Maintenance of Continental Peace and Security," Bulletin of the Pan American Union, LXXXI (October 1947): 538–42.

22. For documents and analysis, see Department of State, "Ninth International Conference of American States, Bogota," Colombia, March 30–May 2, 1948: Report of the Delegation of the United States of America with Related Documents (Washington, D.C., 1948); FR 1948 IX: 1–72; Alberto Lleras Camargo, "Report on the Ninth International Conference of American States," in *Annals of the Organization of American States* I (1949): 1–75.

23. The text of PPS-26, dated 22 March 1948, is printed as an attachment to Secretary of State to Diplomatic Representatives in the American Republics, 21 June 1948, FR 1948 IX: 194–201. The National Security Council incorporated PPS-26 in NSC 16, dated 28 June 1948. At the author's request the NSC declassified NSC 16 and made it available to him in a "sanitized form" in November 1976. Only after receiving the copy did the author discover that it was identical to PPS-26. In what must have been a bureaucratic mix-up, the NSC still maintained as classified a document that was published in the Foreign Relations series in 1972.

24. The author obtained a copy of NSC 7 from Record Group 341 in Modern Military Records in the National Archives, Washington, D.C. NSC 68, "United States Objectives and Programs for National Security," 14 April 1950, was declassified in February 1975. It has been published in the *Naval War College Review* (May–June 1975), 51–108.

25. Marshall to Acting Secretary of State, 30 March 1948, FR 1948 IX: 24; Ambassador Willard S. Beaulac to Acting Secretary of State, 4 April 1948, ibid., 31.

26. Beaulac to Secretary of State, 22 March 1948, ibid., 22–23; Beaulac to Secretary of State, 25 March 1948, in Record Group 59, General Records of the Department of State, Decimal File 1945–1949, 710.J/3-2548, National Archives, Washington, D.C. (documents in this collection hereafter cited as DS followed by file number); Willard L. Beaulac, *Career Ambassador* (New York: Macmillan, 1951), 235–37.

27. Beaulac to Acting Secretary of State, 9 April 1948, FR 1948 IX: 39; top secret telegram, Marshall to Acting Secretary of State, 9 April 1948, DS 710.J/4-948; Marshall to Acting Secretary of State, 10 April 1948, FR 1948 DC: 39–40 (source of the Marshall quotation); Beaulac to Acting Secretary of State, 11 April 1948, ibid., 40–41; Beaulac to Acting Secretary of State, 11 April 1948, ibid., 42; Beaulac to Acting Secretary of State, 13 April 1948, ibid., 43; Beaulac, *Career Ambassador*, 241–61; Clissold, *Soviet Relations with Latin America*, 207–8 (Soviet documents).

28. Beaulac, *Career Ambassador*, 256; Marshall to Acting Secretary of State, 20 April 1948, FR 1948 IX: 53. The text of Resolution XXXII can be found on an enclosure in Secretary of State to Diplomatic Representatives in the American Republics, 21 June 1948, ibid., 193–94.

29. The text of the OAS Charter is in Burr, ed., *Latin America*, 49–70. The Charter's main features are summarized in Acting Secretary of State Lovett to Truman, 31 December 1948, FR 1948 IX: 69–72. For the history of the OAS, see Slater, *The OAS and United States Foreign Policy*, 38–289.

30. Norman T. Ness, Director, Office of Financial and Development Policy, to Assistant Secretary of State for Economic Affairs Willard L. Thorp, 19 February 1948, FR 1948 IX: 5–9; Commercial Attaché Lew B. Clark to Secretary of State, 1 March 1948, DS 710.J/3–148; Beaulac, *Career Ambassador*, 240; Pawley to Truman, 12 February 1948, Truman Papers, WHCF-CF, Box #35, Folder #11.

31. The text of Marshall's address of 1 April 1948 is in Bun, ed., *Latin America*, 42–48; Beaulac's comments on the address are in *Career Ambassador*, 239. The text of the Economic Agreement of Bogotá, 2 May 1948, is in Burr, *Latin America*, 85–101. See also Department of State, Foreign Relations of the United States, 1949, vol. 2, The United Nations; the Western Hemisphere (Washington, 1975), editorial note, 429 (about non-ratification of the Economic Agreement).

32. For a devastating critique of foreign aid, see William and Elizabeth Paddock, *We Don't Know How: An Independent Audit of What They Call Success in Foreign Assistance* (Ames, Iowa: 1973). The United Nations Economic Commission for Latin America (ECLA), in *Development Problems in Latin America* (Austin: University of Texas Press, 1970), 109, argues that the Latin American countries could not expect and did not need subsidies but rather "productive loans with long amortization periods and at rates of interest as low as those prevailing on the money markets."

33. When Secretary of State Acheson presented the North Atlantic Treaty Organization charter to President Truman for submission to the Senate, he wrote: "The North Atlantic Treaty is patterned on the Treaty of Rio de Janeiro." See "The North Atlantic Treaty Organization: Report of Secretary of State Dean G. Acheson to President Truman, April 7, 1949," in *From Isolation to Containment, 1921–1952*, ed. Richard D. Challener, 154–60 (New York: Edward Arnold, 1970).

PART V

1. Margaret Daly Hayes, "The U.S. and Latin America: A Lost Decade?" *Foreign Affairs* 57 (1988–1989).

CHAPTER 18

1. Reprinted from Public Papers of the President of the United States, 1961 (Washington, D.C.: U.S. Government Printing Office, 1962), 170–81.
2. From 1964 to 1985 Brazil was ruled as a military dictatorship (editors' note).

CHAPTER 22

1. See Robert S. Leiken, "End of an Affair: Immigration, Security and the U.S.-Mexican Relationship," *National Interest* (Winter 2002–2003).
2. See C. Ford Runge, "The Farm Bill From Hell," *National Interest* (Summer 2003).

CHAPTER 23

1. Juan González, *Harvest of Empire: A History of Latinos in America* (New York: Viking, 2000), 103.
2. Ibid.
3. Michael C. Meyer, William L. Sherman, and Susan M. Deeds, *The Course of Mexican History,* 7th ed. (New York: Oxford University Press, 2003), 662.
4. González, *Harvest of Empire,* 234.
5. The PRI (Partido Revolucionario Institucional—or the Party of the Institutional Revolution) was created in 1929 and all of Mexico's presidents emerged through its structure until Mr. Fox's election in 2000.
6. Samuel P. Huntington, "The Hispanic Challenge," *Foreign Policy* (March–April 2004): 40. The article was released shortly before publication of Huntington's book dealing with the same topic, *Who Are We? The Challenges to America's National Identity* (New York: Simon & Schuster, 2004).
7. See Valdés-Ugalde and Curzio, "A Reply to Samuel Huntington's 'Hispanic Challenge'" in *Voices of Mexico* 67 (2004).
8. B. Lindsay Lowell and Roberto Suro, "How Many Undocumented: The Numbers behind the U.S.-Mexico Migration Talks." Report of the Pew Hispanic Center, March 21, 2002.

Selected Bibliography

PART I

Alba, Victor. *The Latin Americans*. New York: Praeger, 1967.

Cardoso, Fernando H., and Enzo Faletto. *Dependency and Development in Latin America*. Los Angeles: University of California Press, 1979.

Connell-Smith, Gordon. *The United States and Latin America: An Historical Analysis of Inter-American Relations*. New York: Wiley, 1974.

Dealy, Glen Caudjil. *The Public Man: An Interpretation of Latin American and Other Catholic Countries*. Amherst: University of Massachusetts Press, 1977.

———. *The Latin Americans: Spirit and Ethos*. Boulder, Colo.: Westview, 1992.

Fagg, John Edwin. *Pan Americanism*. Malabar: Krieger, 1982.

Furtado, Celso. *The Economic Development of Latin America*. New York: Cambridge University Press, 1970.

Garcia, Francisco. *Latin America: Its Rise and Progress*. London: Cassell, 1913.

Gaspar, E. *The United States and Latin America: A Special Relationship?* Washington, D.C.: AEI-Hoover, 1978.

Gil, Federjco. *Latin American–United States Relations*. New York: Harcourt Brace Jovanovich, 1971.

Hanke, Lewis, ed. *Do the Americas Have a Common History?* New York: Knopf, 1964.

Harrison, Lawrence. *Underdevelopment Is a State of Mind: The Latin American Case*. Lanham, Md.: Madison Books and Center for International Affairs, Harvard University, 1985.

———. *The Pan American Dream: Do Latin America's Cultural Values Discourage True Partnership with the United States and Canada?* New York: Basic Books, 1997.

Kenworthy, Eldon. *America/Americas: Myth in the Making of U.S. Policy toward Latin America*. College Park: Penn State University Press, 1995.

LaFeber, Walter. *The New Empire*. Ithaca, N.Y.: Cornell University Press, 1963.

Langley, Lester. *America and the Americas: The United States in the Western Hemisphere*. Athens: University of Georgia Press, 1989.

339

Liss, Peggy. *Atlantic Empires: The Network of Trade and Revolution, 1713–1826.* Baltimore: Johns Hopkins University Press, 1983.

Mathews, Herbert, ed. *The United States and Latin America.* New York: Prentice-Hall, 1959.

Onís, Juan de. *The United States as Seen by Spanish American Writers, 1776–1890.* New York: Hispanic Institute of the United States, 1952.

Parker, James W. *Latin American Underdevelopment: A History of Perspectives in the United States, 1877–1965.* Baton Rouge: Louisiana State University Press, 1995.

Perkins, Dexter. *The United States and Latin America.* Baton Rouge: Louisiana State University Press, 1961.

Rama, Carlos. *La imagen de los Estados Unidos en la América Latina: De Simón Bolívar a Salvador Allende.* Mexico City: Secretaria de Educación Pública, 1975.

Rangel, Carlos. *The Latin Americans: Their Love-Hate Relationship with the United States.* New Brunswick: Transaction, 1987.

Shapiro, Samuel, ed. *Cultural Factors in Inter-American Relations.* South Bend, Ind.: Notre Dame University Press, 1968.

Stein, Stanley, and Barbara Stein. *The Colonial Heritage of Latin America.* New York: Oxford University Press, 1970.

Tannenbaum, Frank. *Ten Keys to Latin America.* New York: Knopf, 1962.

Veliz, Claudio. *The Centralist Tradition of Latin America.* Princeton, N.J.: Princeton University Press, 1980.

Vernon, Raymond. *How Latin America Views the U.S. Investor.* New York: Praeger, 1966.

Wagley, Charles. *The Latin American Tradition.* New York: Columbia University Press, 1968.

Whitaker, Arthur. *The Western Hemisphere Idea: Its Rise and Decline.* Ithaca, N.Y.: Cornell University Press, 1954.

Wiarda, Howard, ed. *Politics and Social Change in Latin America: Still a Distinct Tradition?* 3d ed. Boulder, Colo.: Westview, 1992.

Willems, Emílio. *Latin American Culture: An Anthropological Synthesis.* New York: Harper and Row, 1975.

Williams, Edward, J. *The Political Themes of Inter-American Relations.* Belmont, Calif.: Duxbury Press, 1971.

Winn, Peter. *The Americas.* New York: Pantheon, 1992.

Worcester, David, and W. Schaeffer. *The Growth and Culture of Latin America.* New York: Oxford University Press, 1970.

Zea, Leopoldo. *The Latin American Mind.* Norman: University of Oklahoma Press, 1963.

PART II

Aguilar, Alonso. *Pan-Americanism from Monroe to the Present: A View from the Other Side.* New York: *Monthly Review,* 1968.

Bingham, Hiram. *The Monroe Doctrine, an Obsolete Shibboleth.* New Haven, Conn.: Yale University Press, 1913.

Burns, Bradford. *The Poverty of Progress: Latin America in the Nineteenth Century.* Berkeley: University of California Press, 1979.

Bushnell, David, and Neill Macaulay. *The Emergence of Latin America in the Nineteenth Century.* New York: Oxford University Press, 1988.

Dozer, Donald, ed. *The Monroe Doctrine: Its Modern Significance.* New York: Knopf, 1965.

Foner, Philip. *The Spanish-Cuban-American War and the Birth of American Imperialism, 1895–1902,* 2 vols. New York: *Monthly Review,* 1972.

Griffin, Charles. *The United States and the Disruption of the Spanish Empire, 1810–1822.* New York: Columbia University Press, 1937.

Healy, David. *U.S. Expansionism: The Imperialist Urge in the 1890s.* Madison: University of Wisconsin Press, 1970.

Johnson, John. *A Hemisphere Apart: The Foundations of United States Policy toward Latin America.* Baltimore: Johns Hopkins University Press, 1990.

Langley, Lester. *Struggle for the American Mediterranean, 1776–1904.* Athens: University of Georgia Press, 1976.

———. *The Americas in the Age of Revolution, 1750–1850.* New Haven, Conn.: Yale University Press, 1996.

Latane, John. *The Diplomatic Relations of the United States and Spanish America.* Baltimore: Johns Hopkins University Press, 1920.

Lockey, Joseph. *Pan-Americanism: Its Beginnings.* New York: Macmillan, 1920.

Logan, John. *No Transfer: An American Security Principle.* New Haven, Conn.: Yale University Press, 1961.

MacCorkle, William. *The Personal Genesis of the Monroe Doctrine.* New York: Putnam's Sons, 1923.

Manning, William, ed. *Diplomatic Correspondence of the U.S. Concerning the Independence of the Latin American Nations.* 3 vols. New York: Carnegie Endowment for International Peace, 1925.

May, Ernest. *The Making of the Monroe Doctrine.* Cambridge: Harvard University Press, 1975.

McGann, Thomas. *Argentina, the United States, and the Inter-American System, 1880–1914.* Cambridge: Harvard University Press, 1958.

Merk, Frederick. *Manifest Destiny and Mission in American History: A Reinterpretation.* New York: Knopf, 1963.

Perez, Louis. *Cuba between Empires, 1878–1902.* Pittsburgh: University of Pittsburgh Press, 1983.

Quintanilla, Luis. *A Latin American Speaks.* New York: Macmillan, 1934.

Rappaport, Armin, ed. *The Monroe Doctrine.* Huntington: Krieger, 1976.

Robertson, William. *Hispanic-American Relations with the United States.* New York: Oxford University Press, 1923.

Weinberg, Albert. *Manifest Destiny: A Study of Nationalist Expansionism in American History.* Baltimore: Johns Hopkins University Press, 1935.

Whitaker, Arthur. *The United States and the Independence of Latin America, 1800–1830.* Baltimore: Johns Hopkins University Press, 1930.

Zea, Leopoldo. *Positivismo y la circunstancia mexicana.* Mexico City: Siglo Ventiuno, 1985.

PART III

Bemis, Samuel Flagg. *Latin American Policy of the United States*. New York: Harper and Row, 1942.

Black, George. *The Good Neighbor: How the United States Wrote the History of Central America and the Caribbean*. New York: Pantheon, 1988.

Calcott, Wilfred Hardy. *The Caribbean Policy of the United States, 1890–1920*. Baltimore: Johns Hopkins University Press, 1942.

————. *The Western Hemisphere: Its Influence on United States Policies to the End of World War II*. Austin: University of Texas Press, 1968.

De Conde, Alexander. *Herbert Hoover's Latin American Policy*. Stanford, Calif.: Stanford University Press, 1951.

Delpar, Helen. *The Enormous Vogue of Things Mexican: Cultural Relations between the United States and Mexico, 1920–1935*. Tuscaloosa: University of Alabama Press, 1992.

Dozer, Donald. *Are We Good Neighbors? Three Decades of Inter-American Relations, 1930–1960*. Gainesville: University of Florida Press, 1959.

Drake, Paul, ed. *Money Doctors, Foreign Debts, and Economic Reforms in Latin America from the 1890s to the Present*. Wilmington, Del.: SR Books, 1994.

Duggan, Laurence. *The Americas: The Search for Hemisphere Security*. New York: Holt, Rinehart, and Winston, 1948.

Espinosa, Manuel. *Inter-American Beginnings of U.S. Cultural Diplomacy, 1936–1948*. Washington, D.C.: Bureau of Educational and Cultural Affairs, 1976.

Francis, Michael. *The Limits of Hegemony: United States Relations with Argentina and Chile in World War II*. South Bend, Ind.: Notre Dame University Press, 1977.

Fuentes, Carlos. *The Death of Artemio Cruz*. New York: Farrar, Straus, 1962.

Gardner, Lloyd. *The Economic Aspects of New Deal Diplomacy*. Madison: University of Wisconsin Press, 1964.

Geliman, Irwin. *Good Neighbor Policy: United States Policies in Latin America, 1933–1945*. Baltimore: Johns Hopkins University Press, 1979.

Gilderhus, Mark. *Pan American Visions: Woodrow Wilson in the Western Hemisphere, 1913–1921*. Tucson: University of Arizona Press, 1986.

Green, David. *The Containment of Latin America: A History of the Myths and Realities of the Good Neighbor Policy*. Chicago: Quadrangle, 1971.

Grieb, Kenneth. *The Latin American Policy of Warren G. Harding*. Fort Worth: Texas Christian University Press, 1976.

Guerrant, Edward. *Roosevelt's Good Neighbor Policy*. Albuquerque: University of New Mexico Press, 1950.

Haring, C. H. *South America Looks at the United States*. New York: Macmillan, 1929.

Hill, Howard. *Roosevelt and the Caribbean*. Chicago: University of Chicago Press, 1927.

LaFeber, Walter. *The Panama Canal*. New York: Oxford University Press, 1978.

Langley, Lester. *The Banana Wars: The United States Intervention in the Caribbean, 1889–1934*. Lexington: University Press of Kentucky, 1983.

Macaulay, Neill. *The Sandino Affair*. Chicago: Quadrangle, 1967.

Mecham, Lloyd. *The United States and Inter-American Security, 1889–1960*. Austin: University of Texas Press, 1961.

———. *A Survey of United States–Latin American Relations.* Boston: Allen and Unwin, 1965.

Meyer, Lorenzo. *Mexico and the United States in the Oil Controversy, 1917–1942.* Austin: University of Texas Press, 1977.

Munro, Dana. *Intervention and Dollar Diplomacy in the Caribbean, 1900–1921.* Princeton, N.J.: Princeton University Press, 1964.

Nearing, Scott, and Joseph Freeman. *Dollar Diplomacy: A Study of American Imperialism.* New York: Huebesch and Viking, 1925.

Perez, Louis. *Cuba: Between Reform and Revolution.* New York: Oxford University Press, 1988.

Peterson, Harold. *Argentina and the United States, 1810–1960.* Albany: State University of New York Press, 1964.

Pike, Fredrick. *Chile and the United States, 1880–1962.* South Bend, Ind.: University of Notre Dame Press, 1963.

———. *FDR's Good Neighbor Policy: Sixty Years of Generally Gentle Chaos.* Austin: University of Texas Press, 1995.

Randall, Stephan. *The Diplomacy of Modernization: Colombian-American Relations, 1920–1940.* Toronto: University of Toronto Press, 1977.

Schmidt, Hans. *The United States Occupation of Haiti, 1915–1934.* New Brunswick: Rutgers University Press, 1971.

Seidel, Robert. *Progressive Pan Americanism: Development and United States Policy toward South America.* Ithaca, N.Y.: Cornell University, 1973.

Smith, Robert. *The United States and Cuba: Business and Diplomacy, 1917–1960.* New York: Bookman, 1961.

———, ed. *The United States and the Latin American Sphere of Influence.* Vol. 1, *Era of Caribbean Intervention, 1890–1930.* Malabar, Fla.: Krieger, 1981.

Steward, Dick. *Trade and Hemisphere: The Good Neighbor Policy and Reciprocal Trade.* Columbia: University of Missouri Press, 1975.

Tulchin, Joseph. *The Aftermath of War: World War I and U.S. Policy toward Latin America.* New York: New York University Press, 1971.

Whitaker, Arthur. *The United States and South America: The Northern Republics.* Cambridge: Harvard University Press, 1948.

———. *The United States and Argentina.* Cambridge: Harvard University Press, 1954.

Wood, Bryce. *The Making of the Good Neighbor Policy.* New York: Columbia University Press, 1961.

———. *The United States and Latin American Wars, 1932–1942.* New York: Columbia University Press, 1966.

PART IV

Arévalo, Juan Jose. *The Shark and the Sardines.* New York: Lyle Stewart, 1961.

Blasier, Cole. *The Hovering Giant: U.S. Responses to Revolutionary Change in Latin America.* Pittsburgh: University of Pittsburgh Press, 1976.

Bonsal, Philip. *Cuba, Castro, and the United States.* Pittsburgh: University of Pittsburgh Press, 1971.

Gleijeses, Piero. *Shattered Hope: The Guatemalan Revolution and the United States, 1944–1954.* Princeton, N.J.: Princeton University Press, 1991.

Immerman, Richard. *The CIA in Guatemala: The Foreign Policy of Intervention.* Austin: University of Texas Press, 1982.

Mathews, Herbert. *The Cuba Story.* New York: George Braziller, 1961.

McCann, Thomas. *An American Company: The Tragedy of United Fruit.* New York: Crown, 1976.

Needler, Martin. *The United States and Latin American Revolution.* Boston: Allyn and Bacon, 1972.

Rabe, Stephen. *Eisenhower and Latin America: The Foreign Policy of Anticommunism.* Chapel Hill: University of North Carolina Press, 1988.

Schlesinger, Stephen, and Stephen Kinzer. *Bitter Fruit: The Untold Story of the American Coup in Guatemala.* Garden City, N.Y.: Anchor, 1983.

Smith, Wayne. *The Closest of Enemies: A Personal and Diplomatic History of the Castro Years.* New York: Norton, 1987.

Szulc, Tad. *Fidel: A Critical Portrait.* New York: Morrow, 1986.

Welch, Richard. *Response to Revolution: The United States and the Cuban Revolution, 1959–1961.* Chapel Hill: University of North Carolina Press, 1985.

Wilkie, J. W. *The Bolivian Revolution and U.S. Aid since 1952.* Los Angeles: University of California Press, 1969.

Wyden, Peter. *Bay of Pigs.* New York: Simon and Schuster, 1979.

PART V

Bailey, Samuel. *The United States and the Development of South America, 1945–1975.* New York: New Viewpoints, 1976.

Bianchi, Andres, Robert Devlin, and Joseph Ramos. *External Debt in Latin America: Adjustment Policies and Renegotiation.* Boulder, Colo.: Lynne Rienner, 1985.

Biles, Robert, ed. *Inter-American Relations: The Latin American Perspective.* Boulder, Colo.: Lynne Rienner, 1988.

Blachman, Morris J., William Leogrande, and Kenneth Sharpe, eds. *Confronting Revolution: Security through Diplomacy in Central America.* New York: Pantheon, 1986.

Black, Jan Knippers. *United States Penetration of Brazil.* Philadelphia: University of Pennsylvania Press, 1977.

———. *Sentinels of Empire: The United States and Latin American Militarism.* New York: Greenwood, 1986.

Canak, William, ed. *Lost Promises: Debt, Austerity, and Development in Latin America.* Boulder, Colo.: Westview, 1989.

Child, Jack. *Unequal Alliance: The Inter-American Military System, 1938–1978.* Boulder, Colo.: Westview, 1980.

Commission on U.S.–Latin American Relations (Linowitz Commission). *The Americas in a Changing World.* New York: Haisted, 1974.

Cotler, Julio, and Richard Fagen, eds. *Latin America and the United States.* Stanford, Calif.: Stanford University Press, 1974.

Dreier, John. *The Alliance for Progress.* Baltimore: Johns Hopkins University Press, 1962.

Eisenhower, Milton. *The Wine Is Bitter: The United States and Latin America.* Garden City, N.Y.: Doubleday, 1963.

Etchison, Don. *The United States and Militarism in Central America.* New York: Praeger, 1975.

Falcoff, Mark, and Robert Royal, eds. *The Continuing Crisis: U.S. Policy in Central America and the Caribbean.* Washington, D.C.: Ethics and Public Policy Center, 1987.

Farer, Tom. *The United States and the Inter-American System.* St. Paul: West, 1974.

———. *The Grand Strategy of the United States in Latin America.* New Brunswick: Transaction, 1988.

Gordon, Lincoln. *A New Deal for Latin America: The Alliance for Progress.* Cambridge: Harvard University Press, 1963.

Gutman, Roy. *Banana Diplomacy: The Making of American Policy in Nicaragua, 1981–1987.* New York: Simon and Schuster, 1988.

Hansen, Roger. *U.S.-Latin American Economic Policy.* Washington, D.C.: Overseas Development Council, 1975.

Hayes, Margaret Daly. *Latin America and the U.S. National Interest: A Basis for U.S. Foreign Policy.* Boulder, Colo.: Westview, 1984.

Huntington, Samuel P. *Political Order in Changing Societies.* New Haven, Conn.: Yale University Press, 1968.

Johnson, John. *Latin America in Caricature.* Austin: University of Texas Press, 1980.

Karnes, Thomas, ed. *Readings in Latin American Policy of the United States.* Tucson: University of Arizona Press, 1972.

Kirkpatrick, Jeane. "Dictatorship and Double Standards." *Commentary* 70 (November 1979): 34–45.

Kuczynski, Pedro Pablo. *Latin American Debt.* Baltimore: Johns Hopkins University Press, 1988.

Lake, Anthony. *Somoza Falling.* Boston: Houghton Mifflin, 1989.

Levinson, Jerome, and Juan de Onís. *The Alliance That Lost Its Way.* Chicago: Quadrangle, 1970.

Lieuwen, Edwin. *U.S. Policy in Latin America.* New York: Praeger, 1965.

Loveman, Brian, and Thomas Davies, eds. *The Politics and Antipolitics: The Military in Latin America.* Lincoln: University of Nebraska Press, 1978.

Lowenthal, Abraham F. *The Dominican Intervention.* Cambridge: Harvard University Press, 1972.

———, ed. *Exporting Democracy: The United States and Latin America. Themes and Issues.* Baltimore: Johns Hopkins University Press, 1991.

———, ed. *Exporting Democracy: The United States and Latin America. Case Studies.* Baltimore: Johns Hopkins University Press, 1991.

Lowenthal, Abraham, and Samuel Fitch, eds. *Armies and Politics in Latin America.* Rev. ed. New York: Holmes and Meier, 1986.

Manger, William, ed. *The Alliance for Progress: A Critical Appraisal.* Washington, D.C.: Public Affairs Press, 1963.

Martz, John, ed. *United States Policy in Latin America: A Quarter Century of Crisis and Challenge, 1961–1986.* Lincoln: University of Nebraska Press, 1988.

Martz, John, and Lars Schoultz, eds. *Latin America, the United States and the Inter-American System.* Boulder, Colo.: Westview, 1981.

McNeil, Frank. *War and Peace in Central America.* New York: Scribners, 1988.

Middlebrook, Kevin, and Carlos Rico, eds. *The United States and Latin America in the 1980s.* Pittsburgh: University of Pittsburgh Press, 1986.

Molineau, Harold. *U.S. Policy toward Latin America from Regionalism to Globalism.* Boulder, Colo.: Westview, 1986.

Moreno, Dario. *U.S. Policy in Central America: The Endless Debate.* Gainesville: University Presses of Florida, 1990.

Newfarmer, Richard, ed. *From Gunboats to Diplomacy: New U.S. Policies for Latin America.* Baltimore: Johns Hopkins University Press, 1984.

Parkinson, Fred. *Latin America, the Cold War, and the World Powers, 1945–1973.* Beverly Hills: Sage, 1974.

Pastor, Robert. *Condemned to Repetition: The United States and Nicaragua.* Princeton, N.J.: Princeton University Press, 1987.

——, ed. *Latin America's Debt Crisis: Adjusting to the Past or Planning for the Future?* Boulder, Colo.: Westview, 1987.

Pastor, Robert, and Jorge Castañeda. *Limits to Friendship: The United States and Mexico.* New York: Knopf, 1988.

Perloff, Harvey. *Alliance for Progress.* Baltimore: Johns Hopkins University Press, 1969.

Petras, James, and Morris Morley. *The United States and Chile: Imperialism and the Overthrow of the Allende Government.* New York: Monthly Review, 1975.

Pike, Fredrick. *The United States and the Andean Republics: Peru, Bolivia and Ecuador.* Cambridge: Harvard University Press, 1977.

Poitras, Guy. *The Ordeal of Hegemony: The United States and Latin America.* Boulder, Colo.: Westview, 1990.

Rockefeller, Nelson. *The Rockefeller Report on the Americas.* Chicago: Quadrangle, 1969.

Roett, Riordan, ed. *Mexico and the United States: Managing the Relationship.* Boulder, Colo.: Westview, 1988.

Rogers, William D. *The Twilight Struggle: The Alliance for Progress and the Politics of Development in Latin America.* New York: Random House, 1967.

Scheman, Ronald, ed. *The Alliance for Progress: A Retrospective.* New York: Praeger, 1988.

Schoultz, Lars. *Human Rights and United States Policy toward Latin America.* Princeton, N.J.: Princeton University Press, 1981.

——. *National Security and United States Policy toward Latin America.* Princeton, N.J.: Princeton University Press, 1987.

Scott, Peter Dale, and Jonathan Marshall. *Cocaine Politics: Drugs, Armies, and the CIA in Central America.* Berkeley: University of California Press, 1991.

Sigmund, Paul. *The United States and Democracy in Chile.* Baltimore: Johns Hopkins University Press, 1993.

Slater, Jerome. *The OAS and United States Foreign Policy.* Columbus: Ohio State University Press, 1967.

Smith, Gaddis. *The Last Years of the Monroe Doctrine.* New York: Hill and Wang, 1994.

Smith, Robert, ed. *The United States and the Latin American Sphere of Influence*. Vol. 2, *Era of Good Neighbors, Cold Warriors, and Hairshirts, 1930–1982*. Malabar, Fla.: Krieger, 1983.

Stallings, Barbara, and Robert Kaufman. *Debt and Democracy in Latin America*. Boulder, Colo.: Westview, 1989.

Szulc, Tad, ed. *The United States and the Caribbean*. Englewood Cliffs, N.J.: Prentice-Hall, 1971.

Tulchin, Joseph. *Argentina and the United States: Conflicted Relationship*. Boston: Twayne, 1990.

Varas, Augusto, ed. *Hemispheric Security and U.S. Policy in Latin America*. Boulder, Colo.: Westview, 1989.

Wagner, R. Harrison. *U.S. Policy toward Latin America*. Stanford, Calif.: Stanford University Press, 1970.

Walker, William. *Drug Control in the Americas*. Albuquerque: University of New Mexico Press, 1989.

Wesson, Robert, ed. *U.S. Influence in Latin America in the 1980s*. Boulder, Colo.: Westview, 1982.

Wesson, Robert, and Heraldo Muñoz, eds. *Latin American Views of U.S. Policy*. New York: Praeger, 1986.

Wiarda, Howard. *Finding Our Way: Maturity in U.S.–Latin American Relations*. Washington, D.C.: University Press of America, 1987.

———. *Latin America at the Crossroads: Debt, Development and the Future*. Boulder, Colo.: Westview, 1987.

———. *American Foreign Policy toward Latin America in the 80s and 90s: Issues and Controversies from Reagan to Bush*. New York: New York University Press, 1992.

Williams, Edward. *The Political Themes of Inter-American Relations*. Belmont: Duxbury, 1971.

Wood, Bryce. *The Dismantling of the Good Neighbor Policy*. Austin: University of Texas Press, 1985.

PART VI

Bouvier, Virginia, ed. *The Globalization of U.S.-Latin American Relations: Democracy, Intervention and Human Rights*. Westport: Praeger, 2002.

Bulmer-Thomas, Victor, and James Dunkerley, eds. *The United States and Latin America: The New Agenda*. Cambridge: Harvard University Press, 1999.

Carpenter, Ted Galen. *Bad Neighbor Policy: Washington's Futile War on Drugs in Latin America*. New York: Palgrave MacMillan, 2003.

Coerver, Don, and Linda B. Hall. *Tangled Destinies: Latin America and the United States*. Albuquerque: University of New Mexico Press, 1999.

Crandall, Russell. *Driven by Drugs: U.S. Policy toward Colombia*. Boulder, Colo.: Lynne Rienner, 2002.

Dominguez, Jorge, ed. *The Future of Inter-American Relations*. New York: Routledge, 1999.

Dominguez, Jorge, and Rafael Hernandez, eds. *U.S–Cuban Relations in the 1990s*. Boulder, Colo.: Westview, 1989.

Friedman, Max Paul. *Nazis and Good Neighbors: The United States Campaign against the Germans of Latin America in World War II*. New York: Cambridge University Press, 2003.

Fuentes, Carlos. *The Crystal Frontier*. London: Bloomsbury, 1998.

Gilderhus, Mark T., *The Second Century: U.S.-Latin American Relations since 1889*. Wilmington: Scholarly Resources, 2000.

Hall, Michael. *Sugar and Power in the Dominican Republic: Eisenhower, Kennedy and the Trujillos*. Westport, Conn.: Greenwood Press, 2000.

Hartlyn, Jonathan, Lars Schoultz, and Augusto Varas, eds. *The United States and Latin America in the 1990s: Beyond the Cold War*. Chapel Hill: University of North Carolina Press, 1992.

Healy, David. *James G. Blaine and Latin America*. Columbia: University of Missouri Press, 2001.

Jorge, Antonio, ed. *Economic Development and Social Change: United States–Latin American Relations in the 1990s*. New Brunswick: Transaction, 1993.

Joseph, Gilbert M., Catherine C. LeGrand, and Ricardo D. Salvatore, eds. *Close Encounters of Empire: Writing the Cultural History of U.S.-Latin American Relations*. Durham, N.C.: Duke University Press, 1998.

Kryzanek, Michael. *U.S–Latin American Relations*. 3d ed. New York: Praeger, 1996.

Leonard, Thomas. *United States–Latin American Relations, 1850–1903: Establishing a Relationship*. Tuscaloosa: University of Alabama Press, 1999.

Longley, Kyle. *In the Eagle's Shadow: The United States and Latin America*. New York: Harlan Davidson, 2002.

Lowenthal, Abraham. *Partners in Conflict: The United States and Latin America*. Rev. ed. Baltimore: Johns Hopkins University Press, 1990.

Lowenthal, Abraham, and Gregory Treverton, eds. *Latin America in a New World*. Boulder, Colo.: Westview, 1994.

MacLeod, Dag. "Privatization and the Limits of State Autonomy in Mexico: Rethinking the Orthodox Paradox," in *Latin American Perspectives* 32, no. 4 (July 2005).

McPherson, Alan. *Yankee No! Anti-Americanism in US-Latin American Relations*. Cambridge: Harvard University Press, 2003.

Mitchel, Nancy. *The Danger of Dreams: German and American Imperialism in Latin America*. Chapel Hill: University of North Carolina, Press, 1999.

Mitchell, Christopher, ed. *Western Hemisphere Immigration and United States Foreign Policy*. University Park: Penn State University Press, 1992.

Pastor, Robert. *Exiting the Whirlpool: U.S. Foreign Policy toward Latin America and the Caribbean*. Boulder, Colo.: Westview Press, 2001.

Rabe, Stephen. *The Most Dangerous Area in the World: John F. Kennedy Confronts Communist Revolution in Latin America*. Chapel Hill: University of North Carolina Press, 1999.

Raymont, Henry. *Troubled Neighbors: The Story of US-Latin American Relations from FDR to the Present*. Boulder, Colo.: Westview Press, 2005.

Sánchez-Ancochea, Diego. "Domestic Capital, Civil Servants and the State: Costa Rica and the Dominican Republic Under Globalization," in *Journal of Latin American Studies* 37, no. 4 (November 2005).

Scheman, Ronald. *Greater America: A New Partnership for the Americas in the Twenty-First Century.* New York: New York University Press, 2003.

Schoultz, Lars. *Beneath the United States: A History of U.S. Policy toward Latin America.* Cambridge: Harvard University Press, 1998.

Schwartzberg, Steven. *Democracy and US Policy during the Truman Years.* Gainesville: University of Florida Press, 2003.

Shaw, Carolyn. *Cooperation, Conflict and Consensus in the Organization of American States.* New York: Palgrave Macmillan, 2004.

Shulz, Donald. *The United States and Latin America: Shaping an Elusive Future.* Carlisle Barracks, Pa.: Strategic Studies Institute, Army War College, 2000.

Sicker, Martin. *The Geopolitics of Security in the Americas: Hemispheric Denial from Monroe to Clinton.* Westport, Conn.: Praeger Publishers, 2002.

Sikkink, Kathryn. *Mixed Signals: United States Human Rights Policy and Latin America.* Ithaca, N.Y.: Cornell University Press, 2004.

Smith, Joseph. *The United States and Latin America: A History of American Diplomacy, 1776–2000.* New York: Routledge, 2005.

Stolle-McAllister, John. "What *Does* Democracy Look Like? Local Movements Challenge the Mexican Transition," in *Latin American Perspectives* 32, no. 4 (July 2005).

Credits

Chapter 2 is reprinted from Josiah Strong, *Our Country: Its Possible Future and Its Present Crisis* (New York: Baker and Taylor, 1885). Excerpt from Chapter 12, "The Anglo-Saxon and the World's Future," 159–78.

Chapter 3 is from José Enrique Rodó, *Ariel*, trans. Margaret Sayers Peden (Austin: University of Texas Press, 1988). Reprinted by permission of the University of Texas Press.

Chapter 4 is from Fredrick B. Pike, *The United States and Latin America: Myths and Stereotypes of Civilization and Nature* (Austin: University of Texas Press, 1992). Reprinted by permission of the University of Texas Press.

Chapter 5 is from Dexter Perkins, *The Monroe Doctrine, 1823–1826* (Cambridge, MA: Harvard University Press, 1927), 3–4, 40–47, 144–61. Reprinted by permission of the publisher.

Chapter 6 is reprinted from Jaime Suchlicki, *Cuba: From Columbus to Castro*, fifth ed. (McLean, VA: Brassey's, 2002), 79–84.

Chapter 7 is reprinted from Elihu Root, "The Real Monroe Doctrine," *American Journal of International Law* 8, no. 3 (July 1914): 427–42.

Chapter 8 is reprinted from Gaston Nerval [Raul Diez de Medina], *Autopsy of the Monroe Doctrine: The Strange Story of Inter-American Relations* (New York: Macmillan, 1934). Excerpted from Donald Marquand Dozer, ed., *The Monroe Doctrine: Its Modern Significance* (New York: Knopf, 1965), 127–32.

Chapter 9 is reprinted from Lester D. Langley, ed., *The Banana Wars: United States Intervention in the Caribbean, 1898–1934* (Woodbridge, CT: Scholarly Resources Inc., 2002), 3–12.

Chapter 10 is reprinted from Samuel Flagg Bemis, *A Diplomatic History of the United States*, rev. ed. (New York: Henry Holt, 1942), excerpts from Chapter 28, "Cuba and Panama," 513–18.

Chapter 11 is from Link, Arthur S., *The Papers of Woodrow Wilson* (Princeton, NJ: Princeton University Press). Reprinted by permission of Princeton University Press.

Chapter 12 is from Bryce Wood, *The Making of the Good Neighbor Policy* (New York: Columbia University Press, 1961), excerpts from 118–20, 123–31. Reprinted by permission of the publisher.

Chapter 13 is reprinted from Roger R. Trask, "The Impact of the Cold War on U.S.–Latin American Relations: 1945–1949," *Diplomatic History* 1, no. 3: 271–84.

Chapter 14 is reprinted from George Kennan, "Latin America as a Problem in United States Foreign Policy," in *Foreign Relations of the United States, 1950*, vol. 2 (Washington, D.C.: Government Printing Office, 1976), excerpts from 598–624.

Chapter 15 is from Cole Blasier, *The Hovering Giant: U.S. Responses to Revolutionary Change in Latin America, 1910–1985*, rev. ed. (Pittsburgh: University of Pittsburgh Press, 1976), 128–45. Reprinted by permission of the publisher.

Chapter 16 is reprinted from Stephen Schlesinger and Stephen Kinzer, *Bitter Fruit: The Untold Story of the American Coup in Guatemala* (Garden City, NY: Anchor, 1983), 11–23, 70–77, 104–8.

Chapter 17 is reprinted from Alan Luxenberg, "Did Eisenhower Push Castro into the Arms of the Soviets?" *Journal of Interamerican Studies and World Affairs* 30, no. 1 (Spring 1988): 37–71.

Chapter 18 is reprinted from Jerome Levinson and Juan de Onís, *The Alliance That Lost Its Way: A Critical Report on the Alliance for Progress* (Chicago: Quadrangle, 1970), excerpts from Chapter 1 and the Epilogue.

Chapter 19 is reprinted from Robert Pastor, *Condemned to Repetition: The United States and Nicaragua* (Princeton: Princeton University Press, 1987), excerpts from Chapter 14, "Nightmares Come True: An Explanation."

Chapter 20 is reprinted from Riordan Roett, "The Debt Crisis and Economic Development," in *United States Policy in Latin America: A Decade of Crisis and Challenge*, ed. John D. Martz (Lincoln: University of Nebraska Press, 1995), 249–66.

Chapter 21 is from Bruce M. Bagley and Juan G. Tokatlian, "Dope and Dogma: Explaining the Failure of U.S.–Latin American Drug Policies," in *The United States and Latin America in the 1990s: Beyond the Cold War*, eds. Jonathan Hartlyn, Lars Schoultz, and Augusto Varas (Chapel Hill: University of North Carolina Press, 1993), 214–34. Reprinted by permission of the publisher.

Chapter 22 is reprinted from Luisa Angrisani, "More Latin, Less America?" *The National Interest* (Summer 2003), 77–84.

Chapter 24 is reprinted from Jorge G. Castañeda, "The Forgotten Relationship," *Foreign Affairs* (May/June 2003).

Chapter 25 is reprinted from Michael Shifter, "The U.S. and Latin America Through the Lens of Empire," *Current History* 103, no. 670 (February 2004): 61–67.

Chapter 27 is from Richard L. Harris, "Resistance and Alternatives to Globalization in Latin America and the Caribbean," *Latin American Perspectives* 29, no. 127 (2002): 136–51. Reprinted by permission of Sage Publications, Inc.

Chapter 28 is reprinted from Arturo Valenzuela, "Beyond Benign Neglect: Washington and Latin America," *Current History* (February 2005): 58–63.

Index

About the Contributors

Luisa Angrisani is regional editor for Latin America at the Economic Intelligence Unit in London.

Laura Ávila is a graduate student of interdisciplinary ecology at the School of Natural Resources at the University of Florida at Gainesville.

Bruce M. Bagley is professor of international studies at the University of Miami at Coral Gables, Florida.

Samuel Flagg Bemis (1891–1973) was professor of diplomatic history and international relations at Yale University.

Cole Blasier, a political scientist, was founding director of the Center for Latin American Studies at the University of Pittsburgh.

Jorge G. Castañeda is professor of political and social sciences at the Universidad Nacional Autónoma (UNAM) in Mexico and former foreign minister of Mexico.

Richard L. Harris is professor of global studies at California State University, Monterey Bay, and editor of the *Journal of Developing Studies*.

Lance R. Ingwersen is director of policy and programs at Latino-Memphis, Inc., in Memphis, Tennessee.

Wesley Ingwersen is a graduate student of environmental engineering at the University of Florida at Gainesville.

George Kennan (1904–2005) was a U.S. diplomat and principal architect of American foreign policy following World War II.

Stephen Kinzer is a veteran foreign correspondent who writes for the *New York Times*.

Lester D. Langley is professor emeritus of history at the University of Georgia and editor of The United States and the Americas, a book series.

Michael LaRosa is associate professor of history at Rhodes College in Memphis. LaRosa specializes in contemporary Latin American history, with an emphasis on contemporary Colombia.

Jerome Levinson is distinguished lawyer in residence at the Washington College of Law at American University.

Alan Luxenberg is vice president of the Foreign Policy Research Institute in Philadelphia.

Frank O. Mora is professor of national security strategy at the National War College, National Defense University in Washington, D.C. Mora specializes in Latin American foreign policy, hemispheric security, and civil-military relations in Latin America.

Gaston Nerval is the pseudonym for Raúl Díez de Medina, a Bolivian diplomat and journalist born in 1909.

Juan de Onís is a former correspondent for the *New York Times* and the *Los Angeles Times*.

Robert Pastor is vice president of international affairs and professor of international relations at American University.

Dexter Perkins (1890–1984) was professor of history at the University of Rochester.

Fredrick Pike is professor emeritus of history at the University of Notre Dame.

José Enrique Rodó (1872–1917) was an essayist and philosopher from Uruguay. His most influential work was *Ariel*, published in 1900 and translated into English in 1988.

Riordan Roett is professor of political science and director of the Western Hemisphere Program at Johns Hopkins University's Paul H. Nitze School of Advanced International Studies (SAIS) in Washington, D.C.

Elihu Root (1845–1937) was secretary of state from 1905 to 1909 during Theodore Roosevelt's second administration.

Stephen Schlesinger, an attorney, is director of the World Policy Institute in New York City.

Michael Shifter is vice president for policy at the Inter-American Dialogue in Washington, D.C.

Josiah Strong (1847–1916) was a U.S. protestant clergyman who published *Our Country: Its Possible Future and Its Present Crisis* in 1885.

Juan G. Tokatlian is professor of international relations at Universidad de San Andrés in Victoria in the Provincia de Buenos Aires, Argentina.

Roger R. Trask is a historian who works at the historical office of the Office of the Secretary of Defense.

Arturo Valenzuela is professor of government and director of the Center for Latin American Studies at Georgetown University in Washington, D.C.

Bryce Wood taught diplomatic history at Columbia University and Swarthmore College.